Presidential Libraries and Museums

Presidential Libraries and Museums

Christian A. Nappo

ROWMAN & LITTLEFIELD
Lanham • Boulder • New York • London

Published by Rowman & Littlefield
A wholly owned subsidiary of The Rowman & Littlefield Publishing Group, Inc.
4501 Forbes Boulevard, Suite 200, Lanham, Maryland 20706
www.rowman.com

Unit A, Whitacre Mews, 26-34 Stannary Street, London SE11 4AB

British Library Cataloguing in Publication Information Available

Library of Congress Cataloging-in-Publication Data Available

ISBN 9781442271357 (hardback : alk. paper) | ISBN 9781442271364 (electronic)

♾™ The paper used in this publication meets the minimum requirements of
American National Standard for Information Sciences—Permanence of Paper
for Printed Library Materials, ANSI/NISO Z39.48-1992.

Printed in the United States of America

Contents

List of Figures   vii

Preface   ix

Acknowledgments   xi

Introduction: A Brief History of Presidential Libraries and Museums   xiii

1   Fred W. Smith National Library for the Study of George Washington and
the Donald W. Reynolds Museum Education Center at Mount Vernon   1

2   John Adams Library at the Boston Public Library   7

3   James Monroe Museum and Memorial Library   13

4   Stone Library at the Adams National Historical Park   18

5   Abraham Lincoln Presidential Library and Museum   24

6   President Andrew Johnson Museum and Library   32

7   Ulysses S. Grant Presidential Library   37

8   Rutherford B. Hayes Presidential Library and Museums   44

9   Research Library at the Benjamin Harrison Presidential Site   50

10 William McKinley Presidential Library and Museum   57

11 Woodrow Wilson Presidential Library and Museum   65

12 Calvin Coolidge Presidential Library and Museum at the Forbes Library   73

13 Herbert Hoover Presidential Library and Museum   79

14 Franklin D. Roosevelt Presidential Library and Museum   89

15 Harry S. Truman Presidential Library and Museum   102

16 Dwight D. Eisenhower Presidential Library, Museum, and Boyhood Home   119

17 John F. Kennedy Presidential Library and Museum   129

18   Lyndon Baines Johnson Presidential Library and Museum   144

19   Richard Nixon Presidential Library and Museum   154

20   Gerald R. Ford Presidential Library and Museum   167

21   Jimmy Carter Presidential Library and Museum   175

22   Ronald Reagan Presidential Library and Museum   186

23   George Bush Presidential Library and Museum   198

24   William J. Clinton Presidential Library and Museum   206

25   George W. Bush Presidential Library and Museum   215

26   Future Presidential Libraries and Museums   223

Appendix: Presidential Libraries by State   229

Index   231

About the Author   241

Figures

George Washington, lithograph, c. 1828   1

John Adams by Gilbert Stuart   7

James Monroe by Gilbert Stuart   13

John Quincy Adams   18

Stone Library, c. 1962 by Charles E. Peterson   21

Abraham Lincoln and family, c. 1865   24

Andrew Johnson   32

Ulysses S. Grant, c. 1880   37

The seven-mile funeral cortege of General Grant   40

Rutherford B. Hayes, c. 1870s   44

Benjamin Harrison, c. 1896   50

William McKinley, c. 1900   57

President Theodore Roosevelt delivering oration at the dedication of the
    McKinley National Memorial, c. 1908 by John W. Finnell   61

Woodrow Wilson, c. 1912 by Pach Brothers   65

President Woodrow Wilson's birthplace in Staunton, Virginia, with his
    original car parked out front, c. 2006 by Carol Highsmith   69

Calvin Coolidge and wife, 1924   73

Herbert Hoover and Mrs. Hoover, 1929   79

Herbert Hoover Presidential Library and Museum   83

Franklin D. Roosevelt by Elias Goldensky   89

Franklin D. Roosevelt Presidential Library and Museum   95

FDR Reading Room by Thomas Kletecka   97

Harry S. Truman   102

Exterior of the Harry S. Truman Library, 1958   107

Truman's replica Oval Office by Cecil Schrepfer   109

Benton's mural in progress   109

Dwight D. Eisenhower, c. 1953   119

Dwight D. Eisenhower Presidential Library and Museum 125

John F. Kennedy, c. 1960 129

John F. Kennedy Presidential Library and Museum, Boston 135

Kennedy's replica Oval Office by Carol Highsmith 137

LBJ and Lady Bird by Yoichi Okamoto, 1968 144

The front (facing south) of the Lyndon Baines Johnson Presidential Library
and Museum 148

The Oval Office exhibit at the Lyndon Baines Johnson Library
by Gary Phelps 150

Richard Nixon 154

Pat Nixon's beloved rose garden frames the birthplace of her husband,
President Richard Nixon, in Yorba Linda, California, by Carol Highsmith 159

Gerald R. Ford and Betty Ford at the Republican National Convention
by John T. Bledsoe, 1976 167

Gerald R. Ford Presidential Library in Ann Arbor, Michigan 171

Gerald R. Ford Presidential Museum in Grand Rapids, Michigan 172

Ford's replica Oval Office by William Hebert 172

Jimmy Carter by Karl Schumacher, 1977 175

Jimmy Carter Presidential Library and Museum 180

Carter's replica Oval Office 181

Ronald Reagan 186

Ronald Reagan Presidential Library and Museum 191

Reagan's replica Oval Office 192

View of the Air Force One Pavilion at the Reagan Library 193

George H. W. Bush by David Valdez 198

George Bush Presidential Library and Museum on the Texas A&M
University campus, College Station, Texas, by Carol Highsmith 202

Hillary and Bill Clinton at the 1997 dedication of the
Franklin Delano Roosevelt Memorial in Washington, DC,
by Carol Highsmith 206

William J. Clinton Presidential Library, Little Rock, Arkansas,
by Carol Highsmith 209

George W. Bush and Laura Bush 215

George W. Bush Presidential Library on the campus of Southern
Methodist University in Dallas, Texas, by Carol Highsmith 219

Michelle and Barack Obama watch the parade from the viewing stand
in front of the White House, by Carol Highsmith, 2009 224

Theodore Roosevelt by Levin C. Handy 225

Preface

The first presidential library was dedicated in Fremont, Ohio, on May 29, 1916. The library belonged to President Rutherford B. Hayes, who willed his home estate, Spiegel Grove, into a historical site with its own library.[1] Twenty-four more presidential libraries and museums opened in the subsequent 101 years.

Presidential Libraries and Museums covers the histories, collections, and exhibits located in America's twenty-five presidential libraries and museums. The book is like a chronological encyclopedia where each library is presented based on which president, not library, came first. This means George Washington's library is found in the first chapter and George W. Bush's is the last chapter. The book begins with an introduction to the history of presidential libraries and museums. Every chapter starts with a brief biography of the president. The purpose of the biographies is to present key facts about each president as they relate to the exhibits and artifacts visitors will see at his library. The book also contains a list of libraries by state, dates of each president's administration, party affiliation, and dates of birth and death. Also included are the physical addresses, phone numbers, websites, social media, administration, affiliations, and hours of operation of the libraries. The book also features photographs of all presidents with libraries, some photographs of presidential library buildings, and selected photographs of museum exhibits and artifacts. The book concludes with a brief chapter highlighting future presidential libraries and museums that were being planned at the time of the book's publication: the Barack Obama Presidential Library and Museum in Chicago, Illinois, and the Theodore Roosevelt Presidential Library in Dickinson, North Dakota.

The main purpose of this book is to give young adults and college students a ready-reference source of information for research. In many ways this book is interdisciplinary because it covers history, politics, archival studies, architecture, and tourism. Historians will enjoy reading stories about presidents and why they built libraries. Archivists will find detailed information about each library's collection useful for research. Those interested in architecture will find images of actual presidential library buildings interesting. Travelers enjoying presidential history will find this book useful when planning trips too. I hope you'll find this book to be a one-stop source of information about America's presidential libraries and museums.

NOTE

1. Thomas A. Smith, "Before Hyde Park: The Rutherford B. Hayes Library," *American Archivist* 43, no. 4 (Fall 1980): 485.

Acknowledgments

Personal acknowledgment and thanks to my mother for her help on the LBJ chapter. She was employed at the Office of Economic Opportunity from 1968 to 1971. Her insights on the War on Poverty were very helpful to me. Acknowledgments also go to Laura Ripper for doing my proofreading and to all staff members at the various presidential libraries and museums who assisted me in my research for this book.

Introduction

A Brief History of Presidential Libraries and Museums

At the time of publishing this book, there are twenty-five presidential libraries and museums in operation. Thirteen are administered by the National Archives and Records Administration in Washington, DC, and the remaining twelve are controlled by private organizations. One exception is the Abraham Lincoln Presidential Library and Museum, which is administered by the state of Illinois. This figure does not include presidential libraries in the planning and development stage. For example, at the time of writing, the National Archives is working with former president Barack Obama to construct his library and museum.

This chapter gives readers a brief history of the development of presidential libraries and museums. Before the establishment of presidential libraries and museums, there were collections of presidential papers and manuscripts. Ever since the end of George Washington's administration, the papers, letters, and manuscripts of presidents have been "regarded as personal property."[1] However, with no law mandating the disposition of these documents, presidents were free to do as they pleased after their presidencies came to an end. The traditional practice was to donate presidential papers to the Library of Congress. However, the papers of one president deviated from this trend: Rutherford B. Hayes placed his papers in what became the first presidential library.[2]

In 1939, the Executive Office of the President was established with the purpose of "maintaining and archiving of presidential records."[3] President Franklin Delano Roosevelt established this office because he was considering establishing a library of his own. Unfortunately for Roosevelt, however, there were only two "prototype libraries" for him to base his library on: the Rutherford B. Hayes Memorial Library and the Hoover Institution on War, Revolution, and Peace.[4] The Hoover Institution was established by former president Herbert Hoover at Stanford University, from which he had graduated. The original library was created to store information that Hoover had collected in Europe during World War One, before his presidency.[5] Roosevelt used the libraries of both Hayes and Hoover as models for his own. In 1939, Congress passed legislation for the construction of Roosevelt's library. On July 4, 1940, the archivist of the United States accepted the library "on behalf of the federal government."[6] Roosevelt's library was formally opened to the public in the spring of 1946—a year after his death.

Establishing presidential libraries became a trend in the 1950s. Presidents Harry Truman and Dwight David Eisenhower both constructed their own libraries during this decade. As interest in presidential libraries grew, Congress decided to legislate a government system for the "preservation and administration" of presidential papers.[7] In 1955, Congress took the first step in implementing a law governing the creation of presidential libraries when Congressman Edward Herbert Reese of Kansas proposed a law for the "acceptance and maintenance of Presidential libraries."[8] Reese's law was passed by Congress and became known as the Presidential Libraries Act of 1955. Under this act, the administrator of the General Services Administration (GSA) was granted the "authority to accept for preservation" the papers of current or former presidents.[9] Perhaps the most important aspect of this law was to create a decentralized system that allowed each president to decide where his papers would ultimately be located.[10] As will be explained later in this chapter, Congress became concerned about the rising costs of maintaining several libraries. Besides giving the GSA administrator authority to accept papers from presidents, the administrator also had the authority to "accept title" to land and buildings, "enter into agreements" with "any state, political subdivision, university" or "foundation" to be used as a "presidential archival depository," operate the libraries under the National Archives system, and "accept gifts or bequests of money or other property" to maintain a presidential library.[11]

In 1964 the Office of Presidential Libraries was created as an "entity" within the National Archives and Records Administration.[12] According to the National Archives, this office helps to develop policies for presidential libraries regarding the "acquisition, preservation, and use of historical materials, and the development of new Presidential libraries."[13] It also "provides oversight of budgetary and management controls within the libraries and regularly convenes staff in the libraries to establish and review strategies for implementing the mission and goals of Presidential libraries."[14] Today the Office of Presidential Libraries operates thirteen presidential libraries, and it will operate the one currently being planned and constructed for former president Barack Obama.[15]

From Herbert Hoover's to Dwight Eisenhower's presidential libraries, there was a similar pattern: the libraries were built near the president's hometown. In the 1960s, President Lyndon Johnson started a new trend of building presidential libraries on university campuses. Other presidents, such as Gerald Ford, George H. W. Bush, and George W. Bush, followed Johnson's lead. As presented in the chapters on these libraries, these presidents wanted their libraries to be centers of scholarship and research, given that they created schools of public affairs and service in their names.

In the mid to late 1970s, Congress passed new laws regarding presidential papers due to the Watergate scandal involving President Richard M. Nixon. Nixon made an agreement with GSA administrator Arthur F. Sampson, known as the Nixon–Sampson agreement, which gave Nixon ownership of his papers and audio recordings. The agreement was controversial and, ultimately, nullified the Presidential Recordings and Preservation Act of 1974, signed by President Gerald Ford. The question of who owns presidential papers was finally settled with the enactment of the Presidential Records Act of 1978. That law mandated all presidential records as property of the United States, with effect from January 20, 1981.[16] President Ford said the 1978 law made him, along with President Jimmy Carter, the last presidents "to dispose of our papers and memorabilia in any way we saw fit."[17]

By the 1980s, the number of federally operated presidential libraries had grown, and so had their cost. In 1955 the presidential library system cost $63,745. Thirty years later the cost had metastasized to $15,743,000.[18] Naturally, Congress was alarmed and sought to curb the rising expenditure. The first effort to cap costs came in 1981, when Senator Lawton Chiles of Florida introduced a bill to limit the size of presidential libraries by mandating certain "architectural and design standards."[19] Senator Chiles feared presidents were trying "to build ever grander edifices."[20] One example was President Lyndon B. Johnson, who built the largest presidential library, located in Austin, Texas.[21] Three years later Senator David L. Boren of Oklahoma proposed a law to prevent the GSA administrator from accepting land for a presidential library "unless" there was an "endowment" that was "large enough" to sustain the expense of the library.[22] Ultimately, neither of the bills proposed by Chiles and Boren was enacted.[23] However, Congress eventually agreed to a new law on presidential libraries.

On October 19, 1984, Congress passed the National Archives Administration Act. This law revamped parts of the 1955 Presidential Libraries Act by transferring certain duties from the GSA administrator to the archivist of the United States.[24] The archivist was given the power to make agreements to use state, university, or foundation land and property for presidential libraries; the archivist also had the authority to accept gifts for the libraries.[25] By 1986 Congress was still concerned about the impact that presidential libraries were having on taxpayers, and it continued to grapple with the problem. Senator Chiles tried to convince Congress to adopt a "single centralized library" for presidents, but was unsuccessful.[26] Instead, Congress passed the Presidential Libraries Act of 1986. The law had been proposed a year earlier by Congressman Glenn English of Oklahoma. It shifted the "burden of on-going building operations costs of future libraries from the taxpayer to endowment funds."[27] The law also limited the size of presidential libraries to seventy thousand square feet and required the archivist of the United States to make sure that any endowment covered at least 20 percent of the costs associated with acquiring the land by title and constructing the library.[28] In 2008 Congress amended the required endowment for constructing a presidential library from 20 percent to 60 percent of the associated costs.[29] The amendment was binding on any president taking office on or after July 1, 2002.[30] This means the libraries of presidents Barack Obama and Donald J. Trump will be subject to the requirements of the amendment.

Two of the most common features of almost every presidential library and museum, especially those operated by the federal government, are gift shops for visitors and educational programs for students and teachers. However, the educational programs are a relatively new invention. In the late 1980s, presidential libraries faced problems as the government sought to cut spending. The libraries, and the Hoover library in particular, saw their visitor numbers dwindle.[31] In 1991 the archivist of the United States said that struggling presidential libraries had a choice of "either settling for the status of an archival warehouse or else building on what we have already done."[32] The problem to be solved was how to reinvent the presidential libraries. Former director of the Hoover library Tim Walch discusses the situation of the libraries:

> The concept of "reinventing" government is very much in the news these days. . . . Presidential libraries are among the agencies that have embraced this process. To be sure, these libraries have always served many different constituents. Scholars,

schoolchildren, tourists, conference participants, seniors, and members of civic or-ganizations are just a few of the many users who have streamed through the doors of presidential libraries.[33]

In 1987 historian Richard Norton Smith, who was the director of the Hoover library at the time, came up with a solution that rejuvenated presidential libraries. Walch says that Smith, who was "brimming with enthusiasm and blessed with a staff eager to work," "implemented a plan of large-scale temporary exhibits that galvanized the pub-lic."[34] Smith's idea was to create a temporary exhibit about the thirty-nine presidents of the United States. This exhibit was called "39 Men" and it was very popular at the Hoover library. Smith describes its success as follows:

> From 54,000 in 1987 to 115,000 in 1988, "39 Men" more than doubled our annual attendance. It brought four times as many schoolchildren to West Branch as usual, laying the groundwork for an ambitious follow-up program of educational outreach. It tripled sales in the museum gift shop.[35]

Soon the Hoover library began to introduce new temporary exhibits every year. For example, they held exhibits about World War One and an exhibit on the sixtieth anniversary of Hoover's White House Conference on Child Health.[36] Private donors interested in the temporary exhibits gave $3 million to the Hoover library, which helped it to create more exhibits to satisfy visitors.[37]

When discussing visitors to the Hoover library, Walch explains, "There is no more important group of visitors to the Hoover Library than school children. In fact, school children constitute the largest single group of visitors to the Library each year."[38] All presidential libraries administered by the National Archives run educational programs for students. In 2006 Lee Ann Potter, who was then head of education and volunteer programs at the National Archives and Records Administration, said, "Many of these programs demonstrate an awareness of educational research into multiple intelligences, and embrace educational methods that include cooperative learning, authentic as-sessments, and project- and performance-based learning."[39] Potter gives examples: for preschoolers, the Hoover library's program Your First Museum Experience "offers hands-on experiences."[40] Older students who visit the Kennedy library can participate in the Profiles in Courage Essay Contest by writing "an essay of 1,000 words or less on the meaning of political courage."[41] Potter believes that educational programs at presi-dential libraries are successful because each one is run by an educational specialist. She says, "Most of the education specialists in the libraries . . . are energetic, creative former classroom teachers who possess first-hand knowledge of the needs of classroom teachers and students in their communities."[42]

The scholarly expansion of archives was another consideration for an overhaul at the Hoover library. Previously the library held the papers of Hoover only. However, the archivist decided to enhance the collection with the papers of "agricultural economists and famine relief administrators," those involved in the "development of the nuclear energy industry," and "a number of conservative publishers and journalists."[43] After all, Hoover was involved in agriculture, famine relief, engineering, and conservative politics.

As will be discussed in later chapters of this book, presidential libraries have their share of controversies. Since federal presidential libraries are decentralized, the National Archives and Records Administration have little control over the exhibits at these libraries.[44] According to Dr. Benjamin Hufbauer, decentralized federal presidential libraries have allowed some libraries to present intentionally positive images of the president in question. Hufbauer is a professor of fine arts at the University of Louisville, in Kentucky. He identified a phenomenon occurring at some libraries, which he calls the "Mc President" or the "Happy Meal version of presidential history."[45] Hufbauer praises the Harry Truman library for presenting the controversies surrounding the use of the atomic bomb.[46] On the other hand, he criticizes the Ronald Reagan library for failing to present the Iran–Contra scandal that blighted his administration.[47]

As mentioned at the beginning of this introduction, not all presidential libraries and museums are administered by the National Archives. With the exception of Lincoln's library, the rest are administered and owned by private nonprofit associations, universities, or local public libraries. Those who visit the private libraries, as this book refers to them, will find that the majority of these mirror their federal counterparts. Many have archival manuscripts, books, exhibits, galleries, educational programs for students, and gift shops. However, as readers will discover, some of the smaller private libraries located in public libraries do not have exhibits, educational programs, or gift shops.

NOTES

1. Wendy R. Ginsberg, Erika K. Lunder, and Daniel J. Richardson, *The Presidential Libraries Act and the Establishment of Presidential Libraries* (CRS Report No. R41513) (Washington, DC: Congressional Research Service, 2015), 6.

2. Thomas A. Smith, "Before Hyde Park: The Rutherford B. Hayes Library," *American Archivist* 43, no. 4 (Fall 1980): 485.

3. Ginsberg et al., *Presidential Libraries Act*, 6.

4. Ginsberg et al., *Presidential Libraries Act*, 6.

5. Ginsberg et al., *Presidential Libraries Act*, 6.

6. Ginsberg et al., *Presidential Libraries Act*, 8.

7. Ginsberg et al., *Presidential Libraries Act*, 9.

8. Ginsberg et al., *Presidential Libraries Act*, 9.

9. Ginsberg et al., *Presidential Libraries Act*, 9.

10. Ginsberg et al., *Presidential Libraries Act*, 10.

11. Ginsberg et al., *Presidential Libraries Act*, 10.

12. Frank L. Schick, Renee Schick, and Mark Carroll, *Records of the Presidency: Presidential Papers and Libraries from Washington to Reagan* (Phoenix, AZ: Oryx Press, 1989), 11.

13. "Presidential Libraries: Office of Presidential Libraries," National Archives, accessed May 17, 2017, https://www.archives.gov/presidential-libraries/about/office.html.

14. "Presidential Libraries: Office of Presidential Libraries."

15. "Presidential Libraries: Office of Presidential Libraries."

16. Schick et al., *Records of the Presidency*, 16–18.

17. Schick et al., *Records of the Presidency*, xii.

18. Ginsberg et al., *Presidential Libraries Act*, 12.
19. Ginsberg et al., *Presidential Libraries Act*, 12.
20. Ginsberg et al., *Presidential Libraries Act*, 12.
21. "Presidential Libraries: Frequently Asked Questions," National Archives, accessed May 17, 2017, https://www.archives.gov/presidential-libraries/about/faqs.html.
22. Ginsberg et al., *Presidential Libraries Act*, 12.
23. Ginsberg et al., *Presidential Libraries Act*, 12.
24. Ginsberg et al., *Presidential Libraries Act*, 12.
25. Ginsberg et al., *Presidential Libraries Act*, 10.
26. Ginsberg et al., *Presidential Libraries Act*, 20.
27. Ginsberg et al., *Presidential Libraries Act*, 13.
28. Ginsberg et al., *Presidential Libraries Act*, 13–18.
29. Ginsberg et al., *Presidential Libraries Act*, 13–18.
30. Ginsberg et al., *Presidential Libraries Act*, 13–18.
31. Richard Norton Smith, "A Presidential Revival: How the Hoover Library Overcame a Mid-Life Crisis," *Prologue: Quarterly of the National Archives* 21 (Summer 1989): 116.
32. Don W. Wilson, "Presidential Libraries: Developing to Maturity," *Presidential Studies Quarterly* 21, no. 4 (Fall 1991): 775.
33. Timothy Walch, "Reinventing the Herbert Hoover Presidential Library," *Government Information Quarterly* 12, no. 1 (1995): 113.
34. Walch, "Reinventing," 115.
35. Smith, "Presidential Revival," 118.
36. Smith, "Presidential Revival," 119.
37. Walch, "Reinventing," 116.
38. Walch, "Reinventing," 112.
39. Lee Ann Potter, "Education Programs in the Presidential Libraries: A Report from the Field," *Public Historian* 28, no. 3 (Summer 2006): 134.
40. Potter, "Education Programs," 135.
41. Potter, "Education Programs," 136.
42. Potter, "Education Programs," 138.
43. Walch, "Reinventing," 119.
44. Benjamin Hufbauer, *Presidential Temples: How Memorials and Libraries Shape Public Memory* (Lawrence: University Press of Kansas, 2005), 173.
45. Hufbauer, *Presidential Temples*, 173.
46. Hufbauer, *Presidential Temples*, 156–57, 172–73.
47. Hufbauer, *Presidential Temples*, 143, 173.

BIBLIOGRAPHY

Ginsberg, Wendy R., Erika K. Lunder, and Daniel J. Richardson. *The Presidential Libraries Act and the Establishment of Presidential Libraries* (CRS Report No. R41513). Washington, DC: Congressional Research Service, 2015.

Hufbauer, Benjamin. *Presidential Temples: How Memorials and Libraries Shape Public Memory*. Lawrence: University Press of Kansas, 2005.

Potter, Lee Ann. "Education Programs in the Presidential Libraries: A Report from the Field." *Public Historian* 28, no. 3 (Summer 2006): 133–42.

Schick, Frank L., Renee Schick, and Mark Carroll. *Records of the Presidency: Presidential Papers and Libraries from Washington to Reagan.* Phoenix, AZ: Oryx Press, 1989.

Smith, Richard Norton. "A Presidential Revival: How the Hoover Library Overcame a Mid-Life Crisis." *Prologue: Quarterly of the National Archives* 21 (Summer 1989): 115–23.

Smith, Thomas A. "Before Hyde Park: The Rutherford B. Hayes Library." *American Archivist* 43, no. 4 (Fall 1980): 485–87.

Walch, Timothy. "Reinventing the Herbert Hoover Presidential Library." *Government Information Quarterly* 12, no. 1 (1995): 113–25.

Wilson, Don W. "Presidential Libraries: Developing to Maturity." *Presidential Studies Quarterly* 21, no. 4 (Fall 1991): 771–79.

Fred W. Smith National Library for the Study of George Washington and the Donald W. Reynolds Museum Education Center at Mount Vernon

Address: 3600 Mount Vernon Memorial Highway, Mount Vernon, VA 22121
Phone: (703) 780-2000
Website: http://www.mountvernon.org/library/
Social media: https://www.facebook.com/TheWashingtonLibrary/
Administration: Mount Vernon Ladies' Association
Hours: 9 a.m. to 5 p.m., Monday–Friday

BIOGRAPHY OF GEORGE WASHINGTON

February 22, 1732–December 14, 1799
First President: April 30, 1789–March 4, 1797
Federalist

George Washington, lithograph, c. 1828. *LC-USZ62-7265*

George Washington was born to Augustine and Mary Ball Washington at Pope's Creek in Westmoreland County, Virginia. Augustine Washington was a land speculator and slaveholder. George received his education from his mother. Augustine died when George was only eleven years old, making him the young heir to ten slaves and two thousand acres of land.[1] In his twenties, George lost his teeth to "diet and disease" and was forced to wear dentures made of ivory.[2]

When Washington reached adulthood he worked as a surveyor. Later he became an officer in the English army during the French and Indian War (the North American part of the Seven Years' War). He also served as an elected representative to the Virginia House of Burgesses in 1758.[3] Washington married Martha Dandridge on January 6, 1759. They never had any children together, but George helped raise Martha's children from her previous marriage.

1

During the American Revolution, Washington supported the American cause and was appointed commander of the Continental Army. Washington held his army together during the precarious early years of the war, when the Americans suffered several humiliating defeats at the hands of superior English forces, and retreated to Valley Forge in 1777.[4] However, Washington did secure one important victory on December 25, 1776, when his army quietly crossed the Delaware River to launch a sneak attack on Hessian mercenaries in Trenton, New Jersey. The English enlisted Hessian solders from Germany to try to quell the revolution.[5] The American Revolution took a dramatic turn when the French sent troops to help defeat the English. America made an alliance with England's enemy, France, whom England had previously defeated in the French and Indian War. With the help of the French, Washington led his troops to a major victory against the English at the Battle of Yorktown in 1781.[6] With peace and independence at hand, the nation turned to forming a government. In 1787, the United States ratified the Constitution, making the country a democratic republic. A year later it would hold its first presidential election.

In 1788 George Washington, who ran largely unopposed, was elected America's first president after receiving 43,782 popular votes and 69 electoral votes. As president, Washington was well aware that he could not exceed the authority vested in him by the newly minted Constitution. He said that the Constitution would "mark the line of [his] official conduct."[7] In 1792 Washington was unanimously elected to a second term as president with 28,579 popular votes and all 132 electoral votes. During his second term, Washington signed Jay's Treaty with England. The treaty was named after the American John Jay, who negotiated it. It was controversial in America, because England refused to stop conscripting American sailors into its navy and England could also tax American imports.[8] Opponents criticized Washington for signing a treaty that they believed damaged America's "national self-esteem."[9]

Washington refused to run for a third term as president. In doing so, he set a presidential precedent that only two terms should be held.[10] The only president to break this precedent was Franklin Delano Roosevelt in 1940. In his Farewell Address, published in September 1796, Washington warned against forming permanent alliances with foreign nations. He said, "It is our true policy to steer clear of permanent alliances with any portion of the foreign world; so far, I mean, as we are now at liberty to do it."[11] Washington feared that such alliances would force Americans to be "subjected to the policy and will" of another country.[12] Washington also condemned the formation of political parties, which he feared would lead to "disorders and miseries."[13]

After his presidency came to an end, Washington retired to his plantation at Mount Vernon. Though he was a slave owner, Washington had begun to question whether slavery should have a future in America. During the revolution, he allowed black people to join the army. In 1786 Washington wrote to a friend he hoped that "Slavery in this Country may be abolished by slow, sure and imperceptible degrees."[14]

The Washington library's website tells the story of how, on December 12, 1799, Washington supervised Mount Vernon on horseback on a very cold and wet day. The next day he suffered from a sore throat, but he decided to go outdoors again. That night, however, he had breathing problems. The physicians who tended Washington decided that the best treatment was to bleed him, which was still a common medical practice in the late eighteenth century. Washington is believed to have lost thirty-two ounces of blood. On the night of December 14, 1799, Washington passed away.[15] He was buried at Mount Vernon. His wife, Martha, who died on May 22, 1802, is buried next to him.

LIBRARY AND MUSEUM

The history of the Fred W. Smith National Library for the Study of George Washington goes all the way back to Mount Vernon, where George and Martha Washington lived. Mount Vernon is a plantation and sits on thirty acres of "gardens and forests."[16] The mansion was built in the 1740s by Washington's half-brother Lawrence, who named the estate in honor of Admiral Edward Vernon, whom Lawrence served under in the navy. Washington took possession of the estate from Lawrence's widow in 1754. He made improvements to the mansion by adding two and a half stories. The extension to the mansion was completed in 1787 and is considered an "excellent example of colonial architecture."[17] The tombs of Washington and wife Martha are in Mount Vernon for visitors to view.[18]

By 1853, Mount Vernon was in disrepair. Upon seeing the "decrepit state of George Washington's home," a woman named Louisa Bird Cunningham wrote to her daughter Ann Pamela to say, "If the men of America have seen fit to allow the home of its most respected hero to go to ruin, why can't the women of America band together to save it?"[19]

Upon reading her mother's letter, Ann Pamela Cunningham was inspired to save Mount Vernon. She immediately created a society whose mission was to preserve the plantation, naming the society the Mount Vernon Ladies' Association. Cunningham created her own board of regents of women. She sought a particular caliber of women to serve as vice regents: "women who were smart, creative and perhaps most of all, connected."[20] Cunningham and her board of regents raised $200,000 toward the purchase of Mount Vernon and began their task of preserving the home of George Washington for future generations.[21]

Today, 150 years after its founding, the Mount Vernon Ladies' Association continues to fund Mount Vernon. In 2006 the Donald W. Reynolds Museum Education Center was constructed there.[22] Seven years later the Fred W. Smith National Library was opened at Mount Vernon too.[23] The library is "funded by $106 million in private contributions raised from more than 7,000 individuals, foundations and corporations by the not-for-profit Mount Vernon Ladies' Association."[24]

The Donald W. Reynolds Museum and Education Center contains twenty-three exhibits, seven hundred objects, and several movies about George Washington. The museum and its exhibits are part of the Mount Vernon estate.[25] The first of its two theaters, which is located in the Ford Orientation Center, screens a movie called *We Fight to Be Free*, which presents key moments in George Washington's life. The film was "made possible by the generosity of the Ford Motor Company Fund and Donald and Nancy de Laski."[26]

The second theater is located in the Museum and Education Center. Here, short films and documentaries about George and Martha Washington are screened for visitors. The first of these is *A 40-Year Romance*, which was produced by the History Channel and documents the courtship and marriage between George and Martha. The second, *General Washington, Commander in Chief*, uses multimedia to present Washington's military campaigns during the American Revolution. Finally, in *Grand Finale*, former secretary of state General Colin Powell and historian David McCullough reflect on Washington's legacy.[27]

The entire exhibit area covers forty-four hundred square feet. Most of the exhibits focus on the artifacts, documents, artwork, and archaeology concerning Washington's life. However, an important exhibit focuses on a more controversial aspect of Washington's life: his ownership of slaves. This exhibit is called *Lives Bound Together: Slavery at George Washington's Mount Vernon*. The exhibit made its debut at the museum in October 2016. The library's website says that "Nineteen enslaved individuals are featured throughout the exhibit, represented with life-size silhouettes and interactive touch screens providing biographical details."[28]

Visitors to the museum will see real objects that once belonged to George Washington. Among the most notable on display are the Houdon Bust of Washington, the bedstead he used during the American Revolution, his dress sword, his presidential chair, and the ivory dentures that he wore. Also included are objects belonging to Martha Washington and the Washington household, such as Martha's chair cushion, their house bell, chinaware cups, and a key to the Bastille in Paris, France, which was given to Washington by General Marquis de Lafayette. Visitors can also see a painting of Mount Vernon by Benjamin Henry Latrobe, a British architect.[29] There are 350 archaeological artifacts found at Mount Vernon, including animal bones, seeds, metal buttons, and ceramic fragments "unearthed" at the estate.[30]

According to the website, the Fred W. Smith National Library owns "1,000 documents written or received by George and Martha Washington."[31] These papers were part of a collection of 140,000 compiled by the Mount Vernon Ladies' Association and the University of Virginia. Since 1968 the association and the university have sought to locate and identify Washington's papers worldwide for publication. However, Washington's personal collection of papers is held at the Library of Congress. Originally, Washington bequeathed his personal collection of papers to his nephew George Corbin Washington. Corbin held them until January 3, 1834, when he sold them to the Department of State.[32] Washington's papers stayed at the State Department for seventy years before they were transferred to the Library of Congress in 1904. By 1964 the library had microfilmed the papers and they were subsequently digitized in 1998.[33]

The library also contains fifteen hundred books from the eighteenth century. The books originally belonged to Washington and were passed down through the generations to his heirs. The majority of Washington's books are on legal topics. One of particular note is about navigation, *A Treatise on the Improvement of Canal Navigation*. Washington's collection also contains classics, such as *The Iliad* and *Don Quixote*. The library is also home to newspapers and manuscripts from the nineteenth century.[34]

NOTES

1. James MacGregor Burns and Susan Dunn, *George Washington*, the American Presidents Series (New York: Times Books, 2004), 7.

2. "False Teeth," George Washington's Mount Vernon, accessed May 25, 2017, http://www .mountvernon.org/digital-encyclopedia/article/false-teeth/.

3. "Key Facts about George Washington," George Washington's Mount Vernon, accessed May 25, 2017, http://www.mountvernon.org/george-washington/key-facts/.

4. Burns and Dunn, *George Washington*, 26.

5. "Battles of Trenton and Princeton," accessed May 25, 2017, http://www.history.com/top ics/american-revolution/battles-of-trenton-and-princeton.

6. Burns and Dunn, *George Washington*, 27.

7. Burns and Dunn, *George Washington*, 65.

8. Burns and Dunn, *George Washington*, 110–15.

9. Burns and Dunn, *George Washington*, 115.

10. Burns and Dunn, *George Washington*, 128.

11. George Washington, "Farewell Address 1796," Lillian Goldman Law Library at Yale Law School, http://avalon.law.yale.edu/18th_century/washing.asp.

12. Burns and Dunn, *George Washington*, 130.

13. Burns and Dunn, *George Washington*, 129.

14. Burns and Dunn, *George Washington*, 155.

15. "The Death of George Washington," George Washington's Mount Vernon, accessed May 25, 2017, http://www.mountvernon.org/digital-encyclopedia/article/the-death-of-george -washington/.

16. William G. Clotworthy, *Homes and Libraries of the Presidents: An Interpretive Guide*, third edition (Blacksburg, VA: McDonald & Woodward, 2008), 29.

17. Clotworthy, *Homes and Libraries*, 30.

18. "The Tombs," George Washington's Mount Vernon, accessed May 25, 2017, http://www .mountvernon.org/the-estate-gardens/the-tombs/.

19. "Mount Vernon Ladies' Association," George Washington's Mount Vernon, accessed May 25, 2017, http://www.mountvernon.org/preservation/mount-vernon-ladies-association/.

20. "The Birth of the Mount Vernon Ladies' Association," George Washington's Mount Ver-non, accessed May 25, 2017, http://www.mountvernon.org/preservation/mount-vernon-ladies -association/birth-of-the-mount-vernon-ladies-association/.

21. "The Kindness of Strangers," George Washington's Mount Vernon, accessed May 25, 2017, http://www.mountvernon.org/preservation/mount-vernon-ladies-association/the-kindness -of-strangers/.

22. Clotworthy, *Homes and Libraries*, 30.

23. Christopher Klein, "Mount Vernon Opens New George Washington Presidential Library," *History in the Headlines*, October 2, 2013, http://www.history.com/news/mount-vernon-opens -new-george-washington-presidential-library.

24. Klein, "Mount Vernon."

25. "Museum and Education Center," George Washington's Mount Vernon, accessed May 25, 2017, http://www.mountvernon.org/the-estate-gardens/museum/.

26. "Movie Showtimes," George Washington's Mount Vernon, accessed May 25, 2017, http:// www.mountvernon.org/plan-your-visit/movie-showtimes/.

27. "Movie Showtimes."

28. "Lives Bound Together: Slavery at George Washington's Mount Vernon," George Washington's Mount Vernon, accessed May 29, 2017, http://www.mountvernon.org/plan-your-visit/calendar/exhibitions/lives-bound-together-slavery-at-george-washingtons-mount-vernon/.

29. "Top Ten Objects in Mount Vernon's Collection," George Washington's Mount Vernon, accessed May 25, 2017, http://www.mountvernon.org/preservation/collections-holdings/top-ten-objects-in-mount-vernons-collection/.

30. "Top Ten Objects."

31. "The Papers of George Washington Documentary Editing Project," George Washington's Mount Vernon, accessed May 25, 2017, http://www.mountvernon.org/library/research-library/washington-papers.

32. Frank L. Schick, Renee Schick, and Mark Carroll, *Records of the Presidency: Presidential Papers and Libraries from Washington to Reagan* (Phoenix, AZ: Oryx Press, 1989), 43–44.

33. "The Papers of George Washington."

34. "About the Library," George Washington's Mount Vernon, accessed May 25, 2017, http://www.mountvernon.org/library/about-the-library/.

BIBLIOGRAPHY

Burns, James MacGregor, and Susan Dunn. *George Washington*. The American Presidents Series. New York: Times Books, 2004.

Clotworthy, William G. *Homes and Libraries of the Presidents: An Interpretive Guide*. Third edition. Blacksburg, VA: McDonald & Woodward, 2008.

Klein, Christopher. "Mount Vernon Opens New George Washington Presidential Library." *History in the Headlines*, October 2, 2013. http://www.history.com/news/mount-vernon-opens-new-george-washington-presidential-library.

Schick, Frank L., Renee Schick, and Mark Carroll. *Records of the Presidency: Presidential Papers and Libraries from Washington to Reagan*. Phoenix, AZ: Oryx Press, 1989.

Solis, Steph. "George Washington Presidential Library to Open Sept. 27." *USA Today*, September 3, 2013. http://www.usatoday.com/story/news/nation/2013/07/12/george-washington-presidential-library/2510295/.

Washington, George, "Farewell Address 1796." Lillian Goldman Law Library at Yale Law School. http://avalon.law.yale.edu/18th_century/washing.asp.

John Adams Library at the Boston Public Library

Address: 700 Boylston Street, Boston, MA 02116
E-mail: johnadamslibrary@bpl.org
Website: http://www.johnadamslibrary.org/
Administration: Boston Public Library

BIOGRAPHY OF JOHN ADAMS

October 19, 1735–July 4, 1826
Second President: March 4, 1797–March 4, 1801
Federalist

John Adams by Gilbert Stuart.
LC-DIG-ppmsca-19162

John Adams was born in Braintree, Massachusetts, to John Adams Sr. and Susanna Boylston Adams. The home that John was born in is now preserved by the National Park Service. As a child, John attended local schools. He entered Harvard University at the age of sixteen; four years later, he graduated and decided to embark on a career as a lawyer. He apprenticed himself to an attorney and was admitted to the bar by the Massachusetts Superior Court in 1761. On October 25, 1764, he married his third cousin, Abigail Smith.

After the French and Indian War ended in 1763, England began taxing the American colonies in order to pay the war debt. Adams, along with many Americans, was against the taxes. He believed that England could not implement taxes upon the colonies without proper representation in Parliament. Over the eleven years that followed, a series of protests against the taxes took place, which eventually culminated in the American Revolution.

On March 5, 1770, British soldiers opened fire on a mob of citizens in Boston. The incident, known as the Boston Massacre, claimed the lives of five colonists, including Crispus Attucks, a man of African descent. As an attorney, Adams defended some of the British soldiers who were on trial for the massacre. Six soldiers were acquitted and two were convicted. Then, on December 16, 1773, the Boston Tea Party took place. Rather than pay taxes on tea, the colonists decided to throw it into Boston Harbor. This worsened relations with England. Eventually, on April 19, 1775, British soldiers exchanged fire with colonists at Lexington, Massachusetts, initiating the American Revolution.

Adams, along with Thomas Jefferson, was involved in writing the Declaration of Independence. The declaration was signed on July 4, 1776, but America remained at war with the British until 1783, with General George Washington leading the troops. While the war raged on, Adams and Benjamin Franklin went to France to seek support. France agreed to join the war on the American side in order to avenge "forfeiting" some of her colonies to the British during the previous French and Indian War.[1]

After the war, a constitution was drafted in 1787 and George Washington was elected the nation's first president. Adams became the first vice president. After eight years as president, Washington humbly turned down the opportunity to run for a third term. His departure made it possible for Adams to be elected the second president in 1796.

Perhaps the most turbulent problem during Adams's administration was the Quasi-War with France, which lasted from 1798 to 1800. During the revolution, America and France were allies against the British. After the war, America and Great Britain signed a peace treaty and sought friendlier relations. France became upset with the new treaty, known as Jay's Treaty.[2] In response, France expelled America's minister, Charles Pinckney, and began to harass American trading vessels at sea. Adams attempted a settlement by sending a delegation to France to negotiate. However, unknown French officials demanded that America pay them before they would formally negotiate. Since Adams did not know the names of the French officials, he called them X, Y, and Z.[3] For the next two years America and France fought an undeclared war at sea. Back home, disputes erupted between pro-British and pro-French politicians. Adams was pro-British, whereas his vice president, Thomas Jefferson, was pro-French. Jefferson argued that "France's true enemy was England, not America."[4]

As Americans became more divided over this issue, Congress passed a series of laws known as the Alien and Sedition Acts. Americans had become suspicious of French immigrants in America, fearing that they may be enemies. The Alien Act allowed the president to "expel" foreigners he believed were "dangerous."[5] Then there was the Sedition Act, which outlawed any "False, scandalous, and malicious" writings against government officials with the intent to "excite against them . . . the hatred of the good people of the United States."[6] In 1800 the Quasi-War ended when Napoleon signed a peace treaty with America.

Back in America, the election of 1800 was taking place and Jefferson was challenging Adams for the presidency. The nation became divided between Adams's Federalists and Jefferson's new Democratic-Republicans. The Federalists were pro-British and the Democratic-Republicans supported France. The election saw four candidates square off: Adams, Jefferson, Aaron Burr, and Charles Pinckney. That year there was no clear winner in the electoral college. Jefferson and Burr were tied at seventy-three votes each, Adams received sixty-four votes, and Pinckney received sixty-five. This meant the House of Representatives would have to elect the president. In 1801 they elected Thomas Jefferson, making Adams the first sitting president not to be reelected. Embittered toward Jefferson, Adams refused to attend his inauguration.[7]

Adams retired to his home in Quincy, where he lived for the rest of his life. In 1824 he saw his son, John Quincy, elected to the presidency. Eventually, there was a rapprochement between Adams and Jefferson, with the two exchanging letters. Coincidentally, both men died on the same day: July 4, 1826.[8]

LIBRARY

The history of the John Adams Library goes back to 1822, when Adams was eighty-six years old. He made arrangements for his three thousand books, deeding to

> the inhabitants of the Town of Quincy in their corporate capacity, and their successors, the fragments of my library, which still remain in my possession, excepting a few that I shall reserve for my consolation in the few days that remain to me.[9]

Adams also stipulated that his books be "deposited in an apartment of the building to be hereafter erected for a Greek and Latin School or Academy."[10]

Five people were commissioned as custodians to ensure that the books would be kept as requested. Adams wanted his books to be used for educational purposes. Therefore, he did not bequeath his personal Bible or his wife's books. One year later, a list of Adams's books was published in a catalog: *Deeds and Other Documents Relating to the Several Pieces of Land, and to the Library Presented to the Town of Quincy by President Adams.* People found the catalog difficult to use, because his books were cataloged according to their size and the language they were printed in, rather than by title or author.[11]

When Adams died on July 4, 1826, the books were stored in a farmhouse known as the "office room" behind the family mansion (the Old House) in Quincy. Though the town had officially inherited the books, they never built the library Adams had requested. In 1832 Adams's grandson Charles Francis Adams viewed the books with concern. He said:

> The books are very much out of order. Exposed to the injury of time, of damp and mice and utter neglect. I felt an emotion of grief whenever I think of the misapplication of the valuable funds in this instance.[12]

His fears were shared by Adams's great-grandson Alex Smith Johnson, who, in 1844, said:

> The town has never taken any steps towards [the library's] preservation, or to render it available for use. Indeed I suppose there are few persons in Quincy who are capable of using it, as for the most part, it consists of works in foreign and the dead languages.

The disorder in which the books are kept is extreme, and the whole scene an apt comment on being a benefactor of the public.[13]

In February 1848 Charles Francis Adams took the initiative and moved the books to the newly constructed Quincy Town Hall for temporary storage. The books were kept on the second floor of the hall, where they even survived a fire that broke out on August 23, 1851.[14] In 1870 the academy in which Adams wanted his books to be stored was finally built. By 1872 the Adams Academy was open and his books were made available to students. However, they made ill use of the books, tearing the pages and defacing them.[15] Two years later the books were removed to create more space for the growing student population. From the academy the books were moved to the vacant Evangelical Congregational Church. Adams's great-grandson Charles Francis Adams III edited the book catalog, *Catalogue of the Public Library of Quincy*.

In 1882 the wealthy Crane family from New York built the Thomas Crane Library in Quincy and the books were moved there. Thomas Crane was a rich stone contractor and hired noted architect Henry Hobson Richardson to build the library. Four years later the Boston Public Library constructed a new building, designed by architect Charles Follen McKim, in Copley Square. After the building was complete, the library's president, Samuel A. B. Abbott, wrote to the supervisor who managed Adams's books—the Adams Temple and School Fund—to ask if they would be interested in storing the books at the Boston Public Library. The supervisor approved the request, and in 1894 Adams's entire collection was moved to Boston, where it has been ever since.[16]

Since being moved to the Boston Public Library Adams's books have been preserved and cared for. A new catalog for the books was published in 1917, and in 1974 a new building designed by Philip Johnson was constructed to house the library's rare books and manuscripts department, which included Adams's books. In 1982 the library established a laboratory for the continuing preservation of the books. The laboratory is funded by the National Endowment for the Humanities. Unfortunately, funding limited the number of books that could be conserved.[17]

Not all of Adams's books are kept at Boston Public. About 10 percent of the collection is housed at the Stone Library in the Adams National Historic Park.[18] The park contains the "New England saltbox" homes in Quincy, Massachusetts, where John Adams and his son John Quincy were born.[19] The Stone Library, located on the property of the Adams National Historic Park, was built in 1870 and holds twelve thousand books belonging to the family—mostly to John Quincy Adams.[20] Readers can find more information about the Stone Library in the chapter on the John Quincy Adams Library.

Collections

The John Adams Library at the Boston Public Library holds a collection of "1,900 titles and 3,500 volumes."[21] The majority of these books were collected personally by Adams, while others belonged to members of his family. Most of the books in the library were printed in North America or Europe between 1700 and 1825. The books cover the subjects of classical literature, mathematics, history, law, science, religion, agriculture, economics, and travel. The oldest book, *De Nola Opusculum* by Ambrogio Leone, was printed in 1514 and focuses on the architecture of the Renaissance era.[22]

The books are kept in the Boston Public Library's rare books department because of their uniqueness, historical significance, and importance to the history of Boston, and because the books resonate with scholars. The library states that Adams's annotations make the books even more unique:

> What makes the collection exceptional is Adams' scrupulous recording of thousands of interpretive and critical comments in hand written notes throughout the margins of hundreds of his books. Not only are the volumes extensively annotated in Adams' own hand, but they are also often the repository of other personal objects, such as letters, bills of sale, and the autumnal pressed leaves of familiar New England trees.[23]

A separate collection of Adams's books is Jeremiah Gridley's Law Library. Gridley was Adams's tutor when he trained to become a lawyer. Adams purchased his books after Gridley died in 1767. Today thirty volumes of Gridley's law books are found here. Most are from the eighteenth century and are written in English, Latin, or French. Two of them were written by the famous British jurist Sir Edward Coke.[24]

Unlike other presidential libraries, the Adams library does not have any exhibits. However, from 2009 to 2012 the library sent a traveling exhibition, *Adams Unbound*, to several public libraries around the country where visitors could view "photo reproductions" of the books showing Adams's personal annotations.[25]

NOTES

1. John Patrick Diggins, *John Adams*, the American Presidents Series (New York: Times Books, 2003), 33.

2. Diggins, *John Adams*, 96.

3. Diggins, *John Adams*, 97.

4. Diggins, *John Adams*, 105.

5. David McCullough, *John Adams* (New York: Simon and Schuster, 2001), 505.

6. McCullough, *John Adams*, 505.

7. Diggins, *John Adams*, 150.

8. Diggins, *John Adams*, 155.

9. "History of the Adams Library," John Adams Library at the Boston Public Library, accessed March 28, 2017, http://www.johnadamslibrary.org/about/mission/.

10. "History of the Adams Library."

11. "History of the Adams Library."

12. "History of the Adams Library."

13. "History of the Adams Library."

14. "History of the Adams Library."

15. "History of the Adams Library."

16. "History of the Adams Library."

17. "History of the Adams Library."

18. "Adams National Historic Park: Places," National Park Service, accessed March 28, 2017, https://www.nps.gov/adam/learn/historyculture/places.htm.

19. William G. Clotworthy, *Homes and Libraries of the Presidents: An Interpretive Guide*, third edition (Blacksburg, VA: McDonald & Woodward, 2008), 34–35.

20. "Adams National Historic Park: Places."

21. Beth Prindle, "John Adams Library," accessed March 28, 2017, http://www.bpl.org/distinction/files/2013/04/john_adams_library.pdf.

22. Prindle, "John Adams Library."

23. Prindle, "John Adams Library."

24. "Jeremiah Gridley's Law Library," John Adams Library at the Boston Public Library, accessed March 28, 2017, http://www.johnadamslibrary.org/explore/highlights/highlights2.aspx.

25. "Exhibitions: John Adams Unbound: On the Road!" John Adams Library at the Boston Public Library, accessed March 28, 2017, http://www.johnadamslibrary.org/explore/exhibition/.

BIBLIOGRAPHY

Clotworthy, William G. *Homes and Libraries of the Presidents: An Interpretive Guide*. Third edition. Blacksburg, VA: McDonald & Woodward, 2008.

Diggins, John Patrick. *John Adams*. The American Presidents Series. New York: Times Books, 2003.

McCullough, David. *John Adams*. New York: Simon and Schuster, 2001.

Prindle, Beth. "John Adams Library." Accessed March 27, 2017. http://www.bpl.org/distinction/files/2013/04/john_adams_library.pdf.

James Monroe Museum and Memorial Library

Address: 908 Charles Street, Fredericksburg, VA 22401
Phone: (540) 654-1043
Website: http://jamesmonroemuseum.umw.edu/
Social media: https://www.facebook.com/James-Monroe-Museum-and-Memorial
  -Library-177543148635/
Administration: Mary Washington University
Hours: 10 a.m. to 5 p.m. Monday to Saturday; 1 p.m. to 5 p.m. on Sundays

BIOGRAPHY OF JAMES MONROE

April 28, 1758–July 4, 1831
Fifth President: March 4, 1817–March 4, 1825
Democratic-Republican Party

James Monroe by Gilbert Stuart.
LC-USZ62-117118

James Monroe is one of America's Founding Fathers. When the Constitution was written in 1787, future president James Madison proposed a set of amendments, known as the Bill of Rights, in order to protect the interests of the people.[1] Article Five of the Constitution allowed for amendments to be made. However, opponents of the Constitution, including Monroe and another Founding Father, Patrick Henry, still voted against its ratification. Monroe and Henry were both anti-federalists: they believed that the Constitution would place too much power in the hands of a central government.[2] Eventually, the anti-federalists formed the Democratic-Republican Party, under which both Thomas Jefferson and James Monroe were elected.

On February 16, 1786, Monroe married Elizabeth Kortright. James and Elizabeth would have three children: Eliza, James, and Maria Hester. From the 1790s until 1816, Monroe served his country in various capacities, including minister to France, senator from Virginia, governor of Virginia, secretary of state, and secretary of war. In 1816 he ran for president and beat his Federalist opponent, Rufus King. Monroe received 76,592 popular votes and 183 electoral votes, while King received only 34,740 popular votes and 34 electoral votes.

As president, Monroe was concerned about the security of America. His experiences during the American Revolution and in the War of 1812, when Washington was burned, had convinced him to "put security above ideology."[3] His main achievements during his first term were to sign treaties with Great Britain. The Rush-Bagot Treaty of 1817 demilitarized the Great Lakes, and the Treaty of 1818 fixed the border between Canada and the United States at the forty-ninth parallel.[4] Monroe's domestic policy involved promoting the construction of new canals, bridges, and roads to strengthen the infrastructure of the ever-expanding nation.[5]

In 1820 Monroe ran for reelection. He was largely unopposed and was successful in winning a second term. Historians have referred to Monroe's second term as the Era of Good Feelings because he received such solid support from the nation.[6] Monroe's most significant accomplishment during his second term was the Monroe Doctrine. This provided a statement to the rest of the world that the United States was "the dominant power in the entire Western Hemisphere."[7] The doctrine called for an end to the foreign colonization of the New World and warned Europe that the United States would not "tolerate foreign incursions in the Americas."[8]

Though Monroe enjoyed a successful presidency, his post-presidency was difficult. He was in debt, and he spent his retirement sorting through his presidential papers in order to seek reimbursements.[9] Monroe died on July 4, 1831, which made him, along with John Adams and Thomas Jefferson, one of three presidents and Founding Fathers to die on Independence Day.

LIBRARY AND MUSEUM

In the 1920s Monroe's descendants thought that the present brick building, which is today the library and museum, once housed James Monroe's law office. However, the present building is more recent; the original was demolished long ago.[10]

The history of the library and museum goes back to the final days of James Monroe's administration in 1825. Monroe was bankrupt and he was seeking reimbursement from the government for his expenses as president.[11] He even wrote a memoir titled *The Memoir of James Monroe, Esq. Relating to His Unsettled Claims upon the People and Government of the United States.*[12] In 1827, he published two more books for profit. One was a study comparing the American government with other republican governments; the other was his autobiography.[13]

Upon his death in July 1831, Monroe's claims were still not settled. However, he named his grandson James L. Gouverneur Jr. as the heir to his papers.[14] In the late 1840s, Gouverneur turned over some of James Monroe's papers to Henry O'Reilly, editor of the *Rochester Daily Advertiser*. Gouverneur later learned that Congress had apparently purchased the papers that he had loaned to O'Reilly. On February 29, 1849,

Gouverneur came to an agreement with Congress to sell the rest of Monroe's papers in exchange for $20,000.[15] However, it was not until 1889 that the Library of Congress helped to publish the papers, which were presented in a set of seven volumes.

Gouverneur's daughter, Rose de Chine Gouverneur Hoes, played an important role in the development of the presidential library and museum. When she learned that the existing building was to be demolished, she purchased it and sent Monroe's remaining papers and personal possessions there.[16] Rose's two sons, Gouverneur Hoes and Laurence Gouverneur Hoes, along with Laurence's wife, Ingrid Westesson, spent fifty years constructing the museum and establishing the James Monroe Memorial Foundation to govern it.[17] The museum was known as the James Monroe Law Office and Memorial Library until it was transformed into the present-day named library and museum.[18] Today the library is owned by the Commonwealth of Virginia and administered by Mary Washington University.[19]

Collections and Exhibits

The James Monroe Museum and Memorial Library has several online exhibits, which have been created using 3-D scans. The first of these, *James Monroe*, is a bust of Monroe. This bust was sculpted in bronze by Peggy French Cresson in honor of her husband, William Penn Cresson. William had written a scholarly biography on Monroe, which was published by the University of North Carolina Press.[20]

The second online exhibit, *Diplomacy*, presents 3-D scans of artifacts related to Monroe's diplomatic achievements, including the Louisiana Purchase Bas Relief. This work was unveiled in 1904 to commemorate the one-hundredth anniversary of the Louisiana Purchase. The statue was designed by Karl Bitter for the St. Louis World's Fair and shows Monroe with American and French diplomats signing the purchase treaty. Visitors can also see images of the Peace Medals that the president awarded to the chiefs of Native American tribes whom he made peace with.[21]

In the third exhibit, *White House Experience*, website visitors can view 3-D scans of the desk that Monroe sat at to write the Monroe Doctrine. Also included is an early nineteenth-century chair from France, which was used by Cardinal Joseph Fesch, the half-brother of Napoleon's mother. The chair was designed by Dionisio and Lorenzo Santi. It was also used in the White House during Monroe's administration.[22]

The fourth online exhibit, *Personal Possessions*, displays images of the telescope that Monroe used during the War of 1812 and the snuffbox where he kept his tobacco.[23] The following exhibit is about Monroe's youngest daughter, *Maria Hester Monroe Gouverneur*. Among the artifacts that visitors can view online in 3-D are her childhood teapot, a bas relief profile, and her pianoforte.[24] The final online exhibit is *Plantation Life*. Monroe lived on a twelve-hundred-acre plantation, and two items from the plantation are on display. One is a brass candlestick holder and the other is a Betty lamp, which burned oil to light up a house at night.[25]

The public can visit most of the library and museum virtually in 3-D scans;[26] however, there are some permanent exhibits that can only be seen by visiting in person. One of these is titled *James Monroe: An American Life*. This exhibit is dedicated to telling the story of Monroe's professional and private life. Visitors can find out about Monroe's major accomplishments and learn about his family, including his wife, Elizabeth, and his daughters, Eliza and Maria Hester.[27] The next permanent exhibit is *Making of a Revolutionary*, where visitors can learn about the contributions Monroe made as a soldier during the American Revolution. Weapons that Monroe used during the revolution are on display. Of particular interest in this exhibit is an interactive called "The Continental Soldier: Young and Far Away from Home," where visitors can learn what life was like for ordinary soldiers in the American Continental Army.[28] The third exhibit, *The Era of Good Feelings: The Monroe Family in Washington*, shows visitors what life was like in the White House for Monroe and his family. According to the library, the family was "responsible for establishing the style of living in the White House that is still the standard today."[29] The Monroes had the job of refurbishing the White House after it was damaged by fire during the War of 1812. Inside the exhibit, visitors can see the chinaware used by the Monroe family and the desk (which can also be viewed online) that Monroe used when he penned the Monroe Doctrine.[30] The final permanent exhibit is *Americans in Paris: Monroe as Diplomat.* This exhibit tells the story of Monroe as the American ambassador to France, in the late eighteenth century. Visitors can see the French furniture that can also be viewed in the online exhibit.[31]

Unlike other presidential libraries, the James Monroe Museum and Memorial Library only holds a re-creations of the books he once owned. Monroe had three thousand books when he died. He even kept a handwritten inventory, which was handed down to Laurence Hoes. Using the inventory, Hoes was able to locate eighty books that Monroe had owned, which still displayed his personal nameplate inside. These volumes make up the rare book collection, with titles covering science, history, and law.[32]

The library also has an archive of ten thousand documents written by Monroe and his contemporaries. These documents are known as the Ingrid Westesson Hoes Archives and contain approximately eight hundred documents written by Monroe, Thomas Jefferson, and George Washington.[33]

NOTES

1. Harlow Giles Unger, *The Last Founding Father: James Monroe and a Nation's Call to Greatness* (Cambridge, MA: Da Capo Press, 2009), 79.

2. Unger, *Last Founding Father*, 82.

3. Gary Hart, *James Monroe*, the American Presidents Series (New York: Times Books, 2005), 81.

4. Daniel Preston, "James Monroe: Foreign Affairs," Miller Center, University of Virginia, https://millercenter.org/president/monroe/foreign-affairs.

5. Unger, *Last Founding Father*, 3.

6. Unger, *Last Founding Father*, 271.

7. Hart, *James Monroe*, 81.

8. Unger, *Last Founding Father*, 4.

9. Hart, *James Monroe*, 144–46.

10. "About the Museum," James Monroe Museum, accessed March 29, 2017, http://james monroemuseum.umw.edu/about-the-museum/.

11. Frank L. Schick, Renee Schick, and Mark Carroll, *Records of the Presidency: Presidential Papers and Libraries from Washington to Reagan* (Phoenix, AZ: Oryx Press, 1989), 57–58.

12. Schick et al., *Records of the Presidency*, 58.

13. Schick et al., *Records of the Presidency*, 58.

14. Schick et al., *Records of the Presidency*, 58.

15. Schick et al., *Records of the Presidency*, 59.

16. "About the Museum: Site History."

17. "About the Museum: Site History."

18. Schick et al., *Records of the Presidency*, 59.

19. William G. Clotworthy, *Homes and Libraries of the Presidents: An Interpretive Guide*, third edition (Blacksburg, VA: McDonald & Woodward, 2008), 62.

20. "James Monroe," James Monroe Museum in 3-D, accessed March 29, 2017, http://jmonroe3d.umwhistory.org/exhibit/james-monroe/.

21. "Diplomacy," James Monroe Museum in 3-D, accessed March 29, 2017, http://jmonroe3d.umwhistory.org/exhibit/diplomacy/.

22. "White House Experience," James Monroe Museum in 3-D, accessed March 29, 2017, http://jmonroe3d.umwhistory.org/exhibit/presidents-house-experience/.

23. "Personal Possessions," James Monroe Museum in 3-D, accessed March 29, 2017, http://jmonroe3d.umwhistory.org/exhibit/personal-possessions/.

24. "Maria Hester Monroe Gouverneur," James Monroe Museum in 3-D, accessed March 29, 2017, http://jmonroe3d.umwhistory.org/exhibit/maria-hester-monroe-gouverneur/.

25. "Plantation Life," James Monroe Museum in 3-D, accessed March 29, 2017, http://jmonroe3d.umwhistory.org/exhibit/plantation-life.

26. "James Monroe Museum in 3-D!" James Monroe Museum, accessed March 29, 2017, http://jamesmonroemuseum.umw.edu/james-monroe-museum-in-3-d/.

27. "Permanent Exhibits," James Monroe Museum, accessed March 29, 2017, http://jamesmonroemuseum.umw.edu/exhibitions/permanent-exhibits.

28. "Permanent Exhibits."

29. "Permanent Exhibits."

30. "Permanent Exhibits."

31. "Permanent Exhibits."

32. "Collections." James Monroe Museum, accessed March 29, 2017, http://jamesmonroemuseum.umw.edu/collections/.

33. "Collections."

BIBLIOGRAPHY

Clotworthy, William G. *Homes and Libraries of the Presidents: An Interpretive Guide*. Third edition. Blacksburg, VA: McDonald & Woodward, 2008.

Hart, Gary. *James Monroe*. The American Presidents Series. New York: Times Books, 2005.

Schick, Frank L., Renee Schick, and Mark Carroll. *Records of the Presidency: Presidential Papers and Libraries from Washington to Reagan*. Phoenix, AZ: Oryx Press, 1989.

Unger, Harlow Giles. *The Last Founding Father: James Monroe and a Nation's Call to Greatness*. Cambridge, MA: Da Capo Press, 2009.

Stone Library at the
Adams National Historical Park

Address: 135 Adams Street, Quincy, MA 02169
Phone: (617) 770-1175
Website: https://www.nps.gov/adam/index.htm
Administration: National Park Service
Hours: 9 a.m. to 5 p.m., Monday to Sunday

BIOGRAPHY OF JOHN QUINCY ADAMS

July 11, 1767–February 23, 1848
Sixth President: March 4, 1825–March 4, 1829
Democratic-Republican Party

John Quincy Adams.
LC-D416-520

John Quincy Adams was born to John and Abigail Adams in Braintree (Quincy), Massachusetts. Young John Quincy never attended school but was tutored by his cousin, John Thaxter, and a law clerk, Nathan Rice. They taught him Greek and Latin language and history.[1] John Quincy also accompanied his father on diplomatic missions abroad. On July 26, 1797, Adams married Louisa Johnson. Together they would have four children: George, Charles Francis, John, and Louisa Catherine, who died in infancy.

Adams began his political career as a diplomat. From 1794 to 1817, he served as ambassador to the Netherlands, Prussia, England, and Russia. He also served in the United States Senate, representing Massachusetts. In 1817 he was appointed as secretary of state by President James Monroe. Before that he had helped to negotiate the Treaty of Ghent, which ended the War of 1812 with England. He also negotiated with Spain for the annexation of Florida.[2] According to historian Samuel Flagg Bemis, Adams's successes as secretary of state stemmed from promoting "the fundamentals of American foreign-policy—self-determination, independence, noncolonization, nonintervention, nonentanglement in European politics, [and] Freedom of the Seas."[3] These achievements made Adams a good candidate to run for president in 1824.

In 1824 the nation saw a four-way presidential race between John Quincy Adams, Andrew Jackson, William Crawford, and Henry Clay. Among the electorate, the favored candidate was Jackson, the rugged and tough general who defeated the British in New Orleans in 1815. However, on the day of the election there was a problem: no candidate got a majority in the electoral college. The Twelfth Amendment to the Constitution requires that disputed elections be settled by the House of Representatives, where each state casts its vote as one. Although Jackson had won the popular vote, the House elected Adams to the presidency in 1825. Days later Adams appointed his rival, Henry Clay, as secretary of state. Jackson's supporters believed that Adams had stolen the election, and Jackson accused Adams of making a "corrupt bargain" with Clay.[4]

Adams's presidential policies were rooted in what was then called the "American System," where the government promoted "sound banking" and protectionism for American manufacturers in the world markets.[5] The policies of the American System began with Alexander Hamilton and the Federalist Party. Adams's critics, including Andrew Jackson, opposed the system because they believed that a strong central government put "individual liberty" in peril.[6] During his presidency Adams also invested in infrastructure programs for the construction of highways and canals. In foreign affairs, however, he was less successful. His pro-Jackson opponents in Congress routinely thwarted the efforts he made with foreign nations.[7]

When Adams lost his reelection bid to Jackson in 1828, he refused to attend Jackson's inauguration. However, losing the presidency was not the only problem that he had to face. After Adams returned home to Quincy, Massachusetts, for his retirement, his son George Washington Adams fell into debt and committed suicide.[8] Three years later, in 1833, Adams's retirement came to an abrupt end when his own district elected him to the House of Representatives. He became the first president to hold office in his post-presidency. So delighted was Adams when he was elected that he said, "I am a member-elect of the Twenty-Second Congress. . . . No election or appointment conferred upon me ever gave me so much pleasure."[9]

In Congress, Adams became a vocal abolitionist crusader. On his first day in office, he shocked many by calling for the "abolition of slavery and the slave trade in the District of Columbia."[10] In 1841, Adams took some time away from Congress to defend slaves in the *Amistad* case. A year earlier, the *Amistad*, a Spanish slave ship, had been commandeered by the slaves near Cuba. After killing the captain, they thought they had convinced the remaining sailors to return them to Africa. Instead, the sailors took them to New York.[11] The slaves wanted their freedom and petitioned for it in America's courts. The case went to the United States Supreme Court, where the slaves won their case and their freedom. During the oral arguments, Adams said, "Justice . . . is the constant and perpetual will to secure everyone his own right."[12]

Adams continued to serve in Congress until his death. On February 21, 1848, he collapsed during a session in the House of Representatives. He was moved into the Speaker's office, where he spoke his last words before going into a coma: "This is the end of earth, but I am composed."[13] Adams remained in a coma for the next two days and died on February 23, 1848.

LIBRARY

The Stone Library is near the mansion (known as the Old House) that John Quincy's father, John Adams, purchased in 1787.[14] The Old House is located in Quincy, Massachusetts. It was the family home and John Adams kept his personal collection of books and manuscripts there.[15] John Quincy was born in the house adjacent to the "Old House" and the Stone Library.[16] When John Adams died in July 1826, the collection was moved to a farmhouse behind the mansion for storage.

Shortly before becoming president in 1824, John Quincy Adams visited the family graves in Quincy, where he had an unnerving realization about their legacy. When writing of them, he said, "Four generations, of whom very little more is known, than is recorded upon these stones."[17] The cemetery visit convinced him of the need to preserve the family papers. Like his father, John Quincy Adams was a conspicuous record keeper. He preserved his own personal books and diaries for the future. After leaving the presidency in 1829, Adams considered building a "fireproof" library for his and his father's papers.[18] He began writing a biography on his father, but his work was abruptly cut short when he was elected to the House of Representatives in 1833. In 1842 he was still concerned about the future of his papers, and he bemoaned in his diary that he had "no chests and boxes and bureaus and drawers sufficient in numbers and capacity to contain these documents."[19]

One year before John Quincy Adams died, he willed his manuscripts and those of his father to his son Charles Francis Adams with the stipulation that he construct a fireproof building to keep them safe. He also stipulated that the manuscripts be kept "together as a single collection and in possession of the family."[20] In 1869 Charles Francis selected notable architect Edward C. Cabot to construct the fireproof library, known as the Stone Library, next to the Old House.[21] The building was completed a year later, in 1870. When Charles Francis died in 1886 he left the collection inside the Stone Library to his four sons: John Quincy II, Charles Francis II, Henry, and Brooks. Just after the turn of the century, in 1902, the surviving sons of Charles Francis deposited the papers with the Massachusetts Historical Society in Boston for "safekeeping."[22] They also established the Adams Manuscript Trust to oversee the birthplace of John and John Quincy Adams, the Old House, the Stone Library, and all the papers held by the Massachusetts Historical Society. Though the Stone Library holds the papers of both presidents, its focus is more on the family than on the presidency. The job of preserving the manuscripts went to the son of Charles Francis II, Charles Francis III when he became president of the Massachusetts Historical Society in 1908. Charles Francis III administered the trust as president of the society until 1940 when he deeded the Old House and the Stone Library to the United States Park Service. Today the house and Stone Library are still administered by the National Park Service and are known as the Adams National Historic Park.[23]

Stone Library, c. 1962 by Charles E. Peterson. *LC-HABS MASS,11-QUI,5D*

Collections and Exhibits

The Adams National Historic Park rests on thirteen acres of land and consists of eleven buildings, including the Stone Library, the Adams mansion (the Old House), and the saltbox structures in which Adams and his father were born. The entire collection, including books, manuscripts, and personal items that belonged to the Adams family, is made up of one hundred thousand objects.[24]

The Stone Library holds twelve thousand books belonging to the Adams family. The library's website states that more than twelve languages are represented in the collection, which includes a range of subjects from astronomy, literature, horticulture, natural history and theatre."[25] The library also has a personal copy of George Washington's Farewell Address given to John Quincy's father, John Adams, a Bible given to John Adams, which is inscribed with a "note of gratitude" from the Mendi people of Africa, and a Bible Concordance from 1521.[26]

In addition to the books, the library holds seventeenth-century American art, European and American decorative works of art, an archaeological collection, and photographs from the nineteenth century. Among the artists represented in the library are John Trumbull, Mather Brown, and William Morris Hunt. Ninety-nine percent of the objects in the library are original; examples include the Dutch chairs, the Queen Anne highboy, the Grecian card table, and the Louis XV settee and chairs. Visitors can also view reproduction upholstery, bedspreads, and wallpaper.[27]

NOTES

1. Robert V. Remini, *John Quincy Adams*, the American Presidents Series (New York: Times Books, 2002), 4.

2. Harlow Giles Unger, *John Quincy Adams* (Philadelphia: Da Capo Press, 2012), 174–75, 205–6.

3. Samuel Flagg Bemis, *John Quincy Adams and the Foundations of American Foreign Policy* (New York: Alfred A. Knopf, 1981), 567.

4. Unger, *John Quincy Adams*, 238–39.

5. Remini, *John Quincy Adams*, 81.

6. Remini, *John Quincy Adams*, 81.

7. Margaret A. Hogan, "John Quincy Adams: Foreign Affairs," Miller Center, University of Virginia, accessed March 27, 2017, http://millercenter.org/president/biography/jqadams-foreign-affairs.

8. Saturday Evening Post editors, *The Presidents: Their Lives, Families and Great Decisions: As Told by the* Saturday Evening Post (Indianapolis, IN: Curtis Publishing Company, 1989), 33.

9. John F. Kennedy, *Profiles in Courage*, Commemorative edition (New York: Harper & Row, 1964), 53.

10. Unger, *John Quincy Adams*, 266.

11. Unger, *John Quincy Adams*, 287–88.

12. Unger, *John Quincy Adams*, 291.

13. Unger, *John Quincy Adams*, 310.

14. Frank L. Schick, Renee Schick, and Mark Carroll, *Records of the Presidency: Presidential Papers and Libraries from Washington to Reagan* (Phoenix, AZ: Oryx Press, 1989), 27.

15. Schicket al., *Records of the Presidency*, 120.

16. "Plan Your Visit." National Park Service, accessed March 27, 2017, https://www.nps.gov/adam/learn/historyculture/places.htm.

17. Schick et al., *Records of the Presidency*, 121.

18. Schick et al., *Records of the Presidency*, 121.

19. Schick et al., *Records of the Presidency*, 121.

20. Schick et al., *Records of the Presidency*, 121.

21. Schick et al., *Records of the Presidency*, 122.

22. Schick et al., *Records of the Presidency*, 122.

23. "Collections," National Park Service, accessed March 27, 2017, https://www.nps.gov/adam/learn/historyculture/collections.htm.

24. "Collections."

25. "Collections."

26. "Collections."

27. "Collections."

BIBLIOGRAPHY

Bemis, Samuel Flagg. *John Quincy Adams and the Foundations of American Foreign Policy*. New York: Alfred A. Knopf, 1981.

Clotworthy, William G. *Homes and Libraries of the Presidents: An Interpretive Guide*. Third edition. Blacksburg, VA: McDonald & Woodward, 2008.

Diggins, John Patrick. *John Adams*. The American Presidents Series. New York: Times Books, 2003.

Kennedy, John F. *Profiles in Courage*. Commemorative edition. New York: Harper & Row, 1964.

Remini, Robert V. *John Quincy Adams*. The American Presidents Series. New York: Times Books, 2002.

Saturday Evening Post editors. *The Presidents: Their Lives, Families and Great Decisions: As Told by the* Saturday Evening Post. Indianapolis, IN: Curtis Publishing Company, 1989.

Schick, Frank L., Renee Schick, and Mark Carroll. *Records of the Presidency: Presidential Papers and Libraries from Washington to Reagan*. Phoenix, AZ: Oryx Press, 1989.

Unger, Harlow Giles. *John Quincy Adams*. Philadelphia: Da Capo Press, 2012.

Abraham Lincoln
Presidential Library and Museum

Address: 112 N. Sixth St., Springfield, IL 62701
Social media: https://www.facebook.com/Lincoln.Museum/
Administration: Illinois Historic Preservation Agency
Museum hours: 9 a.m. to 5 p.m., every day; closed on Thanksgiving Day, Christmas
  Day, and New Year's Day
Library hours: 9 a.m. to 5 p.m., Monday to Friday; closed on Thanksgiving Day,
  Christmas Day, and New Year's Day

BIOGRAPHY OF ABRAHAM LINCOLN

February 12, 1809–April 15, 1865
Sixteenth President: March 4, 1861–April 15, 1865
Republican Party

Abraham Lincoln and family, c. 1865.
LC-DIG-pga-03267

Abraham "Abe" Lincoln was born in a log cabin to Thomas and Nancy Hanks Lincoln in Hodgenville, Kentucky. Two years after his birth, the family moved to Knob Creek, Kentucky, and later to Spencer County, Indiana. In the fall of 1818, tragedy struck the family when Nancy died of "milk sickness" after one of their milking cows ate a poisonous snakeroot, causing its milk to be contaminated.[1] After Nancy died, Thomas Lincoln married Sara Bush Johnston, who became Abe's stepmother. Abe's childhood was tough, as he often did hard farm work. He had little formal education, as living on the frontier meant that teachers came and went. Instead, Abe educated himself by reading books. He read as much as he could, even borrowing books from neighbors. On one occasion he borrowed a book and tucked it into the loft of his log cabin. That night, the book was damaged by rain that seeped in through the logs. To compensate for the book, Abe worked the man's farm for three days.[2] By age twenty-one, he could "read, write, do arithmetic, and cipher to the rule of three, which was as much as most teachers in Indiana could do."[3] In the 1830s, the Lincolns relocated to Illinois, which became the state that Abe Lincoln is associated with.

As an adult, Lincoln took on many jobs to support himself. He worked on flatboats, worked as a store clerk, and briefly served as an officer during the Black Hawk War between the United States and Native Americans in 1832. In 1828 Lincoln sailed down the Mississippi River to deliver goods. While in New Orleans, he witnessed firsthand the horrors of a slave auction. Lincoln had always believed that "slavery was morally wrong and should be placed on the road to extinction."[4] But his experiences in New Orleans may have influenced his decision as president to formally emancipate them.[5]

No matter what job Lincoln did, he always had a book with him to read. He educated himself further by reading law books, which enabled him to go on to become a reputable lawyer in Illinois. On November 4, 1842, Lincoln married Mary Todd of Kentucky. Together they had four children: Robert, Edward, Willie, and Tad. Sadly, Edward died at age four and Willie at age eleven. To add to this tragedy, his youngest, Tad, would die at eighteen, leaving only Robert to live a full life.

Lincoln became interested in politics and was elected to the United States House of Representative in 1846, representing the Whig Party. In Congress, Lincoln openly opposed the declaration of war against Mexico in 1848. He feared that America was being too aggressive toward Mexico. He also became a vocal critic of slavery and tried to end slavery in Washington, DC, but without success.[6]

After serving in Congress, Lincoln decided to run for the senate from Illinois. He faced Democratic congressman Stephen A. Douglas. Lincoln and Douglas debated each other in what became known as the Lincoln-Douglas debates. The debates came on the heels of the infamous Dred Scott decision. The United States Supreme Court had ruled that a slave named Dred Scott "possessed no rights" and, therefore, could not sue his owner for freedom when he was "transported to a free state."[7] Douglas supported slavery, and said that he would "stand on the great principle of Popular Sovereignty."[8] Under popular sovereignty, the people of the states, and not the government, should decide on the question of slavery. This was in contrast to Lincoln, who vehemently opposed slavery. He said, "A house divided against itself cannot stand. I believe this government cannot endure permanently half *slave* and half *free*."[9] Lincoln lost the election to Douglas that year. However, two years later in 1860 the candidates would once again face off against each other for the presidency.

The presidential election of 1860 was turbulent. The Republicans nominated Abraham Lincoln for president and Hannibal Hamlin of Maine for vice president. The Democrats were split between Vice President John C. Breckinridge and Stephen A. Douglas. When the convention nominated Douglas, Southern delegates left in protest, fearing that he would not be a unifier.[10] They reconvened and nominated Breckinridge instead. This split in the Democratic Party led to a Republican victory in 1860. Lincoln won 1,865,908 popular votes and 180 electoral votes. Douglas won 1,380,202 popular votes and only 12 electoral votes. Douglas's Democratic rival Breckinridge fared better, winning 848,019 popular votes and 72 electoral votes. A third-party candidate named John Bell, representing the Constitutional Union Party, won 590,901 popular votes and 39 electoral votes.

Lincoln's victory angered the South, as they feared that he would abolish slavery. On December 20, 1860, the legislature of South Carolina voted in favor of secession.[11] Soon, other states from the South left the Union to form their own independent nation, which they called the Confederate States of America. The Confederate attack on Fort Sumter, South Carolina, on April 12, 1861, precipitated the Civil War. Union general George B. McClellan saw the war as insurrection and recommended that Lincoln fight a limited war. However, this strategy ultimately failed, as the Confederacy won victories at the battles of Bull Run, Fredericksburg, and Chancellorsville. Lincoln had dismissed McClellan after he won the Battle of Antietam but suffered large numbers of casualties.

After Antietam, Lincoln signed the Emancipation Proclamation, which formally freed the slaves in the South. Still having problems with his generals, Lincoln appointed others, including Ambrose Burnside and Joseph Hooker, both of whom failed to bring about a swift Union victory. In 1863, Lincoln finally appointed General Ulysses S. Grant to head the Union Army. Grant believed that the Confederacy had to be destroyed and advocated total war.[12] His tough tactics had won him victories in such places as Shiloh and Vicksburg. In spite of this, Grant was unpopular in the army and he was known to be a drinker. When Lincoln was informed of this, however, he joked, "Find out what he's drinking and order it for my other generals."[13] On July 3, 1863, the Union won the first decisive victory over the Confederates during the bloody three-day Battle of Gettysburg in Pennsylvania. Four months after the battle, on November 19, 1863, Lincoln would visit the battlefield to deliver his famous Gettysburg Address, dedicating a cemetery there to the fallen troops.

In 1864 the Republican Party nominated Lincoln to run for a second term. Rather than renominate his running mate, Hamlin, Lincoln picked Democratic military governor of Tennessee Andrew Johnson. Unlike his compatriots, Johnson had remained loyal to the Union. Lincoln chose him as a gesture of "kindness to the South."[14] The Democrats nominated former Union general McClellan, who advocated peace and "maintain[ing] slavery in the South."[15] With the exception of Louisiana, which was under Union occupation, the South did not participate in this election. The result was another victory for Lincoln, who won 2,218,388 popular votes and 212 electoral votes. McClellan won 1,812,807 popular votes and 21 electoral votes, with only Kentucky and New Jersey supporting him.

Lincoln wanted the South to return to the Union peacefully after the war. In his second inaugural address, he said:

> With malice toward none, with charity for all, with firmness in the right as God gives us to see the right, let us strive on to finish the work we are in, to bind up the nation's wounds, to care for him who shall have borne the battle and for his widow and his orphan, to do all which may achieve and cherish a just and lasting peace among ourselves and with all nations.[16]

In January 1865, the Thirteenth Amendment was passed, legally abolishing slavery. Four months later, the war ended when Confederate general Robert E. Lee surrendered to General Grant at Appomattox Court House in Virginia. With the war over, Lincoln started working on returning the South to the Union and helping former slaves adjust to freedom. However, tragedy struck on April 14, 1865, when actor and Confederate sympathizer John Wilkes Booth shot Lincoln in the back of the head while he was watching a play with his wife, Mary. Booth was tracked down and shot dead twelve days later. The nation was saddened by Lincoln's death, and his funeral train sent him for burial in Springfield, Illinois. Mary died seventeen years later, on July 16, 1882. Mary and Abe are buried in the Lincoln Tomb at the Oak Ridge Cemetery in Springfield.

LINCOLN'S PAPERS AND THE LIBRARY AND MUSEUM

The story of Lincoln's papers begins a few days after his assassination on April 15, 1865. Lincoln's oldest son, Robert Todd Lincoln, asked United States Supreme Court justice David Davis to administer his father's estate. The president's secretaries, John G. Nicolay and Colonel John Hay, stored the papers at the National Bank of Bloomington. In 1874, Robert Lincoln had the papers sent back to Nicolay and Hay, who were writing the authorized biography of his father. After Nicolay died in 1901, Hay had the papers moved to the Department of State. When Hay died in 1905, the papers were returned to Robert Lincoln, who initially stored them in his father's office at the Pullman Building in Chicago. Since Robert moved around a lot, he took the papers with him to his various homes in Georgetown and Manchester, Vermont. In late 1901, Librarian of Congress Herbert Putnam failed to persuade Robert Lincoln to donate the papers to the library. On Robert Lincoln's death in 1926, his will stated that the papers would go to the Library of Congress, but it stipulated that they must not be released publicly until twenty-one years after his death. Why Robert Lincoln ordered this is unknown. However, in 1947, the Library of Congress finally made the papers public.[17]

The Abraham Lincoln Presidential Library and Museum was established as the Illinois State Historical Library, and it kept this name until 2004. This presidential library is divided into two separate buildings on opposite sides of the street: the library and the museum. The library has worked hard to collect Lincoln's papers. Its website states:

> For more than 25 years, the Illinois State Historical Library and its successor, the Abraham Lincoln Presidential Library, have supported a long-term effort to locate, image, annotate, and publish comprehensive collections of papers relating to Abraham Lincoln's legal, political, and presidential career.[18]

The buildings are situated on the Old State Capitol, which was abandoned in 1876. The library planners visited several presidential libraries across the nation, seeking inspiration. The planners decided to create the exhibits first and have an architect build a facility around them. Architect Gyo Obata of the firm Hellmuth, Obata, and Kassabaum was chosen to design the library and museum. The library building is ninety-eight thousand square feet and features "buff-colored limestone from Egypt," a skywalk, and curved walls of glass.[19] Formal construction of the buildings began in 2001. The library opened to the public in 2004, followed by the museum one year later.

The museum building is across the street from the library. The museum was formally dedicated on April 19, 2005, at a ceremony attended by President George W. Bush and First Lady Laura Bush, United States senator and future president Barack Obama, and twenty-five thousand guests. On August 21, 2012, the museum welcomed its three-millionth visitor.[20] The library is administered by the Illinois Historic Preservation Agency, an Illinois state governmental agency. Its overall mission is supported by the Abraham Lincoln Presidential Library Foundation, a private nonprofit organization. The foundation also accepts donations.[21]

Collections and Exhibits

Visitors entering the Lincoln museum begin their tour in *The Plaza*, where they can see lifelike figures of Lincoln and his family. Next, visitors will move on to *The Treasures Gallery* to view items from Lincoln's family life. Inside the gallery are photos, china, and crystal.[22] The next exhibit is *The Illinois Gallery*, where visitors can view artifacts related to Lincoln's life and legacy. Children will enjoy *Mrs. Lincoln's Attic*. In this gallery, you can try on Lincoln's suit and Mary Lincoln's dress, rearrange the furniture inside the Lincoln Home dollhouse, and have your picture taken with a young Abraham Lincoln, his sister, and parents.[23]

The first major section is *Journey One: The Pre-Presidential Years*. This is divided into nine exhibits that re-create scenes to tell the story of Lincoln, from his childhood in Kentucky to his presidency in Washington, DC. Visitors touring this exhibit will see a young Lincoln reading a book outside his log cabin. This exhibit is named *Self-Taught*. The next two exhibits, *On the River* and *New Salem*, show some of the odd jobs that Lincoln did, such as "plying flatboats" and working as a store clerk.[24] The next exhibit captures the drama of a slave auction in New Orleans, where a father, mother, and child are all sold to separate bidders. Lincoln's trip to New Orleans in the late 1820s may have shaped his antislavery convictions. The next exhibit, *Life in Springfield*, presents Lincoln as a lawyer, suitor, husband, and father. There are also exhibits re-creating the Lincoln-Douglas debates, with two replicas of the men. *The Permissive Parent* shows Lincoln as a parent to his children.[25] Finally, *Journey One* concludes with *On to Washington*, showing Lincoln delivering his farewell speech to the people of Springfield shortly before he left for the White House.[26]

After leaving *Journey One*, visitors will enter the *Union Theater*, where digital-projection screens present the story of *Lincoln's Eyes*. Special effects are used "to capture the sorrow, hope, vision, resolve, and forgiveness in Lincoln's eyes."[27]

Journey Two: The White House Years is the second main section, which is divided into sixteen exhibits. It gives visitors an exclusive insight into the hardships that Lincoln faced as a wartime president. Within the exhibits visitors will see re-created scenes of Mary Lincoln being fitted for a dress, Lincoln's office at the White House, citizens of Washington expressing their dissatisfaction with Lincoln, and a mural of the Confederate attack on Fort Sumter (which was the formal beginning of hostilities). They will also see the Lincolns at the South Portico of the White House; Mary Lincoln grieving the sad death of the Lincolns' youngest son, Willie; the White House kitchen staff spreading rumors and gossip; the Emancipation Proclamation; Lincoln receiving telegrams about high casualty counts during battles; information about the Battle of Gettysburg; and Lincoln's reelection victory of 1864. Finally, there is information about Lincoln's assassination, including scenes of his funeral train, the president lying in state, and how his memory has been preserved with "souvenirs and other objects."[28]

After the story in the theater, visitors move on to *Ask Mr. Lincoln.* Visitors select questions from a "pre-programmed" list and view a film that answers their questions. Lincoln historian Tom Schwartz provides the background, while actor William Schallert "provides" the voice of Lincoln.[29]

The next stop is *Ghosts of the Library.* A host will welcome visitors and explain that they will see ghostly images. The museum utilizes Holavision, which releases "smoke and vapors" that are manipulated by the host to form the ghostly characters of Lincoln, his wife, Mary, and soldiers from the Civil War.[30] When the show is over, visitors will go to the final rooms of the museum, *The Gateway.* Here, visitors will find information about Lincoln-related historical sites in central Illinois and a gift shop for souvenirs.[31]

According to the website, the Lincoln library holds "the world's largest archive of papers and artifacts on Abraham Lincoln and an unparalleled collection on the history of the Prairie State."[32] There are approximately "172,000 books and pamphlets, 3,000 maps, and 1,200 periodical series."[33] Topics covered by the books include the Civil War, family genealogies, Native American history, Illinois history, and local history. There are also military rosters and pension indexes from the American Revolution to World War II. The library holds original maps from the 1700s, including pre-statehood maps of Illinois, the Great Lakes region, and the Louisiana Territories.[34]

In 1985 librarians of the Illinois State Historical Library began compiling and annotating papers related to Lincoln's career in law and politics. In the year 2000 the librarians published a collection of ninety-six thousand documents containing court records and legal correspondences relating to Lincoln's law practice. The librarians are now compiling a collection of papers for two additional series. The first will contain papers about Lincoln's life before he became president in 1861. The second will focus on his presidency, which lasted until his assassination in 1865.[35]

An interesting feature of this library's website is a section dedicated to bibliographic sources on Lincoln and his era. The library calls it their Selected Bibliographies; thirteen bibliographies are available in PDF format. For example, the selected bibliography on the 1860 Republican National Convention gives researchers information on books and journal articles that have been written about this event. Other relevant bibliographies include the 1864 Republican National Convention, Illinois Regiments, the letters of Lincoln and General Grant, Lincoln's Tomb, the Lincoln-Douglass Debates, and even White House Dinners.[36]

NOTES

1. George McGovern, *Abraham Lincoln,* the American Presidents Series (New York: Times Books, 2009), 16.

2. Brian Burns, "A Real Education," *Illinois History: A Magazine for Young People*, February 1995, 29–30, accessed May 19, 2017, http://www.lib.niu.edu/1995/ihy950229.html.

3. Burns, "Real Education," 29–30.

4. LaWanda Cox, *Lincoln and Black Freedom: A Study in Presidential Leadership* (Columbia: University of South Carolina Press, 1994), 5.

5. Christ Balich, "Flatboating Down the Mississippi," *Illinois History: A Magazine for Young People*, February 1995, 33, accessed May 19, 2017, http://www.lib.niu.edu/1995/ihy950233.html.

6. McGovern, *Abraham Lincoln*, 32–34.

7. McGovern, *Abraham Lincoln*, 40.

8. Benjamin P. Thomas, *Abraham Lincoln: A Biography* (Carbondale: Southern Illinois University Press, 2008), 177.

9. Thomas, *Abraham Lincoln*, 180.

10. James C. Klotter, *The Breckinridges of Kentucky* (Lexington: University Press of Kentucky, 1986), 115.

11. McGovern, *Abraham Lincoln*, 46–51.

12. McGovern, *Abraham Lincoln*, 80–89.

13. McGovern, *Abraham Lincoln*, 87.

14. McGovern, *Abraham Lincoln*, 104.

15. William E. Gienapp, "The 1864 Election in Illinois," *Illinois History Teacher* (2001), http://www.lib.niu.edu/2001/iht820144.html.

16. Abraham Lincoln, "Abraham Lincoln: Second Inaugural Address," in *Inaugural Addresses of the Presidents of the United States*, http://www.bartleby.com/124/pres32.html.

17. Frank L. Schick, Renee Schick, and Mark Carroll, *Records of the Presidency: Presidential Papers and Libraries from Washington to Reagan* (Phoenix, AZ: Oryx Press, 1989), 80–81.

18. "Papers of Abraham Lincoln," Abraham Lincoln Presidential Library and Museum, accessed May 18, 2017, https://www.illinois.gov/alplm/library/lincoln/Pages/PapersofAbraham Lincoln.aspx.

19. Myron Marty, "The Abraham Lincoln Presidential Library and Museum," *Public Historian* 28, no. 3 (Summer 2006): 186.

20. "Museum History," Abraham Lincoln Presidential Library and Museum, accessed May 18, 2017, https://www.illinois.gov/alplm/museum/About/Pages/Museum-History.aspx.

21. "Abraham Lincoln Presidential Library Foundation," Abraham Lincoln Presidential Library and Museum, accessed May 18, 2017, https://www.illinois.gov/alplm/library/aboutus/Pages/AbrahamLincolnPresidentialLibraryFoundation.aspx.

22. "Interactive Map of Museum: The Plaza," Abraham Lincoln Presidential Library and Museum, accessed May 18, 2017, https://www.illinois.gov/alplm/museum/visit/Pages/Interac tiveMap.aspx#Plaza.

23. "Interactive Map of Museum: The Plaza."

24. "Journey One: The Pre-Presidential Years," Abraham Lincoln Presidential Library and Museum, accessed May 18, 2017, https://www.illinois.gov/alplm/museum/visit/Pages/Journey -One.aspx.

25. Marty, "Abraham Lincoln Presidential Library," 187.

26. "Journey One: The Pre-Presidential Years."

27. "Interactive Map of Museum: Union Theater," Abraham Lincoln Presidential Library and Museum, accessed May 18, 2017, https://www.illinois.gov/alplm/museum/visit/Pages/Interac tiveMap.aspx#Union.

28. "Journey Two: The White House Years," Abraham Lincoln Presidential Library and Museum, accessed May 18, 2017, https://www.illinois.gov/alplm/museum/visit/Pages/Journey -Two.aspx.

29. "Interactive Map of Museum: Union Theater."

30. "Ghosts of the Library," Abraham Lincoln Presidential Library and Museum, accessed May 18, 2017, http://www.lincolnlibraryandmuseum.com/ghosts.htm.

31. "The Museum Store," Abraham Lincoln Presidential Library and Museum, accessed May 18, 2017, https://www.illinois.gov/alplm/museum/visit/Pages/InteractiveMap.aspx#Store.

32. "About Us," Abraham Lincoln Presidential Library and Museum, accessed May 18, 2017, https://www.illinois.gov/alplm/library/aboutus/Pages/default.aspx.

33. "Printed Materials," Abraham Lincoln Presidential Library and Museum, accessed June 5, 2017, https://www.illinois.gov/alplm/library/collections/printedmaterials/Pages/default.aspx.

34. "Printed Materials."

35. "Papers of Abraham Lincoln," Abraham Lincoln Presidential Library and Museum, accessed May 18, 2017, https://www.illinois.gov/alplm/library/lincoln/Pages/PapersofAbrahamLincoln.aspx.

36. "Subject Bibliographies," Abraham Lincoln Presidential Library and Museum, accessed May 18, 2017, https://www.illinois.gov/alplm/library/lincoln/Pages/SubjectBibliographies.aspx.

BIBLIOGRAPHY

Balich, Christ. "Flatboating Down the Mississippi." *Illinois History: A Magazine for Young People*, February 1995: 33. Accessed May 19, 2017. http://www.lib.niu.edu/1995/ihy950233.html

Burns, Brian. "A Real Education." *Illinois History: A Magazine for Young People*, February 1995. Accessed May 19, 2017. http://www.lib.niu.edu/1995/ihy950229.html.

Cox, LaWanda. *Lincoln and Black Freedom: A Study in Presidential Leadership*. Columbia: University of South Carolina Press, 1994.

Gienapp, William E. "The 1864 Election in Illinois." *Illinois History Teacher* (2001): 44–63. Accessed May 19, 2017. http://www.lib.niu.edu/2001/iht820144.html.

Klotter, James C. *The Breckinridges of Kentucky*. Lexington: University of Kentucky Press, 1986.

Lincoln, Abraham. "Abraham Lincoln: Second Inaugural Address." In *Inaugural Addresses of the Presidents of the United States*. http://www.bartleby.com/124/pres32.html.

Marty, Myron. "The Abraham Lincoln Presidential Library and Museum." *Public Historian* 28, no. 3 (Summer 2006): 185–89.

McGovern, George. *Abraham Lincoln*. The American Presidents Series. New York: Times Books, 2009.

Schick, Frank L., Renee Schick, and Mark Carroll. *Records of the Presidency: Presidential Papers and Libraries from Washington to Reagan*. Phoenix, AZ: Oryx Press, 1989.

Thomas, Benjamin P. *Abraham Lincoln: A Biography*. Carbondale: Southern Illinois University Press, 2008.

· 6 ·

President Andrew Johnson Museum and Library

Address: 60 Shiloh Road, Greeneville, TN 37743
Phone: (423) 636-7348 or (800) 729-0256 ext. 5348
Website: http://ajmuseum.tusculum.edu/
Social media: https://www.facebook.com/President-Andrew-Johnson-Museum-and
  -Library-138121451797/
Administration: Tusculum College
Hours: 9 a.m. to 5 p.m., Monday to Friday; closed during holidays recognized by
  Tusculum College

BIOGRAPHY OF ANDREW JOHNSON

December 29, 1808–July 31, 1875
Seventeenth President: April 15, 1865–March 4, 1869
Democratic Party

Andrew Johnson.
LC-USZ62-13017

Andrew Johnson was born in Raleigh, North Caro-lina. Being poor, he apprenticed himself as a tailor and moved to Greeneville, Tennessee, where he found much success. He married Eliza McCardle, who would give him five children, and became active in local politics. Presenting himself as a common man, Johnson became an alderman in Greeneville and eventually climbed the political ladder to the Tennessee legislature, the gover-norship, and the United States Senate.

When the Civil War broke out in 1861, the senators and congressmen from the South abandoned Washington for the Confederacy. Senator Johnson was the sole exception: bravely, he remained loyal to the Union, despite being a Southerner and a Democrat. Johnson challenged fellow Southerners to stay loyal, too. In a speech explaining his position, he stated:

I will not give up this government. . . . No; I intend to stand by it . . . and I entreat every man who is a patriot . . . to come forward . . . and rally around the altar of our common country, and lay the Constitution upon it as our last libation, and swear by our God, and all that is sacred and holy, that the Constitution shall be saved, and the Union preserved.[1]

When President Abraham Lincoln sought reelection in 1864, he was up against the popular former general George B. McClellan. Lincoln wanted a vice president who would be acceptable to the North and the South. This made Senator Johnson an attractive running mate. Writing on the subject, David O. Stewart explained, "By adding Johnson to their ticket, Republicans hoped to appeal to Democrats and show that they were not just a Northern party."[2] Lincoln's decision paid off and he was elected to a second term. However, on April 14, 1865, President Lincoln was assassinated by John Wilkes Booth. The president's death in the early hours of the following morning made Johnson president.

President Johnson wanted to implement Lincoln's plan for a peaceful rapprochement with the South after the war. But a segment of the Republican Party known as the Radical Republicans had other plans for the South—they wanted punishment and military rule. The Radical Republicans were led by Congressman Thaddeus Stevens of Pennsylvania. Stevens was an ardent abolitionist who called for a "radical reorganization of southern institutions, habits, and manners."[3] Stevens sought to treat the South as a conquered nation of enemies and proposed legislation to divide it into five military districts. To make matters worse for Johnson, his secretary of war, Edwin Stanton, was a Radical Republican who favored Stevens's plan. This created much friction between Johnson and Stanton.

Historians have argued that Johnson was a flawed character. Hans L. Trefousse said Johnson was "stubborn,"[4] while John F. Kennedy said his "own belligerent temperament soon destroyed any hope that Congress might now join hands in carrying out Lincoln's policies of permitting the South to resume its place in the Union with as little delay . . . as possible."[5] In 1867 Congress passed the Tenure of Office Act over Johnson's veto. The act prevented presidents from removing sitting cabinet members. This caused an enraged Johnson to remove Secretary Stanton and set the stage for impeachment.

The impeachment of Andrew Johnson is a historical milestone in America: it was the first time a sitting president was impeached. The impeachment has become a part of American popular culture; the event was portrayed in the 1942 movie *Tennessee Johnson*, where actor Van Heflin played Johnson and Lionel Barrymore (whose grandniece is Drew Barrymore) played Thaddeus Stevens. The future president John F. Kennedy presented the impeachment in his book *Profiles in Courage*, arguing that Republican senator Edmund G. Ross of Kansas was courageous for going against the wishes of his party to acquit Johnson.

On February 24, 1868, the House of Representatives voted in favor of eleven articles of impeachment. A few weeks later, on March 13, 1868, the trial began in the Senate chambers, with Chief Justice Salmon P. Chase presiding. The main Republican prosecutors were Thaddeus Stevens and his radical colleague Congressman Benjamin Butler of Massachusetts. Johnson's defense team consisted of former attorney general Henry Stanbery and former Supreme Court justice Benjamin Curtis. The United States

Constitution says that presidents can be impeached only if they are guilty of "high crimes and misdemeanors."[6] The Republicans believed Johnson's removal of Stanton was a high crime and argued just that. Over the next two months, inflamed and impassioned speeches for and against Johnson were made in the Senate. The climax came on May 26, 1868, when the Senate acquitted Johnson "35 to 19, exactly one vote short of the required two-thirds for conviction."[7] Among those voting for acquittal were seven Republican senators, including Edmund G. Ross.

That summer, Johnson actively sought the Democratic nomination. However, the convention nominated New York governor Horatio Seymour, who lost to the Republican Ulysses S. Grant. In 1875 Johnson was reelected to the United States Senate. Johnson was happy to return to his former seat.

On July 31, 1875, at the age of sixty-six, Andrew Johnson died from a stroke. He is buried at the Andrew Johnson National Cemetery in Greeneville, Tennessee.

LIBRARY AND MUSEUM

The President Andrew Johnson Museum and Library is located at Tusculum College. The college was established in 1794 near the Great Smoky Mountains of Greeneville. Tusculum is a private Presbyterian college and the first established in Tennessee.[8] Johnson was a trustee of the college from 1844 to 1875.

The library and museum is housed in the Old College building. In 1835 the Reverend Samuel Witherspoon Doak built a two-room academic building on the campus. However, the humble building did not keep pace with the growth of the college and by 1840 a new building was needed. That year a fund of $4,245.62 was raised by donors, including then Tennessee state legislator Andrew Johnson. When the new brick building was completed one year later, Reverend Doak made a dedication speech stating:

> This institution was revived in the year 1834 and has enjoyed growing prosperity up to the present time and without any expense to the public until the year 1841. The institution is furnished with a convenient, comfortable and handsome brick edifice 68 feet long, 36 feet wide, and two stories high. It is located four miles east of Greeneville, East Tennessee, having all the advantages of a [college] in a town as yet free from all its disadvantages, on a beautiful eminence, that commands a delightful view of the distant mountains and the surrounding farms and forrest [sic].[9]

In 1924 Johnson's great-granddaughter, Margaret Johnson Patterson Bartlett, graduated from Tusculum. Margaret and her father, Andrew Johnson Patterson, were the promoters of Andrew Johnson's legacy and homestead. When Mr. Patterson died, Mrs. Bartlett and her mother, Mattie, donated books and other artifacts to the museum at Tusculum.[10]

Collections and Exhibits

The library is run by the Department of Museum Studies at Tusculum. Inside the presidential library visitors will find President Andrew Johnson's personal library: eight hundred volumes he owned, along with another five hundred that belonged to his children and grandchildren. The majority are reference books from his era, and the personal collections of his granddaughter Margaret are also on display. Those interested in President Johnson's personal papers will find "fifteen linear feet" of papers written by Johnson and his family.[11] Visitors can also see photographs, along with a life-mask of President Abraham Lincoln and Johnson's own top hat.[12]

As of 2015 the museum contains five exhibits. The first exhibit is *Andrew Johnson: Heritage, Legacy, and Our Constitution*, which includes Johnson's personal library. Visitors will also find personal objects that belonged to the Johnson family. A coffee and tea warmer can be seen in the exhibit, along with Johnson's personal desk and flags.[13]

The second exhibit is *Scholars Then Soldiers: Tusculum College during the American Civil War*. The exhibit was opened in 2012 to commemorate the sesquicentennial of the Civil War. Visitors can learn about the nineteen Tusculum alumni who fought in the war and find out how the war affected the college when the Greeneville campus was devastated by combat damage.[14]

The third exhibit is *Reaper: Nettie McCormick and the Machine That Built Tusculum*. Nettie McCormick's husband was Cyrus McCormick, who invented the McCormick mechanical reaper. The invention helped to revolutionize the business of agriculture by making the harvesting of grains less laborious. Throughout her life, Nettie McCormick made several donations to Tusculum and this exhibit celebrates the contributions of this couple.[15]

The fourth exhibit is a work in progress. It will be named *Glimpses of Tusculum: A Storied History* and will showcase artifacts and photos of past Old Oak Festivals the college celebrates annually.[16]

The fifth and final exhibit is a temporary one: *Sittin' Pretty: Selections from the Doak House Furniture Collection*. A collection of Appalachian chairs was presented at the 2015 Old Oak Festival at Tusculum.[17]

In January 2015 the library received a grant of $800 from the Tennessee Historical Records Advisory Board. The money will be used to add extra shelves for the library's collection of rare books and its "backlogged collections."[18]

NOTES

1. Hans L. Trefousse, *Andrew Johnson: A Biography* (New York: W. W. Norton, 1989), 131.

2. David O. Stewart, *Impeached: The Trial of President Andrew Johnson and the Fight for Lincoln's Legacy* (New York: Simon & Schuster, 2009), 7.

3. Stewart, *Impeached*, 17.

4. Trefousse, *Andrew Johnson*, 42.

5. John F. Kennedy, *Profiles in Courage*, Commemorative edition (New York: Harper & Row, 1964), 133.

6. Stewart, *Impeached*, 79.

7. Trefousse, *Andrew Johnson*, 326.

8. "My Tusculum College," Tusculum College, accessed March 28, 2016, http://www.tusculum.edu/mytusculum/quickfacts.html.

9. "President Andrew Johnson Museum and Library: About the Museum Building," Tusculum College, accessed March 28, 2016, last modified October 20, 2014, http://ajmuseum .tusculum.edu/?page_id=40.

10. "President Andrew Johnson Museum and Library: The Andrew Johnson Collection," Tusculum College, accessed March 28, 2016, last modified April 1, 2015, http://ajmuseum.tusculum .edu/?page_id=6.

11. "President Andrew Johnson Museum and Library: The Andrew Johnson Collection."

12. "President Andrew Johnson Museum and Library: The Andrew Johnson Collection."

13. "Current Exhibits," Tusculum College, accessed May 26, 2016, last modified April 9, 2015, http://ajmuseum.tusculum.edu/?page_id=358.

14. "Current Exhibits."

15. "Current Exhibits."

16. "Current Exhibits."

17. "Current Exhibits."

18. "President Andrew Johnson Museum and Library: Tusculum College Receives Grant from the Tennessee Historical Records Advisory Board," Tusculum College, accessed 28 March 2016, last modified July 1, 2015, http://ajmuseum.tusculum.edu/?page_id=396.

BIBLIOGRAPHY

Kennedy, John F. *Profiles in Courage*. Commemorative edition. New York: Harper & Row, 1964.

Stewart, David O. *Impeached: The Trial of President Andrew Johnson and the Fight for Lincoln's Legacy*. New York: Simon & Schuster, 2009.

Tennessee Johnson. Directed by William Dieterle. 1942, Culver City, CA: Metro-Goldwyn-Mayer Studios.

Trefousse, Hans L. *Andrew Johnson: A Biography*. New York: W. W. Norton, 1989.

Ulysses S. Grant Presidential Library

Address: 395 Hardy Road, Mississippi State, MS 39762-5408
Phone: (662) 325-4552
Website: http://www.usgrantlibrary.org/
Administration: Ulysses S. Grant Association
Partnership: Mississippi State University Libraries

BIOGRAPHY OF ULYSSES S. GRANT

April 27, 1822–July 23, 1885
Eighteenth President: March 4, 1869–March 4, 1877
Republican Party

Ulysses S. Grant, c. 1880.
LC-USZ62-110720

Hiram Ulysses Grant was born in Point Pleasant, Ohio, to Jesse and Hannah Grant. He was one of six children born to this couple. During his childhood, Hiram Ulysses attended local schools and when he was older worked at his father's leather-making tannery. He disliked working there because the "sights and smells of slaughter and blood" disturbed him.[1] Since he could not tolerate the tannery, his father got a congressman to recommend him for West Point in New York.

On May 29, 1839, Grant began his military studies at West Point. His name was inadvertently changed from Hiram Ulysses to Ulysses Simpson because the congressman who recommended him mistook his name.[2] Like Grant, many of his classmates at West Point would become famous generals during the Civil War. Among them were George B. McClellan, Thomas "Stonewall" Jackson, and William Tecumseh Sherman. However, Grant was not a good student at West Point. Historian Josiah Bunting III said, "Minor disciplinary scrapes and misadventures and a manifest indifference to military rigmarole" earned him the rank of "cadet private" upon graduation.[3]

Grant saw his first military exploits during the Mexican War as a lieutenant. After the war he married Julia Dent. Together they would have four children: Frederick Dent, Ulysses Jr., Nellie, and Jessie Root. Grant went on to see a variety of military assignments out west in California and the Oregon Territory. Though he was promoted to captain, Grant earned a reputation for being an alcoholic and was forced to resign his commission in 1854. He then embarked on unsuccessful careers as a farmer and working in a leather store his father owned.[4]

When the Civil War broke out in 1861, Grant was recalled to active service. He was appointed a colonel to a volunteer regiment from Illinois and proved himself to be a capable commander. That same year he was promoted to the rank of general.[5] Grant became famous during the Battle of Shiloh, which was fought April 6–7, 1862, in Tennessee. The Civil War had been raging almost a year and the North was losing. "Shiloh was the severest battle fought at the West during the war."[6] During the battle Grant showed determination and won.[7] The battle was costly for the North and some called on President Lincoln to dismiss him. Lincoln refused by stating, "I can't spare this man; he fights."[8] Fighting and winning is exactly what Grant did. Unlike other Union generals, Grant did not make "excuses" for failures.[9]

From 1862 to 1863, Grant tried and eventually succeeded in taking the strategic town of Vicksburg, Mississippi. Grant said, "Vicksburg was important to the enemy because it occupied the first high ground coming close to the [Mississippi] river below Memphis."[10] He laid a massive siege to the town until the troops there finally surrendered on July 4, 1863. That day the North also defeated the South at Gettysburg. Grant said in his memoirs, "This news, with the victory of Gettysburg won the same day, lifted a great load of anxiety from the minds of the President, his Cabinet, and the loyal people all over the North. The fate of the Confederacy was sealed when Vicksburg fell."[11]

By 1864 Grant had become the commanding general of all Union forces. He won more victories at Chattanooga and at Petersburg which opened the Confederate capital at Richmond, Virginia, to him in March of 1865. A month later on April 9, 1865, he forced Confederate general Robert E. Lee to an unconditional surrender at the Appomattox Courthouse in Virginia. The war was over, but the nation had to face the tragic assassination of President Abraham Lincoln when actor John Wilkes Booth shot him at Ford's Theater six days later on April 15.

For the presidential election of 1868, the Republicans nominated Grant. Democrats nominated former governor Horatio Seymour of New York. The election was a victory for Grant, as he won 3,013,421 popular votes and 214 electoral votes. His opponent Seymour won 2,706,829 popular votes and 80 electoral votes.

Perhaps the most important aspect of Grant's first term was dealing with the South. The South was still under federal military control in what was known as Reconstruction. As president, Grant helped get the Fifteenth Amendment ratified which gave the vote to African American men. He also vigorously supported legislation outlawing the racist activities of the Ku Klux Klan. In 1871 Congress passed the Ku

Klux Klan bill, which promised "swift and sure federal action if violence and intimidation continued."[12]

In 1872 Grant won reelection over Democrat Horace Greeley of New York. Greeley was a famous journalist who had founded the *New York Tribune*. Grant won 3,598,235 popular votes and 286 electoral votes. Greeley won 2,834,761 popular votes and 66 electoral votes. Before the election was finalized, Greeley died on November 29, 1872, and his electoral votes were split up among other candidates.

Grant's second term was plagued by numerous scandals. Perhaps the most infamous was a fake corporation known as Crédit Mobilier, created by the Union Pacific Railroad. In 1872, the nation was constructing the transcontinental railroad, which was subsidized with federal money. Crédit Mobilier took advantage of federal subsidies to enrich themselves and their subcontractors.[13] Another scandal was known as the Whisky Ring because alcohol distillers bribed Treasury agents into "falsifying the quantities of liquor" to avoid higher taxes.[14] Then there was the retroactive congressional pay raise called the "Back Pay Grab."[15]

Most historians agree Grant's administration was corrupt. Josiah Bunting quotes the famous American historian Richard Hofstader, who argued, "Grant's administrations are notorious for their corruption."[16] However, Bunting argues the traditional narrative of Grant's administration as being corrupt overlooks key facts about political life during America's Gilded Age. He says the postwar Gilded Age was a "period richly hospitable to material ambition" and the so-called corruption in the administration was really just "political patronage."[17]

In 1876 Grant refused to seek a third term and went into retirement when his successor Rutherford B. Hayes became president. For the next two years, Grant and his wife went on an international tour. Together they visited Japan, Great Britain, Germany, Russia, India, and China. The tours were chronicled by journalist and future Librarian of Congress John Russell Young in a book titled, *Around the World with General Grant*.

Upon returning home Grant faced two personal crises. One was that he lost money when a bank he invested in crashed. The other was that he had throat cancer.[18] Grant had been a heavy cigar smoker and this was most likely the cause.[19] There was little the medicine of the late nineteenth century could do. He spent his remaining days in pain writing his memoirs, which provided financial support to his family. On July 23, 1885, Grant died. He is buried at the General Grant National Memorial in New York City. His wife, Julia, died on December 14, 1902. She is interned with her husband.

LIBRARY

The Grant library's history began in 1962. That year some states established Civil War Centennial Commissions to promote the history of the war during its one-hundredth anniversary. At the time, most of Grant's papers were "scattered" in various libraries, archives, and museums.[20] Historians concluded Grant's papers should be localized into

The seven-mile funeral cortege of General Grant. *Courtesy of the Ulysses S. Grant Presidential Library, Mississippi State University Libraries*

one library for easy access. Centennial commissions for New York, Illinois, and Ohio got together with some reputable historians and created the Ulysses S. Grant Association. John Y. Simon was named the association's first editor. Originally, the association was based at the Ohio Historical Society and later moved to Southern Illinois University in Carbondale. The association collected and published many of Grant's personal papers as general and president. By 2009, the association had published thirty-one volumes of Grant's papers.[21]

In 2008 Simon died and the papers were moved from Southern Illinois to their current home in the Mitchell Memorial Library at Mississippi State University. Why the papers were transferred from Southern Illinois to Mississippi State was not revealed publicly due to litigation. Four years later the library came under the leadership of John F. Marszalek.[22] Today the library is headed by Frank J. Williams, who helped compile the first scholarly edition of the *Personal Memoirs of U. S. Grant*, the thirty-second volume published by the association.[23] In 2015 the university built a twenty-one-thousand-square-foot addition to the northeast corner of the library for expansion purposes. The new library reopened in late 2017.[24]

Digital Collections

The Grant library holds seventeen thousand linear feet of published and unpublished papers and manuscripts written by Grant. The library also holds artifacts and ten thousand published books about Grant and the Civil War. The combined number of papers and books at the library make it the largest collection in the world on Grant.[25]

The Papers of Ulysses S. Grant consist of thirty-two volumes of Grant's papers and manuscripts, which have been published by the Grant Association. These digital copies can be viewed online. John Y. Simon edited most of the volumes when the library was affiliated with Southern Illinois University. The Grant Association received assistance in their publishing endeavor from the National Historical Publications and Records Commission, and the National Endowment for the Humanities.[26]

The Ulysses S. Grant Collection is a series of digital photographs, music sheets, political cartoons, and other memorabilia donated to the library over the years. Researchers will see digital copies of political cartoons that were printed in *Harper's Weekly* and *Puck*. They can also view "patriotic" music sheets honoring President Lincoln, General Sherman, and Grant.[27]

The Bultema-Williams Collection of Ulysses S. Grant Photographs and Prints is a collection of photographs and postcards of Grant, his home, and his family. They were donated by retired chief justice Frank J. Williams of Rhode Island and "amassed" by James A. Bultema, who served in the Grant Association as the vice president of development.[28]

The Bibliography and Chronology digital archive contains a timeline of Grant's life along with an annotated biography and a bibliography of books published on him.[29]

The Julia Grant World Tour Photographs is a collection of photos taken by Grant's wife during their post-presidential years. The collection contains images of famous heads of state whom Grant and his wife visited abroad, such as King Umberto of Italy, General Saigo of Japan, King Leopold II of Belgium, Queen Victoria of Great Britain, and Maria Feodorovna, Empress of Russia.[30]

The Ida Honoré Grant Correspondence, 1889–1893, is a collection of correspondence from the woman who married Grant's son Frederick Dent Grant. Honoré Grant was a wealthy socialite. The correspondences were written during Frederick Dent Grant's time as the American ambassador to Austria-Hungary. Altogether, the collection consists of 130 letters written between Honoré Grant and her relatives back in the states. The letters were donated by her great-grandson Ulysses Grant Dietz.[31]

The Letters of Private Arthur McKinstry is a personal collection of letters written by a Union soldier to his family. Arthur McKinstry was a Massachusetts native who served as a private in the New York State Volunteers Company D 72nd Regiment. McKinstry joined the army at the age of twenty-one in May 1861. He served until his death one year later on May 5, at the Battle of Williamsburg in Virginia. During his service, he wrote several letters to his mother, aunt, and cousins. The letters were recently donated to the Grant library by Frances Oakley, who is a descendent of McKinstry. The library was pleased to add the letters to its collection, calling them "a significant addition to the Grant collections."[32]

The final digital collection is the Orville Elias Babcock Diaries. Babcock was an army engineer who served under General Grant as an aide-de-camp. Babcock was with Grant at Vicksburg, Nashville, and Chattanooga. He also served as an aide when Grant became president. However, Babcock was involved in several scandals during Grant's administration, including the Whisky Ring. The collection contains several diaries written by Babcock between 1863 and 1869.[33]

NOTES

1. Josiah Bunting III, *Ulysses S. Grant*, the American Presidents Series (New York: Times Books, 2004), 10.

2. Bunting, *Ulysses S. Grant*, 12–14.

3. Bunting, *Ulysses S. Grant*, 17.

4. Bunting, *Ulysses S. Grant*, 28–33.

5. Bunting, *Ulysses S. Grant*, 38–44.

6. Ulysses S. Grant, *Memoirs of Ulysses S. Grant*, ed. John Kirk (East Bridgewater, MA: JG Press, 2012) 49.

7. Bunting, *Ulysses S. Grant*, 47.

8. Bunting, *Ulysses S. Grant*, 47.

9. Bunting, *Ulysses S. Grant*, 38.

10. Grant, *Memoirs*, 59.

11. Grant, *Memoirs*, 85.

12. Bunting, *Ulysses S. Grant*, 113.

13. Bunting, *Ulysses S. Grant*, 132.

14. Bunting, *Ulysses S. Grant*, 136.

15. Bunting, *Ulysses S. Grant*, 134.

16. Bunting, *Ulysses S. Grant*, 129.

17. Bunting, *Ulysses S. Grant*, 131.

18. Bunting, *Ulysses S. Grant*, 152.

19. Bunting, *Ulysses S. Grant*, 153.

20. "Welcome from President Frank J. Williams," Ulysses S. Grant Presidential Library, accessed March 28, 2017, http://www.usgrantlibrary.org/usga/welcome.asp.

21. "Welcome from President Frank J. Williams."

22. "Frequently Asked Questions," Ulysses S. Grant Presidential Library, accessed March 28, 2017, http://www.usgrantlibrary.org/about/faq.asp.

23. "Frequently Asked Questions."

24. "Mitchell Memorial Library Extension Project," Mississippi State University Libraries, accessed June 8, 2017, http://lib.msstate.edu/places/construction/mml-expansion/.

25. "Frequently Asked Questions."

26. "Digital Collections: The Papers of Ulysses S. Grant," Mississippi State University Libraries, accessed March 28, 2017, http://digital.library.msstate.edu/cdm/landingpage/collection/USG_volume.

27. "Digital Collections: Ulysses S. Grant Collection," Mississippi State University Libraries, accessed March 28, 2017, http://digital.library.msstate.edu/cdm/landingpage/collection/usgrant.

28. "Bultema-Williams Collection of Ulysses S. Grant Photographs and Prints," Mississippi State University Libraries, accessed June 6, 2017, http://digital.library.msstate.edu/cdm/landingpage/collection/cdv.

29. "Bibliography and Chronology," Mississippi State University Libraries, accessed June 6, 2017, http://digital.library.msstate.edu/cdm/landingpage/collection/bib.

30. "Julia Grant World Tour," Mississippi State University Libraries, accessed June 6, 2017, http://digital.library.msstate.edu/cdm/landingpage/collection/p16631coll2.

31. "Ida Honoré Grant Correspondence, 1889–1893," Mississippi State University Libraries, accessed June 6, 2017, http://digital.library.msstate.edu/cdm/landingpage/collection/p16631coll6.

32. "The Letters of Pvt. Arthur McKinstry," Mississippi State University Libraries, accessed June 6, 2017, http://digital.library.msstate.edu/cdm/landingpage/collection/p16631coll13.

33. "Orville Elias Babcock," Mississippi State University Libraries, accessed June 6, 2017, http://digital.library.msstate.edu/cdm/landingpage/collection/p16631coll17.

BIBLIOGRAPHY

Bunting III, Josiah. *Ulysses S. Grant.* The American Presidents Series. New York: Times Books, 2004.

Grant, Ulysses S. *Memoirs of Ulysses S. Grant.* Edited by John Kirk. East Bridgewater, MA: JG Press, 2012.

Kennedy-Nolle, Sharon. "Reconstruction on the Imperial Road: John Russell Young's 'Around the World with General Grant.'" *Journal of the Midwest Modern Language Association* 43, no. 2 (Autumn 2010): 75–98.

Rutherford B. Hayes
Presidential Library and Museums

Address: Spiegel Grove, Fremont, OH 43420
Phone: (419) 332-2081
Website: http://www.rbhayes.org/
Social media: https://www.facebook.com/hayespresidentialcenter/
Administration: The Hayes Presidential Center, Inc.
Hours: 9 a.m. to 5 p.m., Monday to Saturday; closed on Sundays

BIOGRAPHY OF RUTHERFORD B. HAYES

October 4, 1822–January 17, 1893
Nineteenth President: March 4, 1877–March 4, 1881
Republican Party

Rutherford B. Hayes, c. 1870s.
LC-BH832-30321 H

Rutherford Birchard Hayes was born in Delaware, Ohio, to Rutherford Hayes Jr. and Sophia Birchard Hayes. Rutherford never knew his father because he died of a fever four months before Rutherford was born.[1] Rutherford was schooled at the Norwalk Seminary, which was run by Methodists. After leaving school, he studied at and graduated from Kenyon College. Wanting to become an attorney, he enrolled at Harvard Law School. Hayes graduated from Harvard in 1843. Upon graduating he returned to Ohio, where he passed the bar exam.

Hayes became a reputable lawyer in Cincinnati. He married Lucy Webb, and he and Lucy went on to have eight children. When the Civil War broke out in 1861, Hayes joined the Twenty-Third Ohio Volunteer Infantry as an officer. After the war he served in Congress and as Governor of Ohio.

In 1876 Hayes was nominated by the Republican Party as their presidential candidate. The Democrats nominated New York governor Samuel J. Tilden. In the election there was no clear winner. Hayes and Tilden were tied in the number of electoral college votes, with 184 each. Tilden won the popular vote, with 4,288,546 compared with 4,034,311 for Hayes. However, what mattered was the electoral college vote, not the popular vote. An Electoral Commission was created and given the task of settling the disputed election, but this was to no avail. A few weeks before Inauguration Day, the Republicans and Democrats in Congress came to an agreement whereby Hayes would receive one extra electoral vote in order to make him president. Historian C. Vann Woodward called this the "Compromise of 1877." According to Woodward, the Republicans promised that Hayes would withdraw Union troops from the South and cut political support for two Republican governors in South Carolina and Louisiana. In return, the Democrats would not use the "filibuster" (talking a bill to death) to stop Hayes from being declared president.[2] This compromise did not please everyone. Many Democrats saw corruption and called Hayes "his fraudulency."[3]

One of the first problems that Hayes had to deal with as president was a series of strikes and riots that erupted in several major cities, including Pittsburgh, Chicago, and St. Louis. The riots stemmed from railroad workers demanding better wages. Hayes was sympathetic to the workers and criticized the railroad managers. However, Hayes did not support workers whom he perceived as being troublemaking agitators, and he sent federal troops to quell the riots in the name of preserving the peace.[4] Back in Washington, First Lady Lucy Hayes earned the nickname "Lemonade Lucy" after she banned alcohol from White House functions.[5]

By and large, Hayes's biographers have viewed him as an "honest" president who helped to unify the country but failed to do enough to protect the rights of African Americans in the South.[6] During his final year as president, rather than seeking reelection, Hayes yearned for his administration to end. He said, "I am now in my last year of the Presidency and look forward to its close as a schoolboy longs for the coming vacation."[7] In his place, the Republicans nominated Congressman James A. Garfield. Garfield won the presidency in 1880 only to be assassinated in 1881.

After leaving the White House, Hayes retired to Spiegel Grove. In his retirement Hayes served on the Board of Trustees of Ohio State University. His wife, Lucy, died in 1889. On January 18, 1893, Hayes died of a heart attack. He is buried with his wife in Spiegel Grove.

LIBRARY AND MUSEUM

The grounds of the Hayes Presidential Library and Museums are located on Hayes's twenty-six-acre Spiegel Grove estate, which is located in Fremont, Ohio. The estate contains the library and Hayes's home. The house was built in 1860 by Hayes's uncle, Sardis Birchard. Visitors to the estate will see a red-brick Victorian home with thirty-one rooms. The German word *Spiegel* means "mirror." Sardis Birchard named the estate Spiegel Grove because he thought it best described "the reflection of pools of sparkling water that formed following rain."[8] Hayes inherited the house in 1873 and immediately added an extra room to use as a library. When Hayes became president he used his home as a "summer White House."[9]

After his presidency, Hayes decided to preserve his books and records. He was a meticulous "collector of historical documents and books" and by 1888 his personal library boasted a collection of six thousand volumes, which he personally cataloged and organized.[10] When Hayes died in 1893, his son Webb C. Hayes inherited the library and transformed it into the nation's first presidential library.[11] Later, President Franklin Roosevelt would use this library as a model for his own.[12] The estate was deeded to the state of Ohio and a fireproof building was constructed to house the books. In 1912 a groundbreaking ceremony was held on the estate for the Hayes Commemorative Library and Museum. The building was completed four years later, on May 29, 1916, when it was formally dedicated to the public. In 1922, on the one-hundredth anniversary of Hayes's birth, the library was extended with the addition of an annex. The building would be extended again in 1967, when east and west wings were added.[13] In 2016 the library and museum was completely renovated and new exhibition galleries presenting the lives of Rutherford and Lucy Hayes were created.[14]

Collections and Exhibits

The museum at the Hayes library has five exhibits. The first is the *Centennial Exposition of 1876 in Philadelphia*. Here visitors will gain insights into what life was like during the final quarter of the nineteenth century, when America celebrated the centennial of its founding. The exhibit focuses on the "ideas and innovations" of the era.[15]

From here, visitors will move into the main area of the museum, where they will see historic photographs and information about the contested election of 1876 and the major issues that Hayes had to deal with as president. The exhibit also contains artifacts, such as the original White House china used by the Hayes family, the actual dresses worn by Lucy and her daughters, and the president's carriage.[16]

Following this exhibit is the *Presidents Gallery*. This exhibit is dedicated to all presidents and contains many of their personal artifacts, from letters and documents to a pair of Abraham Lincoln's slippers. Visitors will also see a replica Resolute desk presented to Hayes by Queen Victoria of Great Britain. Visitors may sit at the desk and take pictures.[17] Following the *Presidents Gallery* is the *Hayes Family Gallery*, which includes two dollhouses belonging to Hayes's oldest daughter, Fanny Hayes, the Hayes family tree, and an interactive video presenting the story of "Hayes family memories."[18] Finally, visitors will descend to the lower level of the museum, where they will see the gallery *Rutherford and Lucy Hayes*. This exhibit presents an intimate look at the early years of the couple, when Rutherford served in the Civil War. Also included is historical information on Spiegel Grove.[19]

The library and museum also hosts "rotating" temporary exhibits. In 2016 there were two. The first of these was *100 Moments: Celebrating a Century of the Nation's First Presidential Library*, which ran from October 2016 to May 2017. The exhibit highlighted the one-hundredth anniversary of the Hayes Library and Museums. The exhibit was divided into three sections: one on President Hayes, one on his son Colonel Webb Cook Hayes, and one on the library itself. On display were photos and artifacts belonging to President Hayes and his son Colonel Hayes, most of which were from the Civil War. Since the Hayes library is considered to be the first presidential library, the third section of the exhibit presented the story of the library and its educational goal of making the president's papers available to the public for research.[20] The second temporary exhibit was the *Hayes Train Special*, which showed a miniature "multi-tiered train" running through an "intricate holiday Victorian scene."[21] The exhibit ran from November 25, 2016, to January 8, 2017.

The Hayes library currently has a collection of ninety thousand books. Within the collection, visitors will find books about genealogy; the local history of Fremont, Ohio; and the Gilded Age (late-nineteenth-century America).[22] Also included in the library is Hayes's personal collection of books, along with archival materials spanning his career in the military and in politics. Nearby Bowling Green State University has cooperated with the Hayes library to allow patrons to search materials from the library through the Bowling Green library catalog.[23]

There are approximately six thousand linear feet of documents inside the library's collection of manuscripts. The Rutherford B. Hayes and the Hayes Family Papers collection is one of the most important collections of manuscripts at the library. It contains the personal, military, and political letters and correspondences of Hayes. Some of the papers are addressed to family members, while others are concerned with Hayes's interests in law, history, education, and prison reform. Most of the manuscripts are now available on microfilm.[24]

The other major category of manuscripts at this library is the Gilded Age Collections. These collections contain seventy-five thousand volumes and seven hundred lineal feet of manuscripts. They include materials written by important Americans of the late nineteenth century, such as cartoonist Thomas Nast, author William Dean Howells, Supreme Court Justice Stanley Matthews, and the editor of *Harper's Weekly*, George W. Curtis.[25]

The remaining manuscript collections are concerned with the local history of Sandusky County, Ohio, civil war memoirs, photographs, genealogies, election memorabilia, and information on America's presidents.[26]

Aside from the manuscripts, the Hayes library has more than one hundred thousand images in photographs, lithographs, and posters. Visitors can see collections of photographs of Hayes; his wife, Lucy Webb Hayes; and their son Webb C. Hayes. There are also collections related to Hayes's cousin Lucy Elliot Keeler and local photographers, such as Charles E. Frohman and Ernst Niebergall. The latter collections contain images of the Lake Erie region of northern Ohio that date from the turn of the century.[27]

NOTES

1. Hans L. Trefousse, *Rutherford B. Hayes*, the American Presidents Series (New York: Times Books, 2002), 3.

2. C. Vann Woodward, *Reunion and Reaction: The Compromise of 1877 and the End of Reconstruction* (New York: Oxford University Press, 1966), 7–8.

3. Roy Morris Jr., "How Rutherford 'His Fraudulency' Hayes Ran (and Stole?) His Election," *Washington Times*, February 23, 2003, http://www.washingtontimes.com/news/2003/feb/23/20030223-085620-3260r/.

4. Ari Hoogenboom, *The Presidency of Rutherford B. Hayes* (Lawrence: University of Kansas Press, 1988), 79–81.

5. Trefousse, *Rutherford B. Hayes*, 99.

6. Trefousse, *Rutherford B. Hayes*, 129.

7. Trefousse, *Rutherford B. Hayes*, 118–19.

8. William G. Clotworthy, *Homes and Libraries of the Presidents: An Interpretive Guide*, third edition (Blacksburg, VA: McDonald & Woodward, 2008), 164.

9. Saturday Evening Post editors, *The Presidents: Their Lives, Families and Great Decisions: As Told by the* Saturday Evening Post (Indianapolis, IN: Curtis Publishing Company, 1989), 68.

10. Frank L. Schick, Renee Schick, and Mark Carroll, *Records of the Presidency: Presidential Papers and Libraries from Washington to Reagan* (Phoenix, AZ: Oryx Press, 1989), 140.

11. Thomas A. Smith, "Before Hyde Park: The Rutherford B. Hayes Library," *American Archivist* 43, no. 4 (Fall 1980): 485.

12. Wendy R. Ginsberg, Erika K. Lunder, and Daniel J. Richardson, *The Presidential Libraries Act and the Establishment of Presidential Libraries* (CRS Report No. R41513) (Washington, DC: Congressional Research Service, 2015), 6.

13. Smith, "Before Hyde Park," 485.

14. "Core Exhibits," Rutherford B. Hayes Presidential Library and Museums, accessed May 17, 2017, http://www.rbhayes.org/estate/core-exhibits/.

15. "Core Exhibits."

16. "Core Exhibits."

17. "Core Exhibits."

18. "Core Exhibits."

19. "Core Exhibits."

20. "Rotating Exhibits," Rutherford B. Hayes Presidential Library and Museums, accessed May 17, 2017, http://www.rbhayes.org/estate/rotating-exhibits/.

21. "Rotating Exhibits."

22. "Research and Collections," Rutherford B. Hayes Presidential Library and Museums, accessed May 17, 2017, http://www.rbhayes.org/main/research-collections/.

23. "The Nation's First Presidential Library," Rutherford B. Hayes Presidential Library and Museums, http://www.rbhayes.org/research/library.

24. "Manuscripts Collections," Rutherford B. Hayes Presidential Library and Museums, accessed May 17, 2017, http://www.rbhayes.org/manuscripts/manuscripts-collections/.

25. "Manuscripts Collections."

26. "Manuscripts Collections."

27. "Prints and Photographs," Rutherford B. Hayes Presidential Library and Museums, accessed May 17, 2017, http://www.rbhayes.org/research/prints-photographs/.

BIBLIOGRAPHY

Clotworthy, William G. *Homes and Libraries of the Presidents: An Interpretive Guide.* Third edition. Blacksburg, VA: McDonald & Woodward, 2008.

Ginsberg, Wendy R., Erika K. Lunder, and Daniel J. Richardson. *The Presidential Libraries Act and the Establishment of Presidential Libraries* (CRS Report No. R41513). Washington, DC: Congressional Research Service, 2015.

Hoogenboom, Ari. *The Presidency of Rutherford B. Hayes.* Lawrence: University of Kansas Press, 1988.

Morris, Roy Jr. "How Rutherford 'His Fraudulency' Hayes Ran (and Stole?) His Election." *Washington Times* (February 23, 2003): http://www.washingtontimes.com/news/2003/feb/23/20030223-085620-3260r/.

Saturday Evening Post editors. *The Presidents: Their Lives, Families and Great Decisions: As Told by the* Saturday Evening Post. Indianapolis, IN: Curtis Publishing Company, 1989.

Schick, Frank L., Renee Schick, and Mark Carroll. *Records of the Presidency: Presidential Papers and Libraries from Washington to Reagan.* Phoenix, AZ: Oryx Press, 1989.

Smith, Thomas A. "Before Hyde Park: The Rutherford B. Hayes Library." *American Archivist* 43, no. 4 (Fall 1980): 485–87.

Trefousse, Hans L. *Rutherford B. Hayes.* The American Presidents Series. New York: Times Books, 2002.

Woodward, C. Vann. *Reunion and Reaction: The Compromise of 1877 and the End of Reconstruction.* New York: Oxford University Press, 1966.

Research Library at the
Benjamin Harrison Presidential Site

Address: 1230 North Delaware Street, Indianapolis, IN 46202
Phone: (317) 631-1888
Webpage: http://www.bhpsite.org/
Social media: https://www.facebook.com/pages/Benjamin-Harrison-Presidential-Site/
177105049004525?ref=hl
Administration: Benjamin Harrison Presidential Site
Hours: 10 a.m. to 3:30 p.m., Monday to Saturday; 12 p.m. to 3:30 p.m. on Sundays
in June and July

BIOGRAPHY OF BENJAMIN HARRISON

August 20, 1833–March 13, 1901
Twenty-Third President: March 4, 1889–March 4, 1893
Republican Party

Benjamin Harrison, c. 1896.
LC-USZ62-134885

Benjamin Harrison was born in North Bend, Ohio, to John Scott and Elizabeth Irwin Harrison. John Scott's father was William Henry Harrison,[1] the famous general who won the Battle of Tippecanoe against the Native Americans during the War of 1812. General Harrison became the ninth president of the United States in 1841, but died of pneumonia thirty days after his inauguration—his was the shortest tenure of any president in American history.

Benjamin Harrison's father was a farmer. John had Benjamin tutored until the age of fourteen, by which time he had saved enough money to send his son to the local Farmers' College, run by Presbyterian ministers. While there, young Harrison met his future wife, Caroline Lavinia Scott. He attended the college for three years before transferring to Miami University in Oxford, Ohio. In 1852 Harrison graduated from Miami and decided to embark on a career in law. Since there was no law school nearby, Harrison had to "read law" as a clerk at a Cincinnati law firm.[2] On October 25, 1853, Harrison married Caroline. Together they had two children: Russell and Mary.

In 1855 Harrison moved to Indianapolis, where he took a position at a prestigious law firm. While in Indianapolis, he became interested in Republican politics and supported the abolition of slavery. In 1857 Harrison was elected city attorney for Indianapolis. Two years later he was elected as reporter for the Indiana Supreme Court.[3]

The Civil War broke out when Harrison was working at the Supreme Court. Governor Oliver P. Morton asked Harrison to help raise a regiment for service. Harrison did so and Morton commissioned him as a colonel in the Seventieth Indiana Volunteer Regiment.[4] Harrison and his regiment were placed under the command of Union general William Tecumseh Sherman and served during the campaign to take Atlanta. Harrison was respected by his troops and fought in many battles. Before the war ended, he was promoted to brigadier general.[5]

After the war Harrison returned to his family in Indianapolis. In the 1870s he continued to work as an attorney, but he also became a rising star in the state's Republican Party, campaigning on behalf of candidates. In 1876 he was asked to run for Indiana governor. Harrison accepted the invitation but lost to his Democratic opponent James D. Williams.[6] Four years later Harrison was elected to the United States Senate, where he served one term.

Senator Harrison supported the federal funding of education and equal education for former slaves. He opposed the anti-immigrant Chinese Exclusion Act of 1882, and he advocated pensions for wounded Union veterans of the Civil War.[7] Harrison was not reelected because Democrats had taaken control of the Indiana legislature.[8]

For the presidential election of 1888, Harrison was nominated to run for the Republican Party. His running mate for the vice presidency was Levi P. Morton, who had served as minister to France. The Democrats renominated President Grover Cleveland. As a Democrat, Cleveland ran on a platform of tariff (import tax) reduction.[9] By contrast, Harrison supported protective tariffs and "pledged generous pensions for veterans."[10] The Democrats tried to poke fun at Harrison's height of five feet, six inches. Comparing him with his presidential grandfather, the Democrats' slogan was: "His Grandfather's Hat—It's Too Big for Ben."[11] On Election Day, Harrison was elected president despite losing the popular vote: Harrison won 5,447,219 popular votes and 233 electoral votes, while Cleveland won 5,537,857 popular votes and 168 electoral votes. Discrepancies in the popular votes were blamed on African American voters in the South being either "barred" from placing their votes or intimidated into not doing so.[12]

As president, Harrison had a reputation of being "aloof" and having an "icy" personality.[13] According to University of North Carolina law professor Michael J. Gerhardt, historian Henry Adams ranked Harrison as a good president because in one term he "signed the Sherman Anti-Trust Act; transformed the federal judiciary by making four Supreme Court appointments [and created] federal circuit courts of appeal."[14] Signing the Sherman Anti-Trust Act, which Congress had passed, is seen as one of Harrison's major achievements. In the late nineteenth century, the public feared the growth of

large trusts (corporations). The Sherman Anti-Trust Act was created to prevent individual trusts from creating monopolies that destroyed "their competition through
price-fixing and other dubious means."[15] Harrison also supported the McKinley Tariff
bill, which was proposed by then congressman and future president William McKinley.
The bill was designed to place more tariffs on imported wool and agricultural goods,
with the exception of sugar.[16]

Harrison is also remembered for his decisions on foreign policy. On two occasions,
he used his diplomatic skills to smooth over tensions between two foreign nations. In
1891, a lynch mob in New Orleans killed eleven Italian American immigrants who
had been acquitted of assassinating the local police chief, David Hennessey. Hennessey's murder, along with the trial and lynching of the Italian Americans, introduced
the nation to the mafia.[17] The Italian government demanded that Harrison bring the
perpetrators of the lynch mob to justice. Secretary of State James G. Blaine informed
the Italian ambassador that the lynching was a state and not a federal matter. The Italian
government became so enraged with Blaine that they recalled their ambassador and cut
diplomatic ties. In 1892 Harrison stepped in and asked Congress to pay an indemnity
to Italy, which finally settled the dispute.[18]

The second diplomatic situation involved Chile. In 1891, two American sailors
from the USS *Baltimore* were killed during a brawl in Valparaiso. Harrison saw the brawl
as an act of "unfriendliness" toward America and demanded answers.[19] In response,
Chile called Harrison's comments "erroneous or deliberately incorrect."[20] As tensions
flared, Harrison and the US Navy prepared for possible war with Chile. At the last minute, however, a diplomatic solution was agreed upon: Chile apologized for its previous
response to Harrison and paid reparations to America.[21]

The year 1892 was unhappy for Harrison. His wife, Caroline, died of tuberculosis
and he lost his reelection bid. The Democrats chose former president Grover Cleveland
to run that year, and he won. Columbia University historian Henry F. Graff says Harrison lost due to the infamous Homestead Strike of steel workers, overwhelming opposition in the South, and Cleveland's position in favor of the gold standard for currency.[22]

After losing the election, Harrison resumed his law practice. On April 6, 1896, he
married his wife's niece, Mary Lord Dimmick, and they had one daughter, Elizabeth.
Harrison died of pneumonia on March 13, 1901, at the age of sixty-seven.

LIBRARY AND MUSEUM

The Benjamin Harrison Presidential Site is a historical landmark that was once his
home. It also contains a research library and museum. The presidential site is governed
by a nonprofit organization whose mission is "to increase public understanding of, ap-
preciation for, and participation in the American system of self-government through life
stories, arts, and culture of an American President."[23]

Harrison and his first wife, Caroline, built the Victorian-style home during 1874
and 1875, and Harrison lived there until his death. The Harrison family continued to
live in the house until 1913, when Mary Lord Harrison turned it into a rental prop-

erty. In 1937 Mary Lord sold the family home to the Jordan Conservatory of Music with the caveat that the artifacts would be preserved and that certain rooms would be maintained as museum spaces. Then, in 1966, care of the home was turned over to a nonprofit organization with the sole purpose of maintaining the property as a historic site. In the past, visitors had to make an appointment to view the house. However, this all changed in 1974, when the home was renovated and opened for daily public tours.[24]

Today the home is still part of the nonprofit Benjamin Harrison Presidential Site. In 2001, elevators were installed to make the home more accessible to visitors with disabilities. The presidential site also attracts grade school children. Beginning in 2013 the home launched "a multi-year Bicentennial grant partnership with the Indiana Statehouse and State Library" to enable local fourth graders to visit the museum and library at no cost.[25]

In 2003, the museum was accredited by the American Alliance of Museums, and the National Park Service awarded it the Save America's Treasures grant to fund repairs.[26] In 2014 Charlie Hyde became the site's new chief executive officer; since then the organization has sought to develop an ambitious plan to make the home "the most innovative, impactful, and civically engaged presidential site in the United States within the next five years."[27]

The research library is part of the Benjamin Harrison Presidential Site. This library contains Harrison's personal collection of books, government reports, Civil War records, Presbyterian Church reports, and periodicals, as well as his father's papers. Researchers will also find the genealogy of the Harrison family and records of the presidency. The records of the Harrison family consist of diaries and personal papers. Those interested in Harrison's political views will enjoy the collection of his political pamphlets, legal cases, and campaign speeches. Also included are history books about Indiana and the Victorian era.[28]

The majority of papers relating to Harrison's presidency are located at the Library of Congress, the Indiana State Library, and the Rutherford B. Hayes Library in Fremont, Ohio.[29] Thanks to the Library of Congress, researchers can also view Harrison's presidential papers on microfilm at the presidential site.[30]

The research library also has a collection of 1,280 photographs of Harrison, his wives Caroline and Mary, his parents, and his children.[31]

Collections and Exhibits

The Harrison presidential site also functions as a museum with exhibits. One exhibit is called *Women's Suffrage: From Bustles to Ballots*. The issue of women's right to vote and participate in electioneering was becoming pressing in the late nineteenth century. American women eventually gained the right to vote with the passage of the Nineteenth Amendment in 1919. This exhibit examines the origins of the suffrage movement from the American Revolution to the early twentieth century. The exhibit also features the views of the Harrison women who supported suffrage.[32]

Another exhibit, *Harrison Christmas Traditions*, displays how the Harrison family celebrated Christmas. Visitors will see a Victorian-style Christmas tree, which was popular during the era.[33] The presidential site also manages a traveling exhibit, which can be rented: *Campaigns and Cartoons: The Role of Caricature in Political Persuasion.* The contents of the exhibit are thirty-six political cartoons and sketches of famous figures from the late nineteenth century. Visitors will see cartoons and sketches of President Ulysses S. Grant and of "Boss" Tweed, who ran the corrupt Democratic Party machine, Tammany Hall. The cartoons and sketches were created by Thomas Nast of *Harper's Weekly* and Matthew Morgan of *Frank Leslie's Weekly.* These periodicals were two of the most popular of the nineteenth century.[34]

The latest exhibit as of this writing, on display from March to December 2016, was *President at a Crossroads.*[35] The exhibit celebrates President Harrison and the past two hundred years of American history.[36]

There were also several previous exhibits at the presidential site. In 2007 an exhibit focusing on Harrison's career, *Benjamin Harrison: Lawyer, Soldier, President,* showcased his legal skills, his military leadership, and his diplomatic accomplishments as president.[37] In 2009 the site celebrated the life of Harrison's presidential grandfather, William Henry Harrison. The exhibit was called *Tippecanoe and History Too!* It featured "letters, documents and other artifacts providing insight into the man from 1790 to his death while in office in 1841."[38] More recently, in 2015, the site held an exhibit titled *Death in the White House,* which was dedicated to presidents who died in office and to first ladies who died while their husbands were president. Featured presidents were William Henry Harrison, Zachary Taylor, Abraham Lincoln, James A. Garfield, William McKinley, Warren G. Harding, Franklin Delano Roosevelt, and John F. Kennedy. First ladies featured were Letitia Tyler, Caroline Harrison, and Ellen Wilson.[39]

Aside from the exhibits, the presidential site hosts plays by Candlelight Theatre in the president's home. The theater company began in 2004 and presents plays from the nineteenth and twentieth centuries, and the current creative director is Dr. Donna Wing. In the past, the theater company has performed many Victorian-era murder mysteries, as well as plays written by Agatha Christie and Anton Chekov.[40]

NOTES

1. Charles W. Calhoun, *Benjamin Harrison*, the American Presidents Series (New York: Times Books, 2005), 9.

2. Calhoun, *Benjamin Harrison*, 14–15.

3. Calhoun, *Benjamin Harrison*, 19.

4. Calhoun, *Benjamin Harrison*, 21.

5. Calhoun, *Benjamin Harrison*, 23–24.

6. Calhoun, *Benjamin Harrison*, 32.

7. Calhoun, *Benjamin Harrison*, 38–40.

8. Calhoun, *Benjamin Harrison*, 43–44.

9. Calhoun, *Benjamin Harrison*, 48–49.

10. Henry F. Graff, *Grover Cleveland*, the American Presidents Series (New York: Times Books, 2002), 93.

11. Graff, *Grover Cleveland*, 93.

12. Calhoun, *Benjamin Harrison*, 58.

13. Michael J. Gerhardt, *The Forgotten Presidents: Their Untold Constitutional Legacy* (New York: Oxford University Press, 2013), 141.

14. Gerhardt, *Forgotten Presidents*, 141.

15. Gerhardt, *Forgotten Presidents*, 146.

16. Calhoun, *Benjamin Harrison*, 87–88.

17. Richard Gambino, *Vendetta: The True Story of the Largest Lynching in U.S. History* (Toronto: ON: Guernica Editions 1998), 4.

18. Calhoun, *Benjamin Harrison*, 126–27.

19. Calhoun, *Benjamin Harrison*, 128.

20. Calhoun, *Benjamin Harrison*, 128.

21. Calhoun, *Benjamin Harrison*, 128–29.

22. Graff, *Grover Cleveland*, 108–10.

23. "About us," Benjamin Harrison Presidential Site, accessed August 2, 2016, http://www.presidentbenjaminharrison.org/about.

24. "About us."

25. "About us."

26. "About us."

27. "About us."

28. "Research Library," Benjamin Harrison Presidential Site, accessed August 2, 2016, http://www.presidentbenjaminharrison.org/learn/collections/research-library.

29. Frank L. Schick, Renee Schick, and Mark Carroll. *Records of the Presidency: Presidential Papers and Libraries from Washington to Reagan* (Phoenix, AZ: Oryx Press, 1989), 98.

30. "Research Library."

31. "Benjamin Harrison," Benjamin Harrison Presidential Site, accessed August 2, 2016, http://presidentbenjaminharrison.org/learn/photograph-collection/benjamin-harrison-photograph-collection.

32. "Women's Suffrage: From Bustles to Ballots," Benjamin Harrison Presidential Site, accessed August 2, 2016, http://presidentbenjaminharrison.org/learn/collections/women-s-suffrage.

33. "Harrison Christmas Traditions: The White House," Benjamin Harrison Presidential Site, accessed August 2, 2016, http://presidentbenjaminharrison.org/learn/exhibits/harrison-christmas-traditions.

34. "Traveling Exhibit," Benjamin Harrison Presidential Site, accessed August 2, 2016, http://presidentbenjaminharrison.org/learn/exhibits/traveling-exhibit.

35. "Current Exhibit: President at the Crossroads," Benjamin Harrison Presidential Site, accessed August 2, 2016, http://www.presidentbenjaminharrison.org/learn/exhibits/current-exhibit.

36. "Exhibits," Benjamin Harrison Presidential Site, accessed August 2, 2016, http://www.bhpsite.org/learn/exhibits.

37. "Benjamin Harrison: Lawyer, Soldier, President," Benjamin Harrison Presidential Site, accessed August 2, 2016, http://presidentbenjaminharrison.org/learn/exhibits/past-exhibits/19-learn/exhibits/past-exhibits/57-benjamin-harrison-lawyer-soldier-president.

38. "William Henry Harrison," Benjamin Harrison Presidential Site, accessed August 2, 2016, http://presidentbenjaminharrison.org/learn/exhibits/past-exhibits/19-learn/exhibits/past-exhibits/60-william-henry-harrison.

39. "Articles: Death in the White House," Benjamin Harrison Presidential Site, accessed August 2, 2016, http://www.bhpsite.org/component/content/article/19-learn/exhibits/past-exhibits/159-death-in-the-white-house.

40. "Articles: Signature Events," Benjamin Harrison Presidential Site, accessed August 2, 2016, http://www.presidentbenjaminharrison.org/component/content/category/20-events.

BIBLIOGRAPHY

Calhoun, Charles W. *Benjamin Harrison.* The American Presidents Series. New York: Times Books, 2005.

Gambino, Richard. *Vendetta: The True Story of the Largest Lynching in U.S. History.* Toronto, ON: Guernica Editions.

Gerhardt, Michael J. *The Forgotten Presidents: Their Untold Constitutional Legacy.* New York: Oxford University Press, 2013.

Graff, Henry F. *Grover Cleveland.* The American Presidents Series. New York: Times Books, 2002.

Schick, Frank L., Renee Schick, and Mark Carroll. *Records of the Presidency: Presidential Papers and Libraries from Washington to Reagan.* Phoenix, AZ: Oryx Press, 1989.

William McKinley
Presidential Library and Museum

Address: 800 McKinley Monument Drive NW, Canton, OH 44708
Phone: 330-455-7043
Website: http://mckinleymuseum.org/
Social media: https://www.facebook.com/McKinley-Presidential-Library-Museum
  -Canton-Ohio-122618678228/
Administration: Stark County Historical Society
Hours: 9 a.m. to 4 p.m., Monday to Saturday; noon to 4 p.m. on Sundays

BIOGRAPHY OF WILLIAM McKINLEY

January 29, 1843–September 14, 1901
Twenty-Fifth President: March 4, 1897–September 14, 1901
Republican Party

William McKinley, c. 1900.
LC-USZ62-13025

William McKinley was born in Niles, Ohio. He was the seventh child of William and Nancy McKinley. His father was an iron worker and moved the family to Poland, Ohio, in 1852. Poland was close to Allegheny College, which William would attend in 1860. Due to depression, however, William left college and returned home, where he worked briefly as a teacher and a postal clerk.[1] When the Civil War broke out in 1861, McKinley joined the Union army.

McKinley served in the Twenty-Third Regiment from Ohio. During the war he saw action at the bloody Battle of Antietam and became friends with his commanding general and future president, Rutherford B. Hayes. General Hayes promoted McKinley to lieutenant. As an officer, McKinley served as assistant quartermaster under Hayes. In 1864 he was again promoted—this time to captain, serving under Hayes and General Philip Sheridan.[2] By the time the war ended in 1865,

McKinley had reached the rank of brevet major. After retiring from the army he spent one year at Albany Law School before leaving to read law (as an apprentice) with Judge Charles Glidden in Ohio.[3]

In 1869 McKinley completed his law apprenticeship and was elected prosecutor of Stark County, Ohio. He remained friends with Rutherford B. Hayes, who by then was governor of Ohio.[4] Two years later, in 1871, McKinley married Ida Saxton and together they had two daughters. Sadly, they both died at a young age: Katie at age four and her sister at five months.

McKinley decided to run for a congressional seat in Ohio and was elected in 1878. The Ohio Democrats saw him as a "rising star" in the Republican Party and tried to sabotage his political career by gerrymandering (redrawing) his congressional seat so that he would lose.[5] However, they were unsuccessful. McKinley was almost elected Speaker of the House in 1889, but he lost to fellow Republican Thomas Reed by one vote. Reed appointed McKinley to head the Ways and Means Committee.[6] One of McKinley's most significant accomplishments in Congress was to pass the Tariff Act of 1890, which gave the president authority to impose tariffs on goods from foreign nations that imposed tariffs on American goods.[7] McKinley supported protective tariffs, believing that the policy helped American businesses and raised wages for workers.[8]

In 1892 McKinley was elected governor of Ohio, which helped propel him to the Republican Party's nomination for president in 1896. At the Republican Convention, McKinley had the support of powerful party chairman Marcus Hanna. As a result, McKinley was nominated with Garret A. Hobart as his running mate. The main issue that influenced the 1896 election was the free coinage of silver (bimetallism). The historian Michael Kazin explained: "Through the 1860s, both gold and silver had been recognized as legal tender, with the white metal pegged at one-sixteenth the value of its more valuable counterpart."[9] Since more gold was in circulation, in 1873 Congress had "retired" silver and put the nation on the gold standard (currency backed by gold) to strengthen its currency. However, a depression in 1873 hurt "debt-ridden farmers," who clamored for the return of silver.[10] The farmers believed the gold standard was having the opposite effect to what Congress had intended, and they referred to the law on retiring silver as the "crime of '73."[11] McKinley and the Republican Party supported the gold standard; the Democrats were split on the issue. The so-called Bourbon Democrats, who supported the gold standard, did not want silver to return, whereas a new populist wing of the party championed silver.[12]

That year, the Democrats nominated former congressman William Jennings Bryan of Nebraska. The delegates at the Democratic Convention were captivated by Bryan's "Cross of Gold" speech, in which he said, "we will answer their demand for a gold standard by saying to them: You shall not press down upon the brow of labor this crown of thorns; you shall not crucify mankind upon a cross of gold."[13]

That summer Governor McKinley did not actively campaign. Being humble, he conducted what is known as a "front porch" campaign.[14] This is when a candidate runs their campaign from home and, every now and then, makes a speech to journalists and spectators who show up on the candidate's lawn. Bryan, on the other hand, broke with tradition and toured the nation, giving fiery speeches in which he promised to help farmers and workers fight against the rich trusts (corporations). When the election was over, McKinley found that he had won, receiving 7,111,607 popular votes and 271 electoral votes while Bryan received 6,509,052 popular votes and 176 electoral votes. Surprisingly, to Bryan's dismay, McKinley won the labor (workers') vote.[15]

As president, McKinley is best remembered for expanding American power and influence abroad during the Spanish–American War of 1898. The roots of the war were in a violent rebellion against Spanish rule that was taking place in Cuba. The island had been in the sights of American expansionists since the 1850s.[16] American newspaper titans, such as William Randolph Hearst of the *New York Journal*, began sensationalizing the war in Cuba. They reported acts of savagery against innocent Cubans at the hands of the Spanish. Journalists like Hearst thought that bringing America into conflict with Spain would boost sales of their newspapers; in fact, Hearst is known to have boasted to painter Frederic Remington that if he "would furnish the pictures, Hearst would furnish the war."[17]

Two events led to war breaking out between the United States and Spain in 1898. The first was a letter written by Spanish ambassador Enrique Dupuy de Lôme, who wrote that McKinley was being pressured by Congress to go to war. American newspapers sensationalized this accusation.[18] The second was the sinking of the USS *Maine*. On the night of February 9, 1898, the battleship mysteriously exploded, killing 266 sailors. Although the cause was believed to have been an "internal malfunction," the newspapers blamed Spain.[19]

On April 11, McKinley asked Congress for a declaration of war, which was approved on April 25. Back then, America was an industrialized nation while Spain was still an agrarian empire. Their military was little match for the Americans. However, the war began with major logistical errors on the part of the Americans. Soldiers were issued winter clothing for use in a tropical climate, food rotted, and supplies were delivered to the wrong army units.[20]

The first American victory of the war was the sinking of the Spanish fleet in Manila Bay in the Philippines. Assistant Secretary of the Navy Theodore Roosevelt dispatched an order to Admiral George Dewey, who was stationed in Hong Kong, to attack the Spanish fleet in Manila Bay.[21] Admiral Dewey steamed into the bay in the early morning hours of May 1, and gave his famous order, "You may fire when ready, Gridley."[22] The victory was remarkable because America now controlled the entire archipelago.

Back in America, preparations were being made to invade Cuba. Theodore Roosevelt resigned his position in the Department of the Navy to muster his own division of volunteers, who were known as the Rough Riders. American soldiers led by General William Shafter landed at Daiquiri in an attempt to seize Santiago on June 22. Nine days later, America scored another famous victory when Roosevelt's Rough Riders charged and captured San Juan Hill. By July 17 the Spanish had surrendered Santiago. Before the war ended, America managed to capture two more Spanish possessions: Guam and Puerto Rico. The war ended with a ceasefire in August 1898.

America now held foreign territories, making it an imperial power. However, this brought new challenges. In 1899, a guerilla war against American rule had broken out in the Philippines. The rebellion was led by Emilio Aguinaldo, who demanded full independence; but President McKinley was determined to keep the Philippines and waged an undeclared war to crush the rebels. According to Kazin, "McKinley and most Republicans argued that the United States had an obligation to 'Christianize' and 'civilize' the seven million inhabitants of the vast archipelago."[23]

The Republicans happily renominated McKinley as their candidate for the presidential election in 1900, but they had to choose a new running mate: Vice President Hobart had died on November 21, 1899. They chose the hero of San Juan Hill, Theodore Roosevelt, who had recently been elected governor of New York. As for the Democrats, they renominated Bryan. One of the major issues during the 1900 presidential election was whether America should be a republic or an empire: instead of campaigning on free silver, Bryan campaigned against imperialism. As mentioned by Kazin, "Opposing the war for empire seemed to offer Bryan a political opening that free silver and anti-trust could not match."[24] However, Bryan's anti-imperialism campaign was not successful: McKinley was reelected with a larger victory that year, winning 7,228,864 popular votes and 292 electoral votes. Bryan received 6,370,932 popular votes and only 115 electoral votes. Sadly, though, McKinley would not live to see much of his second term.

On Friday, September 6, 1901, President McKinley was shaking hands with spectators in the Temple of Music at the Pan-American Exposition. Unknown to the police, a man in the crowd had a revolver in his hand, which was wrapped in a handkerchief to look as if it was bandaged. The man was a Polish-American anarchist named Leon Czolgosz. He shot two bullets at the unsuspecting president. One ricocheted off McKinley's coat button, but the other entered his abdomen. As the wounded president fell into the arms of the exposition president, policemen and security guards tackled and subdued Czolgosz. McKinley was taken by ambulance to a hospital, where doctors attempted to save his life. Despite their best attempts, McKinley died of a gangrene infection on September 14. Medical writer Stewart Marshall Brooks claimed that had the doctors drained McKinley's bullet wound, he might have lived.[25]

Meanwhile, attention turned to Czolgosz, who pleaded insanity before the court. His trial began on September 23. During it, Czolgosz exhibited strange behavior and was reported to have "acted as if dazed" in court.[26] However, he did make the following statement: "I don't believe in the Republican form of government, and I don't believe we should have any rulers. It is right to kill them. [. . .] When I shot him [McKinley] I fully intended to kill him."[27] Czolgosz's trial lasted only three days. He was found guilty by a jury and sentenced to be executed in the electric chair. He was executed just over a month later, on October 29, and showed little remorse.

After the execution, experts continued to debate Czolgosz's sanity. Medical expert Dr. Walter Channing argued that Czolgosz's consistent lack of remorse may have been a manifestation of mental illness. He said:

> Speaking from the standpoint of the medical expert, it is to me very difficult to believe that any American citizen of sound mind could plan and execute such a deed as the assassination of the President, and remain impervious to all influences after his arrest, and up to the time of the execution. . . . Such conduct is however consistent with insanity.[28]

Channing believed that Czolgosz was suffering from either "epileptic seizures" or a sleepiness condition known as "somnolence."[29]

The nation was saddened by the death of President McKinley. However, the charismatic personality of Vice President Theodore Roosevelt, who took the helm of the White House after McKinley died, would ultimately overshadow McKinley and make Roosevelt more beloved.

MEMORIAL, MUSEUM, AND EXHIBITS

Outside the William McKinley Presidential Library and Museum sits the McKinley Memorial, where the president, his wife, and two young daughters rest.[30] Describing the memorial, writer William G. Clotworthy said: "One-hundred-eight broad granite steps lead up to a magnificent mausoleum high above the city [Canton, Ohio] that McKinley served with devotion and love."[31] Originally, McKinley was "interred at the Wertz Receiving Vault in Canton's West Lawn Cemetery."[32] However, his close advisors, William R. Day and Senator Marcus Hanna of Ohio, discussed plans for a monument.[33]

A board was created to raise money to purchase land around the West Lawn Cemetery to build the memorial. President Theodore Roosevelt headed the board and a request was made public to raise $600,000 for the memorial's construction.[34] Ohio governor George K. Nash declared McKinley's birthday, January 29, to be a "special day of observance in schools."[35] Schoolchildren and many other people made donations to the board, which enabled it to purchase the land. The cornerstone to the memorial was laid on November 16, 1902.[36] The library's website explains that the memorial's interior dome has a diameter of fifty feet and is seventy-seven feet above the floor. The skylight has forty-five stars, representing the forty-five states in the Union at the time.[37]

President Theodore Roosevelt delivering oration at the dedication of the McKinley National Memorial, c. 1908 by John W. Finnell. *LC-DIG-ppmsca-35682*

Exhibits and Collections

Mark Holland, archivist at the William McKinley Presidential Library and Museum, estimates that the McKinley presidential library has a collection of four thousand books.[38] Visitors to the library will find books on William McKinley, the Civil War, the Spanish-American War, and the history of Stark County, Ohio. The library also holds an unpublished twelve-volume biography of McKinley, which was written by local writer Edward Thornton Heald.[39]

McKinley's official presidential papers were held by his personal secretary, George B. Cortelyou, until Cortelyou's death in 1940. His son, George B. Cortelyou Jr., took control of the papers and sent them to the University of Virginia for safekeeping during World War II. In the early 1960s, the papers were microfilmed and sent to the Library of Congress.[40]

The McKinley library holds the personal correspondence between McKinley and his brother Abner, which was printed on an old-fashioned printing press between March 30, 1870, and January 2, 1873. In 1964, Mrs. T. K. Harris of Canton, donated 268 letters between the brothers to the library. These papers refer to legal matters the brothers worked on together in their law firm, W. & A. McKinley.[41]

The first exhibition that visitors will come to in the library is *The McKinley Gallery*. Visitors are greeted by two life-size models of President McKinley and his wife, Ida Saxon, dressed in period attire. The rest of the gallery contains artifacts that belonged to McKinley, such as a rocking chair, his piano, some of his home furnishings, and campaign memorabilia from the 1900 presidential election.[42]

The Stark County Story is the next exhibition. In this gallery visitors will see old-fashioned items from Stark County. There is a parlor with a gramophone, a Victrola, a harp, and a piano. Another artifact of interest is a high-wheeler bicycle from the turn of the century. There are also several pictures and drawings from the 1800s and a machine representing the industrial heritage of Stark County.[43]

The Street of Shops exhibit is a replica turn-of-the-century town within the museum. Visitors can walk down its street and see replica storefronts, including a convenience store, a barber shop, a lawyer's office, a gas station, a blacksmith shop, and a cabinet shop.[44] The Keller Gallery follows *The Street of Shops*. This is where temporary exhibits are displayed. Past exhibits shown in the gallery have included old-fashioned toys, children's clothes, and the interior of a Victorian dollhouse.[45]

The fifth exhibit is *Discover World*, which introduces visitors to the world of paleontology and science. The centerpiece is known as Natural History Island, where visitors can see a real mastodon skeleton. Visitors will also see a replica dinosaur—Alice the Allosaurus—and take part in a "simulated fossil dig."[46] Adults and children alike will enjoy the Fascination Station. The library's website says, "Inside Fascination Station you will discover hands-on physical science activities for the young and young at heart. Capture your shadow, experience the power of electricity and discover the properties of light and magnetism."[47]

The William McKinley Presidential Library and Museum is unique because it is the only presidential library to have a planetarium. The Hoover Price Planetarium accommodates sixty-five visitors, who can sit and watch while "over 60 projectors show the aurora, meteor shower, an asteroid, panoramic views of downtown Canton, clouds, snow, phases of the moon, and dozens of constellations during a 30 minute presentation."[48] The planetarium was added in 1964 and uses a Spitz A3P as its main projector during shows.[49]

NOTES

1. Kevin Phillips, *William McKinley*, the American Presidents Series (New York: Times Books, 2003), 20–21.

2. Phillips, *William McKinley*, 21–23.

3. Phillips, *William McKinley*, 23.

4. Phillips, *William McKinley*, 23.

5. Phillips, *William McKinley*, 27.

6. Phillips, *William McKinley*, 27.

7. Phillips, *William McKinley*, 44–45.

8. Phillips, *William McKinley*, 42.

9. Michael Kazin, *A Godly Hero: The Life of William Jennings Bryan* (New York: Anchor Books, 2006), 34–35.

10. Kazin, *Godly Hero*, 35.

11. Kazin *Godly Hero*, 35.

12. Kazin, *Godly Hero*, 35, 41.

13. Kazin, *Godly Hero*, 61.

14. Phillips, *William McKinley*, 75.

15. Phillips, *William McKinley*, 77.

16. Kenneth E. Hendrickson, *The Spanish-American War* (Westport, CT: Greenwood Press, 2003), 2.

17. Hendrickson, *The Spanish-American War*, 7.

18. Hendrickson, *The Spanish-American War*, 8.

19. Hendrickson, *The Spanish-American War*, 8.

20. Hendrickson, *The Spanish-American War*, 10.

21. Hendrickson, *The Spanish-American War*, 11.

22. Hendrickson, *The Spanish-American War*, 45.

23. Kazin, *Godly Hero*, 89.

24. Kazin, *Godly Hero*, 97.

25. Stewart M. Brooks, *Our Assassinated Presidents: The True Medical Stories* (New York: Bell, 1985), 170.

26. Murat Halstead, *Illustrious Life of William McKinley—Our Martyred President* (Lansing, MI: P. A. Stone, 1901), 450.

27. Walter Channing, "The Mental Status of Czolgosz, the Assassin of President McKinley," *American Journal of Insanity* 59 (1902): 254–55.

28. Channing, "Mental Status," 271.

29. Channing, "Mental Status," 263.

30. "McKinley Memorial," William McKinley Presidential Library and Museum, accessed October 25, 2016, http://mckinleymuseum.org/mckinley-memorial.

31. William G. Clotworthy, *Homes and Libraries of the Presidents: An Interpretive Guide*, 3rd edition. (Blacksburg, VA: McDonald & Woodward, 2008), 184.

32. "McKinley Memorial."

33. "McKinley Memorial."
34. "McKinley Memorial."
35. "McKinley Memorial."
36. "McKinley Memorial."
37. "McKinley Memorial."
38. Mark Holland, telephone interview with author, September 22, 2016.
39. Mark Holland telephone interview.
40. Frank L. Schick, Renee Schick, and Mark Carroll, *Records of the Presidency: Presidential Papers and Libraries from Washington to Reagan* (Phoenix, AZ: Oryx Press, 1989), 100.
41. Ramsayer Research Library, "McKinley Letter Press, 1870–1873," McKinley Presidential Library and Stark County Archives—Canton, Ohio, accessed October 25, 2016, https://mckinleystarkcountyresearch.wordpress.com/mckinley-archives/mckinley-letter-press-1870-1873.
42. "The McKinley Gallery," William McKinley Presidential Library and Museum, accessed October 25, 2016, http://mckinleymuseum.org/exhibits/william-mckinley-exhibit.
43. "The Stark County Story," William McKinley Presidential Library and Museum, accessed October 25, 2016, http://mckinleymuseum.org/exhibits/the-stark-county-story.
44. "The Street of Shops," William McKinley Presidential Library and Museum, accessed October 25, 2016, http://mckinleymuseum.org/exhibits/the-street-of-shops.
45. "Keller Gallery," William McKinley Presidential Library and Museum, accessed October 25, 2016, http://mckinleymuseum.org/exhibits/keller-gallery.
46. "Discover World," William McKinley Presidential Library and Museum, accessed October 25, 2016, http://mckinleymuseum.org/exhibits/discover-world.
47. "Discover World."
48. "Hoover Price Planetarium," William McKinley Presidential Library and Museum, accessed October 25, 2016, http://mckinleymuseum.org/exhibits/hoover-price-planetarium.
49. "Hoover Price Planetarium."

BIBLIOGRAPHY

Brooks, Stewart M. *Our Assassinated Presidents: The True Medical Stories.* New York: Bell, 1985.

Channing, Walter. "The Mental Status of Czolgosz, the Assassin of President McKinley." *American Journal of Insanity* 59 (1902): 233–78.

Clotworthy, William G. *Homes and Libraries of the Presidents: An Interpretive Guide.* Third edition. Blacksburg, VA: McDonald & Woodward, 2008.

Halstead, Murat. *The Illustrious Life of William McKinley—Our Martyred President.* Lansing, MI: P. A. Stone, 1901.

Hendrickson, Kenneth E. *The Spanish-American War.* Westport, CT: Greenwood Press, 2003.

Hufbauer, Benjamin. *Presidential Temples: How Memorials and Libraries Shape Public Memory.* Lawrence: University Press of Kansas, 2005.

Kazin, Michael. *A Godly Hero: The Life of William Jennings Bryan.* New York: Anchor, 2006.

Nappo, Christian A. "Presidential Assassination and the Insanity Defense." Unpublished Policy and Practice Paper, University of Alabama, 2000.

Phillips, Kevin. *William McKinley.* The American Presidents Series. New York: Times Books, 2003.

Schick, Frank L., Renee Schick, and Mark Carroll. *Records of the Presidency: Presidential Papers and Libraries from Washington to Reagan.* Phoenix, AZ: Oryx Press, 1989.

Woodrow Wilson
Presidential Library and Museum

Address: 20 N. Coalter Street, Staunton, VA 24401
Phone: (540) 885-0897
Social media: https://www.facebook.com/WoodrowWilsonLibrary/
Website: http://www.woodrowwilson.org/
Administration: Woodrow Wilson Presidential Foundation

BIOGRAPHY OF WOODROW WILSON

December 28, 1856–February 3, 1924
Twenty-Eighth President: March 4, 1913–March 4, 1921
Democratic Party

Woodrow Wilson, c. 1912 by Pach Brothers. *LC-USZ62-132907*

Thomas Woodrow Wilson was born in Staunton, Virginia. He was the third of four children born to Joseph Ruggles Wilson and Jessie Janet Woodrow Wilson. The families were of Scotch Irish heritage. His father, Joseph Wilson, was a Presbyterian minister and briefly served in the Confederate army during the Civil War.[1] When Thomas Woodrow left school, he attended Davidson College in North Carolina. Later, he studied at Johns Hopkins University, where he received his PhD in history. From there, he went on to teach at reputable universities, such as Cornell University, Bryn Mawr College, Wesleyan University, and New York School of Law. In 1883 he married Ellen Louise Axson. The couple would have three daughters: Margaret, Jessie, and Eleanor.

In 1902 Wilson became president of Princeton University, which propelled him to national prominence. By 1910 the Democrats, who had not had a president in the White House since 1897, were encouraging Wilson to run for governor of New Jersey.[2] Wilson ran during a period in American history known as the Progressive era. The Progressives were a group of reformers who sought to root out political and economic corruption. H. W. Brands describes the movement's philosophy as follows: "Progressivism [believed] people could be made better by appropriate encouragement: better education, better working conditions, better housing, better laws."[3] Progressives also supported women's suffrage (right to vote). Wilson won the gubernatorial election, and within two years, the Democrats nominated him as their presidential candidate. At the Democratic Party Convention held in Baltimore, Maryland, Wilson accepted the nomination, stating that "America is not distinguished so much by its wealth and material power as by the fact that it was born with an ideal, to serve mankind."[4]

The presidential election of 1912 was exciting because the electorate had three candidates from which to choose. The Republicans renominated President William Howard Taft. However, former president Theodore Roosevelt ran as a third-party candidate for the Progressive "Bull Moose" Party. With the Republican Party splintered, the Democrats were almost guaranteed a victory that fall. When the election results came in, Wilson and his running mate Governor Thomas Marshall of Indiana found that they had won 6,296,284 popular votes and 435 electoral votes. Roosevelt came in second place, winning 4,122,721 popular votes and 88 electoral votes. Taft won 3,486,242 popular votes and captured only 8 electoral votes. It was very embarrassing for a sitting president to win only Vermont and Utah.

During his first term Wilson successfully proposed and signed progressive reforms. The Sixteenth Amendment to the Constitution was ratified, which made it possible for the federal government to tax income. He also got the Underwood Tariff passed to reduce tariffs, created the Federal Trade Commission in order to prevent unfair business practices, and became the first president since John Adams to give the annual State of the Union address to Congress in person rather than sending a message.[5] Wilson's most significant achievement was the creation of the Federal Reserve System. Wilson signed the Federal Reserve Act into law believing that banking should be "public, not private."[6] Sadly, Wilson's wife, Ellen, died of Bright's disease on August 6, 1914, halfway through Wilson's first term. Ellen passed away at the White House. The following year, on December 18, Wilson married Edith Bolling Galt in Washington, DC.

Over in Europe, World War I broke out in August 1914 following the assassination of the Austro-Hungarian archduke Franz Ferdinand by a Serbian nationalist named Gavrilo Princip. What had begun as a conflict between Austria-Hungary and Serbia escalated into a world war. Serbia was allied with Russia, which in turn was allied with France and Britain. Austria-Hungary was allied with Germany. These nations initiated the most horrific war that had ever taken place. The United States declared neutrality as other nations, including Italy, Turkey, and even Japan, entered the war, but US neutrality could not last for long. On May 7, 1915, a German submarine torpedoed the British liner *Lusitania*, killing 1,198 people, of whom 128 were Americans. The American people were shocked and feared that they too would be entering the war.

In 1916, while the war began to enter a stalemate, the United States held a presidential election. The Democrats renominated Wilson and Marshall. The Republicans nominated Supreme Court justice Charles Evans Hughes of New York and former vice president Charles W. Fairbanks of Indiana. Wilson ran on the campaign slogan:

"He kept us out of war."[7] He was reelected that year, carrying 9,126,868 popular votes and 277 electoral votes. Hughes won only 8,548,728 popular votes and 254 electoral votes.

In his second term, Wilson would be forced to enter the war. Back in Europe, Germany decided to engage in "unrestricted" submarine warfare in February 1917.[8] Germany's logic was that sinking all vessels carrying goods would force Great Britain to surrender. This meant that American ships would now be targeted—and they were. The sinking of American ships by German submarines, in addition to the interception of the Zimmermann telegram, in which Germany proffered to Mexico a military alliance against the United States, forced Wilson to ask for a formal declaration of war on April 2, 1917.[9]

The arrival of the American Expeditionary Force helped to break the stalemate. The Americans had arrived just in time, as one ally, Russia, withdrew from the war due to the Russian Revolution of 1917. Within a year, American forces had helped to repel the German forces. In 1918 Wilson proposed a plan, known as the Fourteen Points, to end the war. The idea behind his Fourteen Points was to achieve a "peace without victory."[10] The points called for peace, "freedom of navigation upon the seas," removal of economic barriers to trade, evacuation from occupied territories, the return of the Alsace-Lorraine region from Germany to France, the establishment of an independent Polish state, and the creation of an international body for the purposes of promoting peace.[11] The latter point created the League of Nations, which was the precursor to the United Nations. All nations involved in World War I, including Germany, accepted the peace terms and an armistice was signed to end the war on November 11, 1918.

All belligerents met at Versailles outside Paris, to discuss a peace treaty in 1919. The peace talks were led by the Council of Four, representing the leaders of the main allied nations: David Lloyd George of Britain, Vittorio Emanuele Orlando of Italy, Georges Clemenceau of France, and Woodrow Wilson. When Germany had signed the armistice a year earlier, it expected to pay the costs of restoring property (battlefields) damaged in battle. However, France and Britain went further and demanded "reparations" to pay for the entire war.[12] Their logic behind the reparations was "punishment, payment and prevention" because "a smaller Germany, and a poorer Germany, would be less of a threat to its neighbors."[13] In sum, the Allies calculated that Germany owed them "$33 billion."[14] But the punishments did not end with the reparations. The treaty negotiated also mandated that Germany return the Alsace-Lorraine region to France, grant Poland a corridor to the sea, demilitarize the German Rhineland, limit its military to one hundred thousand men, and admit to being guilty of causing the war.[15] The terms of the treaty outraged Germans and provided fuel to the "Stab-in-the-Back" legend that Germany was forced to surrender despite the fact that their army remained undefeated on the battlefield.[16] British economist John Maynard Keynes also criticized the treaty, calling it a "Carthaginian Peace."[17]

Back home, the Republicans offered stiff resistance to the Treaty of Versailles. The Republicans opposed the League of Nations because Article X of the treaty required signatories to provide military support to protect other members.[18] The main opponent of the League in the Senate was Henry Cabot Lodge of Massachusetts. However, Wilson felt that the rejection of Article X would effectively "[cut] the very heart out of the treaty."[19] In 1919, Wilson went on a national speaking tour to encourage public support for the League of Nations. During his attempt to resuscitate support for the treaty, Wilson became very sick and suffered a stroke that October. With Wilson being in such poor health, questions arose as to whether Vice President Thomas Marshall should assume power. Many thought that Marshall lacked leadership qualities because he was known to crack jokes, such as "What this country needs is a really good five-cent cigar."[20] However, Wilson's doctors refused to declare him an invalid.[21] As such, the First Lady became the link between the president and the government. Edith used the excuse that "anxiety" might cause further harm and privately briefed him on all political questions. She also relayed information from the president to cabinet officials.[22] Wilson eventually recovered enough to resume his job.

The remaining months of Wilson's second term were not very pleasant. The Senate failed to ratify the Treaty of Versailles and the Democratic candidate, Governor James M. Cox of Ohio, lost the presidential election to Republican senator Warren G. Harding from Ohio. After his presidency ended, Wilson retired to Washington, DC, where he died on February 3, 1924. He is interred at the Washington National Cathedral.

WILSON'S PAPERS AND THE LIBRARY AND MUSEUM

Though the Wilson library holds many of the former president's papers and correspondences, others are housed at the Library of Congress and at the Mudd Manuscript Library at Princeton University. The story of these papers' ultimate destinations began in October 1920. Shortly before leaving office, Wilson met with Charles Moore, who worked in the manuscript division of the Library of Congress. Moore inquired where the president would like to have his papers kept. During the meeting, Wilson suggested that the Library of Congress was the best place, but he would not commit until he wrote his will.[23] Almost four months after Wilson's death on February 3, 1924, his wife, who now controlled the papers, wrote a letter to Librarian of Congress Herbert Putnam, agreeing to donate the papers to the library. Edith liked the idea of donating the papers but wanted to decide which ones would ultimately go there.[24] While negotiating with the Library of Congress, Edith selected her husband's friend Ray Stannard Baker to write his official biography and sent him all the relevant papers for this endeavor.[25]

As the biography was being written, historian J. Franklin Jameson suggested that Baker send any papers that he no longer needed to the Library of Congress. Edith Wilson agreed, but added the following stipulations: no unsealed papers would be opened without her permission, as long as she was alive only she could give permission to access the papers, the papers would automatically pass to the Library of Congress after January 1, 1935, and she would be allowed to remove the papers from the Library of Congress.[26] Baker completed eight volumes of the biography in 1937, which he titled *Woodrow Wilson: Life and Letters*. The first batch of papers was sent to the Library of Congress between 1939 and 1940. In 1946, Edith Wilson donated her husband's personal collection of nine thousand books to the Library of Congress. Then, in 1949, author Arthur

S. Link began editing the papers for a published work known as *The Papers of Woodrow Wilson*. This book was published by Princeton University Press.

At the time of her death in 1961, Edith Wilson still controlled many of her husband's papers. Some of the papers were correspondences between Wilson and his first wife, Ellen. Edith had sent them to Ellen's stepdaughter, Eleanor Wilson McAdoo, who donated them to the Firestone Library at Princeton.[27] Today those papers, along with the papers that Link edited, are known as the Papers of Woodrow Wilson Project, which is located at the Mudd Manuscript Library at Princeton University.[28]

The organization that administers the Wilson library and museum was originally known as the Woodrow Wilson Birthplace Foundation. The foundation was created in 1938 with the purpose of preserving Wilson's birthplace: the Staunton Presbyterian Manse, which was built in 1856. The garden of the Manse was created in 1933 by landscape architect Charles Gillette. Seven years later the Manse had been refurbished; in 1941 it was formally dedicated by President Franklin Delano Roosevelt. In 1964 the Manse was registered as a National Historic Landmark. It was again refurbished in 1970 to more accurately reflect its mid-nineteenth-century Victorian look. The Wilson library has since purchased a building near the Manse to house the exhibits of the Wilson Museum. The building that houses the museum is called the Dolores Lescure Center. In 2004 the birthplace foundation was officially renamed the Woodrow Wilson Presidential Library.[29] There is also a separate building for the Library and Research Center.[30] Robin von Seldeneck is the president and chief executive officer of the library and museum, and Andrew Phillips is its curator.

President Woodrow Wilson's birthplace in Staunton, Virginia, with his original car parked out front, c. 2006 by Carol Highsmith. *Carol Highsmith LC-HS503-3007*

Collections and Exhibits

The Wilson museum has seven exhibits, which are described as follows by curator Phillips. The first of these is centered on Wilson's childhood days in Virginia, and the second focuses on his time at Princeton University. Visitors will see the real desk that Wilson used at Princeton, along with paintings by his first wife. From here, visitors will proceed to an exhibit about Wilson's tenure as governor of New Jersey. The gubernatorial desk that he used is on display in this gallery. The next exhibit is dedicated to Wilson's presidency, with exclusive emphasis on his prewar years, from 1912 to 1917. Inside, visitors will see campaign buttons, telephones from the era, wedding china from Wilson's second marriage, and suffragette buttons advocating women's right to vote. Following this gallery, visitors will see the 1919 Pierce-Arrow limousine that Wilson rode in as president. Finally, in the basement visitors will see a replica World War I trench, where they can learn about the experiences, horrors, and hardships of the war. They will see American military uniforms, weapons and arms, a German antitank gun, and a Chauchat French machine gun on display. In the library there are some small exhibits on the Treaty of Versailles and the League of Nations. At the time of writing, these exhibits are under renovation.[31]

The Wilson library holds several papers from the former president's administration. The majority of these were written by Wilson, his administration officials, and his contemporaries. The Hoover-Wilson Correspondence papers, which are from the Hoover Institute, include a collection of letters exchanged between President Wilson and future president Herbert Hoover, who headed the Belgian relief effort and the US Food Administration during World War I.[32] Visitors can also read presidential letters and telegrams written by Wilson about World War I and the Paris Peace Conference. In addition, the books of Wilson's personal papers edited by Arthur S. Link are available at the library. The library is home to a collection of three thousand books. The collection consists of books belonging to Wilson and his father, Joseph, and titles dealing with the history of Virginia, the legacy of Wilson, and contemporaries such as Theodore Roosevelt.[33] Lastly, there is a collection of photographs from Wilson's college years to the time of his presidency.[34]

NOTES

1. H. W. Brands, *Woodrow Wilson*, the American Presidents Series (New York: Times Books, 2003), 2.

2. Brands, *Woodrow Wilson*, 14–16.

3. Brands, *Woodrow Wilson*, 131.

4. Brands, *Woodrow Wilson*, 18.

5. Brands, *Woodrow Wilson*, 29.

6. Brands, *Woodrow Wilson*, 35.

7. Louis Auchincloss, *Woodrow Wilson*. Penguin Lives Biographies (New York: Viking Penguin, 2000), 80.

8. Hew Strachan, *The First World War* (New York: Penguin Books, 2003), 226.

9. Strachan, *First World War*, 227.

10. James Wilkinson and H. Stuart Hughes, *Contemporary Europe: A History*, eighth edition (Englewood Cliffs, NJ: Prentice Hall, 1995), 104.

11. Margaret MacMillan, *Paris 1919: Six Months that Changed the World* (New York: Random House, 2003), 495–96.

12. MacMillan, *Paris 1919*, 186.

13. MacMillan, *Paris 1919*, 162.

14. MacMillan, *Paris 1919*, 480.

15. Wilkinson and Hughes, *Contemporary Europe*, 115–16.

16. Wilkinson and Hughes, *Contemporary Europe*, 109.

17. John Maynard Keynes, *The Economic Consequences of the Peace* (North Charleston, SC: CreateSpace Independent Publishing Platform, 2010), 20.

18. MacMillan, *Paris 1919*, 492.

19. MacMillan, *Paris 1919*, 492.

20. David J. Bennett, *He Almost Changed the World: The Life and Times of Thomas Riley Marshall* (Bloomington, IN: AuthorHouse, 2007), 186.

21. Brands, *Woodrow Wilson*, 125–26.

22. Auchincloss, *Woodrow Wilson*, 2.

23. Frank L. Schick, Renee Schick, and Mark Carroll, *Records of the Presidency: Presidential Papers and Libraries from Washington to Reagan* (Phoenix, AZ: Oryx Press, 1989), 110.

24. Schick et al., *Records of the Presidency*, 111.

25. Schick et al., *Records of the Presidency*, 111.

26. Schick et al., *Records of the Presidency*, 112.

27. Schick et al., *Records of the Presidency*, 112.

28. "Papers of Woodrow Wilson Project Records," Papers of Woodrow Wilson Project, Princeton University Library, accessed May 17, 2017, http://findingaids.princeton.edu/collec tions/MC178#summary.

29. "History," The Woodrow Wilson Presidential Library and Museum, accessed May 17, 2017, http://www.woodrowwilson.org/about-1/history.

30. "Library and Research Center," The Woodrow Wilson Presidential Library and Museum, accessed May 17, 2017, http://www.woodrowwilson.org/museum/archival-collections-at-the -library.

31. Andrew Phillips (curator, The Woodrow Wilson Presidential Library and Museum), telephone interview with the author, April 14, 2017.

32. "Archive Collections," The Woodrow Wilson Presidential Library and Museum, accessed May 17, 2017, http://www.woodrowwilson.org/museum/archival-collections-at-the-library/ archive-collections.

33. Andrew Phillips, telephone interview.

34. "Archive Collections."

BIBLIOGRAPHY

Auchincloss, Louis. *Woodrow Wilson*. Penguin Lives Biographies. New York: Viking Penguin, 2000.

Bennett, David J. *He Almost Changed the World: The Life and Times of Thomas Riley Marshall.* Bloomington, IN: AuthorHouse, 2007.

Brands, H. W. *Woodrow Wilson*. The American Presidents Series. New York: Times Books, 2003.

Keynes, John Maynard. *The Economic Consequences of the Peace*. North Charleston: South Carolina CreateSpace Independent Publishing Platform, 2010.

MacMillan, Margaret. *Paris 1919: Six Months that Changed the World*. New York: Random House, 2003.

Schick, Frank L., Renee Schick, and Mark Carroll. *Records of the Presidency: Presidential Papers and Libraries from Washington to Reagan*. Phoenix, AZ: Oryx Press, 1989.

Strachan, Hew. *The First World War*. New York: Penguin Books, 2003.

Wilkinson, James, and H. Stuart Hughes. *Contemporary Europe: A History*. Eighth edition. Englewood Cliffs, NJ: Prentice Hall, 1995.

Calvin Coolidge Presidential Library and Museum at the Forbes Library

Address: 20 West St., Northampton MA 01060
Phone: (413) 587-1011
Website: http://forbeslibrary.org/calvin-coolidge-presidential-library-and-museum/
Social media (blog): http://forbeslibrary.org/calvin-coolidge-presidential-library-and
   -museum/coolidge-museum-blog/
Administration: Forbes Library
Hours: 9 a.m. to 5 p.m., Monday and Tuesday; 4 p.m. to 9 p.m. on Wednesdays; 1
   p.m. to 5 p.m. on Thursdays; closed from Friday to Sunday

BIOGRAPHY OF CALVIN COOLIDGE

July 4, 1872–January 5, 1933
Thirtieth President: August 2, 1923–March 4, 1929
Republican Party

Calvin Coolidge and wife, 1924.
LC-USZ62-9327

John Calvin Coolidge was born in Plymouth Notch, Vermont. He was one of two children born to John Calvin Coolidge Sr., a farmer, and Victoria Joseph Moor Coolidge. The Coolidge family was religious and stood fast to the principles of "the Puritan piety, the esteem for hard work and thrift."[1] As a teen, Coolidge attended the Black River Academy, where he had a reputation for being "solitary."[2] In fact, his quiet demeanor would earn him the nickname "Silent Cal."[3] At the age of nineteen, Coolidge attended Amherst College. When he graduated, he went to work as an apprentice in a law firm.[4]

After he became a lawyer, Coolidge started to be active in politics. He was elected to the Northampton City Council in Massachusetts as a Republican in 1898. He married Grace Goodhue in 1905 and they had two sons: John and Calvin Jr. Coolidge's next political venture was getting elected mayor of Northampton in 1909. In 1911 he was elected to the Massachusetts State Senate, which made him a powerful figure in the state.[5]

When former president Theodore Roosevelt split from the Republican Party in 1912 to form the Progressive Party, Coolidge declined to support him and remained loyal to the pro-business wing of his party. A year later, Coolidge became president of the Massachusetts State Senate.[6]

In 1918 Coolidge was elected governor. He governed during the Red Scare that followed World War I. Workers began demanding more rights, such as the right to unionize. One of their principal leaders was Samuel Gompers, who headed the American Federation of Labor. Gompers supported Boston policemen, who wanted to unionize for better working conditions and pay. However, Boston mayor Andrew Peters was against a police union. On September 9, 1919, a strike took place involving 1,117 of the 1,544 men in Boston's police force.[7] Governor Coolidge was against the strike and telegrammed Samuel Gompers a warning: "There is no right to strike against the public safety, anywhere, anytime."[8] Coolidge's decision won him national acclaim.[9]

In 1920 the Republican Party nominated Senator Warren G. Harding of Ohio as their presidential candidate. Initially, the party wanted to nominate Senator Irvine Lenroot as their vice president, but delegates chose Coolidge for his stance on "law and order."[10] Together, Harding and Coolidge won against their Democratic opponents Governor James Cox of Ohio and Franklin Roosevelt.

President Harding's administration is remembered for his untimely death and the Teapot Dome Scandal. The scandal related to federal oil reserves at Teapot Dome, Wyoming. Harding and his secretary of the interior, Albert Fall, "exchanged large sums of money" with "oil moguls."[11] The sale was illegal because the oil was federal property and Harding had no right to sell it. Fall served nine months in prison after being convicted of bribery in 1931.[12]

In 1923 Harding set out on a tour, which took him as far as Alaska. He then went on to San Francisco, where he became ill while staying at the Palace Hotel. Then, suddenly on August 2, 1923, Harding died of an "apoplexy stroke."[13] On the night of Harding's death, Coolidge was visiting his father at his Vermont farm. Upon receiving the news that his son was now president, Coolidge's father, who was also a public notary, administered the oath of office to his son under the "glow of a kerosene lamp" at 2:47 a.m.[14]

As president, Coolidge was a minimalist and proposed little for government to implement. When quizzed why he did so little, Coolidge said, "I didn't see the need to do things that didn't need to be done. Sometimes matters just resolve themselves if you leave them alone long enough. . . . When things are going all right, it is a good plan to let them alone."[15]

The United States was in good shape during the "Roaring Twenties," which encompassed most of Coolidge's administration. The economy was booming and the nation was over World War I. Describing the economic boom of the 1920s, journalist and historian Amity Shlaes writes, "Coal prices were stable and employment was so high that workers were scarce."[16] During his first partial term, Coolidge's major achievement, which precipitated this economic boom, was to sign the Revenue Act of 1924. This act is also known as the Mellon Tax bill, because it was proposed by Secretary of the Treasury Andrew Mellon. The act called for tax cuts for the wealthy on the premise that wealth would "trickle-down" extra money that could be used to create jobs rather than fund the government.[17]

While the rest of the nation was enjoying the good times, Coolidge and his family were not. On July 7, 1924, Coolidge's son Calvin Jr. contracted an infection from a blistered toe, which took his life.[18] Coolidge often blamed himself for Calvin's death, rationalizing that his son would never have blistered his toe while playing tennis in Washington had he not been president.[19]

Coolidge won the next presidential election (in 1924) over his Democratic opponent, the reputable attorney John W. Davis. In his second term, Coolidge continued his minimalist approach to the presidency. One problem he encountered, however, was subsidies for farmers. There were no Roaring Twenties for the farmers, who demanded that the government subsidize farm prices. Congress passed two versions of the McNary-Haugen Farm Relief Act in 1924 and 1926 to provide subsidies. Coolidge vetoed both versions, fearing government subsidies would raise prices for consumers and encourage farmers to grow too many crops, which would have to be dumped.[20]

Civil rights were also a major issue for Coolidge throughout his presidency. The nation had witnessed the resurgence of the Ku Klux Klan, and many African Americans in the South became victims of racism and lynching. During his first State of the Union Address in 1923, Coolidge said:

> Numbered among our population are some 12,000,000 colored people. Under our Constitution their rights are just as sacred as those of any other citizen. It is both a public and a private duty to protect those rights. The Congress ought to exercise all its powers of prevention and punishment against the hideous crime of lynching, of which the negroes are by no means the sole sufferers, but for which they furnish a majority of the victims.[21]

Three years later, on May 31, 1926, Coolidge again reminded the nation of the dangers of racial hatred in a speech he gave during the Memorial Exercises at Arlington, Virginia. He said:

> We all subscribe to the principle of religious liberty and toleration and equality of rights. This principle is in accordance with the fundamental law of the land. It is the very spirit of the American Constitution. We all recognize and admit that it ought to be put into practical operation. We know that every argument of right and reason requires such action. Yet in time of stress and public agitation we have too great a tendency to disregard this policy and indulge in race hatred, religious intolerance, and disregard of equal rights.[22]

Coolidge was popular enough to run for a second full term as president, but he refused. One year before the 1928 elections, he released a one-sentence press statement: "I do not choose to run for president in 1928."[23] On August 27, 1928, Coolidge signed the Kellogg–Briand Pact with fourteen other nations to outlaw war as "an instrument of national policy."[24] The Senate affirmed the treaty in January 1929, making this act one of Coolidge's final achievements as president.

The Republicans nominated Coolidge's secretary of commerce, Herbert Hoover, to run for the presidency in 1928. Hoover won the election and Coolidge went into retirement. The stock market crash of October 22, 1929, marked the beginning of the Great Depression. Some historians felt that Coolidge's minimalist policies were partly to blame for the crash; for example, David Greenberg said Coolidge did nothing to stop risky banking practices, such as "selling stocks on margin."[25] This practice involved buying "stocks with a pittance of a down payment and a loan,"[26] and then quickly reselling them for profit before the loan payment comes due. Coolidge spent his remaining years in Northampton, Massachusetts, and died on January 5, 1933.

LIBRARY AND MUSEUM

The history of the Coolidge library goes back to 1920, when Coolidge was elected vice president. That year Coolidge began donating "documents and memorabilia" to the Forbes Library in Northampton, Massachusetts.[27] During his presidency, Coolidge began to donate more materials to the Forbes Library and continued to do so after he left the White House. Most of his donations were from his time as governor.[28] The most significant donations of his post-presidency are two portraits of him and his wife Grace, painted by Howard Chandler Christy.[29]

In 1956, the Forbes Library, acting upon the request of Grace Coolidge, the Trustees of Forbes Library, and the Commonwealth of Massachusetts, created the "Calvin Coolidge Memorial Room as a separate entity within the Forbes Library."[30] In 1985 Coolidge's son John discovered some presidential papers, which he donated to the library.[31] The majority of Coolidge's presidential papers are stored at the Library of Congress.

President Coolidge did not want his presidential papers to become public, as he feared they could be used against him. In later years, when Mrs. Coolidge was asked why her husband did not keep personal records of his administration, she quoted him as saying, "I have never been hurt by what I have not said."[32] Luckily for historians, Coolidge's private secretary Edward T. Clark saved many of his personal presidential papers. Clark said, "Mr. Coolidge's desire was to destroy everything in the so-called personal files and there would have been nothing preserved if I had not taken some things out on my own responsibility."[33] These papers consist of one hundred eighty thousand items and are known as the Edward T. Clark papers at the Library of Congress.[34]

Collections and Exhibits

According to its website, the Coolidge library is "the largest existing source of primary material on Calvin Coolidge."[35] The Coolidge library occupies four thousand square feet of the left side on the second floor of the Forbes Library.

The library has several permanent exhibits. It houses the original desk that Coolidge worked at when studying law, the desk he used in his law office in 1898, and the one he had when he was at the city council of Northampton.[36]

Visitors can see the headdress that Coolidge was given in 1927 by the Sioux tribe in South Dakota. They made him an honorary chief for signing the Indian (Native American) Citizenship Act in 1924.[37] The library also has on display the hats, boots, and electric riding horse he used for exercise.[38]

The library has educational programs about Calvin Coolidge for people of all ages, from schoolchildren to retirees. The library was renovated in 2001, with modern climate control systems, lighting, and a new audiovisual system for presentations and to help people with hearing impairments installed. The current archivist is Julie Bartlett Nelson, who works part-time alongside local volunteers.[39]

NOTES

1. David Greenberg, *Calvin Coolidge*, the American Presidents Series (New York: Times Books, 2006), 15.

2. Greenberg, *Calvin Coolidge*, 18.

3. Amity Shlaes, *Coolidge* (New York: HarperCollins, 2013), 6–7.

4. Greenberg, *Calvin Coolidge*, 20–21.

5. Greenberg, *Calvin Coolidge*, 21.

6. Greenberg, *Calvin Coolidge*, 24–25.

7. Greenberg, *Calvin Coolidge*, 30.

8. David Pietrusza, *1920: The Year of Six Presidents* (New York: Carroll & Graf, 2007), 100.

9. Greenberg, *Calvin Coolidge*, 32.

10. Greenberg, *Calvin Coolidge*, 37.

11. Greenberg, *Calvin Coolidge*, 49.

12. John W. Dean, *Warren G. Harding*, the American Presidents Series (New York: Times Books, 2004), 160.

13. Dean, *Warren G. Harding*, 152.

14. Greenberg, *Calvin Coolidge*, 43.

15. "Quotations, Inspiration and Philosophy of Calvin Coolidge," Calvin Coolidge: 30th US President, accessed September 7, 2016, http://www.calvincoolidge.us/quotations.html.

16. Shlaes, *Coolidge*, 331.

17. Greenberg, *Calvin Coolidge*, 71.

18. Shlaes, *Coolidge*, 298–300.

19. Shlaes, *Coolidge*, 302.

20. Greenberg, *Calvin Coolidge*, 149.

21. "Calvin Coolidge: First Annual Message," The American Presidency Project, accessed September 7, 2016, http://www.presidency.ucsb.edu/ws/?pid=29564.

22. "Calvin Coolidge: Address at the Memorial Exercises at Arlington, Virginia," accessed September 7, 2016, http://www.presidency.ucsb.edu/ws/?pid=402.

23. Greenberg, *Calvin Coolidge*, 137.

24. Greenberg, *Calvin Coolidge*, 123.

25. Greenberg, *Calvin Coolidge*, 147–48.

26. Greenberg, *Calvin Coolidge*, 148.

27. "Calvin Coolidge Presidential Library and Museum," Forbes Library, accessed September 7, 2016, http://forbeslibrary.org/calvin-coolidge-presidential-library-and-museum/.

28. William G. Clotworthy, *Homes and Libraries of the Presidents: An Interpretive Guide*, third edition (Blacksburg, VA: McDonald & Woodward, 2008), 221.

29. "Calvin Coolidge Presidential Library and Museum."

30. "Calvin Coolidge Presidential Library and Museum."

31. Clotworthy, *Homes and Libraries of the Presidents*, 221.

32. Frank L. Schick, Renee Schick, and Mark Carroll, *Records of the Presidency: Presidential Papers and Libraries from Washington to Reagan* (Phoenix, AZ: Oryx Press, 1989), 115.

33. Schick et al., *Records of the Presidency*, 115.

34. Schick et al., *Records of the Presidency*, 115.

35. "Calvin Coolidge Presidential Library and Museum."

36. "Coolidge Museum Video Tour," Forbes Library, accessed September 7, 2016, http://forbeslibrary.org/calvin-coolidge-presidential-library-and-museum/coolidge-museum-video-tour/.

37. "Coolidge Museum Video Tour."

38. "Coolidge Museum Video Tour."

39. "Julie Bartlett Nelson, Archivist at the Calvin Coolidge Presidential Library and Museum," YouTube video, posted by Comcast Newsmakers NE, March 28, 2016, https://www.youtube.com/watch?v=K5kiGztmU2w.

BIBLIOGRAPHY

Clotworthy, William G. *Homes and Libraries of the Presidents: An Interpretive Guide*. Third edition. Blacksburg, VA: McDonald & Woodward, 2008.

Dean, John W. *Warren G. Harding*. The American Presidents Series. New York: Times Books, 2004.

Greenberg, David. *Calvin Coolidge*. The American Presidents Series. New York: Times Books, 2006.

Pietrusza, David. *1920: The Year of the Six Presidents*. New York: Carroll & Graf, 2007.

Schick, Frank L., Renee Schick, and Mark Carroll. *Records of the Presidency: Presidential Papers and Libraries from Washington to Reagan*. Phoenix, AZ: Oryx Press, 1989.

Shlaes, Amity. *Coolidge*. New York: HarperCollins, 2013.

Herbert Hoover Presidential Library and Museum

Address: 210 Parkside Drive, West Branch, IA 52358
Phone: (319) 643-5301
Website: http://www.hoover.archives.gov/
Social media: https://www.facebook.com/HooverPresLib
Administration: National Archives
Hours: 9 a.m. to 5 p.m., every day; closed on Thanksgiving Day, Christmas Day, and
  New Year's Day

BIOGRAPHY OF HERBERT HOOVER

August 10, 1874–October 20, 1964
Thirty-First President: March 4, 1929–March 4, 1933
Republican Party

Herbert Hoover and Mrs. Hoover, 1929.
LC-USZ62-9327

Herbert Clark Hoover was born in West Branch, Iowa. He was one of three children of Hulda and Jesse Hoover. The family lived in a small one-room cottage. The Hoovers were strict Quakers and allowed their children to read only the "Bible, the encyclopedia, or those great novels where the hero overcomes the demon rum."[1] Hoover and his siblings became orphans at a young age: Jesse died in 1880 and Hulda died four years later. Hoover went on to live with his uncle, Dr. John Minthorn, in Newburg, Oregon. In 1891 he moved south to California and attended the newly established Leland Stanford University. Hoover studied geology and engineering. His time at Stanford established his traditionalist American views. William Leuchtenburg

79

said "[Hoover] never ceased to believe his country was the greatest nation on earth; that Westerners, especially Californians, were the most gifted of Americans."[2] While at Stanford he met fellow Iowan Lou Henry, who would become his wife. Hoover graduated from Stanford in 1895 and found work gold mining in the outback of western Australia. Within the next two years, Hoover would build a financial fortune and marry Lou Henry.

From Australia, Hoover went to mine coal in China during the turbulent Boxer Rebellion against Western influence in 1900. When World War I broke out in August of 1914, Hoover involved himself in a humanitarian effort to assist Belgian civilians. Germany violated Belgian neutrality as a shortcut to invade France. Hoover told stories of how "German armies uprooted more than a million Belgians" who were then facing "mass starvation."[3] Hoover took the initiative and created the Commission for the Relief of Belgium. This organization raised money and sent much-needed food. He was acclaimed for his efforts, which caught the attention of government officials in Washington. When the United States entered the war in April 1917, Hoover was appointed Food Czar and headed the United States Food Administration. In this capacity Hoover used patriotism to encourage Americans to grow their own food in "victory gardens" and limit the amount of meat they bought.

When the Republican senator Warren G. Harding became president in 1921, he chose Hoover as his secretary of commerce. Hoover's biggest achievement as secretary was his 1927 visit to the flood-stricken Mississippi region. Hoover raised relief money and learned about the region's race problems.[4]

Hoover ran for president in 1928 against the Democratic governor of New York, Alfred E. Smith. Many Americans refused to vote for Smith because he was a Catholic. Hoover won the election and took the helm of a nation in the midst of an economic boom known as the Roaring Twenties. Then tragedy struck on October 29, 1929, when speculation caused the stock market to crash. The millions of people whom the crash left unemployed or bankrupt naturally looked to Hoover for help. However, Hoover saw the situation as temporary and held fast to his belief that Washington should refrain from providing welfare. In a speech explaining his position he said, "Prosperity [. . .] cannot be restored by raids upon the public Treasury."[5] The public now blamed Hoover personally for the Great Depression and decried the man who saved Belgium as the "Great Scrooge."[6]

Hoover reluctantly agreed to government investments in public works projects. When this remedy failed, he signed the Smoot-Hawley Tariff of 1930, which raised taxes on imports. However, the tax hike during the Depression had the opposite effect to that intended, making things worse. The next disaster for Hoover was his forceful military expulsion of the Bonus Army from Washington, DC, in 1932. The Bonus Army was made up of desperate World War I veterans who were seeking their promised bonus pay. Hoover's critics condemned him for the action he took against them; Hoover said he was wrongly "portrayed as a murderer and an enemy of the veterans."[7] In the summer of 1932 Hoover created the Reconstruction Finance Corporation (RFC) to lend money to struggling industries, but critics said the RFC was "too little, too late."[8]

The presidential election of 1932 had Hoover pitted against the Democratic New York governor Franklin Delano Roosevelt. Hoover wanted to be reelected, but he was facing difficulties. Governor Roosevelt promised to end the Depression with a series of government spending programs he called the New Deal. That fall, Roosevelt won a landslide victory over Hoover.

Though Hoover lost the presidency, he remained active in public life. He became a vocal critic of the New Deal and considered making a political comeback. Writing on the subject, George H. Nash said, "Hoover in his later years was a man driven by an unceasing quest for vindication."[9] In 1940 Hoover returned to fund-raising, providing relief to Finland during their Winter War with Soviet Russia. He also opposed America entering World War II unnecessarily. After the war, President Harry Truman asked Hoover to head a commission (the Hoover Commission) to identify and eradicate wasteful government spending. Hoover was happy to be of service to the nation again. On October 20, 1964, he died at the age of ninety.

LIBRARY AND MUSEUM

The origins of the Herbert Hoover Presidential Library and Museum are traced to Hoover's $50,000 donation in 1919 to Stanford University for the creation of the Hoover Institution on War, Revolution, and Peace.[10] During World War I, Hoover spent much time in Europe providing relief. He wanted a repository at Stanford to make his personal collection of materials from World War I and the Russian Revolution available. The library at Stanford briefly held President Hoover's public papers until they were transferred to his presidential library and museum in West Branch, Iowa. Today, the Stanford library is part of the larger conservative think tank the Hoover Institution. In 1959 the former president published the mission of the Hoover Institution:

> This Institution supports the Constitution of the United States, its Bill of Rights and its method of representative government. Both our social and economic systems are based on private enterprise from which springs initiative and ingenuity. . . . Ours is a system where the Federal Government should undertake no governmental, social or economic action, except where local government, or the people, cannot undertake it for themselves. . . . The overall mission of this Institution is, from its records, to recall the voice of experience against the making of war, and by the study of these records and their publication, to recall man's endeavors to make and preserve peace, and to sustain for America the safeguards of the American way of life. This Institution is not, and must not be, a mere library. But with these purposes as its goal, the Institution itself must constantly and dynamically point the road to peace, to personal freedom, and to the safeguards of the American system.[11]

Knowing that President Franklin Roosevelt had a presidential library, Hoover used the Presidential Record Act of 1955 to establish his own. On August 10, 1962, the library was dedicated and opened. The library is situated around the cottage where he was born in West Branch, Iowa, which is part of the Herbert Hoover National Historic Site. Twenty-seven years before the library was opened, Hoover's sons bought and restored the cottage. Then in 1939, the cottage was named the Birthplace Cottage and was opened as part of the Hoover Birthplace Society. When the time came for Hoover to construct his presidential library, he chose the land adjacent to the Birthplace Cottage.

The dedication of the Hoover Presidential Library coincided with Hoover's eighty-eighth birthday. Among the dignitaries to attend were former president Harry Truman and Vice President Lyndon B. Johnson. At the dedication ceremony Hoover addressed the audience, saying:

> When members of Congress created these Presidential Libraries, they did a great public service. They made available for research the records of vital periods in American history. Within them are the thrilling records of supreme action by the American people, their devotion and sacrifice to their ideals. [. . .] These institutions are the repositories of such experience—hot off the griddle.[12]

On August 12, 1965, Congress authorized the Herbert Hoover National Historic Site to preserve the Birthplace Cottage and transferred its care to the National Park Service. Today the birthplace society is renamed the Hoover Presidential Society. This society "fosters the collection, interpretation and preservation of historical resources relating to the life, ideas, values, and times of Herbert Hoover by supporting the Historic Site and Presidential Library."[13]

Just as President Hoover struggled during the Great Depression, his library underwent a depression of sorts in the late 1980s. Budget cuts and dwindling visits caused disillusionment. The institution needed to reinvent itself. Former director of the Hoover Library Timothy Walch said:

> The Hoover Library and its programs seemed tired and stale. The number of visitors to the museum had dropped. . . . Budget cuts and programmatic rigidity had undermined the ability of the Library to reach out to students and scholars alike. . . . Everyone agreed that something had to be done to "reinvent" the Library, but the inspiration and the resources were lacking.[14]

The solution came in 1987 when the library ushered in Richard Norton Smith as director. Smith is a presidential historian who wrote *Thomas E. Dewey and His Times*, a biography of the governor of New York who twice ran unsuccessfully for the presidency. Smith's ideas transformed the Hoover Library into the institution it is today.

Smith created a three-pronged plan for the library's revitalization. Under his plan, the library would "maintain a first-rate archival repository, [. . .] raise the visibility of a nationally important center of historical scholarship, and [. . .] establish the Hoover Library–Museum as a major cultural asset."[15] Smith initiated his plan with the year-long *39 Men* exhibition celebrating the thirty-nine men who had served as president. Smith recalls the exhibition:

> By far the largest such event in Hoover Library history, *39 Men* featured everything from Calvin Coolidge's electric horse, Thomas Jefferson's monogrammed silk stock-

ings, and John Adams's baby rattle, to Gerald Ford's football helmet, Ronald Reagan's cowboy boots, and a 102-year-old slice of Grover Cleveland's wedding cake.[16]

The popularity of the *39 Men* exhibition increased the number of visitors to the library. Building on this success, Smith decided the library should always have temporary yearly exhibits. But Smith did not stop there: he also made the library friendlier for children. Smith used videos and computer games to present footage of Hoover to students. Finally, he made the Hoover Library a center of scholarship. One example of this is the library's sponsorship of historian George H. Nash and his biographical series on Hoover's life. The library's scholarship is manifested in conferences; one of the most important of these was held in October of 1989, when former president Gerald Ford and the emeritus librarian of Congress Daniel J. Boorstin discussed the public roles of former presidents.[17]

From November 1993 to April 2011, Timothy Walch served as acting director and director of the Hoover Library. Walch is an author and historian who previously served as editor of *Prologue*.[18] During his tenure, Walch wrote *Uncommon Americans: The Lives and Legacies of Herbert and Lou Henry Hoover*, published in 2003. Walch stepped down in April 2011 and was replaced by the museum and library's current director, Thomas Schwartz. Schwartz had previously served as Illinois State Historian, where he directed research on the Abraham Lincoln Presidential Library in Springfield, Illinois.[19]

Herbert Hoover Presidential Library and Museum. *Courtesy of the Herbert Hoover Presidential Library and Museum*

Collections and Exhibits

Beginning at the rotunda, visitors will find the first gallery: *Years of Adventure*. This gallery tells the story of Hoover's early days in Iowa, Oregon, and Stanford University. The gallery also relays the story of Hoover the engineer, who traveled to Australia and China to mine gold and coal. Visitors will see pictures of Hoover and learn about the historical events he witnessed, such as the Boxer Rebellion of 1900.

The second gallery is *The Humanitarian Years*. Here visitors will see how Hoover became a humanitarian during World War I and administered relief to the besieged nation of Belgium. Later, Hoover started a similar initiative to feed people in Russia. Included in this gallery is Hoover's work for the United States Food Administration, where he encouraged Americans to grow their own food and observe "Meatless Monday" to help ration meat.[20]

The third gallery is titled *The Roaring Twenties*. Here, visitors will learn about the Jazz Age, Prohibition, Hollywood, consumerism, and Charles Lindbergh's solo flight across the Atlantic Ocean to Paris. Pictures of Hoover with famous people of the era are contained in this gallery, too.[21]

The fourth gallery takes visitors to Hoover's days as secretary of commerce for Presidents Warren G. Harding and Calvin Coolidge. The gallery is called *The Wonder Boy*. Hoover was very successful as secretary of commerce. Visitors will see displays of Hoover working on early radios and televisions. Most important is the information on Hoover's 1927 visit to the South, where he raised funds to combat the disastrous flooding of the Mississippi River.[22]

The fifth gallery shows visitors the election of 1928, when Hoover decisively won the presidency. The gallery is called *The Logical Candidate*. It presents Hoover's presidency before the stock market crash of October 1929. Visitors can see pictures and newspaper articles about Hoover's campaign, his inauguration, and his early days in the White House.[23]

Galleries six and seven—*The Great Depression* and *From Hero to Scapegoat*—focus on the Great Depression and its impact on President Hoover. In the sixth gallery, visitors learn how Black Tuesday (October 29, 1929) spelled the end of the Roaring Twenties and the beginning of the decade-long Great Depression. Hoover desperately tried to resolve the Depression through constructive efforts, but they had little impact on the disaster. In addition, the gallery presents questions and answers about what caused the Depression.[24]

The story of the Depression is continued in the seventh gallery. Here visitors learn how disappointed the American public was with Hoover. Images of the Bonus Army of World War I veterans demanding their promised bonus pay are displayed, along with quotations criticizing Hoover. A chained-up front entrance door to a bank helps to tell the story of the numerous bank failures of the era.[25]

The eighth gallery is dedicated to Lou Henry Hoover and is called *The Uncommon Woman*. Here visitors can see pictures of the First Lady and even a statue of her with a Girl Scout. Lou Hoover supported the Girl Scouts and helped organize the first Girl Scout cookie sale.[26]

The final gallery is dedicated to Hoover's life after his presidency and includes a replica of his retirement office at the Waldorf Towers in New York City. This gallery is called *The Counselor of the Republic*. Many thought Hoover was done with public life after he lost the presidency to Franklin Roosevelt in 1932. However, he remained active and this gallery is an illustration of his post-presidential achievements. Visitors will see his goodwill trip to Poland, the establishment of the Hoover Commission to cut the size of government, and the ways in which he advised future presidents. The gallery concludes with pictures of his funeral and burial.[27]

There have also been several temporary exhibits at the Hoover Library. Past exhibits have focused on the achievements of women, how Christmas is celebrated around the world, Chinese-American relations, and life in the 1960s.[28]

In 2016 the Hoover Library opened a temporary exhibit called *Ain't Misbehavin'? The World of the Gangster*. The exhibit explores the Jazz Age and the gangster culture of the Prohibition era. The library's press release describes the exhibit:

> You will enter the exhibit, *Ain't Misbehavin'? The World of the Gangster* through a recreated Hat Shop, and as you leave the back door of the Hat Shop you step into a Speakeasy. Outside of the Speakeasy is a back alley that takes you to a typical street from the 1920s, from here you can explore shops with false fronts, gambling halls, FBI offices, and gangster hangouts.[29]

While visitors can visit the library to see the physical exhibits, anyone can view its virtual exhibits in cyberspace. The library has two virtual exhibits: *History of the Flour Sacks* and *World War I Paintings*. The virtual exhibit on flour sacks celebrates Hoover's major achievement during World War I: delivering sacks of flour to Belgium.[30] He directed the Commission for Relief in Belgium in October 1914 to help Belgian civilians, successfully shipping 5.7 million bags of flour during the war. Visitors to the website can see a picture of a real flour sack Hoover sent to Belgium.[31] The other virtual exhibit on paintings from World War I displays propaganda posters from the United States Food Administration, which encouraged Americans to save as much food as possible.[32]

As of 2015, the Hoover Library has twenty thousand reference books and 305 archival collections.[33] The library also has an oral history collection and museum exhibits that present Hoover's life and times. In 2015 the library welcomed 41,818 visitors.[34]

The Hoover Library has permanent, temporary (past), and virtual exhibits. The permanent exhibits take visitors on a tour of Hoover's life and accomplishments, with a special focus on specific historical events. The Hoover Library website says:

> The Herbert Hoover Museum enables visitors to experience the many sides of Iowa's only President. The tour begins in a rotunda area with a 16 foot red granite map of the world and inserted in the floor are 57 brass sheaves of wheat—one in every nation where Hoover conducted relief efforts.[35]

Special Collections The Hoover Presidential Library and Museum contains the archives of many of Hoover's colleagues and contemporaries. Library director Timothy Walch said the library is "committed to preserving and making archival material available. . . . Beginning in the mid-1960s, archivists at the Hoover Library have devoted their time and attention to the papers of Herbert Hoover and his associates."[36] Some of these associates include Republican senator Gerald Nye of North Dakota; General Robert E. Wood; historian Wayne S. Cole; and Hoover's wife, Lou Henry. The library's special collections contain papers, correspondences, and speeches of these individuals who knew and served with Hoover. Perhaps the most famous is the Rose Wilder Lane collection. Lane was the daughter of Laura Ingalls Wilder, whose *Little House* series of children's novels (1932–1943) inspired the beloved American television series *Little House on the Prairie* that starred Michael Landon. Like Hoover, Wilder briefly lived in a small Iowa town, Burr Oak, in the nineteenth century. Rose Wilder Lane was Hoover's first biographer and long-time friend.[37]

Those who are interested in learning more about Laura Ingles Wilder can access the Laura Ingles Wilder Website Index. This website is maintained by the Hoover Library and is divided into two sections: students and educators. Grade school children can click the student section to find a variety of pictures, maps, and information on Wilder and her travels across the Midwestern prairies. In the educator section, teachers will find teaching units and activities that would be of interest to grade-school children, such as making a nine-patch quilt.[38]

NOTES

1. George M. Nash, *The Life of Herbert Hoover: The Engineer, 1874–1914* (New York: W. W. Norton, 1983), 6.

2. William E. Leuchtenburg, *Herbert Hoover* (New York: Henry Holt, 2009), 6–7.

3. Leuchtenburg, *Herbert Hoover*, 25.

4. Donald J. Lisio, *Hoover, Blacks, and Lily-Whites: A Study of Southern Strategies* (Chapel Hill: University of North Carolina Press, 2012), xiv.

5. Leuchtenburg, *Herbert Hoover*, 112.

6. Leuchtenburg, *Herbert Hoover*, 114.

7. Herbert Hoover, *The Memoirs of Herbert Hoover: The Great Depression, 1929–1941* (New York: Macmillan, 1952), 230.

8. James Stuart Olson, *Historical Dictionary of the Great Depression, 1929–1940* (Westport, CT: Greenwood, 2001), 93.

9. George H. Nash, ed., *Freedom Betrayed: Herbert Hoover's Secret History of the Second World War and Its Aftermath* (Stanford, CA: Hoover Institute Press, 2011), lx.

10. Wendy R. Ginsberg, Erika K. Lunder, and Daniel J. Richardson, *The Presidential Libraries Act and the Establishment of Presidential Libraries* (CRS Report No. R41513) (Washington, DC: Congressional Research Service, 2015), 7.

11. "Mission/History," Hoover Institution, accessed April 1, 2016, http://www.hoover.org/about/missionhistory.

12. Frank L. Schick, Renee Schick, and Mark Carroll, *Records of the Presidency: Presidential Papers and Libraries from Washington to Reagan* (Phoenix, AZ: Oryx Press, 1989), 77–78.

13. Spencer Howard, archives technician for reference and research at the Herbert Hoover Presidential Library-Museum, e-mail message to author, March 20, 2016.

14. Timothy Walch, "Reinventing the Herbert Hoover Presidential Library," *Government Information Quarterly* 12, no. 1: 115.

15. Richard Norton Smith, "A Presidential Revival: How the Hoover Library Overcame a Mid-Life Crisis," *Prologue: Quarterly of the National Archives* 21 (Summer 1989): 117.

16. Smith, "Presidential Revival," 118.

17. Walch, "Reinventing," 121.

18. Richard Norton Smith and Timothy Walch, "The Ordeal of Herbert Hoover," *Prologue* 36, no. 2 (Summer 2004), http://www.archives.gov/publications/prologue/2004/summer/hoover-1.html.

19. "Press Release Archive: 2011," National Archives, https://www.archives.gov/press/press-releases/2011/nr11-115b.html.

20. "The Museum Exhibit Galleries: Gallery Two: The Humanitarian Years," Herbert Hoover Presidential Library and Museum, accessed May 26, 2017, http://hoover.archives.gov/exhibits/Hooverstory/gallery02/index.html.

21. "The Museum Exhibit Galleries: Gallery Three: The Roaring Twenties," Herbert Hoover Presidential Library and Museum, accessed May 26, 2017, https://hoover.archives.gov/exhibits/Hooverstory/gallery03/index.html.

22. "The Museum Exhibit Galleries: Gallery Four: The Wonder Boy," Herbert Hoover Presidential Library and Museum, accessed May 26, 2017, http://hoover.archives.gov/exhibits/Hooverstory/gallery04/index.html.

23. "The Museum Exhibit Galleries: Gallery Five: The Logical Candidate," Herbert Hoover Presidential Library and Museum, accessed May 26, 2017, http://hoover.archives.gov/exhibits/Hooverstory/gallery05/index.html.

24. "The Museum Exhibit Galleries: Gallery Six: The Great Depression," Herbert Hoover Presidential Library and Museum, accessed May 26, 2017, http://www.hoover.archives.gov/exhibits/Hooverstory/gallery06/index.html.

25. "The Museum Exhibit Galleries: Gallery Seven: From Hero to Scapegoat," Herbert Hoover Presidential Library and Museum, accessed May 26, 2017, http://hoover.archives.gov/exhibits/Hooverstory/gallery07/index.html.

26. "The Museum Exhibit Galleries: Gallery Eight: An Uncommon Woman," Herbert Hoover Presidential Library and Museum, accessed May 26, 2017, http://hoover.archives.gov/exhibits/Hooverstory/gallery08/index.html.

27. "The Museum Exhibit Galleries: Gallery Nine: Counselor to the Republic," Herbert Hoover Presidential Library and Museum, accessed May 26, 2017, http://hoover.archives.gov/exhibits/Hooverstory/gallery09/index.html.

28. "Exhibits," Herbert Hoover Presidential Library and Museum, accessed May 26, 2017, http:// hoover.archives.gov/exhibits/.

29. Herbert Hoover Presidential Library and Museum, "Ain't Misbehavin'? The World of the Gangster," news release, accessed May 26, 2017, http://hoover.archives.gov/pressreleases/GangsterPR.pdf.

30. "History of the Flour Sacks," Herbert Hoover Presidential Library and Museum, accessed May 26, 2017, http://hoover.archives.gov/exhibits/collections/flour%20sacks/index.html.

31. "History of the Flour Sacks."

32. "United States Food Administration," Herbert Hoover Presidential Library and Museum, accessed May 26, 2017, http://hoover.archives.gov/exhibits/collections/featureditem/worldwar1paintings.html.

33. Spencer Howard, e-mail message to author, March 28, 2016.

34. Herbert Hoover Presidential Library and Museum, "HHPLM Statistics" (unpublished report, Herbert Hoover Presidential Library and Museum, 2016).

35. "The Herbert Hoover Museum: Herbert Hoover Museum Permanent Galleries," Herbert Hoover Presidential Library and Museum, accessed May 26, 2017, http://hoover.archives.gov/exhibits/Hooverstory/index.html.

36. Dwight M. Miller and Dale C. Mayer, *Historical Materials in the Herbert Hoover Presidential Library* (West Branch, IA: Herbert Hoover Presidential Library, 1996), 3.

37. "The Rose Wilder Lane Collection," National Archives and Records Administration, accessed May 26, 2017, http://www.ecommcode2.com/hoover/research/wilder/index.html.

38. "Laura Ingalls Wilder Website Index," Herbert Hoover Presidential Library and Museum, accessed May 26, 2017, http://hoover.archives.gov/LIW/index.html.

BIBLIOGRAPHY

American Heritage Book of the Presidents and Famous Americans: Volume 10. New York: Dell, 1967.

Ginsberg, Wendy R., Erika K. Lunder, and Daniel J. Richardson. *The Presidential Libraries Act and the Establishment of Presidential Libraries* (CRS Report No. R41513). Washington, DC: Congressional Research Service, 2015.

Hoover, Herbert. *The Memoirs of Herbert Hoover: The Great Depression, 1929–1941.* New York: Macmillan, 1952.

Hufbauer, Benjamin. *Presidential Temples: How Memorials and Libraries Shape Public Memory.* Lawrence: University Press of Kansas, 2005.

Lantzer, Jason S. "The Public History of Presidential Libraries: How the Presidency Is Presented to the People." *Journal for the Association of History and Computing* 6, no. 1. http://hdl.handle.net/2027/spo.3310410.0006.101.

Leuchtenburg, William E. *Herbert Hoover.* New York: Times Books, 2009.

Lisio, Donald J. *Hoover, Blacks, and Lily-Whites: A Study of Southern Strategies.* Chapel Hill: University of North Carolina Press, 2012.

Mayer, Dale C., and Dwight M. Miller. *Historical Material in the Hoover Presidential Library.* West Branch, IA: Hoover Presidential Library Association, National Archives and Records Administration, 1996.

Nash, George M. *The Life of Herbert Hoover: The Engineer, 1874–1914.* New York: W. W. Norton, 1983.

———, ed. *Freedom Betrayed: Herbert Hoover's Secret History of the Second World War and Its Aftermath.* Stanford, CA: Hoover Institution Press, 2011.

Olson, James Stuart. *Historical Dictionary of the Great Depression, 1929–1940.* Westport, CT: Greenwood, 2001.

Schick, Frank L., Renee Schick, and Mark Carroll. *Records of the Presidency: Presidential Papers and Libraries from Washington to Reagan.* Phoenix, AZ: Oryx Press, 1989.

Smith, Richard Norton. "A Presidential Revival: How the Hoover Library Overcame a Mid-Life Crisis." *Prologue: Quarterly of the National Archives* 21 (Summer 1989): 115–23.

Smith, Richard Norton, and Timothy Walch. "The Ordeal of Herbert Hoover." *Prologue* 36, no. 2 (Summer 2004). http://www.archives.gov/publications/prologue/2004/summer/hoover-1.html.

Walch, Timothy. "Reinventing the Herbert Hoover Presidential Library." *Government Information Quarterly* 12, no. 1: 113–25.

Franklin D. Roosevelt
Presidential Library and Museum

Address: 4079 Albany Post Rd., Hyde Park, NY 12538
Phone: (845) 486-7770
Website: http://www.fdrlibrary.marist.edu/
Social media: https://www.facebook.com/fdrlibrary
Administration: National Archives
Partnership: Marist College
Hours: 9 a.m. to 5 p.m. every day, November through March; 9 a.m. to 6 p.m., April through October; closed on Thanksgiving Day, Christmas Day, and New Year's Day

BIOGRAPHY OF FRANKLIN D. ROOSEVELT

January 30, 1882–April 12, 1945
Thirty-Second President: March 4, 1933–April 12, 1945
Democratic Party

Franklin D. Roosevelt by Elias Goldensky. *LC-USZ62-117121*

Franklin Delano Roosevelt was born to Sara and James Roosevelt of Hyde Park, New York. Sara and James were both from wealthy families. Franklin's fifth cousin was President Theodore Roosevelt. Franklin was raised and nurtured by Swiss tutors. At age fourteen he entered Groton, a prestigious boarding school. Because of his cloistered upbringing, Franklin had difficulties establishing strong relationships with his peers and participating in sports. Four years later, he graduated from Groton and went on to attend Harvard. At Harvard he was elected president of the student newspaper, the *Harvard Crimson.* One year after graduating from Harvard, in 1905, he married his distant cousin Eleanor, with President Roosevelt in attendance.[1]

From Harvard, Roosevelt enrolled in, but never graduated from, Columbia Law School. By 1910 he had passed the bar, practiced law, and developed an interest in politics. In that year, Roosevelt was elected to the New York State Senate. In 1913

President Woodrow Wilson appointed Roosevelt as assistant secretary of the navy. When the United States entered World War I in 1917, Roosevelt worked hard to make the navy a fighting force.[2] His work attracted the attention of delegates at the 1920 Democratic Convention, who nominated him to run as vice president with James M. Cox.[3] Unfortunately, Cox and Roosevelt lost the election to the Republican senator Warren Harding. Although he had lost, Roosevelt's political future looked bright.

In August 1921 Roosevelt contracted the poliomyelitis virus while on vacation at his summer home on Campobello Island. For the rest of his life, Roosevelt would need crutches, braces, and a wheelchair for mobility. His ordeal with polio is depicted in the 1960 movie *Sunrise at Campobello*, where Roosevelt is played by Ralph Bellamy. After he contracted polio, many concluded that his political career was over. Fortunately, they were wrong; in 1924 he would go to New York to deliver a speech at the deadlocked Democratic Convention. With the aid of crutches, Roosevelt was able to stand and speak to an ecstatic crowd of delegates.[4] Four years later, he was elected governor of New York.

Roosevelt was governor when the stock market crashed on October 29, 1929, ending an era of prosperity and beginning one of poverty. As governor of New York, he decided to take action. Roosevelt provided aid to the unemployed, reduced taxes, and developed publicly owned electrical companies.[5] This was in sharp contrast to the policies of the president at the time, Herbert Hoover, who called for government restraint. The Democrats took notice of Roosevelt's policies and nominated him to run for the presidency in 1932. For their vice president they chose John Nance Garner of Texas. As a candidate, Roosevelt promised government relief for those who were suffering. President Hoover vigorously campaigned against Roosevelt and was steadfast about his own policies. However, when the election was over, Roosevelt found that he had defeated Hoover in a landslide.[6]

In 1933 the gross national product had fallen by over 30 percent and unemployment rose to 24 percent.[7] The nation was perplexed by the grim economic forecast and looked to the new president, Franklin Delano Roosevelt, for reassurance. On March 4, 1933, Roosevelt was sworn in as the thirty-second president and reassured the nation with his inaugural address, saying: "The only thing we have to fear is fear itself."[8] In that speech, he promised serious action to tackle the problems of the Great Depression. In his first one hundred days in office, Roosevelt worked with Congress to enact and sign legislation helping banks, farmers, and workers. Roosevelt created new government agencies, such as the Federal Deposit Insurance Corporation, the Agricultural Adjustment Administration, and the National Recovery Administration. However, he did not stop there; he created the Civilian Conservation Corps to employ young men to plant trees, and the Tennessee Valley Authority to build dams that would provide electricity to the region.

Overall, Roosevelt's policies were popular and welcomed by the public. However, there were many critics. Herbert Hoover used his post-presidency to openly criticize Roosevelt. Republicans like Hoover believed that the New Deal programs were socialistic. Surprisingly, Roosevelt also encountered criticism from within his own party. Huey Long, the governor of Louisiana, thought the New Deal did not go far enough to help people.[9] Then there were other critics, such as the radio-priest Father Charles Coughlin and the elder activist Dr. Francis Townsend. Being elder himself, Dr. Townsend advocated public pensions for the elderly.[10] Sometimes Roosevelt took the advice of his critics, as he did with Dr. Townsend when he created Social Security. Roosevelt signed the Social Security Act in 1935, creating America's first national pension and providing "grants for the blind, the incapacitated, and for dependent children."[11] A year later, in 1936, Roosevelt enjoyed an overwhelming reelection victory over his Republican opponent, Governor Alfred M. Landon of Kansas. Governor Landon carried only two states: Maine and Vermont.

In his second term Roosevelt continued to expand his New Deal by signing legislation that allowed unionized workers to bargain collectively. Because he had a Congress with a Democratic majority, he rarely encountered serious opposition. However, the United States Supreme Court began to declare some of his New Deal programs unconstitutional.[12] Infuriated, Roosevelt announced plans to pack the court with six extra justices who would naturally rule in his favor. What Roosevelt did not foresee was a major backlash by both Democrats and Republicans. Writing on this, Noah Feldman said, "Roosevelt's court-packing plan encountered greater resistance than any other single program he ever introduced."[13] For some critics the plan only reinforced their preconceived notion that Roosevelt was indeed a "traitor to his class" and a "dictator."[14] Outrage over the court-packing plan subsided when some of the justices of the High Court announced their retirement. However, the damage was done and in 1938 the Republicans made significant gains in the congressional midterm elections.[15]

On September 1, 1939, World War II broke out when Nazi Germany invaded Poland. Roosevelt saw potential for American involvement and ran for an unprecedented third term in 1940. The Republicans nominated corporate attorney Wendell Willkie. As an attorney, Willkie represented the interests of private utility companies, who feared federally owned utilities like the Tennessee Valley Authority being subsidized by the taxpayer.[16] The political novice Willkie had run a vigorous campaign to secure the Republican nomination. The Democrats renominated Roosevelt and made his agriculture secretary, Henry A. Wallace, vice president.

Meanwhile the war in Europe raged on, as Great Britain remained unconquered by the German war machine. In 1941 Roosevelt lent Great Britain some American naval destroyers and prepared the nation for war. During his State of the Union address to Congress on January 6, 1941, he informed the nation of four vital freedoms that America had to protect in a world that was dominated by war.

> The first is freedom of speech and expression—everywhere in the world.
>
> The second is freedom of every person to worship God in his own way—everywhere in the world.
>
> The third is freedom from want—which, translated into world terms, means economic understandings which will secure to every nation a healthy peacetime life for its inhabitants—everywhere in the world.
>
> The fourth is freedom from fear—which, translated into world terms, means a world-wide reduction of armaments to such a point and in such a thorough fashion that no nation will be in a position to commit an act of physical aggression against any neighbor—anywhere in the world.[17]

On December 7, 1941, the Japanese bombed the American naval base at Pearl Harbor, sinking several American battleships, including the *Arizona* and the *Oklahoma*. The next day Roosevelt addressed a joint session of Congress to ask for a declaration of war against Japan. In that famous speech he declared December 7, 1941, to be "a date which will live in infamy."[18] Congress declared war on Japan, and three days later declared war on Japan's allies: Nazi Germany and Fascist Italy.

During the war Roosevelt led a precarious alliance between the United States, Great Britain, France, and the Soviet Union. Though many Americans sympathized with Great Britain and France, few could feel the same way about Josef Stalin and his Communist state. Roosevelt's critics believed that he compromised too much with Stalin. However, the alliance was successful, as the allies scored major victories at El Alamein, Stalingrad, Midway, and Normandy.[19] Throughout the war Roosevelt reassured the nation and its allies of the American commitment to full victory. He even traveled to North Africa, Persia, and Yalta to meet with Winston Churchill and Stalin. Perhaps Roosevelt's most controversial decision during the war was to relocate Japanese American citizens to internment camps—there was much unnecessary fear that these citizens would commit acts of sabotage against the American war effort.

In 1944 Roosevelt was reelected to a fourth term in a campaign against Governor Thomas E. Dewey of New York, who had established a reputation as a prosecutor who sent many criminals and mobsters to the penitentiary. The Democrats did not retain Wallace for vice president because he was too liberal.[20] Fearing that Roosevelt might die during his fourth term, they sought a strong running mate who would finish the war; they chose Senator Harry S. Truman of Missouri. Just as victory was in sight, Roosevelt died suddenly on April 12, 1945, in Warm Springs, Georgia. The United States and her allies were in mourning over his death. Roosevelt and his wife, Eleanor, are buried together near the library at the Home of Franklin D. Roosevelt National Historic Site in Hyde Park, New York.

LIBRARY AND MUSEUM

The Franklin D. Roosevelt Presidential Library and Museum is the first federally administered presidential library.[21] Roosevelt was inspired to build his own presidential library during a visit to his hometown of Hyde Park, New York, in 1934. For most of his life, Roosevelt had been an avid book collector and he sought a safe place to store them. He wrote a letter to his neighbor, Dr. Edward J. Wynkoop, about constructing a "fireproof building in Hyde Park in which historical documents can be safely kept."[22] One year later, in August 1935, Roosevelt decided he would not follow the precedent set by other presidents and have his papers sent to the Library of Congress for storage. He wanted a "repository for manuscripts, correspondences, books, reports, . . . relating to this (New Deal) period of our national history."[23] When Roosevelt was mulling over his idea for a presidential library, there were only two other "prototype libraries" for presidents: the Rutherford B. Hayes Memorial Library in Ohio and the Hoover Institution on War, Revolution, and Peace at Stanford University.[24] Using these two libraries as inspiration, Roosevelt created the blueprints for his.

Though Roosevelt had chosen a library model, he also needed an administrative model. The model he was looking for came from Andrew Mellon, the former treasury secretary. In December 1936 Mellon approached Roosevelt with the idea of building an art gallery in Washington, DC. The gallery was to hold the best art in the world and be financed by Mellon and administered by the public. Roosevelt liked Mellon's idea. He not only agreed to build the National Art Gallery, but used the idea to promote his own presidential library.[25] Excited about his library, Roosevelt showed his architect friend, Henry J. Toombs, some models that he had personally sketched. He also informed Toombs that his archive would have "rooms and exhibitions halls" to attract tourists and historians.[26] Roosevelt's idea of separating the museum from the archives would serve as the general model for all presidential libraries administered by the National Archives.[27]

On December 11, 1939, Roosevelt held a luncheon with a group of scholars, historians, and university professors to devise the formal plans for his archive. Among the people in attendance were archivist Waldo G. Leland; Judge Samuel I. Rosenman; Charles A. Beard of Columbia University; United States Supreme Court Justice Felix Frankfurter; Librarian of Congress Archibald MacLeish; and Marguerite Wells, who was the president of the League of Women Voters.[28] This cabal of experts became known as the Executive Committee. The committee decided to call the building a library rather than an archive; according to Benjamin Hufbauer, the term "library" was perceived as being "less alien to the public."[29] Formal plans for the Franklin D. Roosevelt Library were then submitted to Congress for approval. Since no one could foresee the reaction of Congress to the idea of funding a presidential library, the committee created the Franklin D. Roosevelt Library, Incorporated, to help raise money for its construction. This corporation had the "power to solicit, accept, borrow, invest, and expand money, to transfer property to the United States provided that adequate legislation should have been enacted for the acceptance of such property and for its permanent care and maintenance."[30] In July 1938, the corporation breathed a sigh of relief as Congress passed legislation to create the library. The cornerstone of Roosevelt's library was laid on November 19, 1939, eleven months after he first met with the Executive Committee. The Franklin Roosevelt Library became the first federal library for the presidency.[31]

In 1940, while the library was still being built, questions were raised about what collections were to be kept there. Initially, Roosevelt's collection was divided into four categories. The first of these included Roosevelt's public and personal papers. It contained all of his correspondence in the New York state legislature, as assistant secretary of the navy, as governor of New York, and as president. The second category included the historical manuscripts, maps, and paintings that make up Roosevelt's large collection on the history of the American navy. The third category was smaller and contained information relating to the history of the state of New York. The fourth and final category was Roosevelt's personal library of books.[32]

On June 30, 1941, Roosevelt delivered the dedication speech to formally open his library to the public. He said:

> It seems to me that the dedication of a library is an act of faith. To bring together the records of the past and to house them in buildings where they will be preserved for the use of men and women in the future, a nation must believe in three things: It must believe in the past. It must believe in the future. It must, above all, believe in the

capacity of its own people so to learn from the past that they can gain in judgment in creating their own future.... We hope that millions of our citizens from every part of the land will be glad that what we do today makes available to future Americans the story of what we have lived, and what we are living today, and what we will continue to live during the rest of our lives.[33]

In the years preceding his death, Roosevelt tried to exert control over what material went to the library. In 1943 the library's first director, Fred W. Shipman, received a personal letter from Roosevelt informing him of which papers would be made public. In this letter, Roosevelt said, "Before any of my personal or confidential files are transferred to the Library . . . I wish to go through them and select those which are never to be made public."[34] However, two years after Roosevelt's death, in 1947, Judge Frederick S. Quintero ruled that all of Roosevelt's public papers must be made available at the library.[35] Controlling information to be stored in a presidential library is a controversial issue. As mentioned in the introduction, some presidential libraries, including the Roosevelt library, have tried to cherry-pick exhibits and materials that display their president in the most positive light, which Hufbauer labeled the "Happy Meal version of presidential history."[36]

On March 17, 1950, all of Roosevelt's papers were made available to the public. During the 1960s and 1970s, the library continued to grow. Papers were donated by many of Roosevelt's cabinet members and advisors, such as Harry L. Hopkins, Frances Perkins, Louis M. Howe, and Henry Morgenthau Jr. When Eleanor Roosevelt died in 1962, her papers were also donated and were placed in a special exhibit in her honor.[37] As documents in the library grew, the need to help researchers make their searches less complex became a concern. The Roosevelt library solved this problem by partnering with nearby Marist College in 1993.[38] Together the library and Marist College created "a searchable online finding-aide system and a digitized database" of all documents.[39]

In the early 1990s, many presidential libraries were in a malaise; budget cuts and declining visits were creating problems for them. Just as the Herbert Hoover library changed, so did the Roosevelt library. The director at the time, Verne Newton, decided to overhaul the library; his solution was to make it more like a "mini-Disneyland."[40] Under Newton's management, the library used interactive technologies to allow visitors to see and hear Roosevelt's speeches and newsreels. Newton also created video games that allowed visitors to make decisions on important events in Roosevelt's administration. One game allowed players to decide if Roosevelt should have sent destroyers to Great Britain when the war broke out in 1939.[41] A more recent adaptation has been to embrace criticism of Roosevelt by opening exhibits that question his decisions.

In 2013 the library underwent a further renovation, costing $35 million. The money came from the federal government. The library explained: "The renovation brings the Library's archives and museum up to the National Archives' standards for the preservation of historic collections, while carefully preserving the building's historic appearance."[42] Visitors can now see exhibits that offer debates on the New Deal, Japanese American internment, why Roosevelt did little to help Jewish refugees, and whether he willingly gave Stalin control over Eastern Europe.[43] Even though the library has

Franklin D. Roosevelt Presidential Library and Museum. *Courtesy of the FDR Presidential Library and Museum*

opened the door to criticism, some feel that it did not go far enough. Reporter Edward Rothstein of the *New York Times* said that

> this one [the critical exhibit] could have gone further. In the discussion of the New Deal, in particular, the exhibition is so supportive of Roosevelt's vision that excerpts from critical histories aren't given enough space to develop their counterarguments.[44]

Collections and Exhibits

In the fiscal year 2012, the Franklin D. Roosevelt Presidential Library and Museum welcomed 84,360 visitors.[45] Anyone visiting the Roosevelt library will see the eleven exhibits, which can also be viewed online. Each of these exhibits is divided into thematic galleries about the president and his era. The exhibits begin in the front lobby, where you will see a large photo of President Roosevelt, two bronze busts of Roosevelt and his wife, Eleanor, and a wall of letters to the president from ordinary Americans.[46]

The second exhibit is *America, 1932, A Nation in Fear.* This exhibit explores the Great Depression and the presidential election of 1932. If you visit, you will see the word "Unemployment" in large red neon lights against a wall showing a photograph of unemployed men, possibly standing in a breadline. The exhibit contains many images of breadlines and destitute Americans, and items such as campaign buttons and Roosevelt's lucky campaign hat. There is also a discussion of the causes of the Great Depression.[47]

The third exhibit is *A Promise of Change.* When Governor Roosevelt challenged President Herbert Hoover for the presidency in 1932, he promised change and relief.

This exhibit is dedicated to that promise, which helped Roosevelt to win the presidency. Visitors will view more galleries on the election of 1932, the worsening economic crisis, and Roosevelt's inauguration. Emphasis is placed on the infamous March 4, 1933, inauguration car journey, when Hoover and Roosevelt shared a ride to the Capitol and practically ignored each other. A gallery of particular interest covers a little-known fact: President-elect Roosevelt was almost assassinated on March 15, 1933, in Miami, Florida. The assassin was an Italian anarchist named Giuseppe Zangara. He missed Roosevelt and unintentionally shot and killed the mayor of Chicago, Anton Cermak, who was with Roosevelt at the time. Zangara received a quick execution.[48]

While the first three exhibits focus on Roosevelt the candidate, the fourth, *Foundations of a Public Life*, takes visitors back to his earlier days. Here, you can learn about young Franklin's privileged life, his education, his marriage to Eleanor, his cousin President Theodore Roosevelt, and his struggle to overcome polio. You will also see pictures and paintings of Roosevelt's parents and ancestors, and the hobby horse that he played with as a child.[49]

Exhibit five fast-forwards to President Roosevelt's first one hundred days in office, during which time he initiated the New Deal. The exhibit, *A New Deal*, includes several galleries dedicated to the various government agencies that Roosevelt created in an effort to restore the American economy. The galleries focus on how Roosevelt saved America's failing banks, the repeal of Prohibition, his labor reforms, Social Security, the Works Progress Administration, the Civilian Conservation Corps, and his 1936 reelection victory over Alfred M. Landon. The exhibit also gives attention to the role that Eleanor Roosevelt played in improving race relations, and the beginning of World War II.[50]

This exhibit presents some criticism of President Roosevelt. Two galleries in particular question his policies. One of these, *The New Deal: Did It Work?*, presents the controversies surrounding whether or not the policies halted the depression. Debates are proffered by historians of the New Deal.[51] Liberal historians, such as William Leuchtenburg and Arthur Schlesinger, praise Roosevelt's New Deal, while conservative ones, including Burton Folsom and Amity Shlaes, criticize it. Conservative historians argue that Roosevelt's New Deal did the opposite of what was intended: it prolonged the Great Depression and enlarged the federal government. Another critical gallery concerns Roosevelt's relationship with African Americans, whose cause his wife Eleanor championed. The gallery, *A New Deal: A New Deal for African Americans?*, questions Roosevelt's paradoxical approach to race relations. While the New Deal programs offered relief to African Americans, they still suffered under segregation and they often got the lowest-paid jobs.[52]

The sixth exhibit, *FDR's "Act of Faith": FDR's Private Study*, focuses on Roosevelt's creation of his presidential library. Visitors will see pictures of the library and a replica of Roosevelt's private study. This exhibit also contains Roosevelt's wheelchair, the painting of his mother, Sara Roosevelt, and his personal collection of twenty-two thousand books.[53]

Exhibit seven is dedicated to World War II and is aptly named *War!* The exhibit has two levels. The upper level tells the story of the war from 1939 to 1945. You can see newspaper headlines, photographs from the war, and propaganda posters. Galleries focus on certain aspects of the war, such as Pearl Harbor, Roosevelt's Four Freedoms, the American alliance with Churchill and Stalin, and wartime strategies (displayed in a map room). The exhibit also includes galleries on Roosevelt's third-term reelection in 1940, when he ran against Wendell Willkie, the internment of Japanese Americans, and how the American people mobilized for war. One gallery is dedicated to his beloved dog, Fala.[54]

The lower level of the exhibit examines the final year of the war and its aftermath. It displays information about Roosevelt's fourth-term reelection victory over Thomas E. Dewey, the atomic bomb, the Tehran and Yalta conferences, the Holocaust, and how Roosevelt and the allies planned for a lasting peace by creating the United Nations.[55] The exhibit on World War II praises Roosevelt, but it does pose two important questions: Was the internment of Japanese Americans justified?[56] Why did Roosevelt do nothing to stop the holocaust of European Jews?[57]

The eighth exhibit is *FDR's Death*. Visitors entering this exhibit will see his actual Oval Office desk as it appeared when Roosevelt occupied the room. The exhibit also presents headlines and photos of President Roosevelt's sudden death on April 12, 1945.[58] The following exhibit is solely dedicated to his wife, Eleanor: *First Lady of the World*. Eleanor Roosevelt was an activist First Lady who helped campaign for her husband, reassured the nation during the Great Depression and World War II, and, most importantly, acted as a delegate to the newly established United Nations, where she assisted in writing its charter. Eleanor is also remembered for her efforts to promote world peace and women's rights; visitors will see information about those achievements, too.[59]

The tenth exhibit is dedicated to Roosevelt's legacy and presents galleries on his economic philosophies, America's veterans, the United Nations, and his secretary of labor, Francis Perkins, who was the first woman to hold a cabinet position. The eleventh, and final, exhibit is called *Behind the Scenes* and contains archives and artifacts. The library holds an archive of thirty-five thousand objects and "17 million pages of [archival] documents."[60] You can see artifacts like Roosevelt's 1936 Ford Phaeton, his collection of model ships, and his collection of furniture and sculptures.

FDR Reading Room by Thomas Kletecka. *Courtesy of the FDR Presidential Library and Museum by Thomas Kletecka*

Pare Lorentz Center

In 1993 the Pare Lorentz Center was built on the grounds of the Franklin Delano Roosevelt Presidential Library and Museum in Hyde Park, New York. Lorentz was Roosevelt's personal filmmaker, who made documentaries for the administration. His most famous work is the 1936 documentary *The Plow That Broke the Plains*, which chronicles the dust-bowl conditions on the American farms of the Great Plains. Lorentz also made documentaries about World War II and the Nuremberg Trials. Prior to becoming a filmmaker, Lorentz was a journalist. He died in 1992.[61]

Henry A. Wallace Visitor and Education Center

Also important is the Henry A. Wallace Visitor and Education Center, which was built in 2003 on the Roosevelt estate with the assistance of the National Park Service. Wallace is a controversial figure in American history. He served as Roosevelt's secretary of agriculture from 1933 to 1940 and as vice president from 1941 to 1945. At the 1944 Democratic Convention, the delegates did not renominate Wallace as vice president; instead, they chose Senator Harry S. Truman. Wallace was seen as being too sympathetic to the Soviet Union during the war. In 1948 he splintered from the Democrats to run as the Progressive Party candidate and lost in a four-way race. The Henry A. Wallace Center is used for conferences and for educational purposes.[62]

NOTES

1. Alan Brinkley, *Franklin Delano Roosevelt* (New York: Oxford University Press, 2010), 3–8.
2. Brinkley, *Roosevelt*, 11.
3. Brinkley, *Roosevelt*, 13.
4. Brinkley, *Roosevelt*, 22.
5. Brinkley, *Roosevelt*, 23.
6. Brinkley, *Roosevelt*, 28.
7. Brinkley, *Roosevelt*, 30.
8. Brinkley, *Roosevelt*, 31.
9. Brinkley, *Roosevelt*, 47.
10. Brinkley, *Roosevelt*, 47.
11. William E. Leuchtenburg, *The FDR Years: On Roosevelt and His Legacy* (New York: Columbia University Press, 1995), 253.
12. Brinkley, *Roosevelt*, 56.
13. Noah Feldman, *Scorpions: The Battles and Triumphs of FDR's Great Supreme Court Justices* (New York: Twelve, 2010), 108.
14. Feldman, *Scorpions*, 108.
15. Brinkley, *Roosevelt*, 62.
16. Wendell L. Willkie, "Government and the Public Utilities," *Vital Speeches of the Day* 1 (1935): 295.
17. Franklin D. Roosevelt, "Four Freedoms Speech" (speech, Annual Message to Congress on the State of the Union, Washington, DC, January 6, 1941), accessed June 7, 2016, http://www.fdrlibrary.marist.edu/pdfs/fftext.pdf.

18. Brinkley, *Roosevelt*, 75.

19. Brinkley, *Roosevelt*, 79–83.

20. Brinkley, *Roosevelt*, 92.

21. Benjamin Hufbauer, *Presidential Temples: How Memorials and Libraries Shape Public Memory* (Lawrence: University Press of Kansas, 2005), 29.

22. Frank L. Schick, Renee Schick, and Mark Carroll, *Records of the Presidency: Presidential Papers and Libraries from Washington to Reagan* (Phoenix, AZ: Oryx Press, 1989), 152.

23. Schick et al., *Records of the Presidency*, 151.

24. Wendy R. Ginsberg, Erika K. Lunder, and Daniel J. Richardson, *The Presidential Libraries Act and the Establishment of Presidential Libraries* (CRS Report No. R41513) (Washington, DC: Congressional Research Service, 2015), 6.

25. Hufbauer, *Presidential Temples*, 27–29.

26. Hufbauer, *Presidential Temples*, 29.

27. Hufbauer, *Presidential Temples*, 29.

28. Waldo Gifford Leland, "The Creation of the Franklin D. Roosevelt Library: A Personal Narrative," *American Archivist* 18, no. 1 (January 1955): 10–11.

29. Hufbauer, *Presidential Temples*, 32.

30. Ginsberg et al., *The Presidential Libraries Act*, 8.

31. Hufbauer, *Presidential Temples*, 29.

32. R. D. W. Connor, "The Franklin D. Roosevelt Library," *American Archivist* 3, no. 2 (April 1940): 90–91.

33. Leland, "The Creation," 29.

34. Hufbauer, *Presidential Temples*, 33.

35. Hufbauer, *Presidential Temples*, 33.

36. Hufbauer, *Presidential Temples*, 173.

37. "'One Definite Locality': History of the FDR Presidential Library & Museum," Franklin D. Roosevelt Presidential Library and Museum, accessed June 7, 2016, http://www.fdrlibrary.marist.edu/library/onedefinitelocality.html.

38. Clifford J. Laube, e-mail message to author, July 25, 2016.

39. Hufbauer, *Presidential Temples*, 207.

40. Hufbauer, *Presidential Temples*, 39.

41. Hufbauer, *Presidential Temples*, 39.

42. "Franklin D. Roosevelt Presidential Library and Museum Completes Building Renovation and Opens New Museum," Franklin D. Roosevelt Presidential Library and Museum, May 13, 2013, accessed June 7, 2016, https://fdrlibrary.org/documents/356632/390886/twentythirteenseven.pdf/e2f372c9-e8a9-44b3-a109-1367c20727d8.

43. Edward Rothstein, "Roosevelt's Legacy, Burning Brightly," *New York Times*, June 27, 2013, http://www.nytimes.com/2013/06/28/arts/design/a-revamped-roosevelt-library-and-museum.html?_r=0#.

44. Rothstein, "Roosevelt's Legacy."

45. Ginsberg et al., *The Presidential Libraries Act*, 28.

46. "Museum Lobby," Franklin D. Roosevelt Presidential Library and Museum, accessed June 7, 2016, http://www.fdrlibraryvirtualtour.org/page01-00.asp.

47. "America 1932, A Nation in Fear," Franklin D. Roosevelt Presidential Library and Museum, accessed June 7, 2016, http://www.fdrlibraryvirtualtour.org/page02-00.asp.

48. "The Promise of Change," Franklin D. Roosevelt Presidential Library and Museum, accessed June 7, 2016, http://www.fdrlibraryvirtualtour.org/page03-00.asp.

49. "Foundations of a Public Life," Franklin D. Roosevelt Presidential Library and Museum, accessed June 7, 2016, http://www.fdrlibraryvirtualtour.org/page04-00.asp.

50. "A New Deal," Franklin D. Roosevelt Presidential Library and Museum, accessed June 7, 2016, http://www.fdrlibraryvirtualtour.org/page05-00.asp.

51. "A New Deal: Second Term Setbacks," Franklin D. Roosevelt Presidential Library and Museum, accessed June 7, 2016, http://www.fdrlibraryvirtualtour.org/page05-19.asp.

52. "A New Deal: A New Deal for African Americans?" Franklin D. Roosevelt Presidential Library and Museum, accessed June 7, 2016, http://www.fdrlibraryvirtualtour.org/page05-20.asp.

53. "FDR's 'Act of Faith': FDR's Private Study," Franklin D. Roosevelt Presidential Library and Museum, accessed June 7, 2016, http://www.fdrlibraryvirtualtour.org/page06-01.asp.

54. "War!" Franklin D. Roosevelt Presidential Library and Museum, accessed June 7, 2016, http://www.fdrlibraryvirtualtour.org/page07-00.asp.

55. "War! Leading the World War II Generation," Franklin D. Roosevelt Presidential Library and Museum, accessed June 7, 2016, http://www.fdrlibraryvirtualtour.org/page07-33.asp.

56. "War! Japanese American Internment," Franklin D. Roosevelt Presidential Library and Museum, accessed June 7, 2016, http://www.fdrlibraryvirtualtour.org/page07-15.asp.

57. "War! Holocaust and Liberation, 1942–1945," Franklin D. Roosevelt Presidential Library and Museum, accessed June 7, 2016, http://www.fdrlibraryvirtualtour.org/page07-39.asp.

58. "FDR's Death," Franklin D. Roosevelt Presidential Library and Museum, accessed June 7, 2016, http://www.fdrlibraryvirtualtour.org/page08-00.asp.

59. "First Lady of the World," Franklin D. Roosevelt Presidential Library and Museum, accessed June 7, 2016, http://www.fdrlibraryvirtualtour.org/page09-00.asp.

60. "Behind the Scenes," Franklin D. Roosevelt Presidential Library and Museum, accessed June 7, 2016, http://www.fdrlibraryvirtualtour.org/page11-00.asp.

61. "Who was Pare Lorentz?" Pare Lorentz at the Franklin D. Roosevelt Presidential Library, accessed June 7, 2016, http://www.parelorentzcenter.org/who-was-pare-lorentz/.

62. "Henry A. Wallace Visitor and Education Center," Franklin D. Roosevelt Presidential Library and Museum, accessed June 7, 2016, http://www.fdrlibrary.marist.edu/pdfs/factwallace.pdf.

BIBLIOGRAPHY

American Heritage Book of the Presidents and Famous Americans: Volume Ten. New York: Dell, 1967.

Barnard, Ellsworth. *Wendell L. Willkie: Fighter for Freedom.* Marquette: Northern Michigan University Press, 1966.

Brinkley, Alan. *Franklin Delano Roosevelt.* New York: Oxford University Press, 2010.

Carlin, John W. "FDR, His Library, and the National Archives." *Prologue* 35, no. 4 (Winter 2003): http://www.archives.gov/publications/prologue/2003/winter/archivist.html.

Clotworthy, William G. *Homes and Libraries of the Presidents: An Interpretive Guide.* Third edition. Blacksburg, VA: McDonald & Woodward, 2008.

Connor, R. D. W. "The Franklin D. Roosevelt Library." *American Archivist* 3, no. 2 (April 1940): 81–92.

Feldman, Noah. *Scorpions: The Battles and Triumphs of FDR's Great Supreme Court Justices.* New York: Twelve, 2010.

Folsom, Burton W. *New Deal or Raw Deal? How FDR's Economic Legacy Has Damaged America.* New York: Threshold Editions, 2009.

Ginsberg, Wendy R., Erika K. Lunder, and Daniel J. Richardson. *The Presidential Libraries Act and the Establishment of Presidential Libraries* (CRS Report No. R41513). Washington, DC: Congressional Research Service, 2015.

Hoover, Herbert. *The Memoirs of Herbert Hoover: The Great Depression, 1929–1941.* New York: Macmillan, 1952.

Hufbauer, Benjamin. *Presidential Temples: How Memorials and Libraries Shape Public Memory.* Lawrence: University Press of Kansas, 2005.

Leland, Waldo Gifford. "The Creation of the Franklin D. Roosevelt Library: A Personal Narrative." *American Archivist* 18, no. 1 (January 1955): 11–29.

Leuchtenburg, William E. *The FDR Years: On Roosevelt and His Legacy.* New York: Columbia University Press, 1995.

McCoy, Donald R. *Landon of Kansas.* Lincoln: University of Nebraska Press, 1966.

Olson, James Stuart. *Historical Dictionary of the Great Depression, 1929–1940.* Westport, CT: Greenwood, 2001.

Roosevelt, Franklin D. "Four Freedoms Speech." Annual Message to Congress on the State of the Union in Washington, DC, January 6, 1941.

Rothstein, Edward. "Roosevelt's Legacy, Burning Brightly." *New York Times,* June 27, 2013. http://www.nytimes.com/2013/06/28/arts/design/a-revamped-roosevelt-library-and-museum.html?_r=0#.

Schick, Frank L., Renee Schick, and Mark Carroll. *Records of the Presidency: Presidential Papers and Libraries from Washington to Reagan.* Phoenix, AZ: Oryx Press, 1989.

Shlaes, Amity. *The Forgotten Man: A New History of the Great Depression.* New York: Harper Perennial, 2008.

Smith, Richard Norton. "A Presidential Revival: How the Hoover Library Overcame a Mid-Life Crisis." *Prologue: Quarterly of the National Archives* 21 (Summer 1989): 115–23.

Sunrise at Campobello. Directed by Vincente J. Donehue. DVD. Burbank, CA: Warner Brothers Home Video, 2009.

Weintraub, Stanley. *Final Victory: FDR's Extraordinary World War II Presidential Campaign.* Cambridge, MA: Da Capo Press, 2012.

Willkie, Wendell L. "Government and the Public Utilities." *Vital Speeches of the Day* 1 (1935): 294–95.

Harry S. Truman
Presidential Library and Museum

Address: 500 W. US Highway 24, Independence, MO 64050-1798
Phone: 1-800 833-1225 or (816) 268-8200
Website: https://www.trumanlibrary.org/
Social media: https://www.facebook.com/TrumanPresidentialLibrary/
Administration: National Archives
Hours: 9 a.m. to 5 p.m., Monday to Saturday; noon to 5 p.m. on Sundays; closed on
  Thanksgiving Day, Christmas Day, and New Year's Day

BIOGRAPHY OF HARRY S. TRUMAN

May 8, 1884–December 26, 1972
Thirty-Third President: April 12, 1945–January 20, 1953
Democratic Party

Harry S. Truman.
LC-USZ62-117122

Harry Truman was born in Lamar, Missouri, to John and Martha Truman. He was one of three children in a farming family. Deciding on a middle name for Harry proved to be problematic, as both of his grandfathers—Anderson Shipp Truman and Solomon Young—wanted their name to serve. Truman's daughter, Margaret, wrote in her biography, "To placate their touchy elders, his parents added an S, but studiously refrained from deciding whether it stood for Solomon or Shippe [*sic*]."[1]

In 1890 the family moved to Independence, Missouri, where Harry was able to attend school. He graduated from high school in 1901 and hoped to attend West Point. However, poor eyesight prevented it. After being rejected, Truman decided to stay in Missouri to help on the family farm. From 1906 to 1911, as well as working on the farm, he took jobs as a railroad clerk, a bank clerk, and a National Guard reservist. In his spare time, Truman educated himself by reading the biographies of famous politicians and military figures.[2]

When the United States entered World War I in April 1917, Truman rejoined the Missouri National Guard and became a lieutenant in charge of Battery D of the 129th Field Artillery in the Thirty-Fifth Division in France. His men respected his leadership skills and together they fought in the Argonne offensive. By 1919 the war had ended; in June of that year Truman returned home to marry his girlfriend, Bess Wallace. He briefly ran a haberdashery shop with some friends, but the business failed.

After that, Truman turned to politics. He befriended Tom Pendergast, who ran the Democratic Party's political machine in Missouri. With Pendergast's help, Truman was elected Jackson County judge for the eastern district. However, in 1924 he lost his reelection bid; the Republicans swept the nation that year, returning President Calvin Coolidge to the White House. However, this was only a temporary loss. Two years later Truman was elected presiding judge of Jackson County and held the position for eight years.[3] Truman did not have a law degree, so he briefly attended Kansas City Law School.[4]

The politics in Kansas City were corrupt and Truman was disheartened by this reality. In 1932 Truman asked for, and was refused, Pendergast's support to run for Missouri governor. Then, in 1934, Pendergast supported him to run for the United States Senate. Truman beat the Republican Roscoe C. Patterson and went to Washington.[5] In the Senate, Truman was appointed to chair the Interstate Commerce Committee, which investigated wasteful business spending. In 1939 his friend Tom Pendergast was convicted and sentenced for tax evasion. Truman refused to abandon Pendergast during this ordeal. However, Truman was reelected to the Senate in 1940 despite his harmful connection with Pendergast.[6]

During World War II, Truman built a strong and positive national reputation for himself as head of the Truman Committee, which investigated "profiteering" within the armaments industry.[7] In 1944 President Franklin D. Roosevelt, who was running for an unprecedented fourth term, was seeking a new vice presidential running mate. Many feared that the ailing president would die before the end of the term. However, the current vice president was Henry A. Wallace, whose progressive ideology and pro-Russian attitudes frightened many Democrats. Roosevelt's campaign chairman, Bob Hannegan, suggested alternatives to Wallace, such as United States Supreme Court Justice William O. Douglas, Senator Alben Barkley of Kentucky, and Senator Harry Truman. President Roosevelt and influential party officials saw Truman as the "best alternative."[8] During the convention, Hannegan summoned Truman to speak with Roosevelt over the phone about accepting the vice presidency. At first, Truman was hesitant to accept. When Hannegan relayed the information to Roosevelt, Truman heard him yell over the phone, "Well, tell him if he wants to break up the Democratic Party in the middle of a war, that's his responsibility."[9] After the phone call, Truman accepted the offer. That year, Roosevelt was reelected over the Republican New York governor, Thomas E. Dewey.

Truman was not vice president for very long. On April 12, 1945, President Roosevelt died suddenly of a cerebral hemorrhage in Warm Springs, Georgia. Later that day the unsuspecting vice president was sworn in as the thirty-third president of the United

States. According to Truman, with the nation at war, being handed the presidency felt like "the moon, the stars, and the planets had all fallen on [him]."[10] His daughter recalled how many problems her father would have to grapple with as president:

> It is fascinating to look back on the year 1945 and see the emergence of all the major national and international problems which my father was to grapple with for the next seven years: our relations with Russia, the status of Palestine, the tangle in China, and on the home front, the struggle between a President who was determined to repre-sent all the people and a Congress inclined to serve special interests. All these gigantic headaches demanded attention. . . . It was easy to see why the President worked an eighteen-hour day.[11]

Work is exactly what Truman did. As president, he never refused to take respon-sibility for his actions. In fact, he kept a sign on his desk that read: "The Buck Stops Here."[12] Truman made the decision to use the atomic bomb on Hiroshima and Na-gasaki to end the war, attended the Potsdam Conference to confer with allies about postwar plans, grappled with an economic slowdown in 1946, recognized the Jewish state of Israel, and fought the Cold War against the Soviets.

During the war, the Allies agreed to give Stalin the task of occupying Eastern Europe after the war. Not only did he do this, but he also imposed Communism on the various nations. Stalin wanted to gain full control of Berlin, which, like the rest of Germany, was divided between the Allies. In 1948 he blockaded the city, but Truman would not let him have it: the president flew supplies into the city during the opera-tion known as the Berlin Airlift. This effort prevented West Berlin from becoming a Soviet prize. To help stem the flow of Communism, Truman's secretary of state, George Marshall, designed a major economic plan to rebuild postwar Europe: the Marshall Plan. The Marshall Plan called for massive economic assistance to help Europe recover after the war. According to historian John Lewis Gaddis, the Marshall Plan was also intended to thwart Soviet expansion into Western Europe. Gaddis said, "The gravest threat to western interests in Europe was not the prospect of Soviet military intervention but rather the risk that hunger, poverty, and despair might cause Europeans to vote their own communists into office."[13]

Truman sought the Democratic Party nomination in 1948, but he was challenged. The two most contentious issues for the party were civil rights and the Cold War. Southern Democrats (known as Dixiecrats) were upset over Truman's pro–civil rights platform, while Progressive Democrats sought rapprochement with the Soviet Union to end the Cold War. When Truman was nominated at the Democratic National Con-vention, Southern delegates split and nominated Strom Thurmond of South Carolina as their Dixiecrat candidate. Progressive Democratic delegates also split that year and nominated former vice president Henry A. Wallace.[14] The Republicans renominated Governor Thomas E. Dewey of New York. The pollsters wrongly calculated a Dewey victory in a four-way race.

So certain was Dewey of victory that he was reluctant to waste time campaign-ing.[15] Therefore, Truman redoubled his efforts and took his message directly to the people. He toured the nation on his "Whistle Stop" train and made speeches in every town he could. David Pietrusza writes that the night of the election, the *Chicago Daily*

Tribune wrongly headlined: "Dewey defeats Truman."[16] So how did Truman turn defeat into victory? According to Pietrusza, pollster George Gallup believed that "in the campaign's final ten days, a full third of Wallace's supporters shifted to Truman."[17] Dewey blamed his defeat on losing the "farm vote" and reporter Sam Lubell believed that 13 percent of Dewey's voters "stayed home" instead of voting.[18]

During his second term, one of Truman's first initiatives was to implement his Fair Deal legislation of minimum wage hikes, the expansion of social security, and labor rights. However, little of the Fair Deal became reality because Southern Democrats and Republicans united against it in Congress.[19] As the 1940s drew to a close, more problems evolved. China was taken over by a Communist government and the Soviets got the atomic bomb. Then, in 1950, Communist North Korea crossed the thirty-eighth parallel to invade neighboring South Korea. North Korea had almost captured all of South Korea, with the exception of Pusan. Truman went to the United Nations for help, and received it. On June 27, 1950, the Security Council of the United Nations passed a resolution for member states to "furnish such assistance to the Republic of [South] Korea as may be necessary to repel the armed attack and to restore international peace and security in the area."[20] Truman sent troops under the command of General Douglas MacArthur. On September 18, 1950, MacArthur successfully landed UN troops at Inchon, cutting the North Korean forces in half. Eleven days later, Seoul, South Korea, was recaptured.[21]

On November 1, 1950, tragedy almost struck the president. The White House was undergoing major repairs, so the president and his family were living in the neighboring Blair House. Two Puerto Rican nationalists, Oscar Collazo and Griselio Torresola, tried to storm into the Blair House to assassinate him. The two assassins shot and killed one policeman, Leslie Coffelt, but failed to harm the president. Torresola was killed during the attempt, leaving Collazo to face trial.[22]

Back in Korea, Communist China sent troops across the Yalu River into North Korea when UN forces came too close to the Chinese border in late November 1950. The attack came as a complete surprise. Almost three hundred thousand Chinese soldiers forced the UN forces to fall back, and Seoul came under Communist control once again. The question now was whether to repel the Chinese or declare war on them. General MacArthur wanted a full-scale war to defeat Communist China. However, Truman and his advisors preferred to contain the Chinese at the thirty-eighth parallel. In 1951 UN forces recaptured Seoul again and fought the Chinese back to the thirty-eighth parallel. However, on April 10 that year, Truman relieved MacArthur of command for vocally advocating an invasion of China despite being warned not to do so.[23] Back home, Truman's dismissal of MacArthur was horribly unpopular. A survey revealed that 66 percent of Americans did not approve.[24]

On November 19, 1951, Truman discreetly told his staff that he would not seek a third term.[25] He made the announcement official in January 1952, when General Dwight David Eisenhower announced his intentions to seek the Oval Office.[26] That summer the Democrats nominated Governor Adlai Stevenson of Illinois, who lost the election to Eisenhower. Truman spent the rest of his years in retirement in Independence.

On December 26, 1972, Truman died. He and his wife Bess are buried next to each other in the library courtyard. Their daughter, Margaret Truman Daniel, became a well-known author and died in 2008.[27]

LIBRARY AND MUSEUM

The idea of a presidential library and museum for President Harry S. Truman came from R. B. White, who headed the Kansas City Museum. In July 1945 White wrote Truman to suggest the creation of a "Harry S. Truman Room" as an addition to the museum.[28] Truman visited White in Kansas City to discuss the matter in more detail and ultimately turned the idea down. He believed a future museum must be located in his home town of Independence. A year later, in 1946, he wrote to the mayor of Independence, Roger Sermon, about creating a museum. Sermon took the matter to the city council, which voted in favor and agreed to find a location to store the president's materials.[29] The vote of the city council was the first major step toward the Harry Truman Library and Museum.

Over the next two years, plans for the library were neglected because Truman had to focus on winning the four-way race during the presidential election of 1948. Having won the election, he was inaugurated in January 1949 and was able to focus on his future library again. Truman was concerned about the future of his presidential records for research purposes. He once told Senator Burton K. Wheeler, "If everybody could keep a record of his transactions from day to day it would save a lot of misstatements in history."[30] Truman signed two important pieces of legislation, which required the National Archives to care for all presidential papers from his administration and future administrations. These acts were the Federal Property and Administrative Services Act of 1949 and the Federal Records Act of 1950. Shortly before leaving the White House in 1953, Truman had Jess Larson of the General Services Administration appoint two archivists to arrange and categorize his papers for the library.[31]

Just as President Franklin Roosevelt established a foundation to raise money for his library, Truman created the Harry S. Truman Library, Inc., in 1953. The foundation was administered by attorney Basil O'Connor and former presidential assistant David D. Lloyd. The decision was made to follow the Franklin Roosevelt blueprint for Truman's library.[32] In the spring of 1954, the new mayor of Independence, Robert P. Weatherford, suggested Truman build his library on thirteen acres of land known as Pickwick Park. Truman viewed the land and was very satisfied. A year later, in 1955, President Eisenhower signed legislation passed by Congress allowing the federal government to accept Truman's library and the libraries of future presidents. This law is known as the Presidential Libraries Act.[33]

Construction of the library began on May 8, 1955, which was also Truman's seventy-first birthday. The entire library cost $1,750,000 to build.[34] Truman chose architect Edward F. Neild to plan and build his library. Neild was famous in Kansas City for building the town's courthouse.[35] The library was still being constructed when it partially opened in 1957. Philip C. Brooks was named the first director of the library and served from 1957 to 1971. Brooks was more interested in the library serving as a center of scholarship than as a place of education.[36] David D. Lloyd and the archivist of the United States, Wayne Grover, pushed for the library to include exhibits. Together they consulted the political scientist Clinton Rossiter for ideas. Rossiter had identified six jobs the president had to manage while in office: "the president as chief executive, as legislative leader, as social head of state, as head of his political party, as commander-in-chief, and as head of the nation's foreign policy."[37] Lloyd and Grover decided to build the exhibits around these tasks. These exhibits were small and described the president's duties for each job. For example, the exhibit *Director of Foreign Policy* displayed a portrait of Truman's secretary of state, Dean Acheson, next to a description that stated, "The President must develop programs to strengthen the free world and safeguard the security of the United States."[38] More exhibits were added, which are presented later in this chapter.

On July 6, 1957, the library was formally dedicated at a ceremony attended by President Truman, his friend and former president Herbert Hoover, Eleanor Roosevelt, and chief justice of the United States Supreme Court Earl Warren, who delivered the dedication speech.[39] By the 1960s the library was fully operational and in service to the public. Philip C. Brooks's continuing belief that it should serve the needs of scholars is evident in his statement that: "The mélange of activity at the Truman Library . . . indicates that, four and a half years after its dedication, it is well launched as an institution embodying the research program that is its core and the historical materials that support it."[40]

Though the library opened in 1957, one of its most important attractions had not yet been created: Thomas Hart Benton's mural titled *Independence and the Opening of the West*. Benton was an American regionalist artist born on April 15, 1889, in Neosho,

Exterior of the Harry S. Truman Library, 1958. *Courtesy of the Harry S. Truman Presidential Library and Museum*

Missouri. He gained attention in the 1930s, when he was commissioned to paint murals in the Missouri state capitol building in Jefferson City. Benton's paintings depicted ordinary Americans and realistic landscapes.[41] In 1959 Benton began painting his famous *Independence and the Opening of the West* above the entrance to the replica of Truman's Oval Office at the library. Benton wanted a mural that would illustrate the history of Independence. In the 1830s and 1840s, Independence was one of the last towns that settlers would visit before embarking west on the Santa Fe or Oregon Trails.[42]

At first sight, the mural conjures images of a Technicolor John Wayne western. The mural has two sides. On the right-hand side, white settlers are seen approaching Native Americans. The settlers include a hunter, a trapper, a mother with children, and a French *voyageur*. These people are walking toward some Native American Pawnees on the left. One Native American is friendly and offers a peace pipe. However, the other is wary and has his bow and arrow ready for use. The background of the mural also contains important images: another Native American is seen engaging in trade with a white settler; two African American blacksmiths appear on the right-hand side of the mural; and a Mexican gentleman with a mule appears on the left. Truman liked Benton and the mural so much that he even helped him paint it.[43] Benton completed the mural in March 1961 and was paid $60,000.[44]

Professor Benjamin Hufbauer is critical of *Independence and the Opening of the West* for depicting white American superiority and stereotypical racist images of Native Americans. Hufbauer suggests the juxtaposition of the mural above the entrance to Truman's replica Oval Office, which he called "the nerve center of Cold War America," was planned to show "American steadfastness in the face of a global threat."[45] In the mid-nineteenth century, Americans believed in the manifest destiny of the white American to conquer the west and the Native American. By the middle of the twentieth century, Americans had embraced a new destiny in the face of the Red Scare from the Soviet Union: America would triumph over Communism. Hufbauer says:

> The painting visually expresses the ideology of Manifest Destiny in which both Truman and Benton were steeped. The mural has the effect of surrounding the Oval Office with inevitability, by paralleling the success of earlier generations of white Americans on the western frontier with the success of the twentieth-century Americans on the global stage.[46]

Hufbauer also points out the mural's "dichotomy between 'good' and 'bad' Indians."[47] The "good" Native Americans are depicted as engaging in trade with white settlers, while the "bad" ones "threaten settlers and get drunk."[48] On a more positive note, he believes the depiction of the two African American blacksmiths is a representation that they are freemen in the state of Missouri, which was a slave state before the Civil War.[49]

When President Truman died in 1972, the director at the time, Benedict Zorbist, decided that the library needed a change. Zorbist wanted to create new exhibits, but he was refused funding by the federal government.[50] Though the library was administered by the National Archives, funding for exhibits would have to come from private donations. In 1991 a private donation of $4 million was provided upon the death of a friend of the Truman family, Greta Kempton.[51] Greta, who was a painter, left her entire estate to the library.

Truman's replica Oval Office by Cecil Schrepfer. *Courtesy of the Harry S. Truman Presidential Library and Museum*

Benton's mural in progress. *Courtesy of the Harry S. Truman Presidential Library and Museum*

Three years later, in 1995, the new director, Larry Hackman, took over administration of the library. Hackman was apolitical about presidents and wanted to reinvent the library with exhibits that would "make people think."[52] Because of Hackman's influence, the exhibits at the Truman library are more balanced, thus avoiding the "Happy Meal version of presidential history" that Hufbauer has criticized.[53] Hackman also successfully raised $23 million for renovating the library.[54] Not all of the money raised by Hackman came from private donations: former Democratic senator and vice presidential candidate Thomas F. Eagleton of Missouri convinced Congress to appropriate $8 million.[55]

In early 2000 the library celebrated the twentieth century with a temporary exhibit, *Looking Back on the American Century.* The exhibit presented objects from the last one hundred years that were symbolic of American culture. Among the special features at this exhibit were a Model T roadster from 1915, Charles Lindbergh's flight suit, magician Harry Houdini's handcuffs, Elvis Presley's stage suit, and James Dean's 1955 Triumph 500 motorcycle.[56] According to historian Jason S. Lantzer, however, the exhibit was not very successful because "Visitors were more intrigued by a simple exhibit of photographs of presidential families."[57]

In 2001 Michael J. Devine replaced Hackman as director. Devine helped create the permanent exhibition *Harry S. Truman: His Life and Times* in 2004. He also strengthened the library's existing relationship with the University of Missouri–Kansas City and the Harry S. Truman Little White House historic site in Key West, Florida.[58] The new renovations were celebrated with a "rebirth" ceremony at the library on December 9, 2001.[59]

In 2015 Dr. Kurt Graham was appointed to head the Truman library.[60] Graham holds a PhD in American history from Brown University and previously taught at California State University in San Bernardino. Prior to his appointment Graham was the director of the Church History Museum in Salt Lake City, Utah.[61]

Collections and Exhibits

In 2012 the Truman library welcomed 63,579 visitors.[62] Researchers who visit the library are able to access a large amount of information; according to their website, the Truman library contains:

> 15,000,000 pages of manuscript materials in its custody. . . . In addition . . . the Library also has an audiovisual collection consisting of about 128,000 still pictures, 1,300 hours of audio disc and tape recordings, 500 motion pictures and 1,000 hours of video tape recordings. The Library's collection of printed materials includes more than 10,000 books.[63]

The library also has an oral history collection. Back in 1961, library staff began collecting the oral histories of Truman's assistants, cabinet members, friends, and contemporaries, such as Dean Acheson, Earl Warren, and Ambassador W. Averell Harriman.[64] Aside from the manuscripts, books, and oral history collection, the library has two permanent museum exhibits: *Harry S. Truman: His Life and Times* and *Harry S. Truman: The Presidential Years.*

Harry S. Truman: His Life and Times was created in 2004 as part of the library's Creating a Classroom for Democracy project. The project is aimed at grade-school children who want to understand what it was like to be President Truman. Young students can take part in activities such as wearing 1940s clothing and creating campaign buttons. The exhibit is separated into twelve galleries, which span Truman's life from his childhood to his post-presidential retirement. Unlike the other permanent exhibit, *Harry S. Truman: The Presidential Years*, this focuses more on Truman the man.[65]

The first two galleries are *Boyhood* and *Farm Years*.[66] Together they give visitors a glimpse into Truman's early life, his family, and his ancestors. The Truman family owned the Grandview farm outside Independence. Being a farmer was tough work, and visitors learn the hardships young Harry faced when working on the farm and doing odd jobs at a local drugstore.

The third gallery is *Becoming a Man*. Truman was not able to complete his formal education, so he resorted to teaching himself. Truman wanted to marry his girlfriend, Bess Wallace, so he worked in a series of jobs in the hope of becoming successful. Here visitors can learn how Truman toiled as a haberdasher and a bank clerk and see pictures of Truman working at these jobs. In his spare time he continued his education by joining the local Freemason order.[67] The fourth gallery, *Family*, shows visitors how Truman finally married Bess Wallace and displays information about the couple's one and only child, Margaret Truman.[68]

Gallery five, *Military Service*, focuses on Truman's service in World War I. This gallery shows pictures of Truman serving in the war.[69] The sixth exhibit, *Home from the War*, presents Truman's postwar life in Kansas City, where he tried his hand as a store owner. The gallery also has a photo on display of Truman's wedding to Bess.[70]

After failing in business, Truman turned to the public life of politics. Gallery seven, *County Judge*, explains how Truman befriended the Pendergast family. They were a politically powerful family in Missouri. Pendergast helped Truman get elected as judge for the Jackson County Court. The gallery showcases Truman's *Pickwick Papers*, which he wrote when relaxing at the Pickwick Hotel in Kansas City. In these papers, Truman explains his thoughts about local politics.[71]

The eighth gallery, *Senator*, is centered on Truman's ten years in the United States Senate. Truman was an active senator who led investigations into profiteering during World War II, as highlighted by the exhibit.[72] Truman's solid reputation as senator led to the Democrats nominating him for vice president in 1944. The following gallery is called *Senate to White House* and explains how Truman became vice president in January 1945, only to find himself president by April 12 when President Roosevelt died unexpectedly.[73]

The tenth gallery is about Truman's time at the White House as president. During his presidency he had the White House gutted and remodeled. For a few years in the late 1940s, the adjacent Blair House became the de facto White House. Visitors can see photographs of the White House being remodeled and learn about the failed assassination attempt on November 1, 1950, by two Puerto Rican nationalists.[74]

Gallery eleven is called *Traveling President* because Truman spent so much time outside the White House. Aside from the Blair House, Truman had a home in Key West, Florida, which became known as the Little White House. Visitors will also learn about the USS *Williamsburg*, which Truman used to cruise around the Potomac.[75] The final gallery, *Mr. Citizen*, is dedicated to Truman's post-presidency and retirement in

Independence. The exhibit contains photographs of the senior president and includes information about his death and funeral.[76]

The second permanent museum exhibit is *Harry S. Truman: The Presidential Years.* The exhibit occupies a space of ten thousand five hundred square feet and consists of seventeen galleries from A to Q. Each gallery examines particular key facts and events of the Truman administration.[77] A unique feature of this exhibit is that two of the galleries are "decision theaters," where visitors can watch videos and interact with the information using a keypad.

Visitors first enter Gallery A, where they will see a fifteen-minute introductory film directed by Charles Guggenheim and narrated by actor Jason Robards. The film tells the story of Truman's life from birth to the day he took office when President Roosevelt died.[78] After watching the film, visitors move on to Gallery B, *Taking Office,* where they will see a large picture of President Truman being sworn in with his wife, Bess, and daughter, Margaret. The Bible that was used to swear Truman in is also displayed in this gallery.[79] In Gallery C, *The First Four Months*, billboards adorn the walls with newspaper articles about the end of World War II. Visitors will learn about the surrenders of Germany and Japan, the atomic bomb, the postwar Potsdam Conference, and the signing of the United Nations Charter. Of special interest is an American flag created from parachutes by American prisoners of war in Japan, who were interned under harsh conditions until their liberation.[80]

The most controversial issue during the Truman administration was his decision to use the atomic bomb on Hiroshima and Nagasaki. Even today historians question if using the atomic bomb against Japan was justified. Gallery D, *The Decision to Drop the Bomb*, is entirely dedicated to this world-changing event. When visitors walk into this gallery, they will hear an audio loop of American veterans discussing the use of the bomb. Videos are played of the bloody fighting in Iwo Jima and Okinawa; the firebombing of Tokyo; and America's efforts to produce the atomic bomb.[81] Hufbauer mentions that the anti-Japanese propaganda videos shown in the exhibit highlight the role of racism in the use of the bomb.[82] The gallery also contains President Truman's letters and diary entries about his decision. An interesting feature of this gallery is a comment book in which visitors can write their opinions about Truman's use of the atomic bomb. According to Hufbauer, visitors filled four volumes in two years.[83] Their comments have been positive and negative. However, Hufbauer says that more comments support the use of the bomb than oppose it.[84] The whole idea of this gallery is to challenge people's perceptions of Truman and the atomic bomb.

With the war over, the nation returned to peace. Gallery E, *Postwar America*, presents what this looked like in America. This gallery is divided into two areas. The first of these shows how the nation's economy was transformed from a wartime to a peacetime economy. In this section of the gallery, visitors will see video loops and photographs of veterans returning home. The second part of the gallery focuses on America's postwar economic boom. Displays show the growth in consumerism as postwar Americans bought refrigerators, televisions, and new homes in the expanding suburbs. Visitors can also read Truman's presidential letters and memorandums in which he expressed his concerns about the postwar economy.[85] While America was experiencing good fortune in financial terms after the war, Europe was in the economic doldrums. In Gallery F,

Europe: 1947, visitors can see pictures and videos of how Europeans were struggling to rebuild their war-torn continent. Special information is presented on the spread of Communism in Eastern Europe.[86]

As the Soviet Union expanded Communism across Europe, the Cold War developed. Visitors can learn more about this in Gallery G, *Origins of the Cold War*. Upon entering, there is a nine-screen video wall that tells the story of how the Cold War began. The video highlights the 1948 Berlin Airlift, which involved American cargo planes flying supplies into West Berlin after the Soviets attempted to force the city into submission by blockading it. The video shows the routes taken by the planes. Another interesting part of this exhibition is the 594 miniature airplanes that hang there. These miniature planes represent the real 594 planes that flew over Berlin every day. The background lighting is designed to give the impression that the planes are, in fact, flying.[87] Included in this gallery are the memorandums, letters, telegrams, and speeches of Truman and the important people who served with him during his administration. A special exhibit in this gallery is dedicated to the architects of "containment" (keeping Communism from spreading). The architects were Secretary of State Dean Acheson, Ambassador W. Averell Harriman, Ambassador George F. Kennan, and General George Marshall. Together these men used their military, political, economic, and diplomatic skills to work in a successful effort to stop Communism from spreading into Western Europe.[88]

From Gallery G, visitors will enter Gallery H, *Recognition of Israel*. On May 14, 1948, after being persuaded by prominent Jewish Americans, Truman recognized the newly created state of Israel. At the time, Israel was part of Palestine and was occupied by the British. The gallery contains official letters and memorandums written by Truman on his decision to recognize Israel and whether he should actively promote racial desegregation at home.[89] After viewing Gallery H on Israel, visitors will enter Gallery I, which is the first decision theater. Inside, videos are shown about recognizing Israel and whether the American army should be desegregated. Visitors can make their own decision and vote using an interactive keyboard.[90]

The surprising result of the presidential election of 1948 is the centerpiece of Gallery J, *Upset of the Century*. Pollsters predicted that Truman would lose to the Republican nominee, Thomas E. Dewey. With two factions of the Democrats—the Dixiecrats and the Progressives—splitting from the party, few thought Truman could retain his base in order to win. However, Truman appealed directly to the people by touring the country on his "whistle stop" train. The gallery displays a map of the United States that shows all of the towns, cities, and villages where Truman stopped to make a speech. Visitors can use a keyboard to choose a town and hear excerpts from the speech that Truman made there. There is also an alcove with a political cartoon of Truman trying to straddle a donkey split in two: the donkey is symbolic of the Democratic Party. Also on display is Norman Rockwell's famous painting *Family Squabble*, which depicts a husband and wife arguing over Dewey and Truman while their child sits on the floor between them, crying.[91]

President Truman began his second term in January 1949 and visitors can view the highlights of this term in Gallery K, *Second Term*. Truman grappled with many foreign and domestic problems during this time, including the Cold War, civil rights, and public housing. However, in 1950 the Korean War took center stage as the United States led an international force to liberate South Korea from a Communist invasion by North Korea. Gallery L is called *The Cold War Turns Hot* and focuses on the Korean War, Communist China, and the attainment of the atomic bomb by the Soviets. These problems are at the center of a display called "Ten Fateful Months." Visitors can also read official documents and memorandums about the Korean War, McCarthyism, and Truman's growing frustrations with General Douglas MacArthur, whom he relieved of command.[92]

After viewing this gallery, visitors move directly to the second decision theater. Here they will watch a video called *Spies in Government: How Far Do You Go to Find Them?* During Truman's administration, he wanted federal employees to declare their loyalty to America against Communism. Visitors in the theater are asked whether they think this was a good idea or whether it was an invasion of privacy.[93]

American pop culture of the early 1950s is presented in Gallery N: *America: 1952.* Here visitors can see displays of the covers of *Life* magazine and listen to music from the era.[94] In 1953 President Truman left office with an approval rating of 30 percent. This information is displayed in Gallery O, *Leaving Office.* With a war still raging on the Korean Peninsula, Truman left the presidency to General Dwight David Eisenhower. Visitors can listen to the speech Truman made when he refused to run for a third term and read his diary entries about the inauguration of the next president.[95]

The final two galleries are dedicated to Truman's legacy. In Gallery P, *Legacy Gallery*, visitors will see a life-sized bronze statue of President Truman and information about the original six jobs he was tasked with as president. Just outside this gallery is an eternal flame, which is set on top of a slab of black granite. The flame was donated by Tirey J. Ford of the American Legion Post 21. Visitors will also hear audio loops of President Truman and various historians discussing the issues of the day.[96] Finally, Gallery Q, *A Living Legacy*, shows a video about how today's American politicians "invoke the spirit of Truman."[97] As visitors leave, they will see a large black silhouette of the retired president walking down a street.

Truman Library Institute

The Truman Library Institute is the nonprofit partner of the Truman Presidential Library and Museum. The mission of the institute is to promote President Truman's legacy and "enrich the public understanding of history, the presidency and America's unique form of government."[98] The institute makes sure the Truman library survives as a "classroom for democracy" and serves more than thirty thousand teachers and students every year.[99]

NOTES

1. Margaret Truman, *Harry S. Truman* (New York: William Morrow, 1973), 46.

2. Robert Dallek, *Harry S. Truman*, the American Presidents Series (New York: Times Books, 2008), 2–3.

3. Dallek, *Harry S. Truman*, 5–7.

4. Truman, *Harry S. Truman*, 69.

5. Dallek, *Harry S. Truman*, 8–11.

6. Dallek, *Harry S. Truman*, 10–11.

7. Dallek, *Harry S. Truman*, 13.

8. Dallek, *Harry S. Truman*, 15.

9. David Pietrusza, *1948: Harry Truman's Improbable Victory and the Year That Transformed America's Role in the World* (New York: Union Square Press, 2011), 11–12.

10. Dallek, *Harry S. Truman*, 18.

11. Truman, *Harry S. Truman*, 301.

12. "'The Buck Stops Here' Desk Sign," Harry S. Truman Library and Museum, accessed August 8, 2016, https://www.trumanlibrary.org/whistlestop/qq/ds_7.htm.

13. John Lewis Gaddis, *The Cold War: A New History* (New York: Penguin Books, 2005), 32.

14. Dallek, *Harry S. Truman*, 81–82.

15. Dallek, *Harry S. Truman*, 82.

16. Pietrusza, *1948*, 394.

17. Pietrusza, *1948*, 395.

18. Pietrusza *1948*, 405–6.

19. Dallek, *Harry S. Truman*, 84–86.

20. William Stueck, *Rethinking the Korean War: A New Diplomatic and Strategic History* (Princeton, NJ: Princeton University Press, 2002), 65.

21. Dallek, *Harry S. Truman*, 100–7.

22. J. T. Curry, "They've Killed the President," *Whistle Stop: Harry S. Truman Library Institute Newsletter* 40 (1979).

23. Dallek, *Harry S. Truman*, 112–18.

24. Dallek, *Harry S. Truman*, 120.

25. Truman, *Harry S. Truman*, 527.

26. Truman, *Harry S. Truman*, 529.

27. Bart Barnes, "Margaret Truman Daniel Dies at Age 83," *Washington Post*, January 29, 2008, accessed August 8, 2016, http://www.washingtonpost.com/wp-dyn/content/article/2008/01/29/AR2008012901321.html.

28. Raymond Geselbracht, "Creating the Harry S. Truman Library: The First Fifty Years," *Public Historian* 28, no. 3 (Summer 2006): 38.

29. Geselbracht, "Harry S. Truman Library," 38.

30. Charles T. Morrissey, "Truman and the Presidency—Records and Oral Recollections," *American Archivist* 28, no. 1 (January 1965): 53.

31. Frank L. Schick, Renee Schick, and Mark Carroll, *Records of the Presidency: Presidential Papers and Libraries from Washington to Reagan* (Phoenix, AZ: Oryx Press, 1989), 170–71.

32. Geselbracht, "Harry S. Truman Library," 39.

33. Geselbracht, "Harry S. Truman Library," 47–48.

34. "History of the Truman Library & Museum," Harry S. Truman Library and Museum, accessed August 8, 2016, http://www.trumanlibrary.org/libhist.htm.

35. Geselbracht, "Harry S. Truman Library," 39.

36. Geselbracht, "Harry S. Truman Library," 56.

37. Geselbracht, "Harry S. Truman Library," 51.

38. Benjamin Hufbauer, *Presidential Temples: How Memorials and Libraries Shape Public Memory* (Lawrence: University Press of Kansas, 2005), 145.

39. Geselbracht, "Harry S. Truman Library," 52.

40. Philip C. Brooks, "Harry S. Truman Library—Plans and Reality," *American Archivist* 25 (January 1962): 26.

41. "FAQ: Can you tell me more about Thomas Hart Benton?" Harry S. Truman Library and Museum, accessed August 8, 2016, http://www.trumanlibrary.org/trivia/benton.htm.

42. "*Independence and the Opening of the West* by Thomas Hart Benton," Harry S. Truman Library and Museum, accessed August 8, 2016, http://www.trumanlibrary.org/teacher/benton.htm.

43. "*Independence*," Harry S. Truman Library and Museum.

44. "Thomas Hart Benton," Harry S. Truman Library and Museum.

45. Hufbauer, *Presidential Temples*, 43.

46. Hufbauer, *Presidential Temples*, 45.

47. Hufbauer, *Presidential Temples*, 49.

48. Hufbauer, *Presidential Temples*, 49–53.

49. Hufbauer, *Presidential Temples*, 55–56.

50. Hufbauer, *Presidential Temples*, 146.

51. Hufbauer, *Presidential Temples*, 147.

52. Hufbauer, *Presidential Temples*, 143.

53. Hufbauer, *Presidential Temples*, 173.

54. Geselbracht, "Harry S. Truman Library," 70.

55. Geselbracht, "Harry S. Truman Library," 69.

56. "Looking Back on the American Century," Harry S. Truman Library and Museum, accessed August 8, 2016, http://www.trumanlibrary.org/museum/amerweb2.htm.

57. Jason S. Lantzer, "The Public History of Presidential Libraries: How the Presidency Is Presented to the People," *Journal for the Association of History and Computing* 6, no. 1 (2003): http://hdl.handle.net/2027/spo.3310410.0006.101.

58. Geselbracht, "Harry S. Truman Library," 72.

59. Geselbracht, "Harry S. Truman Library," 72.

60. Brian Burnes, "New Leaders Chosen for Truman Museum and Historic Site," *Kansas City Star*, June 29, 2015, accessed August 8, 2016, http://www.kansascity.com/news/local/article25782277.html.

61. "Truman Library News Releases," Harry S. Truman Library and Museum, accessed August 8, 2016, http://www.trumanlibrary.org/news/index.html.

62. Wendy R. Ginsberg, Erika K. Lunder, and Daniel J. Richardson, *The Presidential Libraries Act and the Establishment of Presidential Libraries* (CRS Report No. R41513) (Washington, DC: Congressional Research Service, 2015), 28.

63. "History of the Truman Library and Museum," Harry S. Truman Library and Museum, accessed August 8, 2016, http://www.trumanlibrary.org/libhist.htm.

64. "Oral History Interviews," Harry S. Truman Library and Museum, accessed August 8, 2016, https://www.trumanlibrary.org/oralhist/oral_his.htm#A.

65. "Harry S. Truman: His Life and Times," Harry S. Truman Library and Museum, accessed August 8, 2016, http://www.trumanlibrary.org/lifetimes/index.html.

66. "Boyhood," Harry S. Truman Library and Museum, accessed August 8, 2016, http://www.trumanlibrary.org/lifetimes/boyhood.htm; Farm Years," Harry S. Truman Library and Museum, accessed August 8, 2016, http://www.trumanlibrary.org/lifetimes/farm.htm.

67. "Becoming a Man," Harry S. Truman Library and Museum, accessed August 8, 2016, http://www.trumanlibrary.org/lifetimes/manhood.htm.

68. "Family," Harry S. Truman Library and Museum, accessed August 8, 2016, http://www.trumanlibrary.org/lifetimes/family.htm.

69. "Military Service," Harry S. Truman Library and Museum, accessed August 8, 2016, http://www.trumanlibrary.org/lifetimes/military.htm.

70. "Home from the War," Harry S. Truman Library and Museum, accessed August 8, 2016, http://www.trumanlibrary.org/lifetimes/home.htm.

71. "County Judge," Harry S. Truman Library and Museum, accessed August 8, 2016, http://www.trumanlibrary.org/lifetimes/county.htm.

72. "Senator," Harry S. Truman Library and Museum, accessed August 8, 2016, http://www.trumanlibrary.org/lifetimes/senate.htm.

73. "Senate to the White House," Harry S. Truman Library and Museum, accessed August 8, 2016, http://www.trumanlibrary.org/lifetimes/whouse.htm.

74. "Living in the White House," Harry S. Truman Library and Museum, accessed August 8, 2016, http://www.trumanlibrary.org/lifetimes/living.htm.

75. "Traveling President," Harry S. Truman Library and Museum, accessed August 8, 2016, http://www.trumanlibrary.org/lifetimes/travel.htm.

76. "Mr. Citizen," Harry S. Truman Library and Museum, accessed August 8, 2016, http://www.trumanlibrary.org/lifetimes/citizen.htm.

77. "Harry S. Truman: The Presidential Years," Harry S. Truman Library and Museum, accessed August 8, 2016, http://www.trumanlibrary.org/hst/index.html.

78. "Introductory Film," Harry S. Truman Library and Museum, accessed August 8, 2016, http://www.trumanlibrary.org/hst/a.htm.

79. "Taking Office," Harry S. Truman Library and Museum, accessed August 8, 2016, http://www.trumanlibrary.org/hst/b.htm.

80. "The First Four Months," Harry S. Truman Library and Museum, accessed August 8, 2016, http://www.trumanlibrary.org/hst/c.htm.

81. "Decision to Drop the Bomb," Harry S. Truman Library and Museum, accessed August 8, 2016, http://www.trumanlibrary.org/hst/d.htm.

82. Hufbauer, *Presidential Temples*, 155–56.

83. Hufbauer, *Presidential Temples*, 157.

84. Hufbauer, *Presidential Temples*, 157.

85. "Postwar America," Harry S. Truman Library and Museum, accessed August 8, 2016, http://www.trumanlibrary.org/hst/e.htm.

86. "Europe: 1947," Harry S. Truman Library and Museum, accessed August 8, 2016, http://www.trumanlibrary.org/hst/f.htm.

87. "Origins of the Cold War," Harry S. Truman Library and Museum, accessed August 8, 2016, http://www.trumanlibrary.org/hst/g.htm.

88. "Origins," Harry S. Truman Library and Museum.

89. "Recognition of Israel," Harry S. Truman Library and Museum, accessed August 8, 2016, http://www.trumanlibrary.org/hst/h.htm.

90. "Decision Theater 1," Harry S. Truman Library and Museum, accessed August 8, 2016, http://www.trumanlibrary.org/hst/i.htm.

91. "Upset of the Century," Harry S. Truman Library and Museum, accessed August 8, 2016, http://www.trumanlibrary.org/hst/j.htm.

92. "The Cold War Turns Hot," Harry S. Truman Library and Museum, accessed August 8, 2016, http://www.trumanlibrary.org/hst/l.htm.

93. "Decision Theater 2," Harry S. Truman Library and Museum, accessed August 8, 2016, http://www.trumanlibrary.org/hst/m.htm.

94. "America: 1952," Harry S. Truman Library and Museum, accessed August 8, 2016, http://www.trumanlibrary.org/hst/n.htm.

95. "Leaving Office," Harry S. Truman Library and Museum, accessed August 8, 2016, http://www.trumanlibrary.org/hst/o.htm.

96. "Legacy Gallery," Harry S. Truman Library and Museum, accessed August 8, 2016, http://www.trumanlibrary.org/hst/p.htm.

97. "A Living Legacy," Harry S. Truman Library and Museum, accessed August 8, 2016, http://www.trumanlibrary.org/hst/q.htm.

98. "About Us," Truman Library Institute, accessed August 8, 2016, http://trumanlibraryinstitute.org/about-us/.

99. "About Us," Truman Library Institute.

BIBLIOGRAPHY

American Heritage Book of the Presidents and Famous Americans: Volume 11. New York: Dell, 1967.

Barnes, Bart. "Margaret Truman Daniel Dies at Age 83." *Washington Post*, January 29, 2008, accessed August 8, 2016, http://www.washingtonpost.com/wp-dyn/content/article/2008/01/29/AR2008012901321.html.

Brooks, Philip C. "Harry S. Truman Library—Plans and Reality." *American Archivist* 25 (January 1962): 25–37.

Burnes, Brian. "New Leaders Chosen for Truman Museum and Historic Site." *Kansas City Star*, June 29, 2015, accessed August 8, 2016, http://www.kansascity.com/news/local/article25782277.html.

Clotworthy, William G. *Homes and Libraries of the Presidents: An Interpretive Guide.* Third edition. Blacksburg, VA: McDonald & Woodward, 2008.

Curry, J. T. "They've Killed the President." *Whistle Stop: Harry S. Truman Library Institute Newsletter* 40 (1979).

Dallek, Robert. *Harry S. Truman.* The American Presidents Series. New York: Times Books, 2008.

Gaddis, John Lewis. *The Cold War: A New History.* New York: Penguin Books, 2005.

Geselbracht, Raymond. "Creating the Harry S. Truman Library: The First Fifty Years." *Public Historian* 28, no. 3 (Summer 2006): 37–78.

Ginsberg, Wendy R., Erika K. Lunder, and Daniel J. Richardson. *The Presidential Libraries Act and the Establishment of Presidential Libraries* (CRS Report No. R41513). Washington, DC: Congressional Research Service, 2015.

Hufbauer, Benjamin. *Presidential Temples: How Memorials and Libraries Shape Public Memory.* Lawrence: University Press of Kansas, 2005.

Lantzer, Jason S. "The Public History of Presidential Libraries: How the Presidency Is Presented to the People." *Journal for the Association of History and Computing* 6, no. 1 (2003): http://hdl.handle.net/2027/spo.3310410.0006.101.

Lloyd. David L. "The Harry S. Truman Library." *American Archivist* 18 (April 1955): 107–10.

Morrissey, Charles T. "Truman and the Presidency—Records and Oral Recollections." *American Archivist* 28, no. 1 (January 1965): 53–61.

Pietrusza, David. *1948: Harry Truman's Improbable Victory and the Year That Transformed America's Role in the World.* New York: Union Square Press, 2011.

Schick, Frank L., Renee Schick, and Mark Carroll. *Records of the Presidency: Presidential Papers and Libraries from Washington to Reagan.* Phoenix, AZ: Oryx Press, 1989.

Stueck, William. *Rethinking the Korean War: A New Diplomatic and Strategic History.* Princeton, NJ: Princeton University Press, 2002.

Truman, Margaret. *Harry S. Truman.* New York: William Morrow, 1973.

Weintraub, Stanley. *Final Victory: FDR's Extraordinary World War II Presidential Campaign.* Cambridge, MA: Da Capo Press, 2012.

Dwight D. Eisenhower Presidential Library, Museum, and Boyhood Home

Address: 200 Southeast Fourth Street, Abilene, KS 67410
Phone: (785) 263-6700 or 877 RING IKE
Website: https://www.eisenhower.archives.gov/
Social media: https://www.facebook.com/IkeLibrary
Administration: National Archives
Hours: 9 a.m. to 4:45 p.m., every day, August through May; 8 a.m. to 5:45 p.m., every day, June and July; closed on Thanksgiving Day, Christmas Day, and New Year's Day

BIOGRAPHY OF DWIGHT D. EISENHOWER

October 14, 1890–March 28, 1969
Thirty-Fourth President: January 20, 1953–January 20, 1961
Republican Party

Dwight D. Eisenhower, c. 1953.
LOC LC-USZ62-13034

Dwight David Eisenhower was born in Denison, Texas. He was one of seven sons born to David Jacob and Ida Elizabeth Eisenhower. Young Dwight was given the nickname "Ike."[1] The Eisenhowers were devout Mennonites of German origin. In 1891 the family moved to Abilene, Kansas. David worked at a local creamery while Ida Elizabeth raised her sons.

As a teen, Eisenhower played football and educated himself reading history books. In 1911, he passed the entrance exam for West Point.[2] He graduated in 1915 and, a year later, married Mamie Geneva Doud. Dwight and Mamie had two sons: Doud Dwight "Icky" and John. When the United States entered World War I in April 1917, Eisenhower was ready to serve as an officer in France. However, he never had the opportunity to see any combat. Instead of serving at the front, he was assigned to various training camps. By the time he received orders to go to France in late 1918,

119

the war had ended.[3] Soon after the war, on January 2, 1921, his young son, Icky, died of scarlet fever.

In between the world wars, Eisenhower served as a clerk for various generals, including Douglas MacArthur, who called him "the best clerk in the Army."[4] During the interwar period, Eisenhower also served with generals John J. Pershing and George C. Marshall and future general George S. Patton. In 1940 he held a command at Fort Lewis, Washington. When the United States entered World War II after the attack on Pearl Harbor, Eisenhower was promoted to general and placed in charge of war plans for the Pacific. However, in June 1942, General Eisenhower was sent to England to work with America's allies.[5]

The question Eisenhower had to answer was where to strike the Germans first. The Soviets were already engaged with them in the east, and a western front was needed. Eisenhower believed that North Africa was the best place to launch the American attack against the Germans. British general Bernard Montgomery was already fighting Hitler's Africa Corps, which was under the control of General Erwin Rommel. On November 8, 1942, Operation Torch was launched as American forces landed in Morocco and Algeria. The landings were successful and by May 1943 the Allies had driven the enemy from North Africa.[6] After the success in North Africa, Eisenhower planned the Allied invasion of Sicily, which took place on July 10, 1943. The invasion frightened the Italians and compelled the king, Victor Emmanuel III, to dismiss the dictator Benito Mussolini. Italy switched its loyalty from Germany to the Allies.[7]

Although the Allies had been successful in Italy, the only way to end the war was to open a second front in Western Europe. As he prepared the Allied invasion of Normandy under Operation Overlord, General Eisenhower's greatest feat was still to come. Biographer Paul Johnson said, "The successful invasion of German-occupied Europe and the destruction of Hitler's regime were to be Ike's contribution to this crusade, and the Battle of Normandy his key moment in history."[8] A few months before the invasion, President Franklin Roosevelt and General Marshall decided that Eisenhower was the best man to lead the invasion force. On December 5, 1943, Roosevelt officially appointed Eisenhower to lead Overlord, making him Supreme Commander of the Allied Forces.[9] On June 6, 1944, the Allied troops landed on the beaches of Normandy. Eisenhower made a public address about the landings:

> People of Western Europe: A landing was made this morning on the coast of France by troops of the Allied Expeditionary Force. This landing is part of the concerted United Nations' plan for the liberation of Europe, made in conjunction with our great Russian allies.[10]

By May 1945 the war in Europe was over. Back home, Eisenhower was treated as a national hero, and questions arose as to whether or not he should be president. However, instead of being president of the United States, Eisenhower chose to be president of Columbia University in New York. He accepted the position because he saw Columbia as a "superb" university that was "turning out young people who were essentially first-class citizens."[11]

In 1952 President Harry S. Truman refused to seek a third term. Problems he was facing in relation to the Korean War convinced him that he could not be reelected.

In his place, the Democrats nominated Governor Adlai E. Stevenson of Illinois. The Republicans nominated General Eisenhower and chose Senator Richard Nixon of California for vice president. The nation was excited for Eisenhower. His campaign created the popular slogan "I like Ike"[12] and was the first to have a television commercial. The cartoon commercial showed an elephant marching down a street with ordinary Americans singing "Ike for President!"[13]

During his first year in office, Eisenhower put an end to the Korean War by successfully negotiating an armistice. Paul Johnson says this was Eisenhower's most "popular act" as president.[14] In 1955 Eisenhower suffered a minor heart attack, but he recovered[15] and ran for reelection in 1956. Once again, he was challenged by former Illinois governor Stevenson—and once again, he won. The problems of the world did not stop for that election, however. In 1956 Eisenhower condemned the invasion of the Suez Canal by Great Britain, France, and Israel, and the Soviet invasion of Hungary.

Further developments in the Middle East became problematic for the United States in the late 1950s as European countries relinquished their colonies. As new nations grew out of the nationalist fervor in the region, the question arose as to where their loyalties lay. Fearing a Communist expansion into the oil-rich Middle East, Eisenhower implemented the Eisenhower Doctrine in 1957. The doctrine offered the Middle East three promises: the use of American military force to assist Middle Eastern nations requesting aid against a Communist nation, free economic assistance from the United States, and $120 million in military and economic assistance to all regional nations approving of the doctrine.[16] A year later, Eisenhower enforced the doctrine when he sent marines to Lebanon in support of a pro-Western regime.

Back home, the battle for civil rights began to boil over as nine African Americans attempted to attend the all-white Central High School in Little Rock, Arkansas, on September 4, 1957. Three years earlier the United States Supreme Court had ruled unanimously against racial segregation in the *Brown v Board of Education* case. Now the decision had to be enforced, and many segregationists in the South stood fast to prevent it. Governor Orval E. Faubus ordered the Arkansas National Guard to prevent the students from enrolling. This action made national headlines. Knowing the law had to be upheld, Eisenhower deployed regular army units comprised of the 101st Airborne to allow the nine students to enroll and attend Central High. Eisenhower said, "Proper and sensible observance of the law . . . demanded the respectful obedience which the nation has the right to expect from all the people."[17] Unfortunately, what happened in Little Rock was just the first in a series of racial clashes over desegregation that rocked the 1960s.

In January 1957 Eisenhower proposed the creation of a large interstate highway system akin to the German autobahn. Congress agreed to fund the interstate, and the "largest public works project in America" began.[18] The interstate system made traveling across the country quicker and easier for millions of Americans. However, the interstate was not built solely for the public; Eisenhower saw it as vital for national security. If America were ever invaded, the interstate would allow rapid transit for troops.[19]

In the 1950s the United States and the Soviet Union were in the midst of an arms race. Each had the hydrogen bomb and had perfected intercontinental missiles that could reach anywhere in the world. Eisenhower knew that in a worst-case scenario involving the Soviets, America would need to be prepared for "an all-out nuclear war."[20] In an attempt to quell tensions, he proposed the idea of an "open sky policy" that would allow each nation to fly "reconnaissance missions" over the other's territories.[21] Soviet leader Nikita Khrushchev rejected the idea.

Tensions increased on October 4, 1957, when the Soviets launched the satellite *Sputnik* into orbit, creating a space race between the two superpowers. Since the Soviets rejected the open sky policy, the only other option was to fly secret reconnaissance flights over Soviet territory. The U-2 spy plane was made for this purpose. On May 1, 1960, the Soviets shot down a U-2 piloted by Francis Gary Powers. The Soviets humiliated Powers in a show trial and imprisoned him; however, a prisoner exchange in 1962 would bring him home. The "U-2 incident," as it was known, increased tensions between the two nations even further during Eisenhower's final months in office. Stephen Kinzer said, "Eisenhower had hoped to end his term with Soviet-American relations improving. Instead they were nearly as frigid as when he took office."[22] On top of this, Eisenhower had to contend with the spread of Communism in Cuba and Vietnam toward the end of his presidency.

Vice President Richard Nixon seemed to be the best man to carry on Eisenhower's fight against Communism, and he was nominated to be the Republican candidate in 1960. The Democrats nominated the young and attractive Massachusetts senator, John F. Kennedy. On January 17, 1961, Eisenhower delivered his Farewell Address to the nation, in which he warned Americans that the growing defense industry might place impositions on a free nation. He said, "In the councils of government, we must guard against the acquisition of unwarranted influence, whether sought or unsought, by the military-industrial complex. The potential for the disastrous rise of misplaced power exists and will persist."[23] The next day, Eisenhower turned over the presidency to Kennedy.

Eisenhower's presidency saw the transformation of America into a nuclear superpower. It also saw the country grow by two more states when Alaska and Hawaii joined in 1959.

Eisenhower and his wife retired to a farm in Gettysburg, Pennsylvania, where the famous battle of the Civil War took place. On March 28, 1969, Eisenhower died of congestive heart failure. He is buried with his wife and his son Doud "Icky" at his presidential library in Abilene, Kansas.

LIBRARY, MUSEUM, AND BOYHOOD HOME

The story of the Eisenhower library began shortly after the Allied victory over Germany in May 1945. Eisenhower's "admirers" wanted to preserve his boyhood home in Abilene, Kansas, as a "reminder of his accomplishments."[24] A nonprofit organization was created by Charles M. Harger of the *Abilene Reflector-Chronicle* and New York artist Albert Reed. A year later Eisenhower's mother died and the family deeded the home to the foundation. The foundation then went on a fund-raising campaign, inviting funds "without respect to race, creed, color, or politics."[25] Over time, diverse individuals and organizations made contributions to the foundation. The museum was built next to Eisenhower's boyhood home in 1952, and it was formally dedicated on November 11, 1954.

That same year Eisenhower made plans to expand his museum to include a library, where his personal papers could be stored. In a memorandum, the National Archives informed the president he should make arrangements for his papers to be transported to his museum in a timely manner:

> Arrangements for the ultimate deposit of Presidential papers ought to be made at the earliest possible time and certainly before the President leaves office. . . . Early determination is desirable to allow completion of construction prior to end of term. . . . A timely decision provides the greatest insurance against later dispersal, loss, misuse, or destruction of the papers.[26]

But not everyone was happy with Eisenhower's papers being deposited in Abilene. A White House report dated January 30, 1954, stated that some scholars did not like having to visit Kansas to do research on the president. A proposal was made to store Eisenhower's papers at Columbia University, since he had served as its president.[27] However, Congress passed the Presidential Libraries Act in 1955, which allowed Eisenhower to build and deposit papers in his library.

Eisenhower decided to turn the whole museum at Abilene into a presidential library. A new foundation was created, which was cochaired by the Kansas governor, George Docking, and former Kansas senator Harry Darby: the Eisenhower Presidential Library Commission. One of the commission's first tasks was to secure land near the museum for the library's construction. The state of Kansas appropriated $275,000 to purchase the land. Altogether, with the appropriation and private donations, the foundation raised $3 million.[28]

On October 14, 1959, on President Eisenhower's sixty-ninth birthday, the library held its "groundbreaking ceremonies."[29] In the speech he delivered during the ceremony, Eisenhower said:

> When this library is filled with documents, and scholars come here to probe into some of the facts of the past half century, I hope that they, as we today, are concerned primarily with the ideals, principles, and trends that provide guides to a free, rich, peaceful future in which all peoples can achieve ever-rising levels of human well-being.[30]

Shortly after Eisenhower left office in 1961, he began the process of sorting through the papers to be sent to his presidential library. His grandson David Eisenhower described this task:

> Since the law regarding presidential papers vested him with full ownership, Eisenhower had ordered, packed, and removed every memorandum, letter, and minute of meetings even remotely connected with his conduct in office, and had had the materials sent to the site of his future presidential library in Abilene, Kansas. The classified materials he shipped to nearby Fort Ritchie, Maryland, for safe storage.[31]

The formal dedication of the library building took place on May 1, 1962. The first director of the Eisenhower library was J. Earl Endacott, who had taught history at

Abilene High School for twenty years. As director, Endacott helped to catalog all materials coming into the library. He even wrote a history of the library. Endacott served as director for twenty-four years and retired in 1969 to make way for his successor, William Jones.[32]

In the fall of 1967, Eisenhower had the remains of his son Doud "Icky" moved from a cemetery in Denver to be reinterred at the library.[33]

By 2014, the library had welcomed 186,307 visitors.[34] At the time of writing this book, the Eisenhower library is celebrating the one-hundredth anniversary of World War I and the seventy-fifth anniversary of World War II. On May 21, 2015, the library held a World Wars concert, with performances of music from World War I. The library invited Kansas State University assistant professor Bryan Pinkall of the School of Music, Theatre, and Dance and pianist Amanda Arrington to perform. The library along with Pinkall said:

> Since it is the 100th anniversary of WWI and the 75th anniversary of WWII, we felt this was a very appropriate time to produce a series like this. . . . The program features music of Alberic Magnard, George Butterworth and F.S. Kelly, who died during World War I. Audio/visuals will help tell the story of these composers.[35]

On May 8, 2015, the library celebrated the seventieth anniversary of the surrender of Germany—Victory in Europe Day. The library invited Robert M. Edsel, an author and the Founder and Chairman of the Monuments Men Foundation for the Preservation of Art, to give a lecture about the cultural treasures stolen by the Germans during the war. In a press release promoting the lecture, the library said:

> Edsel's remarks will provide perspective on the lessons learned about the preservation of cultural treasures during World War II under the leadership of Supreme Allied Commander Dwight D. Eisenhower. He will also discuss the challenges confronting us today as we bear witness to the destruction of cultural treasures in Syria and Iraq by the Islamic State (ISIS).[36]

Two months later on August 14, 2015, the library celebrated the surrender of the Japanese: Victory over Japan Day. An army band played big-band music from the era and there was a special screening of the movie *Unbroken*, which tells the true story of an American Olympic athlete, Louis Zamperini, who survived as a prisoner of war in a Japanese prison camp.[37]

On June 3, 2016, Karl H. Weissenbach stepped down as director of the Eisenhower library. Weissenbach had been director since 2008. During his directorship, the library created successful relationships with the Kansas Humanities Council, American University, Rockhurst University, Kansas Wesleyan University, and Kansas State University.[38] Weissenbach even won the Archivist's Award for Outstanding Achievement in 2010 for his promotion of "civic literacy through public programming."[39] At the time of writing this book, a new director has not yet been named and Deputy Director Tim Rives is acting in that capacity.

Collections and Exhibits

As of 2014, the Eisenhower library's collection contained a total of twenty-six million pages of books, manuscripts, letters, and other relevant presidential documents. This total includes 28,550 books, 33,120 pages of oral history, and 334,500 still photographs.[40]

The library has one temporary exhibit and four permanent ones. The temporary exhibit has three galleries celebrating the seventieth anniversary of World War II. The first of these is *World War II Remembered: Leaders, Battles and Heroes*. This exhibit contains soldiers' personal stories and narratives, including the contributions of minorities, such as the Tuskegee Airmen and the Native American code talkers.[41] The second exhibit is *Be Ye Men of Valour: Allies of World War II*. Here visitors will learn about the contributions made by America's allies, including the British and the Russians, and the roles that underground resistance groups in occupied countries played in winning the war.[42] The third and final exhibit in the group is *Forbidden Art*. This exhibit displays the disquieting art of Holocaust survivors from the infamous Auschwitz concentration camp. The art is on temporary loan from the Auschwitz-Birkenau State Museum in Poland and the Polish Mission of the Orchard Lake Schools.[43] These temporary exhibits will remain at the library until December 2016.

The first permanent exhibit focuses on Eisenhower's early days in Abilene. Exhibit number two is dedicated to his wife and First Lady, Mamie. The third exhibit is the *Military Gallery*, which presents the story of General Eisenhower's role in liberating Europe during World War II. The final exhibit is Eisenhower's *Presidential Gallery*, where visitors can learn about Eisenhower's achievements as president. The exhibit also discusses his post-presidency and death.[44]

Dwight D. Eisenhower Presidential Library and Museum. *Courtesy of Eisenhower Presidential Library, Museum, and Boyhood Home*

Recent Events   In May 2015, the library commemorated the 125th anniversary of Eisenhower's birth with its *Ike 125* lecture series. Guest speakers, including Dominique François, John Robert Greene, Yanek Mieczkowski, and Tim Rives, were invited to lecture on his life.[45]

Oral Histories   Like other presidential libraries, the Eisenhower library has its own collection of oral histories. According to the library's website:

> The oral history collection has been built upon two major components: (1) the Eisenhower Presidential Library's own interviews, and (2) transcripts acquired through a cooperative arrangement with Columbia University's Oral History Project. A third and smaller component consists of a number of oral history interviews donated to the Library by various institutions and individuals.[46]

The oral histories were provided by Eisenhower's friends, family, colleagues, and members of his administration. Some of the more notable histories were given by his chief of staff, Sherman Adams; Connecticut senator and father of President George H. W. Bush, Prescott Bush; Attorney General Thomas C. Clark; General Lucius D. Clay; First Lady Mamie Doud Eisenhower; California senator William F. Knowland; ambassador to Italy Clare Boothe Luce; future vice president and then secretary of health, education and welfare Nelson Rockefeller; James Roosevelt; Minnesota governor Harold Stassen; United States attorney and future Alaska senator Ted Stevens; and Chief Justice Earl Warren.[47]

NOTES

1. Paul Johnson, *Eisenhower: A Life* (New York: Viking Penguin, 2014), 3.
2. Johnson, *Eisenhower*, 4–5.
3. Johnson, *Eisenhower*, 8–9.
4. Johnson, *Eisenhower*, 15.
5. "Army Years," Dwight D. Eisenhower Presidential Library, Museum, and Boyhood Home, accessed October 13, 2016, https://www.eisenhower.archives.gov/all_about_ike/army_years.html.
6. Johnson, *Eisenhower*, 32–35.
7. Johnson, *Eisenhower*, 35.
8. Johnson, *Eisenhower*, 44.
9. Jim Newton, *Eisenhower: The White House Years* (New York: Doubleday, 2011), 42–43.
10. "Pre-Presidential Speeches," Dwight D. Eisenhower Presidential Library, Museum, and Boyhood Home, accessed October 13, 2016, https://www.eisenhower.archives.gov/all_about_ike/speeches/pre_presidential_speeches.pdf.
11. Johnson, *Eisenhower*, 64.
12. Newton, *Eisenhower*, 54.
13. "1952: Eisenhower vs. Stevenson," Museum of the Moving Image, accessed September 1, 2016, http://www.livingroomcandidate.org/commercials/1952.
14. Johnson, *Eisenhower*, 94–95.
15. Johnson, *Eisenhower*, 103.

16. Isaac Alteras, *Eisenhower and Israel: U.S.-Israeli Relations, 1953–1960* (Gainesville: University Press of Florida, 1993), 296.

17. Newton, *Eisenhower*, 251.

18. Newton, *Eisenhower*, 209.

19. Newton, *Eisenhower*, 210.

20. John Lewis Gaddis, *The Cold War: A New History* (New York: Penguin Books, 2005), 66.

21. Gaddis, *The Cold War*, 72.

22. Stephen Kinzer, *The Brothers: John Foster Dulles, Allen Dulles, and Their Secret World War* (New York: Times Books, 2013), 257.

23. "Farewell Radio and Television Address to the American People," Dwight D. Eisenhower Presidential Library, Museum, and Boyhood Home, accessed October 13, 2016, https://www.eisenhower.archives.gov/all_about_ike/speeches/farewell_address.pdf.

24. Frank L. Schick, Renee Schick, and Mark Carroll, *Records of the Presidency: Presidential Papers and Libraries from Washington to Reagan* (Phoenix, AZ: Oryx Press, 1989), 184.

25. Schick et al., *Records of the Presidency*, 184.

26. Schick et al., *Records of the Presidency*, 185.

27. "Some Consideration on Presidential Papers and Libraries," Box 365 of the Official File of the White House Central File, 1953-191, OF 101-PP Presidential Papers (1).

28. Schick et al., *Records of the Presidency*, 185.

29. Schick et al., *Records of the Presidency*, 186.

30. "Home," Dwight D. Eisenhower Presidential Library, Museum, and Boyhood Home, accessed October 13, 2016, https://www.eisenhower.archives.gov/.

31. David Eisenhower and Julie Nixon Eisenhower. *Going Home to Glory: A Memoir of Life with Dwight D. Eisenhower, 1961–1969* (New York: Simon and Schuster, 2010), 14.

32. Dwight D. Eisenhower Library, "Endacott, J. Earl: Papers, 1944–74," Documentary Histories Series, Accession: A91-15 (Abilene, KS: Dwight D. Eisenhower Library), 2–3, https://www.eisenhower.archives.gov/research/finding_aids/pdf/Endacott_Earl_Papers.pdf.

33. Eisenhower and Eisenhower, *Going Home to Glory*, 227.

34. Eisenhower Presidential Library, Museum, and Boyhood Home, "Information Sheet—Fiscal Year 2014" (unpublished information sheet, Eisenhower Presidential Library, Museum, and Boyhood Home, 2015).

35. "K-State Musicians to Present 'World Wars Concert' at Eisenhower Presidential Library," press release, May 12, 2016, Dwight D. Eisenhower Presidential Library, Museum, and Boyhood Home, http://archive.constantcontact.com/fs141/1102308225095/archive/1124470359682.html.

36. "Monuments Men Founder to Keynote VE-Day 70th Anniversary at Eisenhower Presidential Library," press release, May 1, 2015, Dwight D. Eisenhower Presidential Library, Museum, and Boyhood Home, http://archive.constantcontact.com/fs141/1102308225095/archive/1120827139376.html.

37. "Eisenhower Presidential Library to Commemorate V-J Day 70th Anniversary," press release, August 6, 2015, Dwight D. Eisenhower Presidential Library, Museum, and Boyhood Home, http://archive.constantcontact.com/fs141/1102308225095/archive/1121469203379.html.

38. "Retirement of Eisenhower Library Director Karl Weissenbach," press release, April 8, 2016, Dwight D. Eisenhower Presidential Library, Museum, and Boyhood Home, http://archive.constantcontact.com/fs141/1102308225095/archive/1124338244060.html.

39. "Retirement of Eisenhower Library Director Karl Weissenbach."

40. Eisenhower Presidential Library, "Information Sheet—Fiscal Year 2014."

41. "Exhibits Schedule," Dwight D. Eisenhower Presidential Library, Museum, and Boyhood Home, accessed October 13, 2016, https://www.eisenhower.archives.gov/museum/exhibits_schedule.html.

42. "Exhibits Schedule."

43. "Exhibits Schedule."

44. Samantha Kenner, Communications Director, Eisenhower Presidential Library, Museum, and Boyhood Home, telephone interview with the author, September 15, 2016.

45. "Celebrating 125 Years of Dwight Eisenhower," press release, May 18, 2016, Dwight D. Eisenhower Presidential Library, Museum, and Boyhood Home, http://archive.constantcontact .com/fs141/1102308225095/archive/1121103490337.html.

46. "Oral Histories," Dwight D. Eisenhower Presidential Library, Museum, and Boyhood Home, accessed October 13, 2016, https://www.eisenhower.archives.gov/research/oral_histories.html.

47. "Oral Histories."

BIBLIOGRAPHY

Alteras, Isaac. *Eisenhower and Israel: U.S.-Israeli Relations, 1953–1960*. Gainesville: University Press of Florida, 1993.

Brown v. Board of Education of Topeka, 347 US 483 (1954).

Davis, Kenneth S. *The Politics of Honor: A Biography of Adlai E. Stevenson*. New York: Putnam, 1967.

Eisenhower, David, and Julie Nixon Eisenhower. *Going Home to Glory: A Memoir of Life with Dwight D. Eisenhower, 1961–1969*. New York: Simon and Schuster, 2010.

Eisenhower Presidential Library, Museum, and Boyhood Home Information Sheet—Fiscal Year 2014.

Endacott, J. Earl: Papers, 1944–74. Documentary Histories Series, Accession: A91-15. Abilene, KS: Dwight D. Eisenhower Library. https://www.eisenhower.archives.gov/research/finding_ aids/pdf/Endacott_Earl_Papers.pdf.

Gaddis, John Lewis. *The Cold War: A New History*. New York: Penguin Books, 2005.

Johnson, Paul. *Eisenhower: A Life*. New York: Viking Penguin, 2014.

Kinzer, Stephen. *The Brothers: John Foster Dulles, Allen Dulles, and Their Secret World War*. New York: Times Books, 2013.

Newton, Jim. *Eisenhower: The White House Years*. New York: Doubleday, 2011.

Schick, Frank L., Renee Schick, and Mark Carroll. *Records of the Presidency: Presidential Papers and Libraries from Washington to Reagan*. Phoenix, AZ: Oryx Press, 1989.

"Some Consideration on Presidential Papers and Libraries," Box 365 of the Official File of the White House Central File, 1953-191, OF 101-PP Presidential Papers (1).

John F. Kennedy
Presidential Library and Museum

Address: Columbia Point, Boston, MA 02125
Phone: 1-866-JFK-1960
Website: https://www.jfklibrary.org/
Social media: https://www.facebook.com/JFKLibrary
Administration: National Archives
Hours: 9 a.m. to 5 p.m., every day; closed Thanksgiving Day, Christmas Day, and
   New Year's Day

BIOGRAPHY OF JOHN F. KENNEDY

May 29, 1917–November 22, 1963
Thirty-Fifth President: January 20, 1961–November 22, 1963
Democratic Party

John F. Kennedy, c. 1960.
LC-USZ62-13035

John Fitzgerald Kennedy was born to Joseph P. Kennedy Sr. and Rose Fitzgerald Kennedy in Brookline, Massachusetts. Joseph was a businessman who later served as the American ambassador to the United Kingdom. John was one of nine children born to this large and rich Irish American family. John's maternal grandfather, John "Honey Fitz" Fitzgerald, had served as mayor of Boston.

As a child, John was in competition with his eldest brother, Joe, for whom the family had high hopes.[1] John also went through a series of health problems in childhood. He suffered scarlet fever, chicken pox, and various stomach-intestinal ailments.[2] Because of his health, John's schooling proved so problematic that by age thirteen he was lucky to be a "C+" student.[3] In 1930, John briefly attended a Catholic school for boys in New Milford, Massachusetts, but here he suffered more health problems. To make up for lost time, John was tutored at home. A year later, he successfully enrolled at the prestigious boarding school of Choate.[4] Even at Choate, his health problems continued, and he earned a reputation for being "casual and disorderly."[5]

In 1936, Kennedy matriculated at Harvard University and took "courses in political science and international relations."[6] At Harvard he played football and became a voracious reader. A year later he toured Europe, where he saw the rise of Fascism in Italy and Germany. Kennedy was particularly alarmed by the Nazis.[7] In 1940, his thesis, titled "Appeasement at Munich," was accepted and he graduated.[8] His thesis questioned why England did not do more to stop Adolf Hitler's aggression toward Czechoslovakia. After graduation, Kennedy rewrote his thesis, which became his first book, *While England Slept*, and focused on England's military unpreparedness for World War II.[9]

When the United States entered World War II following the Japanese attack on Pearl Harbor, Kennedy decided to serve his nation. In July 1942 he attended a midshipman's school, which trained him as a navy officer. Initially, because of his poor health he was assigned to a noncombat position at the Panama Canal.[10] However, Kennedy wanted to become an officer of a Patrol Torpedo (PT) boat. A year later he got his wish and took command of *PT-109* in the South Pacific. On August 1, 1943, Kennedy's *PT-109* was sent to monitor enemy ships in the Blackett Strait near Kolombangara in the Solomon Islands. That night, a Japanese destroyer accidentally rammed the unsuspecting *PT-109*, causing it to capsize. Two men were killed, and Kennedy and the remaining crew of ten clung to the ship's hull for survival. The following morning, Kennedy led his men to an island for safety. While the crew were recovering on the island, two English-speaking native islanders arrived. Kennedy carved a rescue message onto a coconut shell and asked the islanders to take it to the Allied base at Rendova. The message inscribed on the coconut read:

> NAURO ISL . . . COMMANDER . . . NATIVE KNOWS POS'IT . . . HE CAN
> PILOT . . . 11 ALIVE . . . NEED SMALL BOAT . . . KENNEDY[11]

The commander at Rendova sent the natives to retrieve Kennedy alone, which they did. The following day all the men were rescued by the navy.[12] Kennedy became a hero, as the press printed the story of his crew's ordeal. In 1963 the story was made into a movie, *PT 109*, with actor Cliff Robertson playing Kennedy. While Kennedy was returning home, his older brother, Joseph Jr., died when his dynamite-laden airplane exploded during a mission in Europe.

After the war, Kennedy decided to pursue a career in politics. He ran for the Eleventh Congressional District of Massachusetts as a Democrat. During this election, the issue of Communism was causing fear across the nation as the Cold War emerged between the Soviet Union and America. In a speech against Communism, Kennedy said, "The time has come when we must speak plainly on the great issue facing the world today. The issue is Soviet Russia . . . a slave state of the worst sort . . . embarked upon a program of world aggression."[13] Kennedy won the election, defeating his Republican opponent Lester Bowen with 72 percent of the vote.[14]

In 1952 Kennedy ran for the United States Senate against sitting Republican Henry Cabot Lodge Jr. That year the Republican Party swept the nation when General

Dwight David Eisenhower was elected president. Luckily, Kennedy won the election against Lodge by 3 percent.[15] One year later, on September 12, 1953, Senator Kennedy married Jacqueline Bouvier. Like her husband, Jacqueline hailed from a prominent family and was "socially sophisticated."[16] They had three children together: John (John John) F. Kennedy Jr., Caroline, and Patrick, who died shortly after birth. Caroline was the US ambassador to Japan for three years during the Obama administration. Tragically, John Jr. died in a plane crash in 1999.

Serving in the Senate, Kennedy became very sick, as his back problems got the best of him. During his convalescence, he took leave of the Senate and wrote his celebrated book, *Profiles in Courage*. The book is about the senators and congressmen who were brave enough to make unpopular decisions that, in some cases, cost them their political careers. His book won the Pulitzer Prize in 1957. During the 1956 Democratic Party Convention in Chicago, the delegates renominated former Illinois governor Adlai Stevenson as their candidate. Stevenson did not name a running mate, which meant that the delegates had to choose one for him. Kennedy jumped at the chance to be nominated. The delegates were split between Kennedy and Senator Estes Kefauver of Tennessee. After two ballots, Kefauver was nominated by 755.5 votes to 589.[17] The Democrats ultimately lost to Eisenhower and his running mate Richard Nixon. As for Kennedy, he had set his sights on the presidency.

In 1960, Kennedy ran for the Democratic nomination for president. At just forty-three years old, he represented a new generation. However, he had to overcome the fact that the nation had never elected a Catholic to the presidency. During the primaries his main competition was Senator Hubert H. Humphrey of Minnesota. Kennedy began his campaign in Wisconsin. Since the state borders Minnesota, many presumed that Humphrey would win. However, Kennedy drew "enthusiastic crowds" in Wisconsin and benefited from the state's urban Catholic vote, which helped him secure a victory.[18] The next showdown was in West Virginia. Unlike Wisconsin, West Virginia is a rural state with a small Catholic population, but Kennedy convinced voters in West Virginia that Catholics were as patriotic as Protestants and won.[19] At the Democratic Convention in Los Angeles, Kennedy won the nomination and chose Senator Lyndon Baines Johnson of Texas as his running mate. Kennedy needed a Southerner if he was to be elected, and Johnson was a perfect choice.

The Republicans nominated Vice President Richard M. Nixon and former senator Henry Cabot Lodge Jr., whose Senate seat was now occupied by Kennedy. During the election, the first televised debates were held. The first debate between Kennedy and Nixon is important because of how people perceived the candidates performance. Those who watched the debate on television thought Kennedy won, and those who listened to it on the radio thought Nixon won.[20] Why was this so? Television viewers thought Kennedy looked more confident because his dark suit made him stand out, whereas Nixon's gray one "blended with the background and accentuated the pallor in his face."[21] On election night, Kennedy secured a narrow victory over Nixon. He won by the closet margin in American history: "just over 100,000 votes."[22]

On January 20, 1961, Kennedy was inaugurated as president. At the inauguration, poet Robert Frost recited "The Gift Outright" "to celebrate the new generation's rise to national leadership."[23] The poem was followed by Kennedy's famous inaugural speech, in which he said:

> Let the word go forth from this time and place, to friend and foe alike, that the torch has been passed to a new generation of Americans—born in this century, tempered by war, disciplined by a hard and bitter peace, proud of our ancient heritage—and unwilling to witness or permit the slow undoing of those human rights to which this nation has always been committed, and to which we are committed today at home and around the world.[24]

He concluded his speech by reminding the American people, "ask not what your country can do for you—ask what you can do for your country."[25]

Kennedy's presidency was inspiring for many Americans. He promoted civil rights, created the Peace Corps, and launched America into the space race. However, in October 1962, the Cuban Missile Crisis brought tension to the nation. On the island of Cuba, Communist dictator Fidel Castro allowed Russia to place nuclear missiles there. The Cuban Missile Crisis followed the failed Bay of Pigs invasion of Cuban exiles, which the United States sponsored. Kennedy called for a quarantine of Cuba to prevent more Russian ships from delivering nuclear weapons to the island.[26] The world stood on the brink of nuclear war. On October 22, 1962, Kennedy delivered a speech to the American people, in which he declared his intention to stand up to the Russians. Kennedy said:

> This Government, as promised, has maintained the closest surveillance of the Soviet military build-up on the island of Cuba. Within the past week unmistakable evidence has established the fact that a series of offensive missile sites is now in preparation on that imprisoned island. The purposes of these bases can be none other than to provide a nuclear strike capability against the Western Hemisphere. . . . It shall be the policy of this nation to regard any nuclear missile launched from Cuba against any nation in the Western Hemisphere as an attack by the Soviet Union on the United States, requiring a full retaliatory response upon the Soviet Union.[27]

Thankfully, the Cuban Missile Crisis was resolved peacefully when Russia and America agreed that Russia would remove the missiles in Cuba if America removed its missiles in Turkey.[28] The resolution was a victory for Kennedy. Author Alan Brinkley said that Kennedy's "management of the Cuban missile crisis [had] become the most revered accomplishment of his presidency."[29]

During his presidency, Kennedy also had to deal with race relations. In the American South, African Americans were calling for their constitutional rights against racial segregation. On June 11, 1963, Kennedy delivered a speech about the importance of resolving race relations. He said:

> We face, therefore, a moral crisis as a country and as a people. It cannot be met by repressive police action. It cannot be left to increased demonstrations in the streets. It cannot be quieted by token moves or talk. It is time to act in the Congress, in your State and local legislative body and, above all, in all of our daily lives.[30]

Two weeks later on June 26, 1963, Kennedy visited the divided city of Berlin. Two year earlier, East Germany had built a wall through Berlin to stop people from fleeing to freedom. Standing next to the Brandenburg gate, he spoke his famous words in German, "*Ich bin ein Berliner*."[31]

On November 22, 1963, tragedy struck. Kennedy was assassinated in Dallas, Texas, as his car drove past the Texas School Book Depository Building in Dealey Plaza. Kennedy, along with Texas governor John Connally, was shot. Kennedy received fatal wounds to his neck and head, while Connally was injured but survived. The alleged assassin was Lee Harvey Oswald, who had Communist proclivities and had lived in the Soviet Union. Before Oswald was arrested that fateful day at a Dallas theater, he was also accused of murdering a Dallas police officer named J. D. Tippit. Two days later, Oswald was himself shot while he was being transported to court. His shooter was local nightclub owner Jack Ruby. The murder of Oswald led Americans to believe that Oswald was part of a larger conspiracy to assassinate the president. President Lyndon B. Johnson called for a panel, known as the Warren Commission, to investigate the assassination. The commission was led by Supreme Court chief justice Earl Warren. The commission also included former CIA director Allen Dulles and congressman and future president Gerald R. Ford. In 1964, the commission released the Warren Report, which concluded that Oswald had acted alone.[32] Despite the findings of the report, many still believe that Kennedy was killed in a conspiracy.[33]

President Kennedy was buried on November 25, 1963, at Arlington National Cemetery. Next to his grave is the Eternal Flame, which commemorates his legacy. The legacy of President John F. Kennedy is still very much alive. A *Gallup* poll in 2010 found Kennedy to be the most popular modern president.[34] His wife, Jacqueline, would go on to marry Greek shipping tycoon Aristotle Onassis. But on December 6, 1963, Jacqueline proclaimed to *Life* magazine that Kennedy's administration would forever be known as Camelot. She said, "Don't let it be forgot, that once there was a spot, for one brief, shining moment that was known as Camelot."[35]

LIBRARY AND MUSEUM

The story of the John F. Kennedy Library began on December 19, 1960, when US archivist Wayne C. Grover contacted President-elect Kennedy and offered to help him "securely store" his pre-presidential papers.[36] The Presidential Library Act of 1955, which allowed presidents to have their papers kept in such libraries, made this possible.[37]

Shortly before and after his inauguration on January 20, 1961, Kennedy had been in correspondence with Harvard University president Nathan M. Pusey and the university librarian, Paul H. Buck, about the possibility of storing his presidential papers in Cambridge, Massachusetts.[38] Harvard was a logical choice, as this was Kennedy's alma mater. Pusey felt that having Kennedy's papers at Harvard would be "advantageous to the scholarly world."[39] Five months into his administration, Kennedy had still not made any concrete decisions about his papers. In a letter to Pusey, he said, "While I have made no final decision about the eventual disposition of my papers, I am attracted by the thought of a repository established in association with Harvard."[40] Though Kennedy was interested in Cambridge, he also considered Hyannis Port and Palm Beach as potential locations for his library.[41] He finally settled on Cambridge in December 1961.[42]

During the early days of Kennedy's administration, two of his special assistants, Theodore Sorensen and Arthur M. Schlesinger Jr., worked with Pusey and the National Archives to create plans for his library. Schlesinger wrote letters to administration officials to encourage them to preserve their papers, photos, memorandums, and books. In 1963 Kennedy had chosen the location of his library: a twelve-acre site along the Charles River near Harvard Square.[43] However, although this location was in proximity to Harvard, the land was owned by the Metropolitan Boston Transit Authority (MBTA), which was reluctant to relinquish it to the library. Instead, Kennedy had to settle for a two-acre site near the Harvard Business School in Brighton, which the university donated.[44]

When Kennedy was assassinated, pressure to get the library built grew. On December 5, 1963, the John F. Kennedy Memorial Library was incorporated and his brother Robert F. Kennedy served as its president. He helped raise $18 million for the construction of the library building, which was planned by the architect I. M. Pei.[45] For the next few years, there was an ongoing debate between Kennedy's former assistant Schlesinger and members of the Kennedy family, including Senator Edward Kennedy, about the library's theme. Harvard historian Richard Neustadt suggested they turn the library into a think tank for political studies in the model of the Hoover Institute at Stanford.[46] To make the library a think tank, the land owned by the MBTA would be required. The Commonwealth of Massachusetts did purchase the land for the library, but in the 1970s another dispute broke out. Residents of Boston feared that the library would cause traffic problems, while the General Services Administration calculated that the library would cause "negative environmental impact"; therefore, another location was considered.[47] In November 1975 the land around the MBTA was given back to the commonwealth and a new site near the University of Massachusetts, Boston on the Columbia Point peninsula was briefly considered. However, the high crime rate in that part of the city made it undesirable.[48] Instead, another section of Columbia Point was chosen: the "Ashmont section of Dorchester where the President's mother grew up."[49]

The groundbreaking ceremony took place in 1977, with Kennedy's widow, Jacqueline Kennedy Onassis, present. Two years later, the library was completed and opened to the public.[50] William G. Clotworthy describes the structure as "stark, striking, imposing—stand[ing] beside the sea President Kennedy loved. The park-like surroundings and a unique view of Boston's historic skyline and harbor combine to provide a particularly dramatic setting."[51]

Unfortunately, the library got off on the wrong foot. It was supposed to be inspiring, but the museum's design and displays made visitors feel sad when they saw films about the assassinations of Kennedy and his brother Robert. Carl M. Brauer describes the melancholia of the library:

> The original exhibits mounted in 1979 were intended to inspire visitors, but surveys revealed that sadness was the museum's overriding effect. The somber tone was set by Charles Guggenheim's biographical film ending with Kennedy's shocking death. The tone was reinforced by the museum's gray and beige color scheme and its large glass enclosures. Before leaving the museum, visitors saw a second melancholy film, about Robert Kennedy, who was assassinated in 1968, five years after his brother.[52]

The museum needed an overhaul. In 1992 the library was closed and redesigned using a budget of $6.9 million. The changes included adding more galleries, new exhibits, and video footage of the Kennedys.[53]

On April 15, 2013, terrorists detonated two bombs during the Boston Marathon. While investigators and first responders attended to the injured and searched for the culprits, reports of a third explosion at the Kennedy library were heard. Many feared that terrorists had also attacked the library. However, firefighters discovered that the cause was not terrorism, but "discarded smoking material." The damage to the library was "minimal" but "significant water and other fire protection damage" was seen in parts of the building.[54]

In January 2014, the Kennedy library made history when Heather Campion became the first woman to head the John F. Kennedy Library Foundation. Campion brought an interesting background. Prior to heading the foundation, she had worked for President Jimmy Carter, held important positions in both the Walter Mondale and Michael Dukakis presidential campaigns, and worked at Citizens Bank as the executive vice president for corporate affairs.[55] Campion headed the foundation for just a year and a half before she resigned. The *Boston Globe* reported that several employees had quit their jobs at the library. The employees cited Campion's "leadership style" when explaining their decision to leave.[56]

In August 2016, the library announced Steven Rothstein as the new CEO of the library foundation. Rothstein had formerly led the Perkins School for the Blind.[57] The library has been administered by Acting Director William J. Bosanko since Campion's departure. Before becoming acting director, Bosanko held administrative positions with the National Archives and Records Administration.[58] Despite administrative problems, the library still serves to maintain the life, records, and legacy of President John F. Kennedy. In 2012 the Kennedy library welcomed 208,313 visitors.[59]

John F. Kennedy Presidential Library and Museum, Boston. *Courtesy of the JFK Presidential Library and Museum*

Collections and Exhibits

The John F. Kennedy Presidential Library and Museum has permanent and special temporary exhibits. There are seven permanent exhibits. The first exhibit, *The Campaign Trail*, gives visitors a glimpse of the campaigns run by Senator John F. Kennedy and Vice President Richard Nixon in the run-up to the presidential election of 1960. Inside, visitors can watch the Democratic Convention, where Kennedy gave his acceptance speech, and take a tour of a fictional Main Street USA to see footage of Kennedy campaigning across America. The highlight of this exhibit is Kennedy's message to the electorate about a New Frontier. Included in this exhibit is campaign memorabilia from 1960, such as campaign buttons, convention tickets, posters, and delegate badges.[60]

The second exhibit is aptly named *The Briefing Room*. Here, visitors can view television footage of President Kennedy conducting press conferences. As president, Kennedy gave sixty-four conferences on subjects ranging from Vietnam to the Berlin Wall. Visitors can even see the televised speech that Kennedy gave in Berlin, defying the construction of the Berlin Wall. The exhibit also displays an artifact from Berlin known as the Clock. This clock was given to Kennedy in Berlin and has three dials to show the time in Berlin, Moscow, and Washington.[61]

Exploration of outer space was an important theme throughout Kennedy's presidency. The third exhibit, named *The Space Race*, focuses on two of America's first successful manned space launches. The first spacecraft is Alan B. Shepard's *Mercury Freedom 7*. Shepard's mission lasted only fifteen minutes, but it was an important one, because he was the first American in space. The other spacecraft is John Glenn's *Mercury Friendship 7*. Glenn was the first American to orbit Earth. These successful space flights helped bolster Kennedy's commitment to beat the Soviets in the race to the moon. On display are two replicates of Shepard's and Glenn's spacecrafts.[62]

The fourth exhibit focuses on Kennedy's brother Robert, who served as his attorney general. The *Attorney General's Office* gives visitors a glimpse into Robert Kennedy's tenure heading the Justice Department. As attorney general, Robert Kennedy was a crusader for civil rights. He enforced desegregation laws at universities in Alabama and Mississippi. He also challenged organized crime. In fact, a recent artifact in this exhibit is a toy Teamster truck, which represents RFK's fight against racketeering within the powerful truckers' union. Also included in this exhibit are his personal glasses, pens, and pencils, and his children's drawings.[63] *The Oval Office* is the fifth exhibit. Here, visitors will see a replica of the desk that Kennedy used, along with video clips of speeches he gave from the office about civil rights. This exhibit also displays video footage of Martin Luther King's "I Have a Dream" speech and the enrollment of the first African American students at the University of Alabama.[64]

The final two exhibits are dedicated to the president's family. One is named for his wife, First Lady Jacqueline Bouvier Kennedy. Visitors will see pictures and video clips of the First Lady touring the world and making speeches advocating for the arts. They will also see the famous pink hat and rajah coat she wore during a trip to India.[65] From here, visitors enter the final exhibit, *The Kennedy Family*. This exhibit contains pictures and information about Kennedy's father, Joseph, his grandfather, John "Honey Fitz" Fitzgerald, his mother, Rose Fitzgerald, and his brothers Joseph Jr., Robert, and Edward.[66]

Kennedy's replica Oval Office by Carol Highsmith. *Carol Highsmith LC-HS503-1968*

Special Exhibits   In 2016, the library hosted three special exhibits. One is named *Ernest Hemingway—Between the Wars.* This special exhibit covers the twenty years of Hemingway's life between the two world wars (1919–1939). The exhibit was first held at the Morgan Library & Museum in New York City. Visitors to this special exhibit saw some of the letters written by Hemingway to his father, the notebook he used to write *The Sun Also Rises*, and thirty photographs of Hemingway during this era. The exhibit also contains letters signed by Hemingway's friends, such as Gertrude Stein and F. Scott Fitzgerald, along with some of his personal mementos (dog tags, war medals, and a travel trunk) from the two wars.[67]

The second special exhibit is called *Young Jack*. Here visitors will learn about Kennedy's childhood, his college years, and his time in the navy during World War II. On display is the coconut shell on which he carved a plea for rescue after the *PT-109* was sunk.[68] This exhibit is followed by the actual *Freedom 7* space capsule used by Alan Shepard during his flight into space on May 5, 1961.[69]

Over the years, the library has hosted several temporary exhibits on aspects of Kennedy's presidency. Perhaps the most important was *To the Brink: JFK and the Cuban Missile Crisis.* This exhibit concentrated on the two weeks in October 1962 when it seemed that the United States and the Soviet Union would go to war over the placement of Russian nuclear missiles in Cuba. Visitors saw photos taken during the crisis and heard White House recordings of Kennedy discussing the crisis with his staff.[70]

While the museum primarily showcases exhibits about the Kennedys, it also exhibits art. The library holds twenty thousand artifacts, including busts, vases, portraits of President Kennedy, and dresses owned by Jacqueline Kennedy.[71] There are also interactive video clips on the museum's website, which highlight the major events of Kennedy's administration.[72] Viewers can watch information about the Cuban Missile Crisis, the struggle for civil rights in 1963, and a timeline of Kennedy's life.

The Kennedy library holds a large collection of papers and manuscripts on both the president and his family. According to the library's website, "The Library's holdings include the papers of John F. Kennedy, Robert F. Kennedy, Jacqueline Bouvier Kennedy Onassis, Joseph P. Kennedy and Rose Fitzgerald Kennedy."[73] The library holds fifteen thousand books, graduate theses and dissertations, and periodicals about John F. Kennedy.[74]

Hemingway Collection   The Kennedy library and museum houses the papers of Ernest Hemingway. Kennedy admired Hemmingway's works. The library's website says:

> While Ernest Hemingway and President Kennedy never met, President Kennedy more than once expressed his admiration for Hemingway and his work. In the opening sentence of his own Pulitzer Prize winning book, *Profiles in Courage*, Kennedy cited Hemingway's description of courage, writing that, "This is a book about the most admirable of human virtues—courage. 'Grace under pressure,' Ernest Hemingway defined it."[75]

Hemingway had lived in Cuba. When he died in 1961, many feared that his papers would remain on the island. At that time, Cuba was in the beginning of a long economic embargo. President Kennedy made arrangements for Hemingway's widow, Mary, to visit the island and retrieve his papers. Fidel Castro cooperated with Mary and allowed her to take papers and artwork from Cuba to Florida. A year after Kennedy was assassinated, Mary Hemingway informed Jacqueline Kennedy that she wanted to donate the entire collection to the Kennedy library. The offer was accepted and in 1972 the collection was formally deeded to the library. Mrs. Kennedy Onassis said that the collection would "help to fulfill our hope that the Library will become a center for the study of American civilization, in all its aspects, in these years."[76]

The Hemingway collection consists of one thousand manuscripts, more than ten thousand photos, the first handwritten draft of *The Sun Also Rises,* and forty-four different handwritten endings to *A Farewell to Arms.*[77] It also contains Hemingway's personal collection of bullfighting material, paintings, books from his private library (including a signed copy of *A Draft of XVI Cantos* by Ezra Pound), and the letters of his love interest Agnes von Kurowsky.[78]

Oral History Program

The oral history program at the library is its oldest collection. The collection was started in 1964, funded by the Carnegie Corporation. The goal of the program is to "collect, preserve, and make available interviews conducted with individuals who were associated with the legacy of John F. Kennedy."[79] As of 2016, the program holds a total of sixteen hundred interviews.[80] Some of the more notable oral histories are from Lyndon Johnson, Robert F. Kennedy, and members of the administration.

John F. Kennedy Foundation

The John F. Kennedy Foundation is the organization that raises funds for the library. This foundation was originally the John F. Kennedy Memorial Library Incorporated, which Robert Kennedy initiated to raise money.[81] In 1984 the foundation was reorganized under Massachusetts law and became the nonprofit John F. Kennedy Foundation. According to the library's website, "the Foundation currently employs twenty-six full and part-time staff who worked closely with the Library's federal employees to help fulfill the mission of the John F. Kennedy Presidential Library and Museum."[82] Historian and emeritus foundation director Doris Kearns Goodwin believes the library must preserve Kennedy's legacy for young people. Goodwin said:

> [The library must place Kennedy's] "lifetime into the context of an extraordinary decade when there was a sense of really believing in politics and government and in public action, when people could imagine coming together and doing things to make the country a better place. . . . Even 100 years from now, people coming to see the museum to see the movies will feel connected, not to some stuffy old man, but to a young man who will be forever young.[83]

NOTES

1. Alan Brinkley, *John F. Kennedy,* the American Presidents Series (New York: Times Books, 2012), 8.

2. Brinkley, *John F. Kennedy,* 9.

3. Brinkley, *John F. Kennedy,* 9.

4. Brinkley, *John F. Kennedy,* 9.

5. Brinkley, *John F. Kennedy,* 10.

6. Brinkley, *John F. Kennedy,* 14.

7. Brinkley, *John F. Kennedy,* 13.

8. Brinkley, *John F. Kennedy,* 15.

9. Brinkley, *John F. Kennedy,* 15.

10. Brinkley, *John F. Kennedy,* 19.

11. "MO63.4852 Coconut Shell Paperweight with PT109 Rescue Message," John F. Kennedy Presidential Library and Museum, accessed December 1, 2016, https://www.jfklibrary.org/Asset -Viewer/Ey5l6Vagyk2dwA6BTctDZg.aspx.

12. Robert Dallek, *An Unfinished Life: John F. Kennedy, 1917–1963* (New York: Back Bay Books, 2003), 97.

13. Dallek, *An Unfinished Life,* 132.

14. Seth M. Ridinger, "John F. Kennedy: Public Perception and Campaign Strategy in 1946," *Historical Journal of Massachusetts* 42, no. 2 (Summer 2013): 128.

15. Brinkley, *John F. Kennedy,* 31.

16. Brinkley, *John F. Kennedy,* 33.

17. Brinkley, *John F. Kennedy*, 207.

18. Brinkley, *John F. Kennedy*, 43.

19. Brinkley, *John F. Kennedy*, 42–43.

20. Brinkley, *John F. Kennedy*, 51.

21. Brinkley, *John F. Kennedy*, 51.

22. Brinkley, *John F. Kennedy*, 53.

23. Dallek, *An Unfinished Life*, 323.

24. "John F. Kennedy, XXXV President of the United States: 1961–1963, 1—Inaugural Address," January 20, 1961, The American Presidency Project, accessed December 1, 2016, http://www.presidency.ucsb.edu/ws/?pid=8032.

25. "John F. Kennedy, XXXV President of the United States: 1961–1963, 1—Inaugural Address.".

26. Brinkley, *John F. Kennedy*, 118.

27. "John F. Kennedy: Address on the Cuban Crisis October 22, 1962," Modern History Sourcebook, accessed December 1, 2016, http://sourcebooks.fordham.edu/mod/1962kennedy-cuba.html.

28. Brinkley, *John F. Kennedy*, 123.

29. Brinkley, *John F. Kennedy*, 124.

30. "Radio and Television Report to the American People on Civil Rights, June 11, 1963," John F. Kennedy Presidential Library and Museum, accessed December 1, 2016, https://www.jfklibrary.org/Research/Research-Aids/JFK-Speeches/Civil-Rights-Radio-and-Television-Report_19630611.aspx.

31. "Remarks at the Rudolph Wilde Platz, Berlin," John F. Kennedy Presidential Library and Museum, accessed December 1, 2016, https://www.jfklibrary.org/Asset-Viewer/oEX2uqSQGEGIdTYgd_JL_Q.aspx.

32. Dallek, *An Unfinished Life*, 698.

33. Dallek, *An Unfinished Life*, 698–99.

34. Lydia Saad, "Kennedy Still Highest-Rated Modern President, Nixon Lowest," *Gallup*, December 6, 2010, http://www.gallup.com/poll/145064/Kennedy-Highest-Rated-Modern-President-Nixon-Lowest.aspx.

35. Theodore H. White, "An Epilogue for President Kennedy," *Life*, December 6, 1963, 158–59.

36. Frank L. Schick, Renee Schick, and Mark Carroll, *Records of the Presidency: Presidential Papers and Libraries from Washington to Reagan* (Phoenix, AZ: Oryx Press, 1989), 194.

37. Schick et al., *Records of the Presidency*, 194.

38. Schick et al., *Records of the Presidency*, 195.

39. Schick et al., *Records of the Presidency*, 195.

40. Schick et al., *Records of the Presidency*, 195.

41. Schick et al., *Records of the Presidency*, 195.

42. Schick et al., *Records of the Presidency*, 195.

43. Schick et al., *Records of the Presidency*, 196.

44. Schick et al., *Records of the Presidency*, 196.

45. Schick et al., *Records of the Presidency*, 196.

46. Schick et al., *Records of the Presidency*, 196–97.

47. Schick et al., *Records of the Presidency*, 197.

48. Schick et al., *Records of the Presidency*, 197.

49. Schick et al., *Records of the Presidency*, 197–98.

50. Schick et al., *Records of the Presidency*, 198.

51. William G. Clotworthy, *Homes and Libraries of the Presidents: An Interpretive Guide*, third edition (Blacksburg, VA: McDonald & Woodward, 2008), 271.

52. Carl M. Brauer, "John F. Kennedy Presidential Library and Museum," *Public Historian* 28, no. 3 (Summer 2006): 195.

53. Bauer, "John F. Kennedy," 195.

54. Matt Rocheleau, "Fire at JFK Library Caused by Discarded Smoking Material," *Boston Globe*, April 19, 2013, https://www.bostonglobe.com/metro/2013/04/18/jfk-fire-caused-smoking-materials/Ie17JZl0T0zpSzbMwLuWgL/story.html.

55. Sarah Schweitzer, "JFK Library Foundation Selects First Female Chief." *Boston Globe*, January 28, 2014, https://www.bostonglobe.com/metro/2014/01/28/heather-campion-named-chief-executive-john-kennedy-library-foundation/MyakTuq7tTbD603k42qILM/story.html.

56. Jim O'Sullivan, "JFK Library Sees Exodus as New CEO, Strategy Draw Complaints," *Boston Globe*, August 5, 2015, https://www.bostonglobe.com/metro/2015/08/05/kennedy-library-sees-mass-exodus-new-and-veteran-employees/FL43CXMIIGU397FzS1zwJL/story.html.

57. Jim O'Sullivan, "New Chief Named for JFK Library Foundation," *Boston Globe*, August 30, 2016, https://www.bostonglobe.com/metro/2016/08/30/new-chief-chosen-for-jfk-library/uZJrWj3sgqxf8uFdxjQNMO/story.html.

58. "Administration and Staff," John F. Kennedy Presidential Library and Museum, accessed December 1, 2016, https://www.jfklibrary.org/About-Us/About-the-JFK-Library/Library-Administration-and-Staff.aspx.

59. Wendy R. Ginsberg, Erika K. Lunder, and Daniel J. Richardson, *The Presidential Libraries Act and the Establishment of Presidential Libraries* (CRS Report No. R41513) (Washington, DC: Congressional Research Service, 2015), 28.

60. "Campaign Trail," John F. Kennedy Presidential Library and Museum, accessed December 1, 2016, https://www.jfklibrary.org/Exhibits/Permanent-Exhibits/Campaign-Trail.aspx.

61. "The Briefing Room," John F. Kennedy Presidential Library and Museum, accessed December 1, 2016, https://www.jfklibrary.org/Exhibits/Permanent-Exhibits/Briefing-Room.aspx.

62. "The Space Race," John F. Kennedy Presidential Library and Museum, accessed December 1, 2016, https://www.jfklibrary.org/Exhibits/Permanent-Exhibits/The-Space-Race.aspx.

63. "Attorney General's Office," John F. Kennedy Presidential Library and Museum, accessed December 1, 2016, https://www.jfklibrary.org/Exhibits/Permanent-Exhibits/Attorney-Generals-Office.aspx.

64. "The Oval Office," John F. Kennedy Presidential Library and Museum, accessed December 1, 2016, https://www.jfklibrary.org/Exhibits/Permanent-Exhibits/The-Oval-Office.aspx.

65. "First Lady Jacqueline Bouvier Kennedy," John F. Kennedy Presidential Library and Museum, accessed December 1, 2016, https://www.jfklibrary.org/Exhibits/Permanent-Exhibits/First-Lady-Jacqueline-Bouvier-Kennedy.aspx.

66. "The Kennedy Family," John F. Kennedy Presidential Library and Museum, accessed December 1, 2016, https://www.jfklibrary.org/Exhibits/Permanent-Exhibits/The-Kennedy-Family.aspx.

67. "Ernest Hemingway—Between Two Wars," John F. Kennedy Presidential Library and Museum, accessed December 1, 2016, https://www.jfklibrary.org/Exhibits/Special-Exhibits/Hemingway-Between-Two-Wars.aspx.

68. "Young Jack," John F. Kennedy Presidential Library and Museum, accessed December 1, 2016, https://www.jfklibrary.org/Exhibits/Special-Exhibits/Young-Jack.aspx.

69. "*Freedom* 7 Space Capsule," John F. Kennedy Presidential Library and Museum, accessed December 1, 2016, https://www.jfklibrary.org/Exhibits/Special-Exhibits/Freedom-7-Space-Capsule.aspx.

70. "To the Brink: JFK and the Cuban Missile Crisis," John F. Kennedy Presidential Library and Museum, accessed December 1, 2016, https://www.jfklibrary.org/Exhibits/Past-Exhibits/To-The-Brink-JFK-and-the-Cuban-Missile-Crisis.aspx.

71. "Highlights from the Museum Artifacts Collection," John F. Kennedy Presidential Library and Museum, accessed December 1, 2016, https://www.jfklibrary.org/Exhibits/Museum-Artifacts.aspx.

72. "Interactives," John F. Kennedy Presidential Library and Museum, accessed December 1, 2016, https://www.jfklibrary.org/Exhibits/Interactives.aspx.

73. "About Our Collections," John F. Kennedy Presidential Library and Museum, accessed December 1, 2016, https://www.jfklibrary.org/Research/About-Our-Collections.aspx.

74. Schick et al., *Records of the Presidency*.

75. "History of the Collection: John F. Kennedy and Ernest Hemingway," John F. Kennedy Presidential Library and Museum, accessed December 1, 2016, https://www.jfklibrary.org/Research/The-Ernest-Hemingway-Collection/History-of-the-Hemingway-Collection.aspx.

76. "History of the Collection: John F. Kennedy and Ernest Hemingway."

77. "Highlights," John F. Kennedy Presidential Library and Museum, accessed December 1, 2016, https://www.jfklibrary.org/Research/The-Ernest-Hemingway-Collection/Highlights.aspx.

78. "Highlights."

79. "Oral History Program," John F. Kennedy Presidential Library and Museum, accessed December 1, 2016, https://www.jfklibrary.org/Research/About-Our-Collections/Oral-history-program.aspx.

80. "Oral History Program."

81. "JFK Library Foundation," John F. Kennedy Presidential Library and Museum, accessed December 1, 2016, https://www.jfklibrary.org/About-Us/JFK-Library-Foundation.aspx.

82. "JFK Library Foundation."

83. Schweitzer, "JFK Library Foundation Selects First Female Chief."

BIBLIOGRAPHY

Brauer, Carl M. "John F. Kennedy Presidential Library and Museum." *Public Historian* 28, no. 3 (Summer 2006): 194–97.

Brinkley, Alan. *John F. Kennedy.* The American Presidents Series. New York: Times Books, 2012.

Clotworthy, William G. *Homes and Libraries of the Presidents: An Interpretive Guide.* Third edition. Blacksburg, VA: McDonald & Woodward, 2008.

Dallek, Robert. *An Unfinished Life: John F. Kennedy, 1917–1963.* New York: Back Bay Books, 2003.

Ginsberg, Wendy R., Erika K. Lunder, and Daniel J. Richardson. *The Presidential Libraries Act and the Establishment of Presidential Libraries* (CRS Report No. R41513). Washington, DC: Congressional Research Service, 2015.

Hufbauer, Benjamin. *Presidential Temples: How Memorials and Libraries Shape Public Memory.* Lawrence: University Press of Kansas, 2005.

O'Sullivan, Jim. "JFK Library Sees Exodus as New CEO, Strategy Draw Complaints." *Boston Globe,* August 5, 2015. https://www.bostonglobe.com/metro/2015/08/05/kennedy-library-sees-mass-exodus-new-and-veteran-employees/FL43CXMIIGU397FzS1zwJL/story.html.

———. "New Chief Named for JFK Library Foundation." *Boston Globe,* August 30, 2016. https://www.bostonglobe.com/metro/2016/08/30/new-chief-chosen-for-jfk-library/uZJrWj3sgqxf8uFdxjQNMO/story.html.

Ridinger, Seth M. "John F. Kennedy: Public Perception and Campaign Strategy in 1946." *Historical Journal of Massachusetts* 42, no. 2 (Summer 2013): 112–35.

Rocheleau, Matt. "Fire at JFK Library Caused by Discarded Smoking Material." *Boston Globe*, April 19, 2013. https://www.bostonglobe.com/metro/2013/04/18/jfk-fire-caused-smoking -materials/Ie17JZl0T0zpSzbMwLuWgL/story.html.

Saad, Lydia. "Kennedy Still Highest-Rated Modern President, Nixon Lowest." *Gallup*, December 6, 2010. http://www.gallup.com/poll/145064/Kennedy-Highest-Rated-Modern-President -Nixon-Lowest.aspx.

Schick, Frank L., Renee Schick, and Mark Carroll. *Records of the Presidency: Presidential Papers and Libraries from Washington to Reagan*. Phoenix, AZ: Oryx Press, 1989.

Schweitzer, Sarah. "JFK Library Foundation Selects First Female Chief." *Boston Globe*, January 28, 2014. https://www.bostonglobe.com/metro/2014/01/28/heather-campion-named-chief -executive-john-kennedy-library-foundation/MyakTuq7tTbD603k42qILM/story.html.

White, Theodore H. "An Epilogue for President Kennedy." *Life*, December 6, 1963, 158–59.

Lyndon Baines Johnson
Presidential Library and Museum

BIOGRAPHY OF LYNDON BAINES JOHNSON

August 27, 1908–January 22, 1973
Thirty-Sixth President: November 22, 1963–January 20, 1969
Democratic Party

LBJ and Lady Bird by Yoichi Okamoto, 1968. *Courtesy of the LBJ Presidential Library and Museum*

Lyndon Baines Johnson was born in Stonewall, Texas, to Samuel Ealy Johnson Jr. and Rebekah Baines Johnson. He was one of five brothers and sisters. Young Lyndon knew the meaning of hardship as a child; the family lived in a house with no running water or electricity. When he became president he vowed to help the underprivileged. According to Robert Dallak, Lyndon B. Johnson was the "poor boy from Texas" who "identified with and viscerally experienced the sufferings of the disadvantaged."[1] Lyndon graduated from Johnson City High School at the age of sixteen and went on to attend Southwest State Texas Teachers College in San Marcos. He graduated in 1930 and became a teacher in Houston.

In 1934 Lyndon married Claudia Alta "Lady Bird" Taylor. They would have two daughters: Lynda Bird and Luci Baines. During the same year, he quit teaching to work as a secretary for Congressman Richard Mifflin Kleberg. In 1937 Johnson ran for a congressional seat and won. In Congress he supported President Franklin Roosevelt's New Deal programs. After losing a senate bid in 1941, he went on to serve in the navy. When World War II ended, he left the navy and returned to Texas. He was elected to the United States Senate, where he rose to become the majority leader in 1955. Senator Johnson was chosen by John F. Kennedy to be his running mate in 1960. Together they defeated Republican opponents Vice President Richard Nixon and Ambassador Henry Cabot Lodge Jr.

Johnson served as vice president until Kennedy was assassinated in Dallas on November 22, 1963. Upon assuming the presidency, Johnson had the duty to "convince everyone everywhere that the country would go forward."[2] As president, Johnson saw it as his task to continue the liberal traditions of Roosevelt and Kennedy. On April 24, 1964, Johnson took a trip to Appalachia to view the substandard conditions in the mountain region. He stopped in the town of Inez, Kentucky, where he met with the family of Tom Fletcher. The Fletcher family consisted of Tom, his wife, and eight children, all of whom lived in a three-room shack. According to historian Michael L. Gillette, Johnson was even more astonished by the fact that the family lived on a meager $400 a year and that two of the children had already dropped out of school.[3] President Johnson did not forget the plight of the Fletcher family. When he returned to Washington, he fired the first salvo in his War on Poverty by stating, "I don't know if I'll pass a single law or get a single dollar appropriated, but before I'm through, no community in America will be able to ignore poverty in its midst."[4] The War on Poverty was part of Johnson's larger program known as the Great Society, which provided federal assistance (money) for education, food stamps, and public works projects.[5]

Johnson wanted to create a national program akin to Franklin Roosevelt's New Deal. A month before his Appalachian trip, he signed the Economic Opportunity Act, which created a series of new government programs aimed at fighting poverty. Johnson wanted a program that could be identified with his administration. According to Dallek, a Princeton historian named Eric Goldman proposed the term "Good Society," which was the name of a book written by Walter Lippmann; Johnson liked the name, but changed it to "Great Society."[6] Two of the most noteworthy programs were Volunteers in Service to America (VISTA), which acted like a "domestic Peace Corps," and the Office of Economic Opportunity.[7] The programs were largely community based and aimed to provide education and jobs to people who were less fortunate.

Johnson's Great Society also extended into the realm of health care. Two of the most important federal health programs, Medicare and Medicaid, were created in late 1964. Medicare provided government health care to people aged 65 and over, while Medicaid is a "medical welfare program for the indigent administered through the states."[8]

Despite being a Southerner, Johnson championed civil rights for African Americans. Segregation and discrimination were still obstacles for racial minorities in the American South. After Kennedy's death, Johnson believed that it was imperative to tackle the "moral issue" of civil rights once and for all.[9] Johnson pushed through both the House and the Senate the Civil Rights Act of 1964. He knew how to use the presidency to persuade legislators. To make sure the law met as little resistance as possible, Johnson warned senators that anyone opposing the law would have a "price to pay."[10]

President Johnson sought and won the Democratic Party's nomination for president in 1964. Senator Hubert H. Humphrey of Minnesota was chosen to be his running mate. Meanwhile, there was a revolution of sorts within the Republican Party: Senator Barry Goldwater won the party's nomination over the establishment candidate, Governor Nelson Rockefeller of New York. Goldwater broke ranks with his party by promoting an aggressive anti-Communist foreign policy and strict fiscal conservativism. The Republicans promoted Goldwater with the bumper-sticker slogan: "In your heart you know he's right."[11] The Democrats fought back with a slogan of their own: "Yes, far right."[12] Johnson's campaign strategy involved "emphasizing Goldwater's extremism and the dangers of trusting him with the powers of the presidency."[13] That year, the Democrats used what has become known as the "Daisy" commercial. In this television commercial, a little girl is seen pulling the petals off a daisy while counting them. Suddenly, a man's voice is heard counting down while the camera zooms in on the girl's face. Next, a nuclear bomb is seen exploding. The message was simple: a vote for Goldwater was a vote for nuclear war.[14] On election night, Johnson achieved a resounding victory over Goldwater. Johnson won 43,127,041 popular votes and carried 486 electoral votes, compared with Goldwater's 27,175,754 popular votes and 52 electoral votes.

While Johnson promoted his Great Society at home, the situation in Vietnam grew more intense. The United States had sent American troops as advisors to South Vietnam, which was fighting a war against their communist neighbor, North Vietnam. On the morning of August 2, 1964, the American destroyer *Maddox* reported being attacked by North Vietnamese torpedo boats in the Gulf of Tonkin. The commander of the *Maddox* was not sure if his ship had been attacked and theorized that it may have been a "freak weather event" that had been mistaken as an attack.[15] Either way, the Navy was convinced that there had been an attack and persuaded Johnson to use military action. Johnson went to Congress and obtained approval to use military force with the Gulf of Tonkin Resolution. The resolution gave Johnson a "blank check" to go to war against North Vietnam.[16] The combination of North Vietnam's jungle and guerilla warfare tactics and the Viet Cong rebels in South Vietnam made victory hard to achieve. Also disturbing was the draft, which made many younger Americans fear that they would have to go to war.

By the summer of 1966, America had three hundred twenty-five thousand troops fighting in Vietnam.[17] Johnson used massive American airpower to support the troops. An air operation known as Rolling Thunder called for a bombing campaign against enemy targets. On January 30, 1968, North Vietnamese troops and Viet Cong rebels launched a surprise attack in South Vietnam, known as the Tet Offensive. Up to 1968, popular opinion held that the United States was winning. However, the offensive was so shocking that television journalist Walter Cronkite reacted by asking, "What the hell is going on? I thought we were winning the war."[18] The voices of the anti-war protestors grew louder as they chanted the popular phrase against Johnson and the war: "Hey!

Hey! LBJ! How many kids did you kill today?"[19] However, Johnson refused to stop the war. He remembered how the allies abandoned Czechoslovakia (now the Czech Republic and Slovakia) to Hitler, which eventually led to World War II. To Johnson, "abandoning" South Vietnam to the Communists could lead to World War III.[20]

In 1968 Johnson decided to seek a second term as president. His approval ratings were low as a result of the war in Vietnam. Democratic senator Eugene McCarthy challenged Johnson for the nomination solely on the antiwar issue. During the New Hampshire Democratic primary, Johnson narrowly defeated McCarthy by 7 percent. Johnson knew the results were devastating for a sitting president. Shortly thereafter, in a speech Johnson made from the Oval Office, he said, "I shall not seek, and I will not accept, the nomination of my party for another term as your President."[21] The Democrats nominated Johnson's vice president, Hubert H. Humphrey. Humphrey narrowly lost the election to Richard Nixon.

When Nixon took office in January 1969, Johnson retired to his Texas ranch. He died of a heart attack there on January 22, 1973. Johnson is buried at the Lyndon B. Johnson National Historical Park in Stonewall, Texas. His wife, Lady Bird, died on July 11, 2007. She is buried next to her husband.

LIBRARY AND MUSEUM

Johnson began contemplating his presidential library in the spring of 1965; he said, "I want to have the greatest library ever in the world."[22] Earlier, in 1962, his alma mater, Southwest Texas State University in San Marcos, made a request to store his papers.[23] However, Johnson declined their offer because he "both admired and resented" the college.[24] Attorney General Nicholas Katzenbach suggested that Johnson build his library at Harvard University. Being a Southerner, Johnson thought Harvard had too much of a "hold on government positions."[25] Johnson's wife, Lady Bird, started negotiating with her alma mater, the University of Texas at Austin, as a potential site for the library. University board member William W. Heath, who was related to the president, made an offer to donate land for the library and even fund it.[26] Johnson settled on the University of Texas as the best place. The university promised to put $18 million toward the construction of the library.[27] Most importantly, the university also promised to create a graduate School of Public Affairs "with endowed chairs and projects related to the War on Poverty and other Johnson efforts."[28] On August 9, 1965, Johnson formally accepted the agreement with the university. In his letter of acceptance, he stated:

> The fine public spirit and magnificent generosity that have prompted the University of Texas to make this unexampled offer of a site and structure for use as a Presidential Library should earn it the respect of the entire nation.[29]

A minor problem faced by the library was that the university could not "legally deed its land to the federal government."[30] However, the Presidential Library Act did allow the archivist of the United States to "make agreements" with institutions of higher learning to use land as a depository of presidential materials "without transfer of title to the United States."[31]

In addition to the legal problems, Johnson and his library had a personal one. According to Benjamin Hufbauer, as president, Johnson found himself overshadowed by the legacy of John F. Kennedy.[32] The Johnson library "competed—successfully, in most respects—with the John F. Kennedy Library in Boston for its architectural distinction, attendance, academic affiliation, and completion date."[33] Johnson needed a library that would reflect his personality.[34] He contracted with New York architect Gordon Bunshaft, who built skyscrapers for many reputable corporations. Bunshaft borrowed architectural styles from Roman, Egyptian, and Japanese history. Bunshaft said, "The President was a really virile man, and he ought to have a vigorous, male building."[35] Upon its completion, the Johnson library became the largest federally operated presidential library.[36]

On May 22, 1971, the library was dedicated in front of a crowd of over four thousand spectators, including President Richard Nixon and Vice President Spiro Agnew. In his ceremonial speech, Johnson said: "It is all here: the story of our time with the bark off. . . . This library will show the facts, not just the joy and triumphs, but the sorrow and failures, too."[37]

The current director of the library is Mark K. Updegrove, who has been in the role since October 2009. Previously, Updegrove was manager of *Time* magazine in Los Angeles and president of *Time Canada*. Updegrove was present during the library's Civil Rights Summit in October 2014. The summit was attended by President Barack Obama and his wife Michelle, along with George W. Bush, Laura Bush, Bill Clinton, and Jimmy Carter. In 2016 Updegrove directed the library during the Vietnam War Summit.[38] The library welcomed 87,411 visitors in 2012.[39]

The front (facing south) of the Lyndon Baines Johnson Presidential Library and Museum. *Courtesy of the LBJ Presidential Library and Museum*

Collections and Exhibits

Visitors begin their journey through the permanent exhibits with one titled *Civil Rights*. Here, visitors will be introduced to the various civil rights laws that Johnson implemented as president and the achievements that were made during his presidency. The desk that Johnson sat at when he signed the Voting Rights Act of 1965 is on display, along with an interactive table displaying the social programs he signed into action, such as Head Start, and letters from ordinary Americans who benefited from the programs.[40]

From *Civil Rights*, visitors walk into the next exhibit, titled *November 22, 1963*, where they will see how Johnson made the transition from vice president to president following Kennedy's assassination. The exhibit displays several images from that day, such as a photograph of Johnson taking the oath of office aboard Air Force One. Through a telephone receiver, visitors can listen to some of the real conversations that took place on that day.[41]

Following the *November 22, 1963* exhibit is the *The Legacy Gallery*. Here visitors will learn how much of the legislation implemented under Johnson, known as the Great Society, still affects them today. For example, visitors will learn how Johnson started financial aid for college students, protected civil rights, established the Public Broadcasting Service (the home of *Sesame Street*), and introduced Medicare health insurance for senior citizens.[42]

The Legacy Gallery is followed by the *Social Justice Gallery*. In this exhibit, visitors will learn more about the various legislative initiatives passed by the Johnson Administration. Images and interactive media explore Johnson's contributions to civil rights, national parks, public broadcasting, consumer protection, Medicare, and alleviating poverty.[43]

Following the *Social Justice Gallery* visitors walk into the *White House Years* exhibit, where they can see photographs and artifacts from the time of the Johnson administration. Inside is a pair of cowboy boots owned by the former president, gifts—including a ceremonial sword from Saudi Arabia and two sculptures from China—and information about life on Johnson's ranch in Texas.[44] On a more comical note, visitors will enjoy the *Humor and the Presidency* exhibit, where a life-size "animatronic" president is surrounded by political cartoons. Visitors can also listen to audio recordings of jokes he told during his presidency.[45]

The final two permanent exhibits focus on Johnson's Oval Office and his presidential limousine. *The Oval Office* is on the tenth floor of the library and is on a scale of 7/8 of the size of the original. Inside, visitors will see exactly how the office looked when Johnson used it in the 1960s, including the three television sets that he kept next to his desk.[46] Finally, *LBJ's Presidential Limousine* displays the real custom-built black stretch limousine that he started using in 1968. The limousine weighs fifty-one hundred pounds and has a television, a telephone, and a reserve gas tank. Surprisingly, the limousine is not bulletproof.[47]

In 2016 the library held a temporary exhibit, *The National Parks Photography Project*. The exhibit showcased the photography of Mark Burns, who captured images from all fifty-nine federal parks. The photographs are all black and white.[48]

Online Exhibits   The Johnson library also has several online exhibits allowing remote visits to the library with the use of the Internet. One online exhibit, *Sixty from the 60s*,

The Oval Office exhibit at the Lyndon Baines Johnson Library by Gary Phelps. *Courtesy of the LBJ Presidential Library and Museum*

allows online visitors to zoom in on pictures, posters, and statues of sixty famous people from the 1960s.[49] *The Whistle Stop Tour, 1964* presents a map where you can follow the train route Johnson took to the American South during the presidential election of 1964.[50] *The Vietnam Conflict* allows online visitors to search and view photographs and videos from the time of the Vietnam War, and read information about how Johnson dealt with the conflict. Viewers can listen to speeches and read parts of Johnson's diary.[51] *Tragedy and Transition* focuses on November 22, 1963, the day when Johnson took the helm of the presidency following the assassination of Kennedy. Online visitors can search and view photos and documents related to the transition.[52] *The 1934 Courtship Letters* online exhibit shows some of the love letters written between Johnson and his future wife, Lady Bird.[53] Finally, *Artifact of the Week* publishes information about various artifacts in the museum online. Some of the chosen artifacts include a boxing glove signed by Muhammad Ali, a painting by Dwight D. Eisenhower, stamps, and portraits of famous politicians, including former House Speaker Sam Rayburn.[54]

Manuscripts and Oral Histories   The Johnson library holds around "forty-five million documents related to Johnson and his presidency."[55] Researchers will find the diary Johnson kept every day, photographs, audiovisual materials, recordings of telephone conversations, and oral histories.[56] The library also holds approximately ten thousand "books about history, political science, and military affairs.[57] Like other presidential libraries, the Johnson library holds its own collection of two thousand oral histories.[58] Some of the most notable oral histories are from well-known figures from Johnson's time as president, including Texas congressman Lloyd Bentsen, United

States attorney general Ramsey Clark, television journalist John Chancellor, Evangelist Billy Graham, Vice President Hubert Humphrey, United States Supreme Court justice Thurgood Marshall, Secretary of Defense Robert McNamara, and union leader Asa Philip Randolph.[59]

NOTES

1. Dallek, Robert, *Lyndon B. Johnson: Portrait of a President* (New York: Oxford University Press, 2004), 163

2. Dallek, *Lyndon B. Johnson*, 145.

3. Michael L. Gillette, *Launching the War on Poverty: An Oral History*, second edition (New York: Oxford University Press, 2010), xi.

4. Gillette, *War on Poverty*, xi.

5. Gillette, *War on Poverty*, xi–xii.

6. Dallek, *Lyndon B. Johnson*, 156.

7. Dallek, *Lyndon B. Johnson*, 154.

8. Dallek, *Lyndon B. Johnson*, 199.

9. Dallek, *Lyndon B. Johnson*, 163.

10. Dallek, *Lyndon B. Johnson*, 166.

11. Dallek, *Lyndon B. Johnson*, 184.

12. Dallek, *Lyndon B. Johnson*, 184.

13. Dallek, *Lyndon B. Johnson*, 184.

14. "Peace Little Girl (Daisy) (Johnson, 1964)," The Living Room Candidate: Presidential Campaign Commercials 1952–2016, Museum of the Moving Image, accessed January 14, 2017, www.livingroomcandidate.org/commercials/1964/peace-little-girl-daisy.

15. Dallek, *Lyndon B. Johnson*, 178.

16. Dallek, *Lyndon B. Johnson*, 179.

17. Dallek, *Lyndon B. Johnson*, 255.

18. David F. Schmitz, *Richard Nixon and the Vietnam War: The End of the American Century* (Lanham, MD: Rowman & Littlefield, 2014), 26.

19. Lexington, "Hey! Hey! LBJ! What the Current Fascination for Lyndon Johnson Says about Barack Obama's America," *Economist*, October 3, 2013, http://www.economist.com/news/united-states/21586830-what-current-fascination-lyndon-johnson-says-about-barack-obamas-america-hey-hey.

20. Dallek, *Lyndon B. Johnson*, 209.

21. Dallek, *Lyndon B. Johnson*, 332.

22. Frank L. Schick, Renee Schick, and Mark Carroll, *Records of the Presidency: Presidential Papers and Libraries from Washington to Reagan* (Phoenix, AZ: Oryx Press, 1989), 208.

23. Schick et al., *Records of the Presidency*, 206.

24. Benjamin Hufbauer, *Presidential Temples: How Memorials and Libraries Shape Public Memory* (Lawrence: University Press of Kansas, 2005), 73.

25. Hufbauer, *Presidential Temples*, 73.

26. Hufbauer, *Presidential Temples*, 74.

27. Hufbauer, *Presidential Temples*, 73.

28. Schick et al., *Records of the Presidency*, 207.

29. Schick et al., *Records of the Presidency*, 208.

30. Wendy R. Ginsberg, Erika K. Lunder, and Daniel J. Richardson, *The Presidential Libraries Act and the Establishment of Presidential Libraries* (CRS Report No. R41513) (Washington, DC: Congressional Research Service, 2015), 4.

31. Ginsburg, Lunder, and Richardson, *Presidential Libraries Act*, 4.

32. Hufbauer, *Presidential Temples*, 71.

33. Hufbauer *Presidential Temples*, 71.

34. Hufbauer, *Presidential Temples*, 68.

35. Hufbauer, *Presidential Temples*, 83.

36. "Frequently Asked Questions," National Archives, accessed February 3, 2017, https://www.archives.gov.presidential-libraries/about/faqs.html.

37. "LBJ Presidential Library," LBJ Presidential Library, accessed February 3, 2017, http://www.lbjlibrary.org/page/library-museum/.

38. "About the Director," LBJ Presidential Library, accessed February 3, 2017, http://www.lbjlibrary.org/page/library-museum/about-the-director.

39. Ginsburg, Lunder, and Richardson, *Presidential Libraries Act*, 28.

40. "Civil Rights," LBJ Presidential Library, accessed February 3, 2017, http://www.lbjlibrary.org/exhibits/civil-rights/.

41. "November 22, 1963," LBJ Presidential Library, accessed February 3, 2017, http://www.lbjlibrary.org/exhibits/november-22-1963/.

42. "The Legacy Gallery," LBJ Presidential Library, accessed February 3, 2017, http://www.lbjlibrary.org/exhibits/the-legacy-gallery/.

43. "Social Justice Gallery," LBJ Presidential Library, accessed February 3, 2017, http://www.lbjlibrary.org/exhibits/social-justice-gallery/.

44. "The White House Years," LBJ Presidential Library, accessed February 3, 2017, http://www.lbjlibrary.org/exhibits/the-white-house-years.

45. "Humor and the Presidency," LBJ Presidential Library, accessed February 3, 2017, http://www.lbjlibrary.org/exhibits/humor-and-the-presidency.

46. "The Oval Office," LBJ Presidential Library, accessed February 3, 2017, http://www.lbjlibrary.org/exhibits/the-oval-office/.

47. "LBJ's Presidential Limousine," LBJ Presidential Library, accessed February 3, 2017, http://www.lbjlibrary.org/exhibits/lbjs-presidential-limousine/.

48. "The National Parks Photography Project," LBJ Presidential Library, accessed February 3, 2017, http://www.lbjlibrary.org/exhibits/the-national-parks-photography-project.

49. "Sixty from the '60s," LBJ Presidential Library, accessed February 3, 2017, http://www.lbjlibrary.org/exhibits/sixty-from-the-60s.

50. "Whistle Stop Tour, 1964," LBJ Presidential Library, accessed February 3, 2017, http://whistlestop.lbjlibrary.org/.

51. "Vietnam," LBJ Presidential Library, accessed February 3, 2017, http://www.lbjlibrary.org/exhibits/the-vietnam-conflict.

52. "Nov. 22, 1963: Tragedy and Transition," LBJ Presidential Library, accessed February 3, 2017, http://transition.lbjlibrary.org/.

53. "The 1934 Courtship Letters," LBJ Presidential Library, accessed February 3, 2017, http://www.lbjlibrary.org/exhibits/the-1934-courtship-letters.

54. "Artifact of the Week," LBJ Presidential Library, accessed February 3, 2017, http://www.lbjlibrary.org/exhibits/artifact-of-the-week/.

55. William G. Clotworthy, *Homes and Libraries of the Presidents: An Interpretive Guide*, third edition (Blacksburg, VA: McDonald & Woodward, 2008), 278.

56. "Research," LBJ Presidential Library, accessed February 3, 2017, http://www.lbjlibrary.org/research.

57. Allen Fischer (archivist, LBJ Presidential Library), telephone interview with the author, January 2017.

58. "Research," LBJ Presidential Library, accessed February 3, 2017, http://www.lbjlibrary.org/research/.

59. "Oral Histories," LBJ Presidential Library, accessed February 3, 2017, http://www.lbjlibrary.net/collections/oral-histories/.

BIBLIOGRAPHY

Caro, Robert. *The Path to Power: The Years of Lyndon Johnson, Volume 1.* New York: Vintage, 1990.

Clotworthy, William G. *Homes and Libraries of the Presidents: An Interpretive Guide.* Third edition. Blacksburg, VA: McDonald & Woodward, 2008.

Dallek, Robert. *Lyndon B. Johnson: Portrait of a President.* New York: Oxford University Press, 2004.

Gillette, Michael L. *Launching the War on Poverty: An Oral History.* Second edition. New York: Oxford University Press, 2010.

Ginsberg, Wendy R., Erika K. Lunder, and Daniel J. Richardson. *The Presidential Libraries Act and the Establishment of Presidential Libraries* (CRS Report No. R41513). Washington, DC: Congressional Research Service, 2015.

Hufbauer, Benjamin. *Presidential Temples: How Memorials and Libraries Shape Public Memory.* Lawrence: University Press of Kansas, 2005.

Schick, Frank L., Renee Schick, and Mark Carroll. *Records of the Presidency: Presidential Papers and Libraries from Washington to Reagan.* Phoenix, AZ: Oryx Press, 1989.

Schmitz, David F. *Richard Nixon and the Vietnam War: The End of the American Century.* Lanham, MD: Rowman & Littlefield, 2014.

Richard Nixon Presidential Library and Museum

Address: 18001 Yorba Linda Blvd., Yorba Linda, CA
Phone: (714) 983-9120
Website: https://www.nixonlibrary.gov/
Social media: https://www.facebook.com/NixonPresidentialLibrary
Administration: National Archives
Hours: 10 a.m. to 5 p.m., Monday to Saturday; 11 a.m. to 5 p.m. on Sundays

BIOGRAPHY OF RICHARD NIXON

January 9, 1913–April 22, 1994
Thirty-Seventh President: January 20, 1969–August 9, 1974
Republican Party

Richard Nixon. *LC-USZ62-13037*

Richard Milhous Nixon was born in Yorba Linda, California, to Francis A. and Hannah Milhous Nixon. He was the second of five sons. Nixon's family lived in a home that was built by his father. When Richard was about nine years old, the family moved to Whittier, California, where his father ran a gas station and later a grocery store. The Nixons were Quakers and attended church regularly.[1] Richard taught himself to read; later, he attended a local school, where he performed very well. As early as grade school, Richard took part in debate and politics. Upon graduating from Whittier High School he enrolled at nearby Whittier College. From there, he went on to attend Duke University Law School in 1934.

After graduating from Duke, Nixon returned to Whittier and opened a law practice. In 1938 he married Thelma (Pat) Ryan. They had two daughters: Patricia, known as Tricia, and Julie. In 1942 Nixon took a job in Washington, DC, at the Office of Price Administration, where government rules and bureaucracy left a bitter taste in his mouth.[2] During

World War II, Nixon served in the navy as a lieutenant, but he saw no action.[3] After the war, in 1946, Nixon went into politics, defeating liberal Democratic congressman Horace Jeremiah "Jerry" Voorhis. In Congress, Nixon became a member of the House Un-American Activities Committee and fought Communist infiltration into America. Nixon spearheaded the drive to expose former State Department official Alger Hiss as a Soviet spy. After serving two terms in Congress, Nixon ran for, and won, a seat in the United States Senate. During his senatorial campaign, Nixon earned the nickname "Tricky Dick" for using anti-Communist scare tactics during the Red Scare of the 1950s.[4]

Two years later, in 1952, Nixon was nominated as General Dwight Eisenhower's vice presidential running mate. As soon as Nixon was nominated he was accused of being the beneficiary of a secret fund created by political supporters in California.[5] On the night of September 23, Nixon made a live appearance on television to defend himself in what is known as the "Checkers speech." In this speech, Nixon said that the accusations were false and in "retribution for his recent effectiveness as an anti-communist crusader."[6] Nixon also humanized himself by telling a story about a dog he received as a gift for his daughters:

> One other thing I probably should tell you, because if I don't they will probably be saying this about me, too. We did get something, a gift, after the election. . . . You know what it was? It was a little cocker spaniel dog . . . black and white, spotted, and our little girl Tricia, the six-year-old, named it Checkers. And you know, the kids, like all kids, loved the dog, and I just want to say this, right now, that regardless of what they say about it, we're going to keep it.[7]

The Checkers speech was popular and preserved Nixon's spot as vice president under Eisenhower.[8] That November, Eisenhower was elected president over his Democratic rival, Governor Adlai E. Stevenson of Illinois.

Nixon served two terms as Eisenhower's vice president. His most memorable event as vice president took place in Moscow, in what is known as the Kitchen Debate. In 1959, Nixon visited Soviet premier Nikita Khrushchev at the American exhibition, where replica American kitchens were on display. While the two toured the exhibition they sparred over the virtues of Capitalism and Communism.[9]

In 1960 Nixon won the Republican nomination for president. He chose Ambassador Henry Cabot Lodge Jr. as his running mate. The Democrats nominated Senator John F. Kennedy of Massachusetts and Senator Lyndon B. Johnson of Texas as their candidates. That year, the first televised presidential debates were held. The initial debate did not go well for Nixon. Television viewers thought Kennedy, in his dark suit, looked far more confident than Nixon, who wore a gray suit and whose face looked pale.[10] On the night of the election Kennedy won the narrowest victory in American history by just over one hundred thousand votes.[11] Despite this loss, Nixon did not give up on politics. In 1962 he unsuccessfully challenged Governor Pat Brown for governor of California. Six years later he ran for president once again and won the Republican Party's nomination. His running mate was Governor Spiro Agnew of Maryland. Nixon was running against the Democratic vice president Hubert Humphrey and third-party candidate George Wallace of Alabama. This time, Nixon won by a narrow margin, with "43.4 percent of the vote to Humphrey's 42.7 and Wallace's 13.5."[12]

When Nixon became president he promised to end the Vietnam War by handing over military responsibilities to South Vietnam while gradually withdrawing American forces. He called this policy Vietnamization.[13] To achieve this goal, Nixon initiated Operation Menu, which involved increasing the number of bombings against North Vietnamese targets. Behind Operation Menu was the belief that a sustained bombing campaign would force North Vietnam to seek peace quickly.[14] The operation was also part of Nixon's so-called mad-man theory of using military force to achieve his goals.[15] What Nixon did not tell the American people was that Operation Menu required the secret bombing of North Vietnamese bases in neutral Cambodia.[16] Although to bomb Cambodia was in reality an escalation of the war, Nixon did not fear a public backlash. He believed that most of the American people, whom he referred to as the silent majority and the forgotten majority, supported the war.[17] Unfortunately, Operation Menu and the bombing that ensued did little to compel North Vietnam to attend the peace conference in Paris. Instead, North Vietnam followed the advice of General Võ Nguyên Giáp, who argued that North Vietnam could win by "protracting the conflict" until the day that the United States decided to leave, and then defeating South Vietnam.[18] Back home, protests grew louder. On May 4, 1970, Ohio National Guard troops killed four student-protesters and wounded eleven others when they opened fire at a demonstration on the campus of Kent State University.[19] As for the Vietnam War, it dragged on for more than two and a half years before a peace agreement was eventually signed in Paris on January 27, 1973.

There were other foreign issues that Nixon contended with while he was president. He started détente with the Soviet Union, which was a process of thawing the relations between the two countries, and he recognized and visited Communist China. The late 1960s were turbulent. In 1969 America sent *Apollo 11* into space; the crew were to be the first men on the moon. Also that year, young people flocked to a rock concert held in a field near the small town of Woodstock in upstate New York. Partly due to the Vietnam War, the economy was suffering from unemployment and inflation. A new term, "stagflation," was coined to describe the problem.[20] Nixon reacted by abandoning the old Bretton Woods agreement on "converting dollars into gold at a fixed rate" and imposed "wage and price controls" for a ninety-day period.[21]

On the night of June 17, 1972, a security guard at the Watergate Hotel in Washington, DC, alerted police, who arrested five burglars that had broken into the Democratic Party headquarters there. The burglary ultimately became a political scandal, known as Watergate, that forced Nixon to resign. Watergate boosted the careers of two *Washington Post* journalists who uncovered the truth about the break-in: Carl Bernstein and Bob Woodward. On the afternoon following the burglary, Woodward attended the arraignment of the men who were arrested at Watergate. One of the men told the judge that they were anti-Communists and that he had previously worked for the Central Intelligence Agency (CIA).[22] Woodward was shocked to learn this. He immediately reported what he had learned to his paper. That night, the *Washington Post* reported the following:

> Five men, one of whom said he is a former employee of the Central Intelligence Agency, were arrested at 2:30 A.M. yesterday in what authorities described as an elaborate plot to bug the offices of the Democratic National Committee here.[23]

Bernstein and Woodward used a confidential informant who helped garner more information about Watergate. The informant refused to have his identity publicly revealed. Instead he went by the code name Deep Throat, which was also the title of a popular adult movie at the time.[24] In 2005, the identity of Deep Throat was revealed when former associate director of the Federal Bureau of Investigation Mark Felt took credit for being the mystery man.[25]

Nixon went on to be reelected in 1972 against his Democratic opponent, Senator George McGovern of South Dakota. However, his second term brought more trouble. Vice President Agnew was forced to resign in 1973 due to income tax evasion. Former solicitor general Archibald Cox was appointed as a special prosecutor to investigate Watergate. The scandal mushroomed as reports emerged of shady dealings going on within Nixon's Committee for the Re-election of the President (CREEP) and secret White House tape recordings that Nixon made of his daily meetings were revealed. To add to the suspicion, it was revealed that one of the tapes was missing eighteen minutes, suggesting deliberate erasure.[26] As Cox put pressure on the administration, the White House demanded that Cox be fired. Attorney General Elliot Richardson and his deputy William Ruckelshaus were reluctant to remove Cox, so they resigned. Instead, Cox was formally removed by the acting attorney general, Robert Bork. The removal of Cox on Saturday, October 20, 1973, became known as the Saturday Night Massacre.[27]

Even with Cox gone, Nixon's troubles were still evident, and Congress started impeachment proceedings against him. Nixon tried to defend himself in his famous "I am not a crook" speech in November 1973.[28] By August of the following year, the House Judiciary Committee approved articles of impeachment. Rather than face the humiliation of being impeached, Nixon resigned from the presidency on August 9, 1974. He was succeeded by Vice President Gerald R. Ford, who pardoned Nixon for Watergate a month later.

In his final years, Nixon took up writing and attempted to rehabilitate his image. On April 22, 1994, Nixon died from a stroke. He is buried at his presidential library in Yorba Linda next to his wife, Pat, who died a year before him.

LIBRARY AND MUSEUM

President Nixon made preparations for his presidential library early in his administration. He was the first president to "establish a formal White House liaison office with the National Archives to preserve and organize his administration's records" for transfer to his library.[29] After his resignation, it was feared that Nixon would destroy any presidential papers that would reveal his role in Watergate. According to authors Frank L. Shick, Renee Shick, and Mark Carroll, President Gerald Ford's attorney general, William B. Saxbe, believed Nixon's papers had an important public interest despite being owned by Nixon. To prevent Nixon from destroying the records, Arthur Sampson, who directed the General Services Administration, formed a compromise with Nixon: the Nixon-Sampson agreement. In the agreement, all records would be stored in a General

Services warehouse in California. Unless Nixon and the General Services had "mutual consent" for records to be released, they would not be. The agreement also mandated that Nixon would have to wait three to five years before he could withdraw anything. Finally, any records not claimed or donated would be destroyed. Special provisions were placed on the White House tapes, which required their preservation for either ten years or until Nixon's death. Despite the agreement, Congress intervened and passed the Presidential Recordings and Materials Preservation Act of 1974.[30]

The Presidential Recordings and Materials Act required Nixon's papers and records to be kept in Federal custody near Washington, DC.[31] Nixon quickly took legal action protesting the act. In a suit that made its way to the United States Supreme Court, the court ruled that Nixon had no "executive privilege" to keep the papers as private property.[32] The ruling also nullified the Nixon-Sampson agreement.[33]

In 1978, Nixon's supporters created the Nixon Foundation to raise money to buy the house where Nixon was born and the nine acres of land around it for his library.[34] Five years later, the foundation was incorporated into the Richard Nixon Presidential Archive Foundation. The foundation was headed by Nixon's former Treasury secretary, William E. Simon, and his former undersecretary of the interior, John C. Whitaker.[35] Since the library was planned to be administered privately by the Nixon Foundation through a trust fund, Nixon's papers were stored under the Recordings Act at the National Archives in Alexandra, Virginia, where they were known as the Nixon Presidential Materials Project.[36] The foundation contracted with the New York construction firm DMCD to design the library's original galleries.[37] The cost of construction was $21 million.[38]

The library was formally dedicated on July 19, 1990. Around fifty thousand spectators watched the ceremonies, which were attended by Nixon with former presidents Ronald Reagan and Gerald Ford, and President George H. W. Bush. A "prior commitment" prevented former president Jimmy Carter from attending.[39] The press believed that the dedication was "viewed as a milestone in Nixon's political rehabilitation."[40] At the dedication, President Bush thanked Nixon "for dedicating his life to the greatest cause offered any president—the cause of peace among nations."[41] The legacy of a peacemaker who ended the war in Vietnam is exactly how Nixon perceived his presidency. On Nixon's gravestone an inscription reads, "The greatest honor history can bestow is the title of peacemaker."[42]

In 2006 the Nixon library made the transition from a private library to one administered by the National Archives. Not everyone was happy with the transition. Many prominent scholars feared that the library would fail to protect certain papers and tape recordings. Historians point to an incident in 2005 when the library canceled a conference about Nixon and the Vietnam War. The library cited "lack of interest," but some historians speculate that the conference was canceled to stop information that "might damage Nixon's reputation by telling the truth as they found it."[43] Fears that the Nixon library may be controlling the way in which his presidency is presented are reminiscent of what Benjamin Hufbauer calls the "McPresident" or the "Happy Meal" presidential library, which only represents a president in the most flattering light.[44] Visitors will have to decide for themselves if the Nixon library is indeed a product of that phenomenon.

Pat Nixon's beloved rose garden frames the birthplace of her husband, President Richard Nixon, in Yorba Linda, California, by Carol Highsmith. *Carol Highsmith LC-HS503-5862 (ONLINE)*

On July 20, 2015, the Nixon library underwent a $15 million renovation, which involved creating new galleries. The galleries were closed for more than a year, reopening on October 14, 2016.[45] The new refurbished museum now includes three hundred artifacts, eight thousand square feet of wall murals, six hundred photographs, archival and original films, and digital and multimedia interactives.[46]

The current director of the Nixon library is Michael Ellzey, who took on the role on January 12, 2015. Ellzey holds a juris doctorate from Lincoln University School of Law. Before running the library, he worked for technological companies in Silicon Valley, was the executive director of the San Jose Arena Authority, and served in the United States Marine Corps during Vietnam.[47] In 2012, the Nixon library welcomed 92,590 visitors.[48]

Collections and Exhibits

Visitors begin their journey at the Nixon library at the Orientation Theater and view a multimedia presentation about the president and his life.[49] Then they enter the *Wave of Change* exhibit. "Supergraphics" stretch across the exhibit's walls, highlighting the sights, sounds, and images of the days leading up to Nixon's election victory in the fall of 1968. A large banner with the caption "Nixon's the One" hangs in the exhibit.[50] From here, visitors walk into a replica of the Oval Office as it appeared during Nixon's administration.

One of the most contentious problems during Nixon's presidency was the Vietnam War. The museum has an entire exhibit dedicated to exploring the military and domestic problems that Nixon dealt with while fighting an unpopular and divisive war.[51]

The next exhibit focuses exclusively on Nixon's domestic policies. Inside, visitors will see how Nixon promoted environmental legislation, leading to the creation of the Environmental Protection Agency, his "War on Cancer," which aimed to eradicate the disease, his relationship with the younger generation in the context of the Vietnam War, and his role in fighting racial segregation in schools in the South.[52]

The following exhibit focuses on foreign policy. *Communism and the Cold War* takes visitors back to the time of the Cold War with the Soviet Union. A replica Soviet missile provides the backdrop for issues like détente. Also included is a piece of the Berlin Wall, which was torn down to mark the end of the division between the Capitalist West and the Communist East.[53]

The next exhibit returns home to educate visitors about Nixon's wife, Pat. The *First Lady Pat Nixon* exhibit focuses on her role as ambassador of goodwill. Pat was an active First Lady who welcomed many visitors to the White House.[54] The next exhibit, *The Week That Changed the World*, shifts back to foreign matters, focusing on Nixon's historic trip to Communist China in 1972. Inside there are images and artifacts from China, including photos of Nixon with Chinese premier Zhou Enlai. Visitors can also have their pictures taken behind a photo of Nixon on the Great Wall of China.[55]

Two exhibits show what life was like for Nixon and his family at both the White House in Washington, DC, and his personal Western White House at La Casa Pacifica in San Clemente, California. The exhibits are *Life in the White House* and *The Western White House*. Visitors will see a replica of Nixon's study at La Casa Pacifica.[56]

Visitors then return to foreign policy matters as they view the exhibit *The Middle East* to learn how Nixon dealt with regional leaders like Anwar Sadat of Egypt and Golda Meir of Israel.[57] American politics is the centerpiece of the next exhibit, *1972 Campaign and Victory*. Visitors will learn about Nixon's reelection victory against the Democratic nominee Senator George McGovern of South Dakota. Nixon's second inaugural speech is included in this exhibit.[58] The *Watergate* exhibit is important because this scandal led to Nixon's resignation. Visitors can read information about the break-in at the Watergate Hotel, along with the leak of the Pentagon Papers detailing America's secret activities in Vietnam. Information is also presented about the infamous "plumbers" who broke into the hotel in search of election secrets at Democratic headquarters. This exhibit was created in 2011 and has since been updated with new technologies to "enhance the visitor experience."[59] *Watergate* is followed by an exhibit examining Nixon's resignation, *Farewell Speech and Departure*. The exhibit centers on the day of August 9, 1974, when Nixon resigned and handed the duties of the presidency to Vice President Gerald R. Ford.[60]

The museum then turns back to Nixon's childhood in the exhibit *Back to the Beginning and Early Years*, which presents his life in the family farmhouse. Inside, visitors can see photos of Richard from childhood to his days of service in World

War II.[61] Visitors then view the exhibit *Man in the Arena*, which highlights Nixon's early days in politics from his time in Congress to his vice presidency under Dwight Eisenhower.[62] Nixon ran unsuccessfully for president in 1960, and the exhibit *The 1960 Campaign* looks at the history of that election. Inside, visitors will see a re-creation of the television studio where Kennedy and Nixon debated, along with old-fashioned television cameras and microphones.[63] Visitors then find themselves in a replica of the Lincoln Sitting Room as it looked when Nixon used it as his "favorite room in the White House."[64]

The final four exhibits are about Nixon's post-presidency. *The Eagle's Nest* explores Nixon's New Jersey study, which he used from 1974 to 1994. The following exhibit, *Nixon in Culture* presents the way in which Nixon has been depicted in popular culture. Here, visitors can see many of the books, movies, television shows, and songs created about Nixon. The last two exhibits, *Saying Goodbye* and *Epilogue*, show visitors scenes from Nixon's 1994 funeral and play audio of inspiring words spoken by Nixon.[65]

There are also two permanent exhibits at the museum. One is *The Birthplace* and the other is *The Helicopter*. *The Birthplace* is the original family home where Nixon was born. It was built in 1912 and had several owners before it was sold to the Yorba Linda School District. An elementary school, named after Nixon, was built next to the home in 1948. The school's custodian used it as living quarters. In 1988, the school was demolished and the house became the property of the private Nixon Library and Museum. Today, it belongs to the new public presidential library.[66]

The other permanent exhibit is *The Helicopter*. Here, visitors can step aboard the actual Sikorsky VH-3A Sea King (known as Marine One) used by all presidents from Eisenhower to Ford. The helicopter was built in 1960 and weighs six tons. This helicopter was retired from service in 1976 and has been on display since 2006.[67]

Online Exhibits   Online visitors can view information from the Nixon library in the comfort of their own homes. The library has six online exhibits.[68] The first of these is *Memoirs v Tapes: President Nixon and the December Bombing*. This exhibit critically analyzes the decisions of Nixon and Secretary of State Henry Kissinger to bomb North Vietnam in December 1972 in a desperate attempt to motivate them to sign a peace treaty. Online visitors will see photos of Nixon, Kissinger, and the Vietnam War, along with pertinent information leading to the bombings.[69]

The second online exhibit presents the story of Nixon's decision to visit Communist China: *The Week that Changed the World, February 21–28, 1972: Insights from the Nixon Library*. Online visitors are able to view photos, listen to audiovisuals, and read memorandums, including some in Mandarin.[70]

The third online exhibit is the *Ollie Atkins Slideshow*. Atkins was Nixon's official White House photographer. The full collection contains seven thousand photos spanning the period from the 1940s to the 1970s.[71] The online exhibit presents twenty-six of his photos. In addition to photos of Nixon, among the photos published online are images of war-torn Europe, America in the late 1940s and early 1950s, Harry Truman, and Dwight D. Eisenhower.[72]

The fourth online exhibit is *Nixon Head of State*. Here, visitors can "sample" the thirty thousand gifts that Nixon received as president from foreign leaders.[73] The fifth exhibit, hosted by the National Archives, is *When Nixon Met Elvis*. As well as photos, this includes letters between Nixon and Elvis Presley, who met at the White House on December 21, 1970.[74]

The final online exhibit is *Watergate Files*. Interestingly, the Nixon library offers a link to this file from the Gerald Ford Presidential Library and Museum in Grand Rapids, Michigan. Visitors can access the information, including files and photos, relating to the infamous break-in that cost Nixon his office.[75]

Textual, Audiovisual, and Oral Histories   Currently, the library has an estimated reference collection ranging from three hundred to five hundred books about Richard Nixon, his administration, and the era.[76] The library has a large collection of textual materials in its archive. Most of these texts are in boxes cataloged according to agency, event, or individual who worked for the president. For example, researchers will find boxes of texts from individuals such as Patrick J. Buchanan and John W. Dean. There are also boxes of information from the Committee for the Re-Election of the President, various cabinet posts, and Nixon's earlier political campaigns.[77]

Approximately 2,719 hours of Nixon's infamous White House tapes are stored at the library. Online visitors now have the opportunity to sample them remotely.[78] The library's website has available extracts from the tapes in MP3 format, with transcripts available in PDF. Among the extracts available online are cabinet meetings from July 1972 to July 1973, Nixon's trip to China, and the Watergate tapes.[79] The Nixon library has a collection of audiovisual materials. According to the library's website, the current tally is: "350,000 photographs, 4,000 videotapes, over 4,469 official White House sound recordings, and 2.2 million feet of motion picture film."[80]

The Nixon library contains more than 150 oral interviews with cabinet and administration members. Also included are the interviews with journalists, entertainers, Watergate investigators, members of Nixon's family, and antiwar protesters. The majority of the interviews were conducted from 2006 to 2011 by then director Timothy Naftali. Among the more notable interviewees are John W. Dean, Charles Colson, and John Ehrlichman.[81]

NOTES

1. Elizabeth Drew, *Richard M. Nixon*, the American Presidents Series (New York: Times Books, 2007), 5–6.

2. Drew, *Richard M. Nixon*, 8.

3. Drew, *Richard M. Nixon*, 8.

4. Drew, *Richard M. Nixon*, 11.

5. Drew, *Richard M. Nixon*, 14.

6. Lee Huebner, "The Checkers Speech after 60 Years," *Atlantic*, September 22, 2012, http://www.theatlantic.com/politics/archive/2012/09/the-checkers-speech-after-60-years/262172/.

7. Huebner, "Checkers Speech."

8. Drew, *Richard M. Nixon*, 15.

9. Drew, *Richard M. Nixon*, 26.

10. Brinkley, Alan. *John F. Kennedy*, the American Presidents Series (New York: Times Books, 2012), 51.

11. Brinkley, *John F. Kennedy*, 53.

12. Drew, *Richard M. Nixon*, 22.

13. David F. Schmitz, *Richard Nixon and the Vietnam War: The End of the American Century* (Lanham, MD: Rowman & Littlefield, 2014), 56.

14. Schmitz, *Richard Nixon and the Vietnam War*, 49–50.

15. Schmitz, *Richard Nixon and the Vietnam War*, xiv.

16. Schmitz, *Richard Nixon and the Vietnam War*, 50.

17. Schmitz, *Richard Nixon and the Vietnam War*, 42 and 34.

18. Schmitz, *Richard Nixon and the Vietnam War*. 78.

19. Schmitz, *Richard Nixon and the Vietnam War*, 90–91.

20. Schmitz, *Richard Nixon and the Vietnam War*, 132.

21. Schmitz, *Richard Nixon and the Vietnam War*, 132.

22. Carl Bernstein and Bob Woodward, *All the President's Men* (New York: Pocket Books, 1974), 18.

23. Bernstein and Woodward, *All the President's Men*, 19.

24. Bernstein and Woodward, *All the President's Men*, 71.

25. Carl Bernstein, "Watergate's Last Chapter," *Vanity Fair*, October 1, 2005, http://www.vanityfair.com/news/2005/10/watergate-200510.

26. Drew, *Richard M. Nixon*, 120.

27. Louis W. Liebovich, *Richard Nixon, Watergate, and the Press* (Westport, CT: Praeger, 2003), 96–97.

28. Drew, *Richard M. Nixon*, 121.

29. Frank L. Schick, Renee Schick, and Mark Carroll, *Records of the Presidency: Presidential Papers and Libraries from Washington to Reagan* (Phoenix, AZ: Oryx Press, 1989), 242.

30. Schick et al., *Records of the Presidency*, 243.

31. Maeve Devoy, "Richard Nixon Presidential Library and Birthplace," *Public Historian* 28, no. 3 (Summer 2006): 205.

32. *Nixon v. Administrator of General Services*, 433 US 425 (1977).

33. Schick et al., *Records of the Presidency*, 243.

34. Devoy, "Richard Nixon Presidential Library," 202.

35. Schick et al., *Records of the Presidency*, 247.

36. Schick et al., *Records of the Presidency*, 244–47.

37. Devoy, "Richard Nixon Presidential Library," 203.

38. John Needham and Dave Lesher, "Nixon Library Opens with Pomp, Tributes: Dedication: Three Former Presidents at Yorba Linda Ceremony," *Los Angeles Times*, July 20, 1990, http://articles.latimes.com/1990-07-20/news/mn-178_1_richard-nixon.

39. Needham and Lesher, "Nixon Library Opens."

40. Needham and Lesher, "Nixon Library Opens."

41. Needham and Lesher, "Nixon Library Opens."

42. Devoy, "Richard Nixon Presidential Library," 201–2.

43. Devoy, "Richard Nixon Presidential Library," 205.

44. Benjamin Hufbauer, *Presidential Temples: How Memorials and Libraries Shape Public Memory* (Lawrence: University Press of Kansas, 2005), 173.

45. "Highlights of the New Nixon Library and Museum," Richard Nixon Presidential Library and Museum, accessed January 11, 2017, https://www.nixonlibrary.gov/themuseum/exhibits/current_exhibitions.php.

46. "Orientation Theater," Richard Nixon Presidential Library and Museum, accessed January 11, 2017, https://www.nixonlibrary.gov/themuseum/exhibits/current_exhibitions.php #orientation_theater.

47. "Biography of the Director," Richard Nixon Presidential Library and Museum, accessed January 11, 2017, https://www.nixonlibrary.gov/newsandevents/ellzeybio.php.

48. Wendy R. Ginsberg, Erika K. Lunder, and Daniel J. Richardson, *The Presidential Libraries Act and the Establishment of Presidential Libraries* (CRS Report No. R41513) (Washington, DC: Congressional Research Service, 2015), 28.

49. "Orientation Theater," Richard Nixon Presidential Library and Museum, accessed January 11, 2017, https://www.nixonlibrary.gov/themuseum/exhibits/current_exhibitions.php# orientation_theater.

50. "Orientation Theater."

51. "The Vietnam War," Richard Nixon Presidential Library and Museum, accessed January 11, 2017, https://www.nixonlibrary.gov/themuseum/exhibits/current_exhibitions.php #vietnam_war.

52. "Current Exhibitions," Richard Nixon Presidential Library and Museum, accessed January 11, 2017, https://www.nixonlibrary.gov/themuseum/exhibits/current_exhibitions.php.

53. "Communism and the Cold War," Richard Nixon Presidential Library and Museum, accessed January 11, 2017, https://www.nixonlibrary.gov/themuseum/exhibits/current_exhibi tions.php#communism.

54. "First Lady Pat Nixon," Richard Nixon Presidential Library and Museum, accessed January 11, 2017, https://www.nixonlibrary.gov/themuseum/exhibits/current_exhibitions.php #pat_nixon.

55. "The Week That Changed the World," Richard Nixon Presidential Library and Museum, accessed January 11, 2017, https://www.nixonlibrary.gov/themuseum/exhibits/current_exhibi tions.php#week_that.

56. "Life in the White House" and "The Western White House," Richard Nixon Presidential Library and Museum, accessed January 11, 2017, https://www.nixonlibrary.gov/themuseum/ exhibits/current_exhibitions.php.

57. "The Middle East," Richard Nixon Presidential Library and Museum, accessed January 11, 2017, https://www.nixonlibrary.gov/themuseum/exhibits/current_exhibitions.php#middle_east.

58. "1972 Campaign and Victory," Richard Nixon Presidential Library and Museum, accessed January 11, 2017, https://www.nixonlibrary.gov/themuseum/exhibits/current_exhibitions.php #campaign_victory.

59. "Watergate," Richard Nixon Presidential Library and Museum, accessed January 11, 2017, https://www.nixonlibrary.gov/themuseum/exhibits/current_exhibitions.php#watergate.

60. "Farewell Speech and Departure," Richard Nixon Presidential Library and Museum, accessed January 11, 2017, https://www.nixonlibrary.gov/themuseum/exhibits/current_exhi bitions.php#farewell_speech.

61. "Back to the Beginning and Early Years," Richard Nixon Presidential Library and Museum, accessed January 11, 2017, https://www.nixonlibrary.gov/themuseum/exhibits/cur rent_exhibitions.php#back.

62. "Man in the Arena," Richard Nixon Presidential Library and Museum, accessed January 11, 2017, https://www.nixonlibrary.gov/themuseum/exhibits/current_exhibitions.php#man.

63. "The 1960 Campaign," Richard Nixon Presidential Library and Museum, accessed January 11, 2017, https://www.nixonlibrary.gov/themuseum/exhibits/current_exhibitions.php #campaign_1960.

64. "The Lincoln Sitting Room," Richard Nixon Presidential Library and Museum, accessed January 11, 2017, https://www.nixonlibrary.gov/themuseum/exhibits/current_exhibitions.php #lincoln.

65. "Saying Goodbye" and "Epilogue," Richard Nixon Presidential Library and Museum, accessed January 11, 2017, https://www.nixonlibrary.gov/themuseum/exhibits/current_exhibitions.php.

66. "The Birthplace," Richard Nixon Presidential Library and Museum, accessed January 11, 2017, https://www.nixonlibrary.gov/themuseum/thebirthplace.php.

67. "The Helicopter," Richard Nixon Presidential Library and Museum, accessed January 11, 2017, https://www.nixonlibrary.gov/themuseum/helicopter.php.

68. "Online Exhibits," Richard Nixon Presidential Library and Museum, accessed January 11, 2017, https://www.nixonlibrary.gov/virtuallibrary/onlineexhibits.php.

69. "Memoirs v. Tapes: President Nixon and the December Bombings," Richard Nixon Presidential Library and Museum, accessed January 11, 2017, https://www.nixonlibrary.gov/exhibits/decbomb/splash.html.

70. "The Week that Changed the World: February 21–28, 1972," Richard Nixon Presidential Library and Museum, accessed January 11, 2017, https://www.nixonlibrary.gov/forkids/chinafront.php.

71. "Donated Materials of Ollie Atkins," Richard Nixon Presidential Library and Museum, accessed January 11, 2017, https://www.nixonlibrary.gov/forresearchers/find/av/photo/ollie.php.

72. "Donated Materials of Ollie Atkins."

73. "Nixon Head of State Gifts," Richard Nixon Presidential Library and Museum, accessed January 11, 2017, https://www.nixonlibrary.gov/exhibits/gifts/index.html.

74. "When Nixon Met Elvis," National Archives, accessed January 11, 2017, https://www.archives.gov/exhibits/nixon-met-elvis/.

75. "Watergate Files," Gerald R. Ford Presidential Library and Museum, accessed January 15, 2017, https://www.fordlibrarymuseum.gov/museum/exhibits/watergate_files/index.html.

76. Megan Lee Parker (librarian), telephone interview with the author, December 30, 2016.

77. "Textual Materials," Richard Nixon Presidential Library and Museum, accessed January 11, 2017, https://www.nixonlibrary.gov/forresearchers/find/textual/index.php.

78. "White House Tapes," Richard Nixon Presidential Library and Museum, accessed January 11, 2017, https://www.nixonlibrary.gov/forresearchers/find/tapes/index.php.

79. "White House Tapes."

80. "Audiovisual Materials," Richard Nixon Presidential Library and Museum, accessed January 11, 2017, https://www.nixonlibrary.gov/forresearchers/find/av/index.php.

81. "Oral Histories," Richard Nixon Presidential Library and Museum, accessed January 11, 2017, https://www.nixonlibrary.gov/forresearchers/find/histories.php.

BIBLIOGRAPHY

Bernstein, Carl. "Watergate's Last Chapter." *Vanity Fair*, October 1, 2005, http://www.vanityfair.com/news/2005/10/watergate-200510.

Bernstein, Carl, and Bob Woodward. *All the President's Men.* New York: Pocket Books, 1974.

Brinkley, Alan. *John F. Kennedy.* The American Presidents Series. New York: Times Books, 2012.

Clotworthy, William G. *Homes and Libraries of the Presidents: An Interpretive Guide.* Third edition. Blacksburg, VA: McDonald & Woodward, 2008.

Devoy, Maeve. "Richard Nixon Presidential Library and Birthplace." *Public Historian* 28, no. 3 (Summer 2006): 201–6.

Drew, Elizabeth. *Richard M. Nixon.* The American Presidents Series. New York: Times Books, 2007.

Ginsberg, Wendy R., Erika K. Lunder, and Daniel J. Richardson. *The Presidential Libraries Act and the Establishment of Presidential Libraries* (CRS Report No. R41513). Washington, DC: Congressional Research Service, 2015.

Huebner, Lee. "The Checkers Speech after 60 Years." *Atlantic,* September 22, 2012. http://www.theatlantic.com/politics/archive/2012/09/the-checkers-speech-after-60-years/262172/.

Hufbauer, Benjamin. *Presidential Temples: How Memorials and Libraries Shape Public Memory.* Lawrence: University Press of Kansas, 2005.

Kurlansky, Mark. *1968: The Year That Rocked the World.* New York: Ballantine Books, 2004.

Liebovich, Louis W. *Richard Nixon, Watergate, and the Press.* Westport, CT: Praeger, 2003.

Safire, William. "The Cold War's Hot Kitchen," *New York Times,* July 23, 2009. http://www.nytimes.com/2009/07/24/opinion/24safire.html.

Schick, Frank L., Renee Schick, and Mark Carroll. *Records of the Presidency: Presidential Papers and Libraries from Washington to Reagan.* Phoenix, AZ: Oryx Press, 1989.

Schmitz, David F. *Richard Nixon and the Vietnam War: The End of the American Century.* Lanham, MD: Rowman & Littlefield, 2014.

Gerald R. Ford Presidential Library and Museum

Library address: 1000 Beal Avenue, Ann Arbor, MI 48109
Museum address: 303 Pearl Street NW, Grand Rapids, MI 49504-5353
Library phone: (734) 205-0555
Museum phone: (616) 254-0400
Website: https://www.fordlibrarymuseum.gov/
Library social media: https://www.facebook.com/FordPresidentialLibrary/
Museum social media: https://www.facebook.com/FordPresidentialMuseum/
Administration: National Archives
Library hours: 8:45 a.m. to 4:45 p.m., Monday to Friday.
Museum hours: 9 a.m. to 5 p.m., Monday to Saturday; noon to 5 p.m. on Sundays

BIOGRAPHY OF GERALD R. FORD

July 14, 1913–December 26, 2006
Thirty-Eighth President: August 9, 1974–January 20, 1977
Republican Party

Gerald R. Ford and Betty Ford at the Republican National Convention by John T. Bledsoe, 1976. *LC-U9-33190-22A*

Gerald Rudolph Ford was born in Omaha, Nebraska. His father was Leslie Lynch King Sr., and his mother was Ayer Gardner King, and they named their son Leslie Lynch King, Jr. Shortly after he was born, his mother took him away to live with her parents in Grand Rapids, Michigan. Two years later, his parents divorced. His mother then married Gerald R. Ford Sr., a local salesman. Young Leslie attended school in Grand Rapids, where he did well academically and excelled in sports. In 1931 he attended the University of Michigan in Ann Arbor, where he played football. When Leslie graduated in 1935, he changed his name to Gerald Ford. From Michigan he went to Yale and graduated with a law degree in 1941.[1]

During World War II, Ford served as an officer in the navy. After the war he went into politics and was elected a congressman from Michigan. On October 15, 1948, Ford married Elizabeth "Betty" Anne Bloomer Warren. Together they would have four children: Michael, John, Steven, and Susan. Ford served in Congress until he was chosen to replace Spiro Agnew as Richard Nixon's vice president.[2]

Spiro Agnew was forced to resign in 1973, when evidence came to light that he had taken bribes as Maryland's governor and as vice president.[3] On October 12, 1973, Congress confirmed Ford's appointment as vice president. Little did he know that in a matter of months he would be president. On August 9, 1974, Nixon was forced to resign due to his role in the Watergate scandal and Ford took over. In December, Congress confirmed former governor Nelson A. Rockefeller of New York as Ford's vice president.[4]

Shortly after being sworn in, President Ford made a speech in which he acknowledged that he was the first man to become president without having been elected. Ford said, "I am acutely aware that you have not elected me as your President by your ballots, and so I ask you to confirm me as your President with your prayers."[5] Continuing with his speech, he attempted to heal the nation now that the "long national nightmare" of the Watergate scandal was over. He said that the nation must "bind up the internal wounds of Watergate."[6] However, only a month into his presidency, Ford made the controversial decision to pardon Nixon. At the time many speculated that Nixon and Ford had made an agreement that Ford would pardon him after assuming office. Ford denied the allegation and defended his decision, saying that he had made the pardon for the "good of the country."[7]

As president, Ford promoted a domestic policy of tax cuts and smaller government. His policies often met with fierce resistance from the Democratic-controlled Congress. In foreign affairs, Ford continued many of Nixon's policies, such as détente with the Soviet Union, which aimed to ease tensions between the two nuclear powers. Just as the nation was recovering from the war in Vietnam, America's ally South Vietnam capitulated to North Vietnam in the fall of 1975.[8] Thousands of South Vietnamese were evacuated from the capital, Saigon, by the American army. Ford survived two assassination attempts during his presidency. The first took place on September 5, 1975, in Sacramento, California. Lynette "Squeaky" Fromme managed to point a gun at Ford's chest and pull the trigger, but she had neglected to chamber a round. Fromme was a member of the infamous (Charles) Manson family, which was responsible for gruesome serial killings. She made the assassination attempt to bring attention to the plight of the redwood trees. Less than two weeks later, Sara Jane Moore shot at and missed Ford in San Francisco. A bystander managed to grab the gun before Moore could shoot again. Moore claimed that her motive was to impress her radical friends who had ostracized her when she revealed being a government informant. Fromme and Moore were both convicted and given life sentences.[9]

Ford sought the Republican nomination in 1976, but he faced a serious challenge from former actor governor Ronald Reagan of California.[10] On July 4, 1976, Ford led the nation in celebrating America's Bicentennial of independence. Ford's advisors saw the celebration as an opportunity to "present America at its best—a national salute to freedom that would certify the nation's unity and pay tribute to

America's ideals and values."[11] On August 19, 1976, the Republicans convened in Kansas City, where they chose President Ford over Reagan as their nominee. In his acceptance speech, Ford said:

> We will create a climate in which our economy will provide a meaningful job for everyone who wants to work and a decent standard of life for all Americans. We will ensure that all of our young people have a better chance in life than we had, an education they can use, and a career they can be proud of.[12]

The Democrats nominated former governor Jimmy Carter of Georgia. That fall, Ford and Carter squared off in two memorable debates. However, during the first debate, problems with the audio left the candidates standing in silence behind their podiums for twenty-seven minutes. The second debate saw Ford misspeak when he stated that there was no Soviet domination in East Europe.[13] This mistake may have cost Ford the election. When the results came in on November 2, they made clear that Carter had won the election. Carter received 297 electoral votes and 40,831,881 popular votes, while Ford received 240 electoral votes and 39,148,634 popular votes.

After losing the election, Ford went into retirement. He is remembered as the president who healed America in the aftermath of Watergate.[14] He died on December 26, 2006, and he is buried outside his museum in Grand Rapids. His wife, Betty, died on July 8, 2011, and she is buried next to him.

LIBRARY AND MUSEUM

The history of the Gerald R. Ford Presidential Library and Museum goes back to Ford's days as a congressman representing Michigan. In 1964 Ford met with a staff member representing the Michigan Historical Collections (MHC) to discuss placing his congressional records with them. The MHC was affiliated with Ford's alma mater, the University of Michigan. Ford agreed to have his congressional papers sent to the university under the stipulation that they be kept in a storage facility for five years. The agreement also gave Ford the right to extend the period of storage, and in 1969 he elected to keep his papers in storage until January 1980.[15]

Ford's life changed dramatically on October 12, 1973, when he was confirmed as President Nixon's new vice president after Spiro Agnew resigned in disgrace.[16] On August 9, 1974, Ford was sworn in as president upon Nixon's resignation. For the state of Michigan the event was historic: Ford became the first "Michigander" to hold the high office.[17] Michigan was pleased to have a native in the White House. However, the event also caused a problem for the state, as both Ann Arbor and Grand Rapids competed over which city would host his presidential library.[18]

Although Ford's congressional records were stored in the library at the University of Michigan in Ann Arbor, he had not decided where his presidential papers would be kept. On September 20, 1974, Dr. Robert W. Fleming, who was then the president of the University of Michigan, asked Ford to consider building his presidential library on campus. But the city of Grand Rapids wanted Ford to build his library there. Officials in Grand Rapids believed that a presidential library would bring more tourists to the city and help to stimulate the local economy.[19] The city even established the Gerald Ford Commemorative Committee in anticipation that the library would be built there. Ford was in a dilemma: would he choose his hometown, Grand Rapids, or his alma mater, the University of Michigan in Ann Arbor?[20]

Ford's dilemma was solved by his friend and White House counsel, attorney Philip Buchan. He came up with a compromise—all Ford's presidential papers would go to the University of Michigan, and his presidential memorabilia would go to the Grand Rapids museum.[21] Ford liked the idea of splitting his legacy between the two cities. However, he made a small change to the plans. Instead of using the museum in Grand Rapids to host his memorabilia, he decided to build a separate presidential museum: the Gerald R. Ford Museum.[22]

In 1977 Ford began seeking funding for his buildings and by 1981 he had raised "nearly $12 million."[23] On July 21, 1978, Ford made an agreement with the University of Michigan and the National Archives to build his library on the campus. Eleven months later, on June 19, 1979, the cornerstone was laid. The library was designed by the architectural firm Jickling, Lyman, and Powell, which was located in Birmingham, Michigan. The library covers "40,000 square feet" and is built close to the Bentley Library at the University of Michigan, where Ford's congressional records were located.[24] The library took almost two years to build. It was formally dedicated on April 27, 1981, with the governor of Michigan, William G. Milliken, in attendance.[25]

While the library was being constructed in Ann Arbor, the museum was being built in Grand Rapids. The museum was formally dedicated on September 18, 1981, during a week of events known as the Celebration on the Grand.[26] As well as the opening of the Ford library, events held during the week celebrated the opening of the Grand Rapids Art Center, a convention-symphony hall, and the Amway Grand Plaza Hotel. In attendance with Ford were President Ronald Reagan, Vice President George H. W. Bush, Canadian prime minister Pierre Trudeau, and Michigan governor Milliken.[27]

Between 2014 and 2016 the museum was extensively renovated. The thirteen-hundred-square-foot museum was reopened on June 7, 2016, with new galleries and the DeVos Learning Center for school field trips added to the building. The Gerald R. Ford Presidential Foundation raised $13 million for the renovations. As stated by the foundation's executive director, Joe Cavalruso, this was not just "carpet and paint" but "a whole new experience."[28]

The library and museum have both been administered by Dr. Elaine K. Didier since her appointment in 2005 by the archivist of the United States John W. Carlin. Prior to her appointment, Didier was dean of the Kresge Library at Oakland University in Michigan. She holds a doctorate from Oxford University and taught at the University of Michigan before becoming the dean of the Kresge Library. Ford, who was still alive when Didier was appointed, said:

> I am tremendously pleased by the Archivist's decision to name Elaine Didier as the new Library Director. She has the energy, experience and enthusiasm to sustain and enhance the progress that's been made at the Library and Museum. I am particularly pleased by her interest in partnering with civic leaders and the academic and business communities in Ann Arbor, Grand Rapids and the region to provide new opportunities for educational programming.[29]

Gerald R. Ford Presidential Library in Ann Arbor, Michigan. *Courtesy of the Gerald R. Ford Presidential Library and Museum*

Museum and Collections

The Ford Presidential Museum is divided into nine galleries detailing the life of Ford and his wife, Betty. Visitors will start their tour in a theater, where they will view the short film *A Time to Heal*.[30] The film presents Ford as the president who helped move America forward in the aftermath of the Watergate scandal. Those who are unable to visit the museum can watch the film on the museum's website.[31]

After leaving the theater, visitors enter the first three galleries—*Youth, College,* and *World War II*—where photographs are presented of Ford's childhood, his years at the University of Michigan, and his time in the navy during World War II.[32] From here, visitors will move on to the remaining exhibits detailing Ford's political career: *Congressional* and *Presidential.* Visitors will see letters that Ford signed as congressman and as president, along with photographs of him in his two political roles. Visitors will then enter the gallery *Bicentennial,* which was a year-long celebration of America's two-hundredth anniversary in 1976. Visitors will see a large case where items given to the president during the celebration are on display. Among the many items are American flags, handmade clothes, a quilt, and a caricature of Ford made from river rocks. The display also showcases a can of "Bicentennial air" from Indiana, and a jeweled necklace with the Bicentennial logo of a star. Visitors will also see an actual eighteenth-century French printing press and campaign artifacts from Ford's 1976 Presidential campaign.[33]

The final three galleries—*Mrs. Ford, Post-Presidency,* and *Funeral*—show images of First Lady Betty Ford, Ford's years of retirement, and his funeral.[34] Before they leave the museum, visitors can also see Ford's replica Oval Office and Cabinet Room.

Gerald R. Ford Presidential Museum in Grand Rapids, Michigan. *Courtesy of the Gerald R. Ford Presidential Library and Museum*

Ford's replica Oval Office by William Hebert. *Courtesy of the Gerald R. Ford Presidential Library and Museum*

Library and Collections

The Ford presidential library is an "archival" facility.[35] Its website states that the library has an archive of "approximately 25 million pages of documents, 450,000 photographs, 3,000 hours of audiotape, 3,500 hours of videotape, and 712,027 feet of film."[36] In 2012, the library welcomed 299,189 visitors.[37]

The archive contains various collections of papers on specific subjects related to Ford's administration. The Textual Collection contains information on the Vietnam War, relations between the United States and China, the Nixon presidency, women's rights, and Ford's 1976 presidential campaign.[38] Another important collection is the National Security Adviser's Files. These files contain the reports of Secretary of State Henry Kissinger and of National Security Council meetings on world affairs.[39]

The library also has a collection of oral histories pertaining to the library and Grand Rapids, and from important advisors, such as James M. Cannon.[40]

NOTES

1. "Gerald R. Ford Biography," Gerald R. Ford Presidential Library and Museum, accessed June 1, 2017, https://www.fordlibrarymuseum.gov/museum/EduCenter09/bio_geraldford.html.

2. "Gerald R. Ford Biography."

3. James Cannon, *Gerald R. Ford: An Honorable Life* (Ann Arbor: University of Michigan Press, 2013), 127.

4. Cannon, *Gerald R. Ford*, 293.

5. "Remarks by Gerald Ford on Taking the Oath of Office as President," Watergate.info, accessed June 1, 2017, http://watergate.info/1974/08/09/ford-remarks-on-taking-office.html.

6. Cannon, *Gerald R. Ford*, 27.

7. "Gerald R. Ford Biography."

8. "Gerald R. Ford Biography."

9. Christian A. Nappo, "Presidential Assassination and the Insanity Defense." Unpublished Policy and Practice Paper, University of Alabama, 2000, 26–28.

10. "Gerald R. Ford Biography," Gerald R. Ford Presidential Library and Museum, accessed June 1, 2017, https://www.fordlibrarymuseum.gov/museum/EduCenter09/bio_geraldford.html.

11. Cannon, *Gerald R. Ford*, 416–17.

12. Gerald R. Ford, "Remarks in Kansas City upon Accepting the 1976 Republican Presidential Nomination: August 19, 1976," American Presidency Project, accessed June 1, 2017, http://www.presidency.ucsb.edu/ws/?pid=6281.

13. Julian E. Zelizer, *Jimmy Carter*, American Presidents Series (New York: Times Books, 2010), 51.

14. Peter Baker, "38th President Leaves a Legacy of Healing," *Washington Post*, December 28, 2006, http://www.washingtonpost.com/wp-dyn/content/article/2006/12/27/AR200612 2700727.html.

15. Frank L. Schick, Renee Schick, and Mark Carroll, *Records of the Presidency: Presidential Papers and Libraries from Washington to Reagan* (Phoenix, AZ: Oryx Press, 1989), 220.

16. Schick et al., *Records of the Presidency*, 220.

17. Schick et al., *Records of the Presidency*, 221.

18. Schick et al., *Records of the Presidency*, 222.

19. Schick et al., *Records of the Presidency*, 221.

20. Schick et al., *Records of the Presidency*, 221.

21. Schick et al., *Records of the Presidency*, 222.

22. Schick et al., *Records of the Presidency*, 222–23.

23. Schick et al., *Records of the Presidency*, 223.

24. Schick et al., *Records of the Presidency*, 223.

25. Schick et al., *Records of the Presidency*, 223.

26. Schick et al., *Records of the Presidency*, 223.

27. Schick et al., *Records of the Presidency*, 227.

28. Matt Vande Bunte, "Look Inside $13M Gerald R. Ford Presidential Museum Renovation," *MLive*, http://www.mlive.com/news/grandrapids/index.ssf/2016/01/gerald_r_ford_presidential_mus.html.

29. National Archives, "Didier Named Director of the Gerald R. Ford Presidential Library and Museum," news release, January 10, 2005, https://www.archives.gov/press/press-releases/2005/nr05-33.html.

30. William G. Clotworthy, *Homes and Libraries of the Presidents: An Interpretive Guide*, third edition (Blacksburg, VA: McDonald & Woodward, 2008), 288.

31. https://www.fordlibrarymuseum.gov/biography.aspx.

32. Donald Holloway, Curator, Ford Museum, e-mail message to author, May 25, 2017.

33. Donald Holloway, May 25, 2017.

34. Donald Holloway, May 25, 2017.

35. Clotworthy, *Homes and Libraries*, 288.

36. "Library Collections," Gerald R. Ford Presidential Library and Museum, accessed June 1, 2017, https://www.fordlibrarymuseum.gov/collections-library.aspx.

37. Wendy R. Ginsberg, Erika K. Lunder, and Daniel J. Richardson, *The Presidential Libraries Act and the Establishment of Presidential Libraries* (CRS Report No. R41513) (Washington, DC: Congressional Research Service, 2015), 28.

38. "Textual Collection Subject Guides," Gerald R. Ford Presidential Library and Museum, accessed June 1, 2017, https://www.fordlibrarymuseum.gov/library/guides/subjguid.asp.

39. "Ford Library Textual Collections: National Security Adviser's Files," Gerald R. Ford Presidential Library and Museum, accessed June 1, 2017, https://www.fordlibrarymuseum.gov/library/guides/guidecollectionsnsa.asp.

40. "Oral Histories in the Gerald R. Ford Library," Gerald R. Ford Presidential Library and Museum, accessed June 1, 2017, https://www.fordlibrarymuseum.gov/library/oralhist.asp.

BIBLIOGRAPHY

Baker, Peter. "38th President Leaves a Legacy of Healing." *Washington Post*, December 28, 2006. http://www.washingtonpost.com/wp-dyn/content/article/2006/12/27/AR2006122700727.html.

Cannon, James. *Gerald R. Ford: An Honorable Life*. Ann Arbor: University of Michigan Press, 2013.

Clotworthy, William G. *Homes and Libraries of the Presidents: An Interpretive Guide*. Third edition. Blacksburg, VA: McDonald & Woodward, 2008.

Ginsberg, Wendy R., Erika K. Lunder, and Daniel J. Richardson. *The Presidential Libraries Act and the Establishment of Presidential Libraries* (CRS Report No. R41513). Washington, DC: Congressional Research Service, 2015.

Nappo, Christian A. "Presidential Assassination and the Insanity Defense." Unpublished Policy and Practice Paper, University of Alabama, 2000.

Schick, Frank L., Renee Schick, and Mark Carroll. *Records of the Presidency: Presidential Papers and Libraries from Washington to Reagan*. Phoenix, AZ: Oryx Press, 1989.

Zelizer, Julian E. *Jimmy Carter*. The American Presidents Series. New York: Times Books, 2010.

Jimmy Carter Presidential Library and Museum

Address: 441 Freedom Parkway, Atlanta, Georgia 30307-1498
Phone: (404) 865-7100
Website: https://www.jimmycarterlibrary.gov/
Social media: https://www.facebook.com/CarterPresidentialLibrary/
Administration: National Archives
Hours: 9 a.m. to 4:45 p.m., Monday to Saturday; noon to 4:45 p.m. on Sundays;
  closed on Thanksgiving Day, Christmas Day, and New Year's Day

---

BIOGRAPHY OF JIMMY CARTER

October 1, 1924–
January 20, 1977–January 20, 1981
Democratic Party

Jimmy Carter by Karl Schumacher, 1977. *LC-USZC4-599*

James Earl Carter Jr. was born to James Earl Sr. and Bessie Lillian Gordy. Jimmy's father was a farmer and his mother was a nurse. Both were of the Baptist faith and held progressive antiracist views on African Americans.[1] Young Jimmy grew up in a town called Archery outside Plains, Georgia. He had three siblings: Gloria, Ruth, and Billy. As a boy, Jimmy worked hard on the family farm and selling peanuts. During the Great Depression of the 1930s, the Carters were more fortunate than many others.[2] James Earl Sr. found work on the Sumter County School Board and for the Rural Electrification Administration. When Jimmy was not working, he attended school. He was the first in the family to receive a high school diploma.[3]

Carter graduated from high school in 1941 and went on to study science at Georgia Southwestern College. When America entered World War II following the Japanese bombing of Pearl Harbor, Carter transferred to the

Georgia Technological Institute and enrolled in the school's naval reserve officer training program. A year later, in 1943, Carter received an appointment to the United States Naval Academy in Annapolis, Maryland. He studied naval engineering and graduated in 1946.[4] Carter graduated "fifty-ninth in a class of 820."[5] Before he was assigned to a ship, Carter married Rosalynn Smith. The Carters would have four children: John, James, Donnel, and Amy.

Carter's first assignment was aboard the old battleship USS *Wyoming*. He served on the battleship for two years and then voluntarily transferred to submarine service. The first submarine Carter served aboard was the USS *Pomfret*, which patrolled off the coast of China. During the Korean War, in 1950, Carter transferred to a new class of submarine known as "Killer 1" or USS *K-1*.[6] The *K-1* was assigned to patrol the Atlantic and the Caribbean. In 1952, Carter applied for a position to supervise the construction of nuclear-powered submarines in New York State. The navy required him to supplement his work by studying nuclear physics at Union College.[7] However, in 1953, Carter's father died of pancreatic cancer, and he was forced to leave the navy to help run the family farm.[8]

The American South of the 1950s was a turbulent place, as racial tensions were rising over the issue of civil rights. Carter supported civil rights and became interested in politics. In 1962, Carter ran for a local state senate seat as a Democrat. However, his powerful segregationist opponents tampered with the election results. Carter challenged the results in court and it was ruled that he won the election.[9] During his term in the state senate, Carter worked to promote "government reform and higher education."[10]

In 1966, Carter sought the Democratic nomination for governor of Georgia, but the Georgia Democrats chose the segregationist Lester Maddox instead. Carter returned to his family business and "underwent a born-again experience, which motivated him to devote his life to Christianity."[11] In 1970, Carter again sought the nomination for governor. This time, he won. His "image as an outsider" helped him get elected that year.[12] Carter's major achievement as governor was to allow the US Army Corps of Engineers to construct a dam on the Flint River "to promote development and better water use."[13]

The early 1970s were marred by the Watergate scandal. Nixon was compelled to resign in 1974 because he was implicated in the break-in at the Democratic headquarters at the Watergate Hotel. When Nixon's successor, Gerald Ford, became president, he pardoned Nixon. The pardon made corruption a major issue for the 1976 presidential election.[14] Carter won the Democratic Party nomination and chose Senator Walter F. Mondale of Minnesota as his running mate. During the general election, Carter tried to appeal to "moderates and independents through a centrist agenda."[15] The candidates held two televised debates. In the first, there was a technical problem with the audio, and Carter and President Ford were left standing behind their podiums for twenty-seven minutes. The second debate was an embarrassment for Ford, who made a misstatement about there being no Soviet domination in Eastern Europe during his administration.[16] On election night, the race was close. Carter won with 40,831,881 popular votes and 297 electoral votes, while Ford gained 39,148,634 popular votes and 240 electoral votes. A key demographic that Carter won was evangelicals.[17]

Carter's first two years in office witnessed some important achievements. He signed the Social Security Amendments of 1977, which "resolved a short-term solvency crisis" for the program.[18] Carter also promoted peace in the Middle East and visited Iran to meet with its leader, Mohammad Reza Pahlavi, known as Mohammed Reza Shah. He also made controversial decisions. One was to pardon all drafter dodgers during the Vietnam War.[19] The other was signing a treaty relinquishing control of the Panama Canal to Panama.[20]

Carter's most significant accomplishment was the Camp David Accords in September 1978. Carter invited Israeli prime minister Menachem Begin and Egyptian President Anwar el-Sadat to meet with him at Camp David to discuss peace. Israel and Egypt had previously been at war. The accords successfully ended animosities between the two nations and resolved long-standing disputes over territories.[21]

While Carter's first two years saw some positive achievements, his second two years would witness disappointments. The nation experienced an economic recession in 1979 as "inflation [grew] to 13.4 percent [and] the gross national product (GNP) was nearly flat."[22] To make matters worse, geopolitical troubles in the oil-rich Middle East led to an energy crisis, forcing consumers to pay more at the pump.[23] Carter spent a week and a half at Camp David seeking the opinions of his advisors about the energy crisis.[24] On the night of July 15, 1979, the president, on live television, gave what became known as his "crisis of confidence" or "malaise" speech.[25] Carter said:

> I know, of course, being President, that government actions and legislation can be very important. That's why I've worked hard to put my campaign promises into law—and I have to admit, with just mixed success. But after listening to the American people I have been reminded again that all the legislation in the world can't fix what's wrong with America. So, I want to speak to you first tonight about a subject even more serious than energy or inflation. I want to talk to you right now about a fundamental threat to American democracy.
>
> I do not mean our political and civil liberties. They will endure. And I do not refer to the outward strength of America, a nation that is at peace tonight everywhere in the world, with unmatched economic power and military might.
>
> The threat is nearly invisible in ordinary ways. It is a crisis of confidence. It is a crisis that strikes at the very heart and soul and spirit of our national will. We can see this crisis in the growing doubt about the meaning of our own lives and in the loss of a unity of purpose for our Nation.[26]

Carter concluded his speech by setting goals that he hoped would end the energy crisis. Among the more notable were import quotas, alternative sources of fuel, a requirement for energy companies to cut their use of oil by 50 percent, the creation of an energy mobilization board, and promoting conservation.[27] Two days later, Carter replaced a few members of his cabinet.

The speech was not received well by the public. As historian Daniel Horowitz put it, Carter had accused the public of "falling victim to self-indulgence" and this, along with the reorganization of his cabinet, reinforced a perception that he had no solution to the energy crisis.[28] Matters only became more difficult for Carter. His approval ratings sank to the mid-twenties.[29] Americans felt that the government was failing to help with the energy crisis.[30] Then, on November 4, 1979, Iranian students stormed the American embassy in Tehran and held fifty-five Americans hostage for 444 days. The students were supporters of Ayatollah Khomeini, the new ruler of Iran. Carter made an attempt to rescue the hostages on April 24, 1980, but an army helicopter on the way to Tehran crashed in a sandstorm.[31] Carter took personal responsibility for the mistake and told the American people, "It was my decision to attempt the rescue operation. It was my decision to cancel it when problems developed in the placement of our rescue team for a future rescue operation. The responsibility is fully my own."[32]

Another problem erupted on December 27, 1979, when the Soviet Union invaded Afghanistan in an attempt to help a pro-Moscow regime in Kabul. Carter did not stand by idly as the Soviets ravaged Afghanistan. He immediately postponed further negotiations with the Soviets over the Strategic Arms Limitations Talks (SALT II) and announced an American boycott of the Summer Olympics, which was to be held in Moscow in 1980.[33]

In 1980 Carter ran for a second term. However, he was challenged by a fellow Democrat, Senator Edward Kennedy of Massachusetts. Carter and Mondale were re-nominated after a turbulent primary season. The Republicans nominated the former actor and former governor of California, Ronald Reagan, who wanted to take the party from the center to the right.[34] During the fall of 1980, Carter's approval ratings were still low, but he was tied with Reagan in the polls. Despite this, Carter felt that the electorate would not vote for a conservative candidate like Reagan.[35] On October 28, the two candidates had their one and only presidential debate. During the debate, Reagan asked the voters "Are you better off than you were four years ago," a question that helped him to win the election.[36] On election night, Reagan won the presidency with 43,903,230 popular votes and 489 electoral votes. Carter won just 35,480,115 popular votes and 49 electoral votes. An independent third-party candidate named John B. Anderson won 5,719,850 popular votes but carried no states.

Since leaving the White House, Carter has had an active post-presidency. He returned to Georgia, where he opened his Carter Center. He has written several books, including *Keeping Faith: Memoirs of a President* in 1982. In the mid-1990s, Carter helped to alleviate problems and conflicts in North Korea, Haiti, and Bosnia-Herzegovina.[37] In 2016, Carter was successfully treated for brain cancer.[38] Today, he can be found in Atlanta at his center.

LIBRARY AND MUSEUM

The Jimmy Carter Presidential Library and Museum is located in "a sprawling complex of interconnected buildings set amidst beautifully landscaped rolling hills" in Atlanta.[39] The Carter library is situated next to "four interconnected circular buildings" and two "man-made lakes and a traditional Japanese garden."[40] The Carter Center is the former president's headquarters for his international philanthropic efforts.[41] The other three buildings house the Carter Center of Emory University, the Carter–Menil Human

Rights Foundation, and Carter's executive office, Global 2000.[42] The library, grounds, and buildings are known collectively as the Carter Presidential Center.

The library's origins go back to 1977, when Carter indicated that he would like his library to be located "someplace in Georgia."[43] The following year, Congress passed the Presidential Records and Materials Preservation Act of 1978, which Carter signed into law. The act "ended private ownership of presidential records."[44] Though the law did not come into effect until 1981, Carter decided to bind his papers to the law.[45] In 1979 Carter considered Atlanta, Athens, Macon, Emory University, and the Georgia Institute of Technology (Georgia Tech) as possible locations for his library. The people of his hometown of Plains, urged him to build his library there.[46] After his reelection defeat in 1980, Carter settled on Atlanta.

When Carter left the presidency on January 20, 1981, "a convoy of 19 trailer trucks left Washington for Atlanta" to move his papers to the old Atlanta Post Office Annex.[47] Carter wanted to construct his own presidential library in Atlanta. He chose the current location after leaving office. Originally, the site had been considered a "kudzu-covered wasteland" for a future highway until Governor Carter insisted that the land remain "fallow."[48]

Carter wanted to continue working on human rights after his presidency came to an end, so he formed the nonprofit Carter Center in 1982 for that purpose. The Carter Center's website describes the institution and its mission: "The Carter Center, in partnership with Emory University, is guided by a fundamental commitment to human rights and the alleviation of human suffering. It seeks to prevent and resolve conflicts, enhance freedom and democracy, and improve health."[49]

After raising $26 million from private donors, such as Coca-Cola and Delta Air Lines, Carter's library was built. He contracted with an Atlanta architectural firm, Jova/Daniels/Busby, and a Hawaiian one, Lawton, Umemura & Yamamoto, for the construction.[50]

The Carter Center was formally dedicated on October 1, 1986, on a thirty-five-acre park outside Atlanta.[51] The entire center occupies approximately seventy thousand square feet.[52] Among the five thousand spectators who attended the dedication were President Ronald Reagan and his wife, Nancy. Another attendee was Carter's deputy secretary of state, Warren Christopher, who said that the Carter Center was "not just archives, but a dynamic center of action."[53] The library and museum were opened to the public in January 1987.

From 1986 to 1993, the only way to get to the library by car was on local roads. A new highway was needed if drivers wanted fast and efficient access. In 1993 a $13.3 million road named the Freedom Parkway was constructed to help alleviate traffic problems. It was completed in 1994, making the drive to the library easier in sprawling Atlanta.[54] In 2012, the library welcomed 51,746 visitors.[55]

On November 29, 2015, the National Archives appointed Meredith Evans as director of the Carter library. Evans had previously worked as curator of printed materials at Atlanta University Center's library, where she digitized the papers of Martin Luther King Jr. She had also taught library science at Clark Atlanta University and held leadership positions at George Washington University and the University of North Carolina at Charlotte.[56]

Jimmy Carter Presidential Library and Museum. *Courtesy of the Jimmy Carter Library*

Collections and Exhibits

Visitors walking into the main entrance of the library will see displays of Carter's career from his days in the navy to his presidency. There is also a theater, where visitors can watch an orientation video about the library.[57] Its centerpiece is the replica Oval Office. The library's website describes this as "a full-scale replica of Jimmy Carter's White House Oval Office, furnished exactly as it was during his administration."[58] As visitors walk into the Oval Office, they will see Carter's desk, his yellow-and-orange curtains, and the artwork that decorated his office from 1977 to 1981.

An important artifact on display at the library is the replica Crown of Saint Stephen (the Holy Crown of Hungary). The original crown was given to the United States for safe keeping during the last days of World War II as the Soviet Army approached Budapest. The Hungarians feared they would lose the crown to the unfriendly Soviets. The crown was kept at Fort Knox until Carter returned it to Hungary in 1977. The library's website explains that returning the crown "led to a marked improvement in U.S.-Hungarian relations and was a major factor contributing to the historic changes in Hungary following the fall of communism in Eastern Europe."[59] On March 18, 1998, the Hungarian government thanked Carter for this favor by presenting his library with a special reproduction of the original crown. At the ceremony, Carter said:

> This replica of the Crown of Hungary is a wonderful gift, and I am proud to accept it on behalf of the people of the United States. The people of Hungary trusted us to keep one of their greatest treasures. We returned it when conditions permitted. This replica of the magnificent Crown is a generous and gracious gesture of the abiding faith and trust that exists between our two countries.[60]

Carter's replica Oval Office. *Courtesy of the Jimmy Carter Library*

The library also hosts several temporary exhibits. In 2016 the library exhibited photographer Marie Plakos's *Our Sister's Keeper.* The exhibit is a display of thirty-six "stunning images" of women and children from India, Mexico, Ghana, and Peru.[61] The library also holds regular book signings. On January 17, 2017, the library welcomed author Heather Ann Thompson, who wrote a book about the 1971 Attica prison uprising: *Blood in the Water.*

The manuscripts at the Carter library are divided into three sections: the President's Files, the White House Central Files, and the Staff Office Files.[62] Included in the President's Files is a series of letters known as the Presidential Handwriting File, which contains letters from the president's outbox. Also included in the President's Files are papers from the president's personal secretary, Susan Clough, and the papers that Carter used to write his book *Keeping Faith* in 1982.[63] The White House Central Files contain manuscripts and papers from twenty-five professional staff members using an alphanumeric cataloging scheme. Finally, the Staff Office Files contain the files of officials who worked at the White House. Included are papers from the Press Office, the First Lady's staff, the Chief of Staff, the Council of Economic Advisors, and speechwriters.[64] Aside from the manuscripts, the library holds three thousand two hundred books, of which two thousand seven hundred are from Carter's personal collection.[65]

The library has its own collection of oral histories from Carter's family and members of his administration. The Carter/Smith Oral History Project includes the oral histories of Carter's mother, Lillian, and the First Lady's brother, Jerrold Smith, among other family members.[66] The National Park Service Plains Project Oral Histories contains the histories of Carter; his wife, Rosalynn; and his childhood friends.[67] The Exit Interview Project contains audio recordings of people who served in Carter's White

House administration from June 1978 to January 1981. The library's website explains the importance of the exit interviews:

> In each interview, liaison office staff primarily sought to elicit information about the White House staffer's role during the Carter Administration—daily and long-term projects, important assignments, memorable events, personal interaction with the President, etc. Questions also were asked about the organization of particular White House offices and units. In some instances, specific questions were asked about a staffer's background prior to his/her White House experience, including any service with Carter political campaigns.[68]

Visitors can listen to exit interviews with administration officials, such as National Security Advisor Zbigniew Brzezinski, Deputy Assistant Secretary of State Bob Beckel, and presidential speechwriter Chris Matthews. Readers may be aware that both Beckel and Matthews went on to have successful careers as cable news hosts. Finally, there is a set of oral histories of those who worked at the Carter library. These histories are known as the Carter Library Oral History Project.[69]

In addition to the oral histories, the library has a collection of audiovisual materials. The White House Staff Photographers collection contains 600,000 color and black-and-white photos of Carter, his family, and his administration from 1977 to 1981. The collection also includes a large number of videotapes and audiotapes recorded during the Carter presidency.[70] Among these is a film from the Naval Photographic Center, which includes "1,100,000 feet of 16mm color motion picture film documenting approximately 1,000 Presidential events and appearances."[71] Besides the library's collection of books from Carter's personal library, there are others for research purposes.[72]

NOTES

1. Julian E. Zelizer, *Jimmy Carter*, the American Presidents Series (New York: Times Books, 2010), 7.

2. Zelizer, *Jimmy Carter*, 9.

3. Zelizer, *Jimmy Carter*, 10.

4. Jimmy Carter, *A Full Life: Reflections at Ninety* (New York: Simon and Schuster), 2015, 30–33.

5. Carter, *A Full Life*, 63.

6. Carter, *A Full Life*, 55.

7. Carter, *A Full Life*, 64.

8. Zelizer, *Jimmy Carter*, 12.

9. Zelizer, *Jimmy Carter*, 16–17.

10. Zelizer, *Jimmy Carter*, 17.

11. Zelizer, *Jimmy Carter*, 21.

12. Zelizer, *Jimmy Carter*, 23.

13. Zelizer, *Jimmy Carter*, 26.

14. Zelizer, *Jimmy Carter*, 28–29.

15. Zelizer, *Jimmy Carter*, 47–48.

16. Zelizer, *Jimmy Carter*, 51.

17. Zelizer, *Jimmy Carter*, 113.

18. Zelizer, *Jimmy Carter*, 71.

19. Zelizer, *Jimmy Carter*, 55.

20. Zelizer, *Jimmy Carter*, 69.

21. Zelizer, *Jimmy Carter*, 82–83.

22. Daniel Horowitz, *Jimmy Carter and the Energy Crisis of the 1970s: The "Crisis of Confidence" Speech of July 15, 1979. A Brief History with Documents* (Boston: Bedford/St. Martin's), 2005, 5.

23. Horowitz, *Energy Crisis*, 12.

24. Horowitz, *Energy Crisis*, 18–19.

25. Horowitz, *Energy Crisis*, vii.

26. Jimmy Carter, "Address to the nation on energy and national Goals: 'The Malaise Speech,'" the American Presidency Project, http://www.presidency.ucsb.edu/ws/?pid=32596.

27. Horowitz, *Energy Crisis*, 116.

28. Horowitz, *Energy Crisis*, 25.

29. Horowitz, *Energy Crisis*, 16.

30. Horowitz, *Energy Crisis*, 22.

31. Carter, *A Full Life*, 172.

32. Jimmy Carter, "Statement on the Iran Rescue Mission (April 25, 1980)," Miller Center, http://millercenter.org/president/carter/speeches/speech-3936.

33. Zelizer, *Jimmy Carter*, 103.

34. Zelizer, *Jimmy Carter*, 122.

35. Zelizer, *Jimmy Carter*, 115.

36. Zelizer, *Jimmy Carter*, 123.

37. Carter, *A Full Life*, 214–18.

38. Gillian Mohney, "The Remarkable Treatment That Helped Jimmy Carter Combat Brain Tumor," *ABC News*, March 7, 2016, http://abcnews.go.com/Health/remarkable-cancer-treat ment-helped-jimmy-carter-combat-brain/story?id=37467459.

39. William G. Clotworthy, *Homes and Libraries of the Presidents: An Interpretive Guide*, third edi- tion (Blacksburg, VA: McDonald & Woodward, 2008), 295.

40. Benjamin Hufbauer, *Presidential Temples: How Memorials and Libraries Shape Public Memory* (Lawrence: University Press of Kansas, 2005), 180.

41. Hufbauer, *Presidential Temples*, 180.

42. Frank L. Schick, Renee Schick, and Mark Carroll, *Records of the Presidency: Presidential Papers and Libraries from Washington to Reagan* (Phoenix, AZ: Oryx Press, 1989), 235.

43. "History of the Jimmy Carter Library," Jimmy Carter Presidential Library and Museum, accessed December 19, 2016, https://www.jimmycarterlibrary.gov/library/libhist.phtml.

44. Schick et al., *Records of the Presidency*, 232.

45. Schick et al., *Records of the Presidency*, 233.

46. Schick et al., *Records of the Presidency*, 234.

47. Schick et al., *Records of the Presidency*, 235.

48. Peter Applebome, "Carter Center: More Than the Past," *New York Times*, May 30, 1993, http://www.nytimes.com/1993/05/30/travel/carter-center-more-than-the-past.html?page wanted=all.

49. "Our Mission," the Carter Center, accessed December 19, 2016, https://www.carter center.org/about/index.html.

50. "History of the Jimmy Carter Library."

51. "Where Is the Carter Center Located?" The Carter Center, accessed January 3, 2017, https://www.cartercenter.org/about/faqs/index.html.

52. Schick et al., *Records of the Presidency*, 235.

53. Schick et al., *Records of the Presidency*, 235.

54. Applebome, "Carter Center."

55. Wendy R. Ginsberg, Erika K. Lunder, and Daniel J. Richardson, *The Presidential Libraries Act and the Establishment of Presidential Libraries* (CRS Report No. R41513) (Washington, DC: Congressional Research Service, 2015), 28.

56. Sheila Poole, "Meredith Evans Named New Director of Jimmy Carter Library," AJC.com, November 16, 2015, http://www.ajc.com/lifestyles/meredith-evans-named-new-director-jimmy-carter-library/e3ayqvvckPdKTcxbw4pOiI/.

57. Schick et al., *Records of the Presidency*, 236.

58. "The Oval Office," Jimmy Carter Presidential Library and Museum, accessed December 19, 2016, https://www.jimmycarterlibrary.gov/museum/ovaloffice.phtml.

59. "The Crown of St. Stephen," Jimmy Carter Presidential Library and Museum, accessed December 19, 2016, https://www.jimmycarterlibrary.gov/museum/crown.phtml.

60. "The Crown of St. Stephen."

61. "Special Events at the Jimmy Carter Library and Museum," Jimmy Carter Presidential Library and Museum, accessed December 19, 2016, https://www.jimmycarterlibrary.gov/events/.

62. "Jimmy Carter Library Manuscript Collections," Jimmy Carter Presidential Library and Museum, accessed December 19, 2016, https://www.jimmycarterlibrary.gov/library/listsubj.phtml.

63. "Jimmy Carter Library Manuscript Collections."

64. "Jimmy Carter Library Manuscript Collections."

65. Aisha M. Johnson-Jones, e-mail interview, February 21, 2017.

66. "Oral Histories at the Jimmy Carter Library," Jimmy Carter Presidential Library and Museum, accessed December 19, 2016, https://www.jimmycarterlibrary.gov/library/oralhist.phtml#ohproject.

67. "Oral Histories at the Jimmy Carter Library."

68. "Oral Histories at the Jimmy Carter Library."

69. "Oral Histories at the Jimmy Carter Library."

70. "Jimmy Carter Library Audiovisual Collections," Jimmy Carter Presidential Library and Museum, accessed December 19, 2016, https://www.jimmycarterlibrary.gov/library/av_materials.phtml#descwh.

71. "Jimmy Carter Library Audiovisual Collections."

72. Aisha Johnson-Jones, e-mail message.

BIBLIOGRAPHY

Applebome, Peter. "Carter Center: More Than the Past." *New York Times*, May 30, 1993. http://www.nytimes.com/1993/05/30/travel/carter-center-more-than-the-past.html?pagewanted=all.

Carter, Jimmy. *A Full Life: Reflections at Ninety*. New York: Simon and Schuster, 2015.

———. *Keeping Faith: Memoirs of a President*. New York: Bantam Books, 1982.

Clotworthy, William G. *Homes and Libraries of the Presidents: An Interpretive Guide*. Third edition. Blacksburg, VA: McDonald & Woodward, 2008.

Ginsberg, Wendy R., Erika K. Lunder, and Daniel J. Richardson. *The Presidential Libraries Act and the Establishment of Presidential Libraries* (CRS Report No. R41513). Washington, DC: Congressional Research Service, 2015.

Horowitz, Daniel. *Jimmy Carter and the Energy Crisis of the 1970s: The "Crisis of Confidence" Speech of July 15, 1979.* Boston: Bedford/St. Martin's, 2005.

Hufbauer, Benjamin. *Presidential Temples: How Memorials and Libraries Shape Public Memory.* Lawrence: University Press of Kansas, 2005.

Schick, Frank L., Renee Schick, and Mark Carroll. *Records of the Presidency: Presidential Papers and Libraries from Washington to Reagan.* Phoenix, AZ: Oryx Press, 1989.

Zelizer, Julian E. *Jimmy Carter.* The American Presidents Series. New York: Times Books, 2010.

• *22* •

Ronald Reagan Presidential Library and Museum

Address: 40 Presidential Drive, Simi Valley, CA 93065
Phone: 1-800-410-8354 or (805) 577-4000
Website: https://reaganlibrary.gov/
Social media: https://www.facebook.com/reaganlibraryandfoundation
Administration: National Archives
Hours: 10 a.m. to 5 p.m., every day; closed on Thanksgiving Day, Christmas Day, and
New Year's Day

BIOGRAPHY OF RONALD REAGAN

February 6, 1911–June 5, 2004
Fortieth President: January 20, 1981–January 20, 1989
Republican Party

Ronald Reagan. *Courtesy of the Ronald Reagan Presidential Library and Museum*

Ronald Reagan was born in Tampico, Illinois, to John Edward and Nelle Clyde Wilson Reagan. Ronald was their second son; Neil was Ronald's older brother. John Reagan was an Irish-American Catholic and Nelle was a Protestant of Scottish origin. Ronald was born above the family bakery, where his father worked. The family was poor and they moved many times. Despite these obstacles, Ronald graduated from North Dixon High School and went to Eureka College, Illinois, where he became involved in theater.[1]

After graduating, Reagan worked as a radio announcer in Des Moines, Iowa, where he became a local celebrity.[2] From radio, he moved into filmmaking. Reagan became a notable actor in what were known as low-budget B movies.[3] He worked alongside famous actors, including Errol Flynn and Olivia de Havilland. His most famous role was the football player George Gipp (known as "the Gipper") in the 1940 movie *Knute*

Rockne—All American. The most memorable scene in the film is when Reagan, playing an ailing Gipper, tells his teammates to "win one for the Gipper."[4] Around the time he made that movie, Reagan married his first wife, the actress Jane Wyman. They had two daughters, Maureen and Christine. Christine died in infancy. They also adopted a son, Michael. Today, Michael Reagan is a well-known Republican radio talk-show host. Ronald and Jane divorced in 1948.

During World War II, Reagan served as a lieutenant colonel in the First Motion Picture Unit of the Army Air Force. There, he made use of his acting skills to narrate war documentaries. After the war, Reagan was elected to lead the Screen Actors Guild, which is a labor union for actors. In the late 1940s, fear grew as America plunged into the Cold War. Reagan was concerned that Communists were trying to take over, and he worked with the FBI to help identify potential Communist sympathizers in Hollywood.[5] Reagan was a Democrat who supported President Harry S. Truman, but by 1952 he reversed his course and supported Republican Dwight David Eisenhower. He became more vocal in his anti-Communist rhetoric, too. That same year, Reagan married his second wife, Nancy Davis, who was also an actress. Ronald and Nancy had two children: Patti Davis and Ron Prescott Reagan.

In the 1950s, Reagan became the host of the television anthology series *General Electric Theater.* He also had the complementary job of being a spokesperson for General Electric and toured many of their factories meeting with various employees. Reagan said he considered his time with GE to be a "postgraduate course in political science," which propelled him toward conservative Republican politics.[6] Reagan also started to criticize government taxes.[7] In 1960, Reagan supported Richard Nixon for president rather than John F. Kennedy. Two years later he again supported Nixon, after he lost the presidential election, to run for governor of California. Reagan also formally switched his party affiliation to Republican.[8]

Reagan officially entered politics when he announced his candidacy for California governor in 1966. The platform for his campaign was building a "creative society" where "government would support private initiative rather than supplanting it."[9] Reagan won the election against Democratic incumbent Edmund "Pat" Brown, who was seeking a third term. As governor, Reagan unsuccessfully tried to cut government spending in the state by 10 percent. When the state legislature refused, he successfully proposed introducing a billion-dollar tax increase in return for a decrease in property tax.[10] His most controversial move was to call the National Guard to quell a student protest on the campus of the University of California in Berkeley. This show of force may have been a proving ground for a run at the presidency in 1968.[11] Reagan lost the nomination that year to Richard Nixon.

Ronald Reagan challenged President Gerald Ford for the Republican nomination in 1976. In a close race, Ford secured the nomination over Reagan, but he narrowly lost the presidential election to Democratic former governor Jimmy Carter of Georgia. However, Reagan did not give up. Four years later, he ran for and won the Republican nomination. He chose former CIA director and oilman George H. W. Bush of Texas as his running mate. The Democrats renominated President Carter even though the nation was facing economic troubles and American hostages were being held in Iran. On October 28, 1980, Carter and Reagan debated. Reagan made his case to the American people by asking them one simple question: "Are you better off than you were four years ago?"[12] On election night, it was clear that many citizens believed they were not better off, because they elected Reagan over Carter in a landslide. Reagan won 43,903,230 popular votes and 489 electoral votes. Cater won just 35,480,115 popular votes and 49 electoral votes. A third-party candidate named John B. Anderson won 5,719,850 popular votes. At the age of sixty-nine, Reagan became the oldest man to be elected to the presidency.

Shortly after taking office, Reagan was the victim of an assassination attempt. On March 30, 1981, John Hinckley Jr. shot at Reagan, wounding him and three others as the president left the Washington Hilton Hotel. His press secretary, James Brady, was shot in the head and spent the rest of his life with brain damage. As Reagan was rushed into surgery he joked with his doctors, saying, "Please tell me you're all Republicans."[13] Hinckley faced trial for the assassination attempt. However, the defense testimony showed that Hinckley had planned his assassination attempt to get the attention of actress Jodie Foster, whom he had fallen in love with, and the jury found him "not guilty by reason of insanity."[14]

According to historian Robert Service, the official policy of previous presidents had been to "contain" Soviet expansion. President Nixon introduced the concept of détente to help ease tensions between the two superpowers. However, Reagan thought détente was "a one-way street that the Soviet Union had used to pursue its own aims."[15] He had a different view: he wanted a "victory without [nuclear or military] confrontation."[16] Rather than simply containing Soviet expansion, Reagan's policy change was to "reverse the expansion" of the Soviet Union and its international "influence."[17] In this way, Reagan could pursue his vision for how the Cold War should end: "We win, they lose."[18] A new term was created to describe those who followed Reagan's policy: "Reaganauts."[19] However, not everyone liked Reagan's strong policy against the Soviet Union. For example, the policy frightened foreign leaders, who saw Reagan as a "warmonger."[20]

On March 8, 1983, Reagan made a speech in Orlando, Florida, to the National Association of Evangelicals. In this speech, he denounced the Soviet Union for being an "empire of evil."[21] Reagan was known as the Great Communicator, because he had the "ability to exploit chances to explain himself to the American public."[22] When it came to negotiating nuclear arms limitations with the Soviets, Reagan demanded "arms reductions" instead.[23] For Reagan, the way to stop the Soviet expansionism was to modernize American armed forces.[24] He also called for the development of the Strategic Defense Initiative (SDI), which aimed to place a weapon in space that could "shoot down offensive [Soviet] missiles."[25] Reagan's secretary of defense, Casper Weinberger, believed the SDI would "cause economic stress" for the Soviet Union.[26]

When Reagan was not dealing with the Soviet Union, he was confronting international terrorism. In the mid-1980s, terrorist groups in Lebanon were holding American hostages. The administration decided to enlist the help of one of America's enemies at the time, Iran. Two presidential advisors, Robert McFarlane and Oliver North, helped secure a deal where America would sell weapons to Iran. In return, Iran would convince the terrorists to free the American hostages. America sold 2,008 missiles and the hostages were eventually freed.[27] The proceeds from the sales of the weapons were used to fund Nicaraguan contra rebels, who opposed the socialist Sandinista Junta of National Reconstruction government in power.[28] The deal became known as the Iran-Contra affair. Congress investigated the key players, including McFarlane and North, and the scandal ended with North being convicted of three counts of "accepting an illegal gratuity" and destroying documents relating to the exchange.[29] No evidence was found to indicate that Reagan knew of the exchange.[30]

At home, Reagan pursued a course of what became known as Reaganomics. Jacob Weisberg says that Reagan's conservative economic plan called for "reduced taxes, cutting domestic spending, implementing deregulation, and using monetary policy to combat inflation."[31] Reagan also pursed a government policy that he called New Federalism, where individual states took charge of administering welfare programs, such as food stamps.[32] By 1982, the economy was in a recession. The stock market was down and the homeless population in cities was growing.[33] Reagan's policies helped to reduce inflation and create "a period of economic expansion" during his administration.[34] However, by the same token, the government expanded and as he used deficit spending to fund it.[35]

While Reagan was grappling with the American economy, he also had to negotiate with the new Soviet premier, Mikhail Gorbachev. Reagan began talks with Gorbachev in 1985 after being elected to a second term in a historic landslide against Democrat Walter Mondale. The two met on October 11, 1986, in Reykjavík, Iceland. At the Reykjavík Summit, Reagan and Gorbachev began talks on reducing nuclear arms. The meeting was going well until Gorbachev insisted that Reagan "concede on the Strategic Defense Initiative."[36] The summit ended abruptly in failure and the two leaders left. Before parting Reagan said to Gorbachev, "We were so close to an agreement I think you didn't want to achieve any agreement anyway."[37]

On June 11, 1987, Reagan made an important speech in front of the Brandenburg Gate in West Berlin. He was the second president to make a speech there; the first was John F. Kennedy. In the speech he made demands for Gorbachev to dismantle the wall: "Mr. Gorbachev, open this gate. Mr. Gorbachev, tear down this wall!"[38] However, hope was not lost for a deal between America and the Soviet Union. On December 8, 1987, Reagan and Gorbachev signed the Intermediate-Range Nuclear Forces Treaty (INF Treaty), in which both nations agreed to "limit the number of nuclear weapons they held" and "eliminate an entire category of ballistic missiles."[39]

Constitutionally, Reagan could not run for a third term; instead, he supported his vice president, George H. W. Bush, to run for the presidency. Bush would win the 1988 election against his Democratic rival, Governor Michael Dukakis of Massachusetts. Upon leaving the presidency, Reagan went into retirement in California. Reagan was diagnosed with Alzheimer's and he decided to send a final message to the American people; he said, "In closing let me thank you, the American people for giving me the great honor of allowing me to serve as your President."[40] Reagan died on June 5, 2004; he was buried at his presidential library in Simi Valley, California. His wife, Nancy, died on March 6, 2016, and is buried next to him.

LIBRARY AND MUSEUM

Ronald Reagan began planning for his library shortly after taking office in 1981. Since he donated his gubernatorial papers to the Hoover Institution at Stanford University, he considered having his presidential library and a public affairs center there. Over the next three years, Reagan worked with the director of the Hoover Institution, W. Glenn Campbell, on the logistics of his library. In 1985 the Ronald Reagan Presidential Foundation was created to plan, construct, and fund the library through an endowment. The foundation was headed by Reagan's former attorney generals, William French Smith and Edwin Meese III. Campbell was also a member of the foundation.[41] Reagan wanted a public affairs center to be included in his library at Stanford. However, ultimately the trustees at Stanford turned down the president's request to build a library and public affairs center at the university. Their reasoning was that Reagan's library "when added to the Hoover Institution, would compromise the University's independence and open it up to accusations of partisanship toward right-wing causes."[42]

On November 4, 1991, the Reagan library was formally opened at a dedication ceremony. Four thousand people attended, including then president George H. W. Bush and former presidents Richard Nixon, Gerald Ford, and Jimmy Carter.[43] The Spanish-style library building was built on a "barren hillside" for $60 million.[44] Ted McAllister describes the library and its unique location:

> Sitting atop a hill at the edge of Simi Valley, the Ronald Reagan Library and Museum has a commanding view of surrounding valleys and mountains—the same area used as the location for many of the Hollywood westerns of the 1930s. Befitting Reagan's own cowboy self-image.[45]

In November 2007 the Reagan library was the center of controversy when a National Archives audit discovered that only twenty thousand items out of an estimated one hundred thousand were accounted for.[46] The library had "45 million unprocessed documents" when it opened in 1991.[47] Prior to the audit, a volunteer was fired for stealing from the library. However, the fate of the eighty thousand missing items is not clear. United States senator Chuck Grassley of Iowa speculated that the library "may have experienced loss or pilferage the scope of which will likely never be known."[48] Grassley pushed for audits of other presidential libraries, fearing that priceless and irreplaceable artifacts might go missing in the future. He said, "This report is a wake up. . . . These papers, records and other items have historical value and should be safeguarded for the education and benefit of future generations of Americans."[49]

Historian Ted McAllister explains that the library had a "vision" problem in the past.[50] He argues that the library's central focus is how Reagan ended the Cold War and worked for "nuclear disarmament," but the arrival of Air Force One at the library "provided such a stunning and visually powerful focal point for the museum that it helps overshadow other important events in foreign affairs."[51] McAllister is critical of the Reagan library, as is Benjamin Hufbauer, who says that it has "seriously flawed displays."[52] Hufbauer also criticizes the library for not covering the Iran-Contra affair.[53] Is the Reagan library promoting what Hufbauer calls the "McPresident" or the "Happy

Ronald Reagan Presidential Library and Museum. *Courtesy of the Ronald Reagan Presidential Library and Museum*

Meal" version of presidential history by leaving out critical information?[54] This question is best left to visitors.

The Reagan library has hosted three Republican Party presidential primary debates. On May 3, 2007, Republican candidates debated while seeking to become the Republican nominee for the 2008 presidential election. The debate was presented live from the library and hosted by MSNBC.[55] The second time was September 7, 2011, when Republican candidates debated for the 2012 presidential election. That debate was sponsored jointly by MSNBC and *Politico*.[56] The most recent debate was held in advance of the 2016 presidential election, when Republican candidates met at the library on September 16, 2015. This debate was hosted by CNN.[57]

From February 1 to February 7, 2011, the library celebrated Reagan's centennial by hosting a series of events in honor of the former president. Director John Heubusch said, "The centennial celebration is about more than just one day and one man. It's a year-long historic occasion for people to remember an extraordinary man who restored pride in America and spread freedom throughout the world."[58] The library had a four-part academic symposium where university professors and famous reporters, such as Tom Brokaw, spoke about the president. A concert was also held, at which The Beach Boys and Lee Greenwood played.[59]

Museum and Exhibits

In 2012 the library welcomed 380,570 visitors. The Reagan library has five permanent exhibits. The first exhibit that visitors will see is called *Oval Office*. The replica office is a

Reagan's replica Oval Office. *Courtesy of the Ronald Reagan Presidential Library and Museum*

"full-sized reproduction as it appeared" during Reagan's administration in the 1980s.[60] The following exhibit is *Governor of California*, which highlights Reagan's two terms as governor of California from 1967 to 1975. The information inside covers his achievements as governor, which include lowering taxes and cutting government.[61] The third exhibit is dedicated to Reagan's wife, Nancy. Here, visitors will see paintings and other relevant information pertaining to Nancy's life and her role as First Lady.[62] After learning about the First Lady, visitors will see a replica Berlin Wall and learn what it was like in the divided city of Berlin during the Cold War.[63] The wall came down on November 9, 1989. Outside the library, visitors can see a slab of the original Berlin Wall, complete with the graffiti that had been written on it.[64]

A special exhibit is the actual Air Force One (Boeing VC–137C) airplane used by Ronald Reagan and six other presidents. The plane can be seen in part of the library known as the Air Force One Pavilion, which is open to all. The plane is also known by its tail number, SAM 27000. Reagan used the plane to fly six hundred sixty thousand miles to visit twenty-six foreign countries and forty-six states. The plane is on loan from the United States Air Force.[65]

The final exhibit is dedicated to the Secret Service, which guards the president. Reagan was grateful to the Secret Service for saving his life during the attempted assassination. Inside, visitors will learn about the "not so secret" history of the Secret Service and read information about what it is like to work in the service and how it protects the nation's currency from counterfeiters.[66]

From 2016 to 2017, the library hosted a temporary exhibit: *Interactive! The Exhibition—How Pop Culture Reshapes Technology*. According to the library's website, the exhibit "is a large-scale, hands-on examination of how popular culture in movies, books, TV, and the arts has influenced modern technology and changed the ways we live, work, move, connect, and play."[67] Visitors will learn how fictional movie characters, like "R2D2 from *Star Wars*, a T-800 endoskeleton from *The Terminator*, and a full-size alien from the *Alien* films" operated.[68]

Previously the Reagan library hosted special exhibits on George Washington, baseball, and the Magna Carta, where the original document was on display.[69] The library also hosted five hundred artifacts in an exhibit entitled *D23 Presents: Treasures of the Walt Disney Archives at the Reagan Library*. Visitors were able to see exhibits from the Walt Disney Archives, including the busts of American presidents and costumes, props, and drawings.[70]

Manuscripts and Audiovisuals

Archivists and researchers have access to a large collection of manuscripts at the Reagan library. Among the documents available for research are the White House staff and office inventories, Reagan's gubernatorial collection, the personal papers of Reagan's friends and administrators, federal records, and a digital library of declassified White House staff collections.[71] The library also has a large audiovisual collection of photos and White House videotapes. Not surprisingly, the library holds audiotapes from Reagan's time as California governor and television episodes from the series *General Electric Theater*, which he hosted in the mid-1950s.[72]

View of the Air Force One Pavilion at the Reagan Library. *Courtesy of the Ronald Reagan Presidential Library and Museum*

The Reagan library has a small oral history collection. The Miscellaneous Oral History Interviews were conducted from 2001 to 2004. Roughly half of the histories are from members of the First Motion Picture Unit who served with Reagan during World War II. The other half includes Reagan's contemporaries—his friends and people who worked with him in politics.[73] Remote researchers will benefit from the library's online collection of Reagan's speeches. The collection spans the period 1964–1989 and contains speeches he made as governor and president.[74]

Reagan Foundation

The library is administered in part by the Ronald Reagan Foundation. The foundation "is a non-profit, non-partisan organization dedicated to the promotion of individual liberty, economic opportunity, global democracy, and national pride. It sustains the Ronald Reagan Presidential Library and Museum."[75] The foundation also administers the Center for Public Affairs, which hosts forums and lectures about Ronald Reagan.[76] The current director of the foundation is John Heubusch, who previously worked as a businessman, as chief of staff to Secretary of Labor Elizabeth Dole, and as an Air Force research analyst at the Pentagon.[77]

NOTES

1. Jacob Weisberg, *Ronald Reagan*, the American Presidents Series (New York: Times Books, 2016), 9–12.

2. Weisberg, *Ronald Reagan*, 18.

3. Weisberg, *Ronald Reagan*, 20.

4. Weisberg, *Ronald Reagan*, 21.

5. Weisberg, *Ronald Reagan*, 25.

6. Weisberg, *Ronald Reagan*, 34.

7. Weisberg, *Ronald Reagan*, 38.

8. Weisberg, *Ronald Reagan*, 39.

9. Weisberg, *Ronald Reagan*, 46.

10. Weisberg, *Ronald Reagan*, 47.

11. Weisberg, *Ronald Reagan*, 48.

12. Weisberg, *Ronald Reagan*, 66.

13. Weisberg, *Ronald Reagan*, 71.

14. Christian A. Nappo, "Presidential Assassination and the Insanity Defense," Unpublished Policy and Practice Paper, University of Alabama, 2000, 75–78.

15. James Mann, *The Rebellion of Ronald Reagan: A History of the End of the Cold War* (New York: Viking, 2009), 27.

16. Weisberg, *Ronald Reagan*, 39.

17. Robert Service, *The End of the Cold War: 1985–1991* (New York: Public Affairs, 2015), 14.

18. Mann, *Rebellion*, 16.

19. Service, *Cold War*, 34.

20. Service, *Cold War*, 33.

21. Service, *Cold War*, 43.

22. Service, *Cold War*, 218.

23. Service, *Cold War*, 15.

24. Service, *Cold War*, 22.

25. Service, *Cold War*, 44.

26. Service, *Cold War*, 45.

27. Weisberg, *Ronald Reagan*, 130.

28. Weisberg, *Ronald Reagan*, 130.

29. Weisberg, *Ronald Reagan*, 134.

30. Weisberg, *Ronald Reagan*, 133.

31. Weisberg, *Ronald Reagan*, 69.

32. Weisberg, *Ronald Reagan*, 76.

33. Weisberg, *Ronald Reagan*, 76.

34. Weisberg, *Ronald Reagan*, 78.

35. Weisberg, *Ronald Reagan*, 78–79.

36. Service, *Cold War*, 217.

37. Service, *Cold War*, 218.

38. Service, *Cold War*, 321.

39. Service, *Cold War*, 299–300.

40. Weisberg, *Ronald Reagan*, 145.

41. Frank L. Schick, Renee Schick, and Mark Carroll, *Records of the Presidency: Presidential Papers and Libraries from Washington to Reagan* (Phoenix, AZ: Oryx Press, 1989), 249–50.

42. Schick et al., *Records of the Presidency*, 250.

43. Seth Mydans, "Elite Group to Dedicate Reagan Library," *New York Times*, November 1, 1991, http://www.nytimes.com/1991/11/01/us/elite-group-to-dedicate-reagan-library.html.

44. Mydans, "Elite Group to Dedicate Reagan Library."

45. Ted McAllister, "The Ronald Reagan Library and Museum," *Public Historian* 28 (Summer 2006): 209.

46. Steve Chawkins and Catherine Saillant, "The Talk of the Reagan Library," *Los Angeles Times*, November 9, 2007, http://articles.latimes.com/2007/nov/09/local/me-reagan9.

47. McAllister, "The Ronald Reagan Library," 208.

48. Ricardo Alonso-Zaldivar and Catherine Saillant, "Reagan Library Has Lost Thousands of Artifacts," *Tampa Bay Times*, November 10, 2007, http://www.tbo.com/ap/world/reagan-library-has-lost-thousands-of-artifacts-163909.

49. Alonso-Zaldivar and Saillant, "Reagan Library Has Lost Thousands of Artifacts."

50. McAllister, "The Ronald Reagan Library," 208.

51. McAllister, "The Ronald Reagan Library," 211.

52. Benjamin Hufbauer, *Presidential Temples: How Memorials and Libraries Shape Public Memory* (Lawrence: University Press of Kansas, 2005), 173.

53. Hufbauer, *Presidential Temples*, 143.

54. Hufbauer, *Presidential Temples*, 173.

55. Adam Nagourney, "Republican Candidates Hold First Debate, Differing on Defining Party's Future: Correction Appended," *New York Times*, May 4, 2007, http://query.nytimes.com/gst/fullpage.html?res=9C07EFDB113EF937A35756C0A9619C8B63&scp=14&sq=reagan+library+debate&st=nyt.

56. *New York Times*, "The Republican Debate at the Reagan Library," September 7, 2011, http://www.nytimes.com/2011/09/08/us/politics/08republican-debate-text.html.

57. Jonathan Martin and Patrick Healy, "Candidates Use Second G.O.P. Debate to Taunt Donald Trump," *New York Times*, September 16, 2015, http://www.nytimes.com/2015/09/17/us/politics/candidates-use-second-gop-debate-to-taunt-trump.html.

58. Reagan Foundation, "Ronald Reagan's Centennial to Be Celebrated at the Ronald Reagan Presidential Library," news release, January 19, 2011, https://www.reaganfoundation.org/media/50867/birthday-celebration-week-lead-relase-1-18-11.pdf.

59. Reagan Foundation, "Ronald Reagan's Centennial to Be Celebrated."

60. "Permanent Exhibits," Ronald Reagan Presidential Library and Museum, accessed February 3, 2017, https://reaganlibrary.gov/museum/permanent-exhibits.

61. "Permanent Exhibits."

62. "Permanent Exhibits."

63. "Permanent Exhibits."

64. "Permanent Exhibits."

65. "Air Force One," Ronald Reagan Presidential Library and Museum, accessed February 3, 2017, https://www.reaganfoundation.org/library-museum/permanent-exhibitions/air-force-one/.

66. "Secret Service," Reagan Foundation, accessed February 3, 2017, https://www.reaganfoundation.org/library-museum/permanent-exhibitions/secret-service/.

67. "Interactive! The Exhibition," Ronald Reagan Presidential Library and Museum, accessed February 3, 2017, https://reaganlibrary.gov/museum/current-exhibits.

68. "Interactive! The Exhibition."

69. "Previous Exhibits," Ronald Reagan Presidential Library and Museum, accessed February 3, 2017, https://www.reaganlibrary.gov/museum/mmprevious-exhibits.

70. "Previous Exhibits."

71. "Document Collections," Ronald Reagan Presidential Library and Museum, accessed February 3, 2017, https://reaganlibrary.gov/document-collection.

72. "Document Collections."

73. "Reagan Library Miscellaneous Oral History Interviews, 2001–2004," Ronald Reagan Presidential Library and Museum, accessed February 3, 2017, https://reaganlibrary.gov/archives/speeches/12-archives/audiovisual/10544-oral-histories.

74. "Document Collections."

75. "About Us," Reagan Foundation, accessed February 3, 2017, https://www.reaganfoundation.org/about-us/.

76. "Center for Public Affairs," Ronald Reagan Presidential Foundation and Institute, accessed February 6, 2017, https://www.reaganfoundation.org/support-us/give-a-gift/center-for-public-affairs/.

77. "John Heubusch," Reagan Foundation, accessed February 3, 2017, https://www.reaganfoundation.org/about-us/executive-team/john-heubusch/.

BIBLIOGRAPHY

Alonso-Zaldivar, Ricardo, and Catherine Saillant. "Reagan Library Has Lost Thousands of Artifacts." *Tampa Bay Times*, November 10, 2001. http://www.tbo.com/ap/world/reagan-library-has-lost-thousands-of-artifacts-163909.

Caplan, Lincoln. *The Insanity Defense and the Trial of John Hinckley Jr.* Boston, MA: Godine, 1984.

Chawkins, Steve, and Catherine Saillant. "The Talk of the Reagan Library." *Los Angeles Times*, November 9, 2007. http://articles.latimes.com/2007/nov/09/local/me-reagan9.

Clotworthy, William G. *Homes and Libraries of the Presidents: An Interpretive Guide.* Third edition. Blacksburg, VA: McDonald & Woodward, 2008.

Ginsberg, Wendy R., Erika K. Lunder, and Daniel J. Richardson. *The Presidential Libraries Act and the Establishment of Presidential Libraries* (CRS Report No. R41513). Washington, DC: Congressional Research Service, 2015.

Hufbauer, Benjamin. *Presidential Temples: How Memorials and Libraries Shape Public Memory*. Lawrence: University Press of Kansas, 2005.

Mann, James. *The Rebellion of Ronald Reagan: A History of the End of the Cold War*. New York: Viking, 2009.

Martin, Jonathan, and Patrick Healy. "Candidates Use Second G.O.P. Debate to Taunt Donald Trump." *New York Times*, September 16, 2015. http://www.nytimes.com/2015/09/17/us/politics/candidates-use-second-gop-debate-to-taunt-trump.html.

McAllister, Ted. "The Ronald Reagan Library and Museum." *Public Historian* 28 (Summer 2006): 208–11.

Mydans, Seth. "Elite Group to Dedicate Reagan Library." *New York Times*, November 1, 1991. http://www.nytimes.com/1991/11/01/us/elite-group-to-dedicate-reagan-library.html.

Nagourney, Adam. "Republican Candidates Hold First Debate, Differing on Defining Party's Future: Correction Appended." *New York Times*, May 4, 2007. http://query.nytimes.com/gst/fullpage.html?res=9C07EFDB113EF937A35756C0A9619C8B63&scp=14&sq=reagan+library+debate&st=nyt.

Nappo, Christian A. "Presidential Assassination and the Insanity Defense." Unpublished Policy and Practice Paper, University of Alabama, 2000.

New York Times. "The Republican Debate at the Reagan Library." September 7, 2011. http://www.nytimes.com/2011/09/08/us/politics/08republican-debate-text.html.

Schick, Frank L., Renee Schick, and Mark Carroll. *Records of the Presidency: Presidential Papers and Libraries from Washington to Reagan*. Phoenix, AZ: Oryx Press, 1989.

Service, Robert. *The End of the Cold War: 1985–1991*. New York: Public Affairs, 2015.

Weisberg, Jacob. *Ronald Reagan*. The American Presidents Series. New York: Times Books, 2016.

Zelizer, Julian E. *Jimmy Carter*. The American Presidents Series. New York: Times Books, 2010.

George Bush Presidential Library and Museum

Address: 1000 George Bush Drive West, College Station, TX 77845
Phone: (979) 691-4000
Website: https://bush41.org/
Social media: https://www.facebook.com/bush41library/
Administration: National Archives
Partnership: Texas A&M University in College Station
Hours: 9:30 a.m. to 5 p.m., Monday to Saturday; noon to 5 p.m. on Sundays

BIOGRAPHY OF GEORGE H. W. BUSH

June 12, 1924–
Forty-First President: January 20, 1989–January 20, 1993
Republican Party

George H. W. Bush by David Valdez. *LC-USZ62-98302*

George Herbert Walker Bush was born in Milton, Massachusetts, to Prescott and Dorothy Bush. Prescott Bush was a businessman and served as a United States Senator representing Connecticut from 1952 to 1963. Young George attended Phillips Academy in Andover, Massachusetts. As soon as he turned eighteen in 1942, he joined the navy, where he served as a pilot in World War II. By 1944 Bush was serving aboard the light aircraft carrier USS *San Jacinto*. Stationed in the Pacific theater, he participated in bombing raids against the Japanese, who held Wake Island and Guam.[1] On September 2, 1944, Bush's plane was shot down during a combat mission off the island of Chichi Jima. He successfully parachuted from the plane and waited in a life raft until an American submarine rescued him.

After the war Bush married Barbara Pierce. They had six children: George W., John "Jeb," Neil, Marvin, Dorothy, and Pauline "Robin," Sadly, Robin died in infancy of leukemia.

Bush entered the oil industry in Midland, Texas, and became a millionaire while working for Zapata Oil.[2] After securing his family financially, Bush followed in the footsteps of his father and entered politics. In 1967 he was elected to the Seventh Texas Congressional District as a Republican. He served two terms in the House of Representatives and was nominated to be the United States ambassador to the United Nations in 1971. Following this, he worked as a diplomat in China. He then went on to direct the Central Intelligence Agency in the late 1970s.

However, Bush had his eyes on the presidency. He sought the Republican nomination in 1980, but he was not successful. That year, the Republicans nominated the former governor of California, Ronald Reagan. Reagan chose Bush as his running mate, and the two were elected in 1980 and reelected in 1984. Eventually, in 1988, Bush was nominated by the Republican Party to be their presidential candidate. When delivering his acceptance speech to the convention, Bush made a promise that would come back to haunt him in 1992: "Read my lips: No new taxes."[3] For vice president he chose Senator Dan Quayle of Indiana. The Democrats nominated Governor Michael Dukakis of Massachusetts and Senator Lloyd Bentsen of Texas as their candidates. The Democrats immediately attacked Quayle's "awkwardness in answering questions" and accused him of being a draft-dodger during the Vietnam War.[4] The Republicans fought back with one of the most controversial campaign advertisements ever when they accused Dukakis of releasing dangerous criminals like Willie Horton, who, during a weekend furlough, raped a woman and beat her fiancé.[5] Bush won the election with 48,886,097 popular votes and 426 electoral votes. Dukakis received 41,809,074 popular votes and 111 electoral votes.

Bush's administration would witness one of the most significant events in many years: the end of the Cold War. In the summer of 1989, Hungary pulled down its border fences and allowed people to cross freely into the West.[6] This act gave East Germans an easy route into West Germany rather than having to risk death by scaling the Berlin Wall. In Poland, Lech Wałęsa's Solidarity Party won elections, beating their Communist rivals.[7] Then, on November 9, 1989, the East German government surprised the world by suddenly announcing that the Berlin Wall "was open."[8] A revolution swept across Eastern Europe as Communist leaders relinquished their power. In Romania, the Communist dictator Nicolae Ceauşescu was overthrown. He and his wife Elena were executed on December 25, 1989.[9] That summer in China, however, the government put a brutal end to an antigovernment uprising in Tiananmen Square in Beijing.[10]

In December 1989 Bush met with Soviet premier Mikhail Gorbachev in Malta. The two agreed to sign the Conventional Forces in Europe Treaty.[11] That same month, Bush launched an invasion of Panama, known as Operation Just Cause, to overthrow the dictator Manuel Noriega.[12] In 1990 East and West Germany were reunited and the Soviet Union eventually broke up on December 25, 1991, ending the Cold War.

On August 2, 1990, new foreign problems emerged when the Iraqi dictator Saddam Hussein invaded neighboring Kuwait. The invasion compelled the United States to form an alliance to force Hussein to withdraw from Kuwait. In what was known as

Operation Desert Shield, allied forces sent troops to Saudi Arabia to quell further aggression by Hussein. The United Nations then passed Resolution 670, which gave Iraq until January 15, 1991, to withdraw from Kuwait or face military action. The resolution was approved by Congress on January 12. When Hussein refused to withdraw by January 15, war became inevitable. Operation Desert Storm was initiated on January 17 to stop Hussein from invading more of his neighbors. Cable news broadcast the bombing of Baghdad live for the entire world to see. America and her allies concentrated on bombing military targets to weaken Iraq's resolve. Iraq fought back not directly against the Allies but by launching Scud missiles into Israel. Hussein thought that this would force Israel to enter the war, and Arab nations sympathetic to Hussein might become motivated to attack Israel.[13] Hussein's strategy proved to be unrealistic, and the war entered its next phase: the ground invasion.

Following the "air war" of Desert Storm, America and her allies initiated the ground offensive on February 24. Rather than launch an amphibious landing in Kuwait, the Allies used the "left hook" strategy of attacking Iraqi forces from the western desert into Kuwait.[14] The strategy worked; large numbers of Iraqi forces "collapsed in front of Marines."[15] Kuwait was liberated four days later. In desperation, what was left of Hussein's army fled north to Iraq. However, the war was still on and many retreating soldiers were attacked. Bush feared an unnecessary "overkill" of enemy forces on a stretch of road that was nicknamed "the highway of death."[16] On February 28, a ceasefire was negotiated, which effectively ended the hostilities. Hussein was not removed from power.

Bush had his fair share of domestic successes and failures as president. He successfully promoted and signed the Clear Air Act, the Americans with Disabilities Act and the Civil Rights Act of 1991.[17] In October 1990 Bush signed a budget deal that included tax increases. Though he had promised not to raise taxes on the campaign trail, the Republicans were not a majority in Congress and the Democrats insisted on them.[18] In June 1991, unemployment reached 6.9 percent and one year later the nation entered a recession.[19] The Republicans were angry with Bush for agreeing to the tax hike and accused him of betraying the policies of Ronald Reagan.[20] During the presidential campaign of 1992, the Republican political commentator Patrick J. Buchanan challenged Bush for the nomination. The Democrats also criticized Bush for going against his promise not to raise taxes.[21] They nominated Governor Bill Clinton of Arkansas for president and Senator Al Gore of Tennessee for vice president. Though Bush secured his party's renomination, he faced a challenge by third-party candidate and billionaire H. Ross Perot from Texas. Once again, Vice President Quayle proved problematic on the campaign trail when he instructed an elementary student to spell the word "potato" incorrectly as "potatoe."[22]

On election night, Bush lost his bid for reelection in the three-way race to Clinton. Bush won 39,104,550 popular votes and 168 electoral votes compared with Clinton's 44,909,806 popular votes and 370 electoral votes. Independent candidate Ross Perot won a stunning 19,743,821 popular votes but did not win any states. One of Bush's final acts as president was to send American troops into war-torn Somalia to help deliver humanitarian aid.[23]

Upon leaving the White House, Bush retired from politics. On January 20, 2001, he attended the presidential inauguration of his son George W. Bush. Five years later his son asked him, along with former president Clinton, to raise relief money for the tsunami-stricken regions of Asia and the victims of Hurricane Katrina at home.[24]

LIBRARY AND MUSEUM

Bush was first approached about locating his presidential library on the campus of Texas A&M University in early 1989 by friend and oil man Michel T. Halbouty. Halbouty was also an alumnus of the university from the Class of 1930.[25] The university was interested in hosting Bush's library, and renamed one of its campus streets George Bush Drive in September 1989.[26] About two years later, Bush informed the university that he would build his library there. The library was built on a ninety-acre park situated on the west side of the campus. The Manhattan Construction Company was contracted to build the library at the cost of $85 million. This cost also covered the construction of the Annenberg Presidential Conference Center and an academic building for use by the university.[27] The funds for building the library had to be raised. In fact, foreign nations, including Japan, Kuwait, and Sudan, graciously offered to provide $1 million each.[28] Texas A&M University agreed to open the George Bush School of Government and Public Service in collaboration with its college of liberal arts. The school's mission is "educating principled leaders, conducting research."[29]

On November 30, 1994, the groundbreaking ceremony was held with Bush and his family. Three years later the library was opened to the public. In attendance with the Bush family were Nancy Reagan, "Lady Bird" Johnson, Bill Clinton (who was president at the time), and former presidents Gerald Ford and Jimmy Carter. Also attending were several senators and congressmen, and the Reverend Billy Graham. Former president Ford said the library was a "classroom of democracy, a place to find inspiration as well as information."[30] Since its opening, the library has hosted several guest speakers, including astronaut Buzz Aldrin, college basketball coach Bob Knight, actor Chuck Norris, General Colin Powell, and journalist Diane Sawyer.[31]

Bush and his wife Barbara have both expressed their wish to be buried within the library grounds. In fact, they had their child Robin reinterred there in May 2000.[32]

Like other presidential libraries, the George Bush Presidential Library and Museum has critics. One of these is history professor Dr. Thomas Clarkin of San Antonio College. Clarkin believes that the museum exhibits highlight Bush's foreign-policy achievements, such as the Gulf War, and downplay the domestic issues he faced, such as the problems with the economy. Because of this, Clarkin concludes, "the museum offers an incomplete portrait of his [Bush's] presidency."[33] Is Clarkin suggesting that this library is guilty of creating what Benjamin Hufbauer calls the "Happy Meal version of presidential history?"[34] We should let visitors decide the answer to this question.

George Bush Presidential Library and Museum on the Texas A&M University campus, College Station, Texas, by Carol Highsmith. *Carol Highsmith LC-HS503-3429 (ONLINE)*

Collections and Exhibits

The Bush library has nine exhibits containing a total of thirty-one galleries. The first exhibit is *Symbols of the Presidency*. The exhibit displays images of the presidential seal, including one made of crystal that is three feet high. Also of interest is a real limousine used by the president.[35] *Family Traditions* is the name of the second exhibit, where visitors will see pictures and mementos from Bush's childhood and his years as a young adult. Among the galleries, visitors will see photos and videos of Bush and his family; information about his wife, Barbara; photos, letters, and a replica wedding gown from the marriage of Bush and Barbara; a restored Studebaker, which is identical to the one Bush drove in 1947, and photos and information about the couple's children, including the tragic death of their daughter Robin.[36]

The third exhibit, *World War II*, focuses on Bush's service during the war. Visitors will see pictures of Bush on active duty. Of particular interest is a restored 1944 TBM Avenger plane, exactly like the one that Bush flew. There is also a simulation game where visitors can land a TBM on the deck of USS *San Jacinto*.[37]

This is followed by the exhibit *Political Itch*, which chronicles Bush's journey into public service. The exhibit begins by telling the story of Bush working in the oil industry. A video shows the cutting-edge drilling equipment of the era. From here, visitors will see a thirty-foot-tall reproduction of the Capitol dome representing Bush's days as a congressman from Texas. Next, the galleries present Bush as the United States ambassador to the United Nations. There are several photos of Ambassador Bush and of the United Nations General Assembly. The exhibit concludes with galleries focusing on Bush's tenure as director of the Central Intelligence Agency and how he became vice president under Ronald Reagan.[38]

The fifth exhibit, *Domestic Leadership*, chronicles Bush's domestic achievements as president. In the galleries in this exhibit, visitors can find out about Bush's election to the presidency, see what dinners were like at the White House, view Bush's replica Oval Office, view artifacts (gifts) that Bush received from foreign dignitaries, and learn about Bush signing the Americans with Disabilities Act and the Clean Air Act. The exhibit also contains a Press Room Theater, where visitors can watch footage from the real press conferences held by Bush and his vice president, Quayle. Visitors can also test their speaking skills by reading a speech off a teleprompter.[39] This exhibit leads to the sixth one, which is dedicated solely to the First Lady, Barbara Bush, *To Help Everyday*. Here visitors can see photos and videos of the First Lady.[40] Of special importance in this exhibit is the Literacy Overlook Room. Inside, visitors can relax with their children as they read a variety of storybooks.[41]

The seventh exhibit is *Crisis Management*, which explores Bush's foreign policy. Visitors will see a twelve-foot section of the actual Berlin Wall, which was pulled down during Bush's administration. There are also video kiosks where visitors can learn about other foreign-policy challenges Bush faced, such as how to deal with the Iraqi invasion of Kuwait. Using interactive technology, visitors can make informed decisions on how they would have managed Operation Desert Shield and Desert Storm. A gallery dedicated to "eco-terrorism" explains how Saddam Hussein blew up several Kuwaiti oil rigs as the Iraqi army retreated. It took America and her allies eight months to put out the flames. Finally, there is a wall displaying the names of the service men and women who gave their lives during the Gulf War.[42]

A Life of Service is the eighth exhibit, and this focuses on Bush's life after his presidency. Inside, visitors can see photos and read information taken from the presidential election of 1992, when Bush lost to Governor Bill Clinton. There are also galleries showing Bush parachute jumping; presenting information on his Points of Light Foundation, dedicated to volunteering; and displaying his speedboat, *Fidelity*, which he sailed off the coast of Kennebunkport, Maine.[43]

The final exhibit is *Before You Go*. Here, visitors can use a computer to ask the president or First Lady a question and have the opportunity to receive a letter from them in answer. The computer also provides information about how you can become a "point of light in your own community by doing the things that are of interest to you."[44]

The Bush library is home to a large collection of research materials. Currently, there are more than four hundred forty million pages of records, two million photographs, ten thousand video recordings, and eight hundred hours of audio. There are also 122,000 artifacts, with 1,377 artifacts from foreign heads of state.[45]

The library also holds the vice presidential records of Bush and Dan Quayle.[46] Some of the archives are available for research online. Among the online collections are papers about national security, meetings of the Bush administration, and selected papers on China and the Gulf War.[47]

From 2015 to 2016 the library held a temporary exhibit called the *National Parks Photography Project*. This exhibit showcased the black-and-white photography of America's national parks taken by Mark Burns. The photographs were viewed in the Ansary Gallery of American History.[48]

NOTES

1. Timothy Naftali, *George H. W. Bush*, the American Presidents Series (New York: Times Books, 2007), 7–8.

2. Naftali, *George H. W. Bush*, 10–12.

3. Naftali, *George H. W. Bush*, 61.

4. Naftali, *George H. W. Bush*, 61.

5. Naftali, *George H. W. Bush*, 61.

6. John Lewis Gaddis, *The Cold War: A New History* (New York: Penguin Books, 2005), 241.

7. Robert Service, *The End of the Cold War: 1985–1991* (New York: PublicAffairs, 2015), 401.

8. Gaddis, *The Cold War*, 246.

9. Gaddis, *The Cold War*, 247.

10. Gaddis, *The Cold War*, 245.

11. Naftali, *George H. W. Bush*, 88.

12. Naftali, *George H. W. Bush*, 88.

13. Naftali, *George H. W. Bush*, 123.

14. Naftali, *George H. W. Bush*, 118–25.

15. Naftali, *George H. W. Bush*, 125.

16. Naftali, *George H. W. Bush*, 126.

17. Naftali, *George H. W. Bush*, 133.

18. Naftali, *George H. W. Bush*, 115–17.

19. Naftali, *George H. W. Bush*, 140.

20. Naftali, *George H. W. Bush*, 140.

21. Helen Dewar and Kenneth J. Cooper, "Democrats Attack Bush for Regretting Tax Boost," *Washington Post*, March 5, 1992, https://www.washingtonpost.com/archive/politics/1992/03/05/democrats-attack-bush-for-regretting-tax-boost/0871af99-e435-4808-afa6-175c26ff861c/?utm_term=.f860ef2d7eb9.

22. "Mr. Quayle's 'E' for Effort," *New York Times*, June 17, 1992, http://www.nytimes.com/1992/06/17/opinion/mr-quayle-s-e-for-effort.html.

23. Naftali, *George H. W. Bush*, 152–53.

24. Naftali, *George H. W. Bush*, 175.

25. Dave McDermand, "How Texas A&M Became Home to the George Bush Presidential Library and Museum," *Eagle*, July 3, 2013, http://www.myaggienation.com/campus_evolution/how-texas-a-m-became-home-to-the-george-bush/article_baa24bb4-e411-11e2-8085-0019bb2963f4.html.

26. McDermand, "How Texas A&M."

27. McDermand, "How Texas A&M."

28. McDermand, "How Texas A&M."

29. McDermand, "How Texas A&M."

30. McDermand, "How Texas A&M."

31. McDermand, "How Texas A&M."

32. McDermand, "How Texas A&M."

33. Thomas Clarkin, "The George Bush Presidential Library and Museum," *Public Historian* 28 (Summer 2006): 208.

34. Benjamin Hufbauer, *Presidential Temples: How Memorials and Libraries Shape Public Memory* (Lawrence: University Press of Kansas, 2005), 173.

35. George Bush Presidential Library and Museum, accessed February 11, 2017, https://bush41.org/exhibits-listing.

36. "Exhibits: Permanent Exhibits," George Bush Presidential Library and Museum, accessed February 11, 2017, https://bush41.org/exhibits-listing.

37. "Exhibits: Permanent Exhibits."

38. "Exhibits: Permanent Exhibits."

39. "Exhibits: Permanent Exhibits."

40. "Exhibits: Permanent Exhibits."

41. "Exhibits: Permanent Exhibits."

42. "Exhibits: Permanent Exhibits."

43. "Exhibits: Permanent Exhibits."

44. "Exhibits: Permanent Exhibits."

45. "Research," George Bush Presidential Library and Museum, accessed February 11, 2017, https://bush41.org/research.

46. "Archives and Research," George Bush Presidential Library and Museum, accessed February 11, 2017, https://bush41library.tamu.edu/.

47. "Textual Archives," George Bush Presidential Library and Museum, accessed February 11, 2017, https://bush41library.tamu.edu/archives/.

48. "The National Parks Photography Project," George Bush Presidential Library and Museum, accessed February 11, 2017, https://bush41.org/exhibit/32.

BIBLIOGRAPHY

Clarkin, Thomas. "The George Bush Presidential Library and Museum." *Public Historian* 28 (Summer 2006): 206–8.

Dewar, Helen, and Kenneth J. Cooper, "Democrats Attack Bush for Regretting Tax Boost." *Washington Post*, March 5, 1992, https://www.washingtonpost.com/archive/politics/1992/03/05/democrats-attack-bush-for-regretting-tax-boost/0871af99-e435-4808-afa6-175c26ff861c/?utm_term=.f860ef2d7eb9.

Gaddis, John Lewis. *The Cold War: A New History*. New York: Penguin Books, 2005.

Hufbauer, Benjamin. *Presidential Temples: How Memorials and Libraries Shape Public Memory*. Lawrence: University Press of Kansas, 2005.

Mann, James. *George W. Bush*. The American Presidents Series. New York: Times Books, 2015.

McDermand, Dave. "How Texas A&M Became Home to the George Bush Presidential Library and Museum." *Eagle*, July 3, 2013, http://www.myaggienation.com/campus_evolution/how-texas-a-m-became-home-to-the-george-bush/article_baa24bb4-e411-11e2-8085-0019bb2963f4.html.

Naftali, Timothy. *George H. W. Bush*. The American Presidents Series. New York: Times Books, 2007.

New York Times. "Mr. Quayle's 'E' for Effort." June 17, 1992, http://www.nytimes.com/1992/06/17/opinion/mr-quayle-s-e-for-effort.html.

Service, Robert. *The End of the Cold War: 1985–1991*. New York: Public Affairs, 2015.

William J. Clinton
Presidential Library and Museum

Address: 1200 President Clinton Ave., Little Rock, AR 72201
Phone: (501) 374-4242
Administration: National Archive and Records Administration
Website: https://www.clintonlibrary.gov/
Social media: https://www.facebook.com/ClintonPresLib/
Hours: 9 a.m. to 5 p.m., Monday to Saturday; 1 p.m. to 5 p.m. on Sundays; closed on
    Thanksgiving Day, Christmas Day, and New Year's Day

BIOGRAPHY OF WILLIAM J. CLINTON

August 19, 1946–
Forty-Second President: January 20, 1993–January 20, 2001
Democratic Party

Hillary and Bill Clinton at the 1997 dedication of the Franklin Delano Roosevelt Memorial in Washington, DC, by Carol Highsmith. *Carol Highsmith LC-HS503-5541 (ONLINE)*

Bill Clinton was born William Jefferson Blythe III to William Jefferson Blythe Jr. and Virginia Cassidy Blythe in Hope, Arkansas. His mother was a nurse, and his father was a salesman. The couple married on September 4, 1943. However, the marriage came to a tragic end in 1946 when William Blythe died in a car accident.[1] On June 19, 1950, Virginia married Roger Clinton. Roger Clinton was a Buick salesman who had a reputation for drinking, which proved to be difficult for the family.[2] Virginia and Roger had one son: Roger Jr. Bill would eventually take his stepfather's surname to become Bill Clinton.[3] In school, Bill was a bright child and did very well.[4]

After finishing school, Bill graduated from Georgetown University and attended, but did not complete, a degree as a Rhodes scholar at Oxford University. He returned to the United States and graduated with his Juris Doctor from Yale Law School. After graduating, Clinton married fellow law student Hillary Rodham. Together they had one child: Chelsea. Bill loved politics and returned to his native Arkansas, where he was elected governor after running as a Democrat in 1978. Although he lost his reelection bid in 1980, he stunned everyone when he made a comeback in 1982. Clinton served as governor of Arkansas from 1983 until he was elected president in 1992.[5]

Clinton sought the Democratic Party's nomination in 1992. While he was campaigning for the nomination in New Hampshire in February, however, accusations were made that he had had an affair with a singer named Gennifer Flowers. Clinton and his wife, Hillary, denied the allegations. Experts believed that Clinton's campaign was over, so when Clinton came in second behind former senator Paul Tsongas of Massachusetts, it was a victory. Clinton quipped, "Tonight, New Hampshire has made me the Comeback Kid."[6]

During the general election, Clinton was up against Republican president George H. W. Bush and Texas businessman H. Ross Perot, who ran as an independent candidate. That summer, unemployment hit 7.8 percent, making life difficult for ordinary Americans, who said they "wanted a change."[7] Clinton campaigned on a simple economic slogan: "It's the economy, stupid."[8] He also promised to "build infrastructure, reform welfare, universalize health care coverage, cut taxes for the middle class, and raise taxes on the upper class and foreign corporations."[9] Clinton won the nomination that summer and chose Senator Al Gore of Tennessee as his running mate. During his acceptance speech, Clinton reached out to children who were being raised with a single parent. In his inspiring acceptance address he reassured these children by stating:

> And I want to say something to every child in America tonight who is out there trying to grow up without a father or a mother: I know how you feel. You are special too.
>
> You matter to America. And don't you ever let anybody tell you can't become whatever you want to be. And if other politicians make you feel like you are not part of their family, come on and be part of ours.[10]

After conducting a strong campaign, Clinton won the election on November 3. He won 370 electoral votes and 44,909,806 popular votes, while President Bush won only 168 electoral votes and 39,104,550 popular votes. Perot failed to win any electoral votes but managed to achieve an astonishing 19,743,821 popular votes.

President Clinton had to deal with some serious foreign-policy issues. History professor Gil Troy of McGill University says: "Clinton confronted violence in Bosnia, instability in Haiti, unrest in the new [post-Soviet] Russia, . . . tensions between Israelis and Palestinians, and . . . peace in Northern Ireland."[11] During the Bosnian War, which took place between Serbia and Bosnia, Clinton helped to negotiate peace and sent troops to stop the violence and the "ethnic cleansing" that was taking place there.[12] Clinton's domestic accomplishments were also successful. Despite failing to achieve universal health care reform, he reformed welfare and showed fiscal responsibility by creating a budget surplus.[13] During his State of the Union Address on January 23, 1996, Clinton even offered to cut government spending to help grow the economy. He said:

> We know big Government does not have all the answers. We know there's not a program for every problem. . . . The era of big Government is over. But we cannot go back to the time when our citizens were left to fend for themselves.[14]

That same year Clinton was reelected to a second term in a victory over Senator Bob Dole of Kansas. Ross Perot ran once again as an independent. Clinton won 379 electoral votes and 47,401,185 popular votes, while Dole won just 159 electoral votes and 39,197,469 popular votes. Perot only won 8,085,294 popular votes and no electoral votes.

Clinton's second term was troubling, as allegations of infidelity surfaced once again.[15] In 1998 he was impeached for lying under oath about an affair with a White House intern.[16] In 1999 Clinton's impeachment trial was conducted in the United States Senate, where he was acquitted of the charges. Clinton went on to serve the remaining years of his presidency with "historically high approval ratings."[17]

After leaving the presidency, Clinton became head of his own William J. Clinton Foundation and the Clinton Global Initiative. These organizations help to promote and solve international issues, such as childhood obesity, education, and clean energy around the world.[18] Hillary Clinton became a rising star in the Democratic Party when she was elected to the United States Senate from New York in 2000. She sought the Democratic presidential nomination in 2008 but lost to Senator Barack Obama of Illinois, who became the first African American president. In 2016 Hillary Clinton ran for president as the first female presidential candidate of a major political party. She narrowly lost the election to businessman Donald Trump of New York.

LIBRARY AND MUSEUM

The William J. Clinton Presidential Library is in Little Rock, Arkansas, next to the Arkansas River on a "thirty-acre riverfront tract."[19] The $165 million complex is called the Clinton Presidential Center. According to author William G. Clotworthy, *Newsweek* said the library building represents Clinton's popular image as "larger than life: bold and dramatic."[20] Reporter Suzi Parker of the *Christian Science Monitor* said, "Like the man himself, Bill Clinton's new presidential library is a mix of substance and flash."[21] According to the library's website, the building was designed by architect James Polshek, covering 157,779 square feet. It was recently "designated as one of the most energy efficient and environmentally friendly places to work in the United States by the U.S. Green Buildings Council."[22]

On November 18, 2004, the library officially opened on a wet day in Little Rock. Thirty thousand people were expected to attend the event. While there was never a formal count of the attendees, former presidents George H. W. Bush, George W. Bush, and Jimmy Carter were there. Former president Gerald Ford was invited but did not attend because of health reasons. There were also many celebrities in attendance, including actor Robin Williams, singer Barbara Streisand, Bono of the band U2, and Senator John Kerry. Also attending were Caroline Kennedy and Clinton's vice president, Al Gore.[23] In his speech during the ceremony Clinton said he hoped his library would allow visitors to see "not only what I did with my life but to see what they could do with their lives, because this is mostly the story of what we, the people, can do when we work together."[24] By 2012 the Clinton library had welcomed 312,396 visitors.[25] The current

William J. Clinton Presidential Library, Little Rock, Arkansas, by Carol Highsmith. *Carol Highsmith LC-HS503-4971*

director of the Clinton library is Ms. Terri Garner, who previously served as the executive director of the Bangor Museum and Center for History in Maine.[26]

Collections and Exhibits

The Clinton Library and Museum has a total of twenty-two exhibits. Beginning on the first-floor lobby, visitors will see one of the three Cadillac Fleetwood limousines that Clinton used as president. The limousines were built in Warren, Michigan, in 1993. It took three years to build the limousines, which have "state of the art protection" and a communication system that gave the president worldwide contact.[27]

From the limousine, visitors will go up to the second floor where sixteen exhibits covering Clinton's presidency await them. The first of these is the *Orientation Theater*, where visitors view a twelve-minute film about Clinton and his life from his early years in Hope, Arkansas, to his election as president. Included in the film are interviews with King Hussein of Jordan and President Nelson Mandela of South Africa, who discuss Clinton's presidency.[28]

The second exhibit is called *The Inauguration* and shows visitors the sights and sounds of Clinton's presidential inauguration on January 20, 1993.[29] The third exhibit is *Restoring the Economy*. This exhibit tells the story of how Clinton's economic policies ushered in the "largest peacetime economic expansion" in American history.[30] Inside the exhibit there is a short video of Clinton explaining his economic plans and a time-line showing the impressive economic growth.[31]

The next exhibit is dedicated to the Little Rock Nine. The exhibit is named *Little Rock Nine* because they were the first group of African Americans to attend an all-white school after the call for the desegregation of schools. They went along to enroll in Little Rock High School on September 25, 1957. When the governor at the time, Orval Faubus, refused to admit the students, President Dwight David Eisenhower sent the United States 101st Airborne Division to safely escort the nine to school. The event inspired a young Bill Clinton, who was eleven years old when it took place. When he became president, Clinton awarded the Little Rock Nine the Congressional Gold Medal for their gallant and brave deed. One of the medals was donated to Clinton's library and is on display, along with President Eisenhower's televised address about the high school.[32] Following this exhibit is a full-scale replica of the Cabinet Room as it looked in the West Wing of the White House during Clinton's administration. Visitors may sit at the table and use a touch-screen to view images of the Executive Office of the president.[33]

After visiting the replica Cabinet Room, visitors proceed to the sixth exhibit, which is named *Expanding Our Shared Prosperity*. The exhibit is dedicated to Clinton's efforts to promote commerce and globalization. Visitors will learn that Clinton negotiated around three hundred treaties, including the North American Free Trade Agreement (NAFTA).[34] After learning about Clinton's achievements in promoting globalization, visitors go to a timeline in the seventh exhibit. *Presidential Timeline* is a display presenting almost three thousand daily schedules that Clinton used in office. Visitors can read them to learn more about the daily activities of the president. Included in this exhibit are letters from celebrities Whoopi Goldberg and Tony Danza.[35]

The exhibit entitled *Science and Technology* tells the story of how Clinton promoted technological advances during his administration. The advent of the Internet was important in the 1990s, and Clinton supported its growth. He made sure schools and libraries could get online. He also promoted the Human Genome Project, which mapped the genetic codes of humans, and signed the Telecommunications Act of 1996. Inside the exhibit visitors will see personal computers from the 1990s and an e-mail that Clinton received from famed astronaut-turned-politician Senator John Glenn from Ohio.[36]

While promoting science and technology were important aspects of Clinton's presidency, so was environmentalism. The next exhibit that visitors will enter is called *Protecting the Earth* and is dedicated to Clinton's environmental achievements. Visitors can see photographs and videos of Clinton discussing his green policies. Among his achievements highlighted are the expansion of national monuments, the introduction of the Clean Car Initiative, which aimed to make automobiles more fuel efficient, and the introduction of clean air policies to decrease pollution.[37]

Building One America, the tenth exhibit, highlights Clinton's efforts to unite Americans across racial and ethnic lines. America's demographics were changing in the 1990s as the nation became more diverse. Unfortunately, some did not welcome this change. Hate crimes targeting homosexuals and racially diverse Americans made headlines. To curb this plague, Clinton signed legislation to make hate crimes federal offenses that would receive stiff sentences. Clinton also tried to unite Americans along economic lines by raising the minimum wage and creating a domestic peace corps service known as AmeriCorps. Visitors will see AmeriCorps memorabilia inside.[38]

The eleventh exhibit, *Campaign for the Future*, takes visitors back to 1991, when then governor Clinton decided to run for president. Inside, visitors can view campaign buttons from the election of 1992 and learn about Clinton's primary and general election victories. The exhibit also tells the story of Clinton's reelection victory in 1996. Visitors can see the sunglasses that Clinton wore when he was a guest on *The Arsenio Hall Show*, too.[39]

This exhibit is followed by *Learning across a Lifetime*, which showcases Clinton's educational achievements as president. Visitors will learn about how Clinton brought the Internet to schools, made federal financial aid more affordable, and pushed to hire more teachers. There are videos, photographs, and a crystal in the shape of an apple as an award to First Lady Hillary Clinton who, like Bill, helped to promote education.[40]

Clinton's educational achievements are followed by the exhibit *Making Communities Safer*, which centers on Clinton's crime-fighting policies. During his administration, Clinton signed the Brady bill, which required background checks on people purchasing firearms. The law was named in honor of Jim Brady, who was paralyzed after being shot in the head by John Hinckley Jr. during an attempted assassination of President Reagan. Clinton also supported tougher penalties for criminals.[41] In the next exhibit, *Putting People First*, visitors will learn about how Clinton reformed welfare and fixed entitlements, like social security, for future generations. The exhibit also highlights Bill and Hillary's failed efforts to reform health care. Visitors can see letters sent to and from Hillary Clinton and ordinary Americans concerned about health care.[42]

The final two exhibits on the second floor are concerned with conflicts and Clinton's foreign policy. *Confronting Conflicts, Making Peace* gives visitors an idea of Clinton's foreign-policy achievements. As president, he negotiated an end to the war in Bosnia and promoted peace talks in the Middle East. The exhibit mentions Clinton's role in ending the conflict in Northern Ireland. The exhibit has numerous photographs and texts.[43] Finally, the exhibit *Preparing for New Threats* gives visitors information about the new post–Cold War threats faced by the world at the turn of the century. Among them were terrorism and the proliferation of weapons of mass destruction. Inside, visitors can see a fragment of a Soviet submarine missile that was destroyed under the treaty.[44]

On the third floor, visitors will find the final five exhibits dedicated to Clinton, his family, and his presidency. *The Early Years* exhibit showcases pictures, letters, newspaper clippings, and campaign memorabilia from Clinton's early political career as governor. Visitors learn about Hillary's mother, Dorothy Howell Rodham, along with pictures from Bill's childhood, his marriage to Hillary Rodham, his early years in law and his failed congressional bid in 1974.[45] The next exhibit is *Making the White House a Home*. Here visitors will see photographs of Bill, Hillary, and daughter Chelsea from when they lived in the White House. Since Clinton is both a sports and music fan, visitors will see sports memorabilia and a saxophone that was gifted to him.[46]

The final three exhibits on the third floor focus on gifts and White House events. *People's Gifts* displays real gifts ordinary Americans sent to the first family. Among those on display are a bike, clothes, and a doll.[47] *Celebrations at the White House* shows photographs of various holiday events that took place during Clinton's administration, such as Christmas, Easter, Saint Patrick's Day, and Chanukah. Visitors will see glass sculptures and other holiday ornaments given to the Clintons.[48] Finally, the exhibit *State Events* shows pictures and objects given to Clinton at various formal meetings with foreign leaders. One such artifact on display is a blue porcelain vase from Japanese emperor Akihito and Empress Michiko.[49] The Clinton library has a large collection, holding 76.8 million pages of documents and 1.85 million photographs.[50] The Clinton School of Public Service is located on the grounds of the library. The University of Arkansas administers the program, which offers students a master of public service degree.

NOTES

1. Nigel Hamilton, *Bill Clinton: An American Journey, Great Expectations* (New York: Random House, 2003), 33.

2. Hamilton, *Bill Clinton*, 55.

3. Hamilton, *Bill Clinton*, 73.

4. Hamilton, *Bill Clinton*, 61.

5. "William J. Clinton Biography," William J. Clinton Presidential Library and Museum, accessed May 19, 2017, https://www.clintonlibrary.gov/clintons/william-j-clinton-biography/.

6. Patrick Healy, "Resurrection: How New Hampshire Saved the 1992 Clinton Campaign," *New York Times*, February 8, 2016, https://www.nytimes.com/interactive/2016/02/08/us/poli tics/bill-hillary-clinton-new-hampshire.html?_r=0.

7. Gil Troy, *The Age of Clinton: America in the 1990s* (New York: Thomas Dunne, 2015), 67.

8. Troy, *Age of Clinton*, 71.

9. Troy, *Age of Clinton*, 71.

10. William J. Clinton, "Address Accepting the Presidential Nomination at the Democratic National Convention in New York: July 16, 1992," the American Presidency Project, http://www.presidency.ucsb.edu/ws/?pid=25958.

11. Troy, *Age of Clinton*, 136.

12. "William J. Clinton Biography."

13. "William J. Clinton Biography."

14. William J. Clinton, "Address before a Joint Session of the Congress on the State of the Union: January 23, 1996," The American Presidency Project, http://www.presidency.ucsb.edu/ws/?pid=53091.

15. "William J. Clinton Biography."

16. Troy, *Age of Clinton*, 248.

17. "William J. Clinton Biography."

18. "William J. Clinton Biography."

19. William G. Clotworthy, *Homes and Libraries of the Presidents: An Interpretive Guide*, third edition (Blacksburg, VA: McDonald & Woodward, 2008), 319.

20. Clotworthy, *Homes and Libraries*, 319.

21. Suzi Parker, "A Library—and Legacy—for Billiophiles," *Christian Science Monitor*, November 17, 2004, http://www.csmonitor.com/2004/1117/p03s01-usgn.html.

22. "LEED Certified Building," William J. Clinton Presidential Library and Museum, accessed May 19, 2017, https://www.clintonlibrary.gov/about/being-green/.

23. Maria Newman, "Thousands Attend Dedication of Clinton's Presidential Library," *New York Times*, November 18, 2004, http://www.nytimes.com/2004/11/18/politics/thousands-attend-dedication-of-clintons-presidential-library.html?_r=0.

24. Newman, "Thousands Attend Dedication."

25. Wendy R. Ginsberg, Erika K. Lunder, and Daniel J. Richardson, *The Presidential Libraries Act and the Establishment of Presidential Libraries* (CRS Report No. R41513) (Washington, DC: Congressional Research Service, 2015), 28.

26. National Archives, "National Archives Names New Director of the Clinton Library," news release, November 5, 2007, https://www.archives.gov/press/press-releases/2008/nr08-11.html.

27. "Presidential Limousine and Secret Service," William J. Clinton Presidential Library and Museum, accessed May 19, 2017, https://www.clintonlibrary.gov/museum/permanentexhibits/limoandsecretservice/.

28. "Orientation Theater," William J. Clinton Presidential Library and Museum, accessed May 19, 2017, https://www.clintonlibrary.gov/museum/permanentexhibits/orientationtheater/.

29. "The Inauguration," William J. Clinton Presidential Library and Museum, accessed May 19, 2017, https://www.clintonlibrary.gov/museum/permanentexhibits/inauguration/.

30. "Restoring the Economy," William J. Clinton Presidential Library and Museum, accessed May 19, 2017, https://www.clintonlibrary.gov/museum/permanentexhibits/restoringeconomy/.

31. "Restoring the Economy."

32. "Little Rock Nine," William J. Clinton Presidential Library and Museum, accessed May 19, 2017, https://www.clintonlibrary.gov/museum/permanentexhibits/littlerocknine/.

33. "The Cabinet Room," William J. Clinton Presidential Library and Museum, accessed May 19, 2017, https://www.clintonlibrary.gov/museum/permanentexhibits/cabinetroom/.

34. "Expanding Our Shared Prosperity," William J. Clinton Presidential Library and Museum, accessed May 19, 2017, https://www.clintonlibrary.gov/museum/permanentexhibits/shared-prosperity/.

35. "Presidential Timeline," William J. Clinton Presidential Library and Museum, accessed May 19, 2017, https://www.clintonlibrary.gov/museum/permanentexhibits/timeline/.

36. "Science and Technology," William J. Clinton Presidential Library and Museum, accessed May 19, 2017, https://www.clintonlibrary.gov/museum/permanentexhibits/scienceandtechnology/.

37. "Protecting the Earth," William J. Clinton Presidential Library and Museum, accessed May 19, 2017, https://www.clintonlibrary.gov/museum/permanentexhibits/protectingtheearth/.

38. "Building One America," William J. Clinton Presidential Library and Museum, accessed May 19, 2017, https://www.clintonlibrary.gov/museum/permanentexhibits/buildingoneamerica/.

39. "Campaign for the Future," William J. Clinton Presidential Library and Museum, accessed May 19, 2017, https://www.clintonlibrary.gov/museum/permanentexhibits/campaignforthefuture/.

40. "Learning Across a Lifetime," William J. Clinton Presidential Library and Museum, accessed May 19, 2017, https://www.clintonlibrary.gov/museum/permanentexhibits/learningacrossalifetime/.

41. "Making Communities Safer," William J. Clinton Presidential Library and Museum, accessed May 19, 2017, https://www.clintonlibrary.gov/museum/permanentexhibits/communitiessafer/.

42. "Putting People First," William J. Clinton Presidential Library and Museum, accessed May 19, 2017, https://www.clintonlibrary.gov/museum/permanentexhibits/puttingpeoplefirst/.

43. "Confronting Conflicts, Making Peace," William J. Clinton Presidential Library and Museum, accessed May 19, 2017, https://www.clintonlibrary.gov/museum/permanentexhibits/conflictspeace/.

44. "Preparing for New Threats," William J. Clinton Presidential Library and Museum, accessed May 19, 2017, https://www.clintonlibrary.gov/museum/permanentexhibits/preparing fornewthreats/.

45. "The Early Years," William J. Clinton Presidential Library and Museum, accessed May 19, 2017, https://www.clintonlibrary.gov/museum/permanentexhibits/earlyyears/.

46. "Making the White House a Home," William J. Clinton Presidential Library and Museum, accessed May 19, 2017, https://www.clintonlibrary.gov/museum/permanentexhibits/making thishouseahome/.

47. "People's Gifts," William J. Clinton Presidential Library and Museum, accessed May 19, 2017, https://www.clintonlibrary.gov/museum/permanentexhibits/peoplesgifts/.

48. "Celebrations at the White House," William J. Clinton Presidential Library and Museum, accessed May 19, 2017, https://www.clintonlibrary.gov/museum/permanentexhibits/celebra tionsatthewhitehouse/.

49. "State Events," William J. Clinton Presidential Library and Museum, accessed May 19, 2017, https://www.clintonlibrary.gov/museum/permanentexhibits/stateevents/.

50. Clotworthy, *Homes and Libraries*, 319.

BIBLIOGRAPHY

Clinton, William J. "Address Accepting the Presidential Nomination at the Democratic National Convention in New York: July 16, 1992." The American Presidency Project. http://www.presidency.ucsb.edu/ws/?pid=25958.

———. "Address before a Joint Session of the Congress on the State of the Union: January 23, 1996." The American Presidency Project. http://www.presidency.ucsb.edu/ws/?pid=53091.

Clotworthy, William G. *Homes and Libraries of the Presidents: An Interpretive Guide.* Third edition. Blacksburg, VA: McDonald & Woodward, 2008.

Ginsberg, Wendy R., Erika K. Lunder, and Daniel J. Richardson. *The Presidential Libraries Act and the Establishment of Presidential Libraries* (CRS Report No. R41513). Washington, DC: Congressional Research Service, 2015.

Hamilton, Nigel. *Bill Clinton: An American Journey, Great Expectations.* New York: Random House, 2003.

Healy, Patrick. "Resurrection: How New Hampshire Saved the 1992 Clinton Campaign." *New York Times*, February 8, 2016. https://www.nytimes.com/interactive/2016/02/08/us/politics/bill-hillary-clinton-new-hampshire.html?_r=0.

Newman, Maria. "Thousands Attend Dedication of Clinton's Presidential Library." *New York Times*, November 18, 2004. http://www.nytimes.com/2004/11/18/politics/thousands-attend-dedication-of-clintons-presidential-library.html.

Parker, Suzi. "A Library—and Legacy—for Billiophiles." *Christian Science Monitor*, November 17, 2004. http://www.csmonitor.com/2004/1117/p03s01-usgn.html.

Troy, Gil. *The Age of Clinton: America in the 1990s.* New York: Thomas Dunne, 2015.

George W. Bush Presidential Library and Museum

Address: 2943 SMU Boulevard, Dallas, TX 75205
Phone: (214) 346-1650
Website: https://www.georgewbushlibrary.smu.edu/
Social media: https://www.facebook.com/GWBLibrary/
Administration: National Archives
Partnership: Southern Methodist University
Hours: 9 a.m. to 5 p.m., Monday to Saturday; noon to 5 p.m. on Sundays; closed on
   Thanksgiving Day, Christmas Day, and New Year's Day

BIOGRAPHY OF GEORGE W. BUSH

July 6, 1946–
Forty-Third President: January 20, 2001–January 20, 2009
Republican Party

George W. Bush and Laura Bush. *Courtesy of the George W. Bush Presidential Library and Museum*

George Walker Bush was born to George Herbert Walker and Barbara Pierce Bush in New Haven, Connecticut. His father had served in the Pacific as a fighter pilot during World War II. The family moved to Midland, Texas, in the 1950s when the father started working in the oil industry. As a child, George W. Bush witnessed the death of his infant sister, Robin. He received his education from Philips Academy in Andover, Massachusetts. He then attended Yale University, graduating with a bachelor's degree, and eventually gained an MBA from Harvard. During the Vietnam War, he briefly served stateside in the Air National Guard and was discharged in 1974.

In 1976 Bush married librarian Laura Welch, who also lived in Midland. George W. and Laura have two children: Barbara and Jenna. Around the time of his marriage, he set up his own oil company, Arbusto. However, when oil prices crashed in the early 1980s, he was forced to shut down his company.[1] Bush's years as a young husband and father were difficult, because he struggled with alcohol. Bush said of himself, "I was a boozy kid."[2] One morning waking up with a hangover in 1986, he decided to come to terms with his alcoholism. Bush said, "My problem was not only drinking; it was selfishness. The booze was leading me to put myself ahead of others, especially my family. . . . Faith showed me a way out."[3] The decision to give up the bottle coincided with a meeting he had with the Reverend Billy Graham. Bush's relationship with Graham inspired him to become an Evangelical Christian.[4]

Life improved for Bush and his family after the conversion. In 1988 he helped co-ordinate his father's campaign for the presidency. After his father's election as president, Bush purchased the Texas Rangers baseball team. He ran the team until 1994, when he decided to run for Texas governor. He was inspired to become governor after his father lost his reelection bid against Governor Bill Clinton.[5] Bush said that running the Texas Rangers was a positive experience that prepared him for public office. He added, "I also gained valuable experience handling tough questions from journalists."[6] Bush won the gubernatorial race against Democratic governor Ann Richards with "53 percent of the electorate."[7] However, he faced criticism from the media because his younger brother, Jeb, was simultaneously running for Florida governor.[8]

Bush was reelected in 1998, eventually serving six years as governor. During this time he focused on improving education in the state and made changes in the juvenile justice system.[9] Controversially, he also approved 152 executions.[10] In 2000 Bush decided to seek the Republican nomination for president. He fought a tough primary campaign against his Republican rival, Senator John McCain of Arizona. When Bush won the nomination, he chose former defense secretary Dick Cheney of Wyoming as his running mate. The Democrats nominated Vice President Al Gore and Senator Joe Lieberman of Connecticut as their candidates. Bush and Gore challenged each other vigorously on the campaign trail. On the night of the election, the returns were close, and while Gore initially conceded, he quickly retracted. Gore won the popular vote, but the election came down to disputed votes in Florida. Many blamed voting discrepancies on the use of the "butterfly ballot," which involved citizens using a punch-card method to vote. There were fears that voters in Palm Beach County, Florida, may have accidentally voted for the wrong candidate.[11]

Bush and Gore fought tenaciously in the legal battle to decide how the votes should be recounted. Bush had a slight lead. That December the dispute went all the way to the United States Supreme Court, which decided that "there was no fair way to recount votes in time for Florida to participate in the Electoral College."[12] This decision meant that Bush was declared the winner of Florida by only 537 votes.[13] The final overall results were affirmed by the Electoral College: Bush won 50,456,002 million popular votes and 271 electoral votes, while Gore won 50,999,897 popular votes and 266 electoral votes. Two third-party candidates also received a significant number of votes. One was consumer advocate Ralph Nader, running for the Green Party, who won 2,882,955 popular votes. The other was conservative commentator Patrick

Buchanan, who ran for the Reform Party and won 448,895 popular votes. Neither candidate won any electoral votes.

As president, one of Bush's key accomplishments was the passage of the No Child Left Behind Act to encourage states to strengthen school testing and graduation requirements. The rationale was to hold teachers more accountable for students' learning.[14] On September 11, 2001, Bush was visiting a grade school in Sarasota, Florida, when he heard the news that two airplanes had crashed into the New York's World Trade Center. On that day, which became known as 9/11, the United States experienced the most horrific terrorist attack in its history. On the same day, two other planes were also hijacked. One crashed into the Pentagon and the other into a field in Shanksville, Pennsylvania. The hijackers were linked to the Al-Qaeda terrorist network led by Osama bin Laden. He was the same terrorist who was responsible for attacks against Americans in Kenya, Tanzania, and Yemen. Bush ordered that bin Laden be brought to justice. However, bin Laden was being protected by the sympathetic Taliban regime in Afghanistan. On September 14, Bush toured the ruins of the World Trade Center, which had become known as Ground Zero. While there, he made a speech through a bullhorn, saying, "I can hear you! I can hear you! The rest of the world hears you! And the people—and the people who knocked these buildings down will hear all of us soon!"[15]

Shortly after 9/11, Bush received congressional support for the use of military force in Afghanistan. On October 7, America and her allies invaded Afghanistan seeking bin Laden. The United States had sympathetic allies in Afghanistan. They were known as the Northern Alliance and led by Hamid Karzai. The Northern Alliance helped to take back the cities of Kabul and Kandahar from the Taliban. In place of the Taliban, a moderate regime took control and Karzai was installed as the new leader. That December, bin Laden was reported to be hiding out in Tora Bora, a mountainous region of Afghanistan located near the Pakistani border. Despite large-scale attacks on the mountains, bin Laden managed to escape to Pakistan.[16]

Bush's policies on terrorism were criticized when he sent Taliban prisoners of war to a detention facility in Guantanamo, Cuba. Bush and his advisors believed the prisoners would have few legal rights in a military base to challenge their detention in court.[17] Controversy also arose when Bush signed the Patriot Act, which allowed law enforcement agencies to examine the credit card statements and library records of suspected terrorists without a warrant.[18]

In his State of the Union address on January 29, 2002, Bush said that the United States would target hostile nations who were "seeking weapons of mass destruction and [who] might be willing to provide them to terrorists."[19] Bush declared that three nations (Iran, Iraq, and North Korea) were part of a larger "axis of evil" that threatened world peace.[20] Bush was setting the stage for the invasion of Iraq, which he believed was still keeping illegal chemical weapons from the 1991 Gulf War. In the meantime, Bush built a military alliance in what was known as a "coalition of the willing."[21] The coalition included Spain, the United Kingdom, Italy, and other nations. One traditional ally, France, refused to support the invasion. Bush gave the Iraqi dictator Saddam Hussein and his family the option of leaving Iraq to avoid war. Hussein refused, so Bush launched Operation Iraqi Freedom on March 20, 2003. The campaign was largely successful, as coalition troops captured Baghdad after three weeks of fighting. Many, including Bush, thought the war was over: Bush even celebrated the victory aboard the USS *Abraham Lincoln*, where a sign was displayed reading: "Mission accomplished."[22] However, the war entered a new phase: Hussein avoided capture until December, and a growing insurgency began attacking and killing coalition troops.

The war and the growing number of casualties caused Bush problems when he ran for a second term in 2004. The main purpose of the war was to seize Hussein's weapons of mass destruction. However, none were found, as Hussein had been "bluffing."[23] The Democrats nominated Senator John Kerry of Massachusetts, a navy veteran. Kerry ran on an antiwar platform but he made a critical error during his campaign. In a speech he made to a veterans' group, Kerry revealed that he originally supported the war in Iraq, saying: "I actually did vote for the $87 billion before I voted against it."[24] The Bush campaign countered by portraying Kerry as a "flip-flopper" who changed positions on issues.[25] In the election, Bush achieved a solid victory. He won 62,040,610 popular votes and 286 electoral votes, whereas Kerry received 59,028,444 popular votes and 251 electoral votes.

Bush's second term would prove to be more difficult than his first. He stepped up the military action against insurgents in Iraq and increased the number of American troops to pacify the nation. Back home, in 2005 America witnessed the devastation of New Orleans when Hurricane Katrina caused levees to burst and flood the city. Bush's reaction to the disaster—to measure the damage by flying over the city aboard Air Force One—was seen as incompetent.[26] There were also problems with the Federal Emergency Management Agency (FEMA), whose job it was to provide relief. In 2005, FEMA was administered by a political appointee named Michael Brown, who had no previous experience running such an agency.[27]

Bush could not seek a third term in 2008. Instead he supported the Republican nominee Senator John McCain. On September 15, 2008, the nation entered the Great Recession when the Lehman Brothers bank collapsed. In part, the recession was caused by banks making risky sub-prime loans to homeowners, which created a housing bubble that eventually burst. It was also partly caused by monetary policy.[28] One of Bush's final acts was to sign the Troubled Asset Relief Program, which allowed the federal government to purchase "billions of dollars in mortgage-backed securities."[29] John McCain lost the 2008 election to Senator Barack Obama of Illinois, who became the first African American to be elected president. Bush and his wife Laura retired to their ranch in Crawford, Texas.

LIBRARY AND MUSEUM

Before Bush left office, he considered several universities in Texas to serve as the home of his presidential library: Baylor University, the University of Texas system, the University of Dallas, Texas Tech University, Texas A&M University, and Southern Methodist University.[30] Bush eventually chose Southern Methodist because it is located in Dallas, "a major metropolitan area in the heartland of the nation."[31] Bush also wanted his library to be home to a research institute. The goal of the George W. Bush Institute, located near to the library, is to focus "on programs and research resulting in action in the areas of education reform, global health, economic growth, and human free-dom."[32] The institute also administers the Women's Initiative to promote opportunities for women to act as "agents of change in society."[33] Most importantly, the "Women's Fellowship program has an initial focus on empowering women of the Middle East."[34] Though the library is administered by the National Archives, the Bush Institute reports to the Bush Foundation.[35]

Together, the library, institute, and foundation make up the larger Bush Center, which is located on the campus of Southern Methodist University. The entire center takes up twenty-three acres of land, with a "226,565-square-foot-building surrounded by grounds featuring Texas prairie landscaping."[36]

On April 25, 2013, the library was dedicated in front of a crowd of ten thousand people. Aside from Bush himself, among the dignitaries were his father, George H. W. Bush; President Barack Obama; former presidents Bill Clinton and Jimmy Carter; and former British prime minister Tony Blair.[37] At the ceremony Bush thanked the university president R. Gerald Turner for running "a fantastic university" with "awe-some" students.[38] President Obama called the dedication a "Texas-sized party" and commended Bush for his "incredible strength and resolve" following the terrorist attack of 9/11.[39] Explaining the purpose of the center, library director Alan Lowe said, "The Bush Library and Museum is a state-of-the-art research center for historians, scholars, students and the public. . . . We provide in-depth access to presidential materials and the presidential decision-making process."[40] Prior to his appointment as the director of the Bush library, Lowe worked at the Ronald Reagan and Franklin Roosevelt presidential libraries. In July 2016, Lowe left the Bush library to become director of the Abraham Lincoln Presidential Library and Museum in Springfield, Illinois.[41]

George W. Bush Presidential Library on the campus of Southern Methodist University in Dallas, Texas, by Carol Highsmith. *Carol Highsmith LC-DIG-highsm-30486 (ONLINE)*

Collections and Exhibits

The first exhibit, *A Nation Under Attack*, is dedicated to the lives lost during the horrific terror attacks of September 11, 2001. Inside visitors will see photos of the attacks, "actual steel" from the World Trade Center, and the bullhorn that Bush used to rally the nation at Ground Zero just days later. Visitors can also read letters that Bush wrote and received in the days following the attacks.[42]

The second exhibit is *Life in the White House*. Here visitors will learn what living in the White House was like for Bush and his family. The exhibit includes information about the family's pets, along with videos showing Camp David, the Bush Ranch in Texas, and Bush and the First Lady, Laura.[43]

The third exhibit is a replica Oval Office. Like offices at other presidential libraries, the replica has been created to look exactly as it was during President Bush's administration. According to the library's website, "Visitors are able to take an up-close look at the paintings, sculptures, and bookcases, and may even sit behind the reproduction of the Resolute Desk for a photograph."[44]

From the replica Oval Office visitors walk into the *Decision Points Theater*. Here they can use interactive technology to make their own decisions about key events of the Bush administration, such as the troop surge in Iraq and dealing with the aftermath of Hurricane Katrina. The interactive exhibit contains audio briefings from presidential advisors who help influence visitors' decisions.[45]

The exhibit *Freedom Hall* has a "massive 20-foot-tall, 360-degree LED screen" showing visitors high-definition multimedia clips that blend history, art, and entertainment.[46] The final exhibit is the outdoors *Native Texas Park*. The exhibit covers fifteen acres of parkland that is home to Blackland Prairie grass, seasonal wildflowers, and tree-shaded grass. In spring visitors can see bluebonnets, and they can see monarch butterflies in fall. There is also an amphitheater and a mile-long walking trail. Twice a year, scavenger hunts are held for schoolchildren. *Native Texas Park* reflects "the President and Mrs. Bush's longstanding commitment to environmental conservation and restoration."[47]

In February 2017 the Bush library, in conjunction with the Multicultural Arts Alliance, celebrated Black History Month by holding a special exhibit dedicated to African American artists. The library featured the art of Nathan Jones, James Kemp, and Carl Sidle alongside some exceptional art created by students of Booker T. Washington High School for the Performing and Visual Arts in Dallas.[48]

According to the library's website, "The George W. Bush Presidential Library holds more than 1,200 cubic feet of audiovisual materials (46,000 audio and video tapes, and 375,000 still photographs) and nearly four million electronic photographs created by the White House Photo Office."[49] The library also holds Bush's gubernatorial records from 1994 to 2000. Though the records are stored at his presidential library, they are still the property of the state of Texas and regulated by the Texas Public Information Act.[50]

NOTES

1. James Mann, *George W. Bush*, the American Presidents Series (New York: Times Books, 2015), 19.

2. Mann, *George W. Bush*, 15.

3. George W. Bush, *Decision Points* (New York: Crown Publishing, 2010), 2.

4. Mann, *George W. Bush*, 21.

5. Mann, *George W. Bush*, 27.

6. Mann, *George W. Bush*, 26.

7. Mann, *George W. Bush*, 29.

8. Mann, *George W. Bush*, 28–29.

9. Mann *George W. Bush*, 29–30.

10. Mann, *George W. Bush*, 31.

11. Jonathan N. Wand, Kenneth W. Shotts, Jasjeet S. Sekhon, Walter R. Mebane Jr., Michael C. Herron, and Henry E. Brady, "The Butterfly Did It: The Aberrant Vote for Buchanan in Palm Beach." *American Political Science Review* 95 (December 2001): 793–810, http://rangevoting.org/butterfly.pdf.

12. Bush, *Decision Points*, 81.

13. Wand et al., "Butterfly," 793–810.

14. Mann, *George W. Bush*, 50–51.

15. "George W. Bush: Bullhorn Address to Ground Zero Rescue Workers," *American Rhetoric*, accessed March 27, 2017, http://www.americanrhetoric.com/speeches/gwbush911groundzero bullhorn.htm.

16. Mann, *George W. Bush*, 66.

17. Mann, *George W. Bush*, 67.

18. Bush, *Decision Points*, 161.

19. Mann, *George W. Bush*, 73.

20. Mann, *George W. Bush*, 73.

21. Mann, *George W. Bush*, 85.

22. Mann, *George W. Bush*, 85.

23. Mann, *George W. Bush*, 93.

24. "2004 Bush vs Kerry," The Living Room Candidate: Presidential Campaign Commercials 1952–2016, Museum of the Moving Image, accessed February 11, 2017, www.livingroomcandidate.org/commercials/2004/troops.

25. Mann, *George W. Bush*, 96.

26. Mann, *George W. Bush*, 101.

27. Mann, *George W. Bush*, 100–101.

28. Scott Summer, "How the Subprime Crisis Morphed into the Great Recession," Library of Economics and Liberty, September 12, 2015, http://econlog.econlib.org/archives/2015/09/how_the_subprim.html.

29. Bush, *Decision Points*, 458.

30. Amy Hall, "The George W. Bush Presidential Library and the Presidential Libraries System," *American Society of Indexers* 17 (April–June 2009): 61–63.

31. "About the George W. Bush Presidential Center," George W. Bush Presidential Center, accessed February 11, 2017, http://www.bushcenter.org/about-the-center/index.html.

32. "Bush Center," Southern Methodist University, accessed February 11, 2017, http://www.smu.edu/bushcenter.

33. "Bush Center," Southern Methodist University, accessed February 11, 2017, http://www
.smu.edu/bushcenter.

34. "Bush Center."

35. "Bush Center."

36. "Bush Center."

37. "Bush Center."

38. "Bush Center."

39. "Bush Center."

40. "Bush Center."

41. Julie Fancher, "Alan Lowe, Director of Bush Library and Museum, Tapped to Head Lincoln Library," *Dallas News*, May 2, http://www.dallasnews.com/news/news/2016/05/02/alan
-lowe-director-of-bush-library-and-museum-tapped-to-head-lincoln-library.

42. "Visit Highlights," George W. Bush Presidential Library and Museum, accessed February
11, 2017, https://www.georgewbushlibrary.smu.edu/Visit/Highlights.aspx.

43. "Visit Highlights."

44. "Visit Highlights."

45. "Visit Highlights."

46. "Visit Highlights."

47. "Native Texas Park," George W. Bush Presidential Library and Museum, accessed February
11, 2017, https://www.georgewbushlibrary.smu.edu/Visit/Plan-Your-Museum-Visit/TX%20
Native%20Park.aspx.

48. "Art Past and Present," George W. Bush Presidential Library and Museum, accessed February 11, 2017, https://www.georgewbushlibrary.smu.edu/~/link.aspx?_id=7FF42D6400424CCB
ADF3E1DA9E652759&_z=z.

49. "Resources and FAQs," George W. Bush Presidential Library and Museum, accessed February 11, 2017, https://www.georgewbushlibrary.smu.edu/Research/Resources.aspx.

50. "Gubernatorial Records," George W. Bush Presidential Library and Museum, accessed
February 11, 2017, https://www.georgewbushlibrary.smu.edu/Research/Gubernatorial%20
Records.aspx.

BIBLIOGRAPHY

Bush, George W. *Decision Points*. New York: Crown Publishing, 2010.

Fancher, Julie. "Alan Lowe, Director of Bush Library and Museum, Tapped to Head Lincoln
Library." *Dallas News*, May 2, 2016. http://www.dallasnews.com/news/news/2016/05/02/
alan-lowe-director-of-bush-library-and-museum-tapped-to-head-lincoln-library.

Hall, Amy. "The George W. Bush Presidential Library and the Presidential Libraries System."
American Society of Indexers 17 (April–June 2009): 61–63.

Mann, James. *George W. Bush*. The American Presidents Series. New York: Times Books, 2015.

Naftali, Timothy. *George H. W. Bush*. The American Presidents Series. New York: Times Books,
2007.

Wand, Jonathan N., Kenneth W. Shotts, Jasjeet S. Sekhon, Walter R. Mebane Jr., Michael C.
Herron, and Henry E. Brady. "The Butterfly Did It: The Aberrant Vote for Buchanan in Palm
Beach." *American Political Science Review* 95 (December 2001): 793–810. http://rangevoting
.org/butterfly.pdf.

· 26 ·

Future Presidential Libraries and Museums

The future of presidential libraries is exciting, as the nonprofit Barack Obama Foundation is planning the construction of the Barack Obama Presidential Center. The center will be located on the South Side of Chicago and will be affiliated with the University of Chicago.

Barack Obama is both the first African American and the first native of Hawaii to be elected president. He was born on August 4, 1961, to Ann Dunham and Barack Obama Sr. in Honolulu. His parents divorced after two years of marriage. When his mother married Lolo Soetoro from Indonesia, young Barack attended school there. This marriage would produce a daughter: Maya Kasandra Soetoro. In the early 1970s, Obama returned to Hawaii and lived with his maternal grandparents. He began his college education at Occidental College in Los Angeles. Later, he would transfer and graduate from Columbia, where he received his undergraduate degree in political science. Obama moved to Chicago, where he worked as a community organizer. In 1988 he attended Harvard Law School, after which he returned to practice law in Chicago. Four years later, Obama married Michelle Robinson. Together they have two daughters: Natasha, who is known as Sasha, and Malia. During the 1990s Obama served in the Illinois State Senate. He was elected to the United States Senate in 2004. Then, in 2008, he ran successfully for the Democratic nomination for the presidency. Obama was elected to two terms as president. His most important achievement as president was the passage of the Affordable Care Act (known as "Obamacare") to provide more health care and make it more accessible. Obama was succeeded as president by Donald J. Trump on January 20, 2017.[1]

Before he left office, many speculated that Obama would build his presidential library in Hawaii. In fact, the University of Hawaii established the Barack Obama Hawaii Presidential Center in anticipation.[2] Ultimately, however, Obama chose Chicago. The *Chicago Tribune* said, "With no insult to Hawaii's respect for the life of the mind, it's fair to say that very few people go there in fierce pursuit of book learning."[3] Obama's choice of Chicago should come as no surprise. As previously discussed in this book, presidents want a library for research, and large cities have proffered the best opportunities.

The library's architectural design was planned by Tod Williams Billie Tsien Architects in New York City. The building will contain "a museum, a forum, and a library—and will sit in close proximity to a lagoon that runs into Lake Michigan in the Jackson Park neighborhood."[4] In a press statement the architectural firm said:

Michelle and Barack Obama watch the parade from the viewing stand in front of the White House, by Carol Highsmith, 2009. *Carol Highsmith LC-DIG-highsm-03843 (ONLINE)*

> The design approach for the Center is guided by the goal of creating a true commu-
> nity asset that seeks to inspire and empower the public to take on the greatest chal-
> lenges of our time. . . . The Obamas were clear that they wanted the Center to seam-
> lessly integrate into the Park and the community, and include diverse public spaces.[5]

When completed, the library will cover "200,000 to 225,000 square feet."[6] Its amenities will include a "circular lawn, a sledding hill, an athletic center, and a children's play area, . . . making the center a destination for students as well as scholars."[7] With a construction cost of "$500 million," the center is expected to open in 2021.[8]

The Barack Obama Presidential Center will be the first library to digitize all its presidential papers. By doing so the Obama library is creating a new paradigm by go-ing digital. Oklahoma State University historian Laura A. Belmonte noted that "the Obama center will be the first fully digitized presidential library. You won't find much in the way of paper files, only electronic ones. The physical documents will remain in the National Archives, at a location to be determined."[9] When the library opens, it is expected that Obama will have "artists like Chance the Rapper and Spike Lee"[10] visit and teach children about the arts.

While the Obama Presidential Center is being built, a library foundation in North Dakota is constructing a private library for President Theodore Roosevelt. Roosevelt was a much-loved president who served two terms in office. Before becoming president, he served heroically in the Spanish–American War. In 1900 he was chosen by the Republican Party to be President William McKinley's running mate. He became president in 1901 following the assassination of McKinley. As president, Roosevelt was known as the "trust buster" as he forced the "dissolution" of large corporations which operated in violation of the Sherman Anti–Trust Act.[11] On the international stage, he used his position as president to help make America a world power. His approach was famously to "speak softly and carry a big stick."[12] He did not run for a third term in 1908 but left the White House to go on an adventurous African safari. In 1912 he ran as a third–party candidate for the Progressive "Bull Moose" Party. However, he lost the election to the Democrat, Governor Woodrow Wilson from New Jersey. Roosevelt died on January 6, 1919.[13]

The Theodore Roosevelt Presidential Library Foundation is planning a library on the grounds of Dickinson State University in Dickinson, North Dakota. The university is already home to the Theodore Roosevelt Center. According to the website, the center "has pursued the bold mission of digitizing and archiving all of TR's letters, diaries, photographs, political cartoons, audio and video recordings, and other media."[14]

Theodore Roosevelt by Levin C. Handy. *LC-DIG-ppmsca-35965*

The North Dakota State Legislature appropriated funds for the construction of the library. Dickinson University was chosen to host the library because it was where Roosevelt hunted bison in 1883. However, feeling remorseful, as bison had been hunted almost to the point of extinction, Roosevelt returned to Dickinson to live and work as a rancher.[15] Aside from the library, the foundation is also reconstructing Roosevelt's Elkhorn Ranch, where he lived while in Dickinson.[16] The Roosevelt library is expected to be completed and opened in 2019.[17]

In future years we can expect to see a Donald Trump Presidential Library and Museum, followed by many more. Despite the debates surrounding the way in which presidential libraries portray presidents, they will remain important landmarks representing America's history.

NOTES

1. "President Barack Obama," Barack Obama Presidential Library, accessed June 17, 2017, https://www.obamalibrary.gov/obamas/president-barack-obama.

2. Ashley Parker, "Hawaii Makes Its Case for Obama's Library: Why Not Bring It to the Beach?" *New York Times*, January 5, 2017, https://www.nytimes.com/2014/01/06/us/hawaii-makes-its-case-for-obamas-library-why-not-bring-it-to-the-beach.html?_r=0.

3. "Editorial: Where to Put the Obama Library," *Chicago Tribune*, July 29, 2013, http://articles.chicagotribune.com/2013-07-29/opinion/ct-edit-library-0729-jm-20130729_1_obama-library-barack-obama-aloha-state.

4. Nick Mafi, "Barack Obama Unveils Bold Plans for His Library in Chicago," *Architectural Digest*, May 3, 2017, http://www.architecturaldigest.com/story/barack-obama-unveils-bold-plans-for-presidential-library-chicago.

5. Mafi, "Barack Obama Unveils Bold Plans."

6. Sam Lubell, "Obama Pioneers a New Approach to the Presidential Library," *Wired*, May 5, 2017, https://www.wired.com/2017/05/obama-pioneers-new-approach-presidential-library/.

7. Lubell, "Obama Pioneers a New Approach."

8. Mafi, " Barack Obama Unveils Bold Plans."

9. Lubell, "Barack Obama Pioneers a New Approach."

10. Lubell, "Barack Obama Pioneers a New Approach."

11. "Theodore Roosevelt," the White House, accessed June 19, 2017, https://www.whitehouse.gov/1600/presidents/theodoreroosevelt.

12. "Theodore Roosevelt."

13. "Theodore Roosevelt."

14. "The Library," Theodore Roosevelt Presidential Library Foundation, accessed June 19, 2017, http://www.trpresidentiallibrary.org/library/.

15. "Why Dickinson, North Dakota?" Theodore Roosevelt Presidential Library Foundation, accessed June 19, 2017, http://www.trpresidentiallibrary.org/faq/#whynd.

16. "Why Start by Reconstructing Roosevelt's Elkhorn Ranch Cabin?" Theodore Roosevelt Presidential Library Foundation, accessed June 19, 2017, http://www.trpresidentiallibrary.org/faq/#elkhorn.

17. "Why Start by Reconstructing Roosevelt's Elkhorn Ranch Cabin?"

BIBLIOGRAPHY

Lubell, Sam. "Obama Pioneers a New Approach to the Presidential Library." *Wired*, May 5, 2017. https://www.wired.com/2017/05/obama-pioneers-new-approach-presidential-library/.

Mafi, Nick. "Barack Obama Unveils Bold Plans for His Library in Chicago." *Architectural Digest*, May 3, 2017. http://www.architecturaldigest.com/story/barack-obama-unveils-bold-plans-for-presidential-library-chicago.

Parker, Ashley. "Hawaii Makes Its Case for Obama's Library: Why Not Bring It to the Beach?" *New York Times*, January 5, 2017. https://www.nytimes.com/2014/01/06/us/hawaii-makes-its-case-for-obamas-library-why-not-bring-it-to-the-beach.html?_r=0.

Appendix

Presidential Libraries by State

Arkansas

William J. Clinton Presidential Library and
  Museum, Little Rock

California

Richard Nixon Presidential Library and
  Museum, Yorba Linda
Ronald Reagan Presidential Library and
  Museum, Simi Valley

Georgia

Jimmy Carter Presidential Library and
  Museum, Atlanta

Illinois

Abraham Lincoln Presidential Library and
  Museum, Springfield

Indiana

Research Library at the Benjamin Harrison
  Presidential Site, Indianapolis

Iowa

Herbert Hoover Presidential Library and
  Museum, West Branch

Kansas

Dwight D. Eisenhower Presidential Library,
  Museum, and Boyhood Home, Abilene

Massachusetts

John Adams Library at the Boston Public
  Library
Stone Library at the Adams National
  Historical Park, Quincy
Calvin Coolidge Presidential Library
  and Museum at the Forbes Library,
  Northampton
John F. Kennedy Presidential Library and
  Museum, Boston

Michigan

Gerald R. Ford Presidential Library, Ann
  Arbor
Gerald R. Ford Presidential Museum,
  Grand Rapids

Mississippi

Ulysses S. Grant Presidential Library,
  Mississippi State, Starkville

Missouri

Harry S. Truman Presidential Library and
  Museum, Independence

New York

Franklin D. Roosevelt Presidential Library
  and Museum, Hyde Park

Ohio

Rutherford B. Hayes Presidential Center,
  Spiegel Grove

William McKinley Presidential Library and
    Museum, Canton

Tennessee

President Andrew Johnson Museum and
    Library, Greeneville

Texas

Lyndon Baines Johnson Library and Museum,
    Austin

George Bush Presidential Library and
    Museum, College Station
George W. Bush Presidential Library and
    Museum, Dallas

Virginia

Fred W. Smith National Library for the Study
    of George Washington, Mount Vernon
James Monroe Museum and Memorial
    Library, Fredericksburg
Woodrow Wilson Presidential Library and
    Museum, Staunton

Index

Note: Page references for figures are italicized.

Abraham Lincoln Presidential Library and
    Museum, xiii, xvii, 24, 27–29, 83, 219
Acheson, Dean, 107, 110, 113
Adams, Abigail, 7, 18
Adams, Charles Francis, 9, 10, 20
Adams, Charles Francis, III, 10, 20
Adams, George Washington, 19
Adams, Henry, 51
Adams, John, 7–9; death of, 14; and John
    Quincy Adams, 18, 20, 22; library, 9–11;
    39 Men exhibition, 83
Adams, John Quincy, *18*–20; collections and
    exhibits, 22; and John Adams, 9, 10; library,
    20–22
Adams, Louisa, 18
Adams Academy, 10
Adams Manuscript Trust, 20
Adams National Historic Park, 10, 18, 20, 22
Affordable Care Act, 223
Afghanistan, 178, 217
Agnew, Spiro, 148, 155, 157, 168, 169
Aguinaldo, Emilio, 59
Air Force One, 192, *193*
Akihito, Emperor, 212
Ali, Muhammad, 150
Alien Act, 8
Al-Qaeda, 217
American Revolution, 2, 4, 7, 8, 14, 16
American System, 19
Amistad (ship), 19
Anderson, John B., 178, 188
Arrington, Amanda, 124
Atkins, Ollie, 161
atomic bomb, xvii, 104, 112, 114

Babcock, Orville Elias, 41
Back Pay Grab, 39
Baker, Ray Stannard, 68
Baltimore (ship), 52
Barack Obama Presidential Library and
    Museum, ix, xiii, xiv, xv, 223–24
Barkley, Alben, 103
Bartlett, Margaret Johnson Patterson, 34
Beckel, Bob, 182
Begin, Menachem, 177
Bell, John, 26
Belmonte, Laura A., 224
Bemis, Samuel Flagg, 18
Benjamin Harrison Presidential Site, 50, 52–54
Benton, Thomas Hart, 107–8, *109*
Bentsen, Lloyd, 150, 199
Berlin Airlift, 104, 113
Berlin Wall, 132, 136, 160, 189, 192, 199, 203
Bernstein, Carl, 156–57
Bill of Rights, 13
bin Laden, Osama, 217
Birchard, Sardis, 45
Bitter, Karl, 15
Blaine, James G., 52
Blair, Tony, 219
Bonus Army, 80, 84
Boorstin, Daniel J., 83
Booth, John Wilkes, 27, 33, 38
Boren, David L., xv
Bork, Robert, 157
Bosanko, William J., 135
Bosnian War, 207, 211
Boston Public Library, 7, 10, 11
Boston Tea Party, 8

Brady, James, 188, 211
Brands, H. W., 66
Brauer, Carl M., 134
Breckinridge, John C., 25
Brinkley, Alan, 132
Brokaw, Tom, 191
Brooks, Philip C., 106, 107
Brooks, Stewart Marshall, 60
Brown, Edmund "Pat," 155, 187
Brown, Lester, 130
Brown, Michael, 218
Brown v. Board of Education, 121
Bryan, William Jennings, 58, 59, 60
Buchan, Philip, 170
Buchanan, Patrick J., 162, 200, 216–17
Buck, Paul H., 133
Bultema, James A., 41
Bunshaft, Gordon, 148
Bunting, Josiah, 37, 39
Burns, Mark, 149, 204
Burr, Aaron, 9
Bush, Barbara, 199, 201, 202, 203, 215
Bush, George H. W., *198*–201; and Clinton,
    207, 208; collections and exhibits, 202–4;
    and Ford, 170; and George W. Bush, 215,
    216, 219; library and museum, xiv, 201–4;
    Nixon library, 158; and Reagan, 187,
    189, 190
Bush, George W., *215*–18; Civil Rights
    Summit, 148; Clinton library, 208;
    collections and exhibits, 220; and George
    H. W. Bush, 199, 201; library and museum,
    xiv, 218–20; Lincoln library, 28
Bush, John "Jeb," 199, 216
Bush, Laura, 28, 148, *215*, 216, 218, 220
Bush, Prescott, 126, 198
Bush Center, 219
Butler, Benjamin, 33

Cabot, Edward C., 20
Calvin Coolidge Presidential Library and
    Museum, 73, 76–77
Camp David Accords, 177
Campion, Heather, 135
Cannon, James M., 173
Carnegie Corporation, 138
Carter, Jimmy, *175*–78; Civil Rights Summit,
    148; Clinton library, 208; collections
    and exhibits, 180–82; and Ford, 169; and

George H. W. Bush, 201; and George W.
    Bush, 219; library and museum, xiv,
    178–182; and Reagan, 187–88, 190
Carter, Lillian Gordy, 175, 182
Carter, Rosalynn, 176, 182
Carter Center, 178, 179
Carter/Smith Oral History Project, 181–82
Castro, Fidel, 132, 138
Cavalruso, Joe, 170
Ceauşescu, Nicolae, 199
Cermak, Anton, 96
Channing, Walter, 60
Chase, Salmon P., 33
Cheney, Dick, 216
Chiles, Lawton, xv
China, 105, 114, 156, 160, 161, 162, 199
Christopher, Warren, 179
Christy, Howard Chandler, 76
Churchill, Winston, 92, 96
civil rights, 75, 104, 121, 136, 145–46,
    148–49, 176
Civil War, 26, 29, 32–33, 38, 51
Clark, Edward T., 76
Clarkin, Dr. Thomas, 201
Clay, Henry, 19
Clemenceau, Georges, 67
Cleveland, Grover, 51, 52, 83
Clinton, Bill (William J.), *206*–8; Civil Rights
    Summit, 148; collections and exhibits,
    209–12; and George H. W. Bush, 200, 201,
    203, 207; and George W. Bush, 216, 219;
    library and museum, 208–12; photograph
Clinton, Hillary Rodham, *206*, 207, 208, 211
Clinton Global Initiative, 208
Clotworthy, William G., 61, 134, 208
Clough, Susan, 181
Coffelt, Leslie, 105
Coke, Sir Edward, 11
Cold War, 104, 113, 114, 130, 160
Cole, Wayne S., 86
Collazo, Oscar, 105
Confederacy, 26, 32
Connally, John, 133
Constitution, 2, 8, 13
Coolidge, Calvin, *73*–76; and Hoover, 84;
    library and museum, 76–77; *39 Men*
    exhibition, 82; and Truman, 103
Coolidge, Calvin, Jr., 74, 75
Coolidge, Grace, *73*, 74, 76

Coolidge, John, 74, 76
Cortelyou, George B., 62
Coughlin, Charles, 91
Cox, Archibald, 157
Cox, James M., 68, 74, 90
Crane, Thomas, 10
Crawford, William, 19
Crédit Mobilier, 39
Cresson, Peggy French, 15
Cresson, William Penn, 15
Cronkite, Walter, 146
Cuba, 59, 122, 132, 137, 138
Cunningham, Ann Pamela, 3
Czolgosz, Leon, 60

Dallek, Robert, 144, 145
Daniel, Margaret Truman, 105, 111, 112
Darby, Harry, 123
Davis, John W., 75
Dean, John W., 162
Declaration of Independence, 8
Devine, Michael J., 110
Dewey, George, 59
Dewey, Thomas E., 92, 97, 103, 104, 105, 113
Didier, Elaine K., 170
Dietz, Ulysses Grant, 41
Doak, Samuel Witherspoon, 34
Docking, George, 123
Dole, Bob, 208
Dolores Lescure Center, 69
Donald W. Reynolds Museum Education
    Center, 3
Douglas, Stephen A., 25
Douglas, William O., 103
Dred Scott decision, 25
Dukakis, Michael, 135, 189, 199
Dulles, Allen, 133
Dwight D. Eisenhower Presidential Library,
    119, 122–26, *125*

Eagleton, Thomas F., 110
Edsel, Robert M., 124
Eisenhower, David, 123
Eisenhower, Doud "Icky," 119, 120, 122, 124
Eisenhower, Dwight David, *119*–22; boyhood
    home, 122–23; collections and exhibits,
    125–26; Johnson museum, 150; and
    Kennedy, 131; library and museum, xiii,
    xiv, 122–26; Little Rock Nine, 210; and

Nixon, 155, 161; and Reagan, 187; and
    Truman, 105, 114
Eisenhower, Mamie Dowd, 119, 122, 125,
    126
Eisenhower Doctrine, 121
Eisenhower Presidential Library Commission,
    123
Ellzey, Michael, 159
Emancipation Proclamation, 26, 28
Endacott, J. Earl, 123–24
English, Glenn, xv
Evans, Charles, 66
Evans, Meredith, 179

Fairbanks, Charles W., 66
Fall, Albert, 74
Family Squabble (Rockwell painting), 113
Faubus, Orval E., 121, 210
FDR. *See* Roosevelt, Franklin Delano
Felt, Mark, 157
Ferdinand, Franz, 66
Fitzgerald, F. Scott, 137
Fitzgerald, John "Honey Fitz" Fitzgerald,
    129, 136
Fitzgerald, Rose, 129, 136, 138
Fletcher, Tom, 145
Flowers, Gennifer, 207
Forbes Library, 73, 76
Ford, Betty, *167*, 168, 169, 171
Ford, Gerald R., *167*–69; Clinton library,
    208; and George H. W. Bush, 201; Hoover
    library, 83; and Kennedy, 133; library and
    collections, 173; library and museum, xiv,
    169–173; museum and collections, 171–72;
    and Nixon, 157, 158, 160, 176; and
    Reagan, 187, 190; *39 Men* exhibition, 83
Ford, Tirey J., 114
Founding Fathers, 13, 14
Fourteen Points, 67
Franklin, Benjamin, 8
Franklin D. Roosevelt Presidential Library
    and Museum, 89, 92–98, *95, 97*
Fred W. Smith National Library for the Study
    of George Washington, 1, 3–4
Fromme, Lynette "Squeaky," 168
Frost, Robert, 131

Gaddis, John Lewis, 104
Gallup, George, 105

Garfield, James A., 45, 54
Garner, John Nance, 90
Garner, Terri, 209
General Services Administration (GSA), xiv,
    xv, 157–58
George Bush Presidential Library and
    Museum, 198, 201–4, *202*
George W. Bush Institute, 219
George W. Bush Presidential Library and
    Museum, 215, 218–20, *219*
Gerald R. Ford Presidential Foundation, 170
Gerald R. Ford Presidential Library and
    Museum, 162, 167, 169–73, *171, 172*
Gettysburg Address, 26
Gilded Age Collections, 47
Gillette, Charles, 69
Gillette, Michael L., 145
Glenn, John, 136, 210
Goldwater, Barry, 146
Gompers, Samuel, 74
Goodwin, Doris Kearns, 139
Gorbachev, Mikhail, 189, 199
Gore, Al, 200, 207, 208, 216
Gouverneur, James L., Jr., 14, 15
Gouverneur Hoes, Rose de Chine, 15
Graham, Reverend Billy, 151, 201, 216
Graham, Kurt, 110
Grant, Frederick Dent, 41
Grant, Ida Honoré, 41
Grant, Julia, 38, 39, 41
Grant, Ulysses S., *37–39*; digital collections,
    40–41; Harrison library, 54; and Johnson,
    34; library, 39–41; Union Army, 26
Great Depression, 76, 80, 84, 90, 95, 96
Great Society program, 145, 149
Greeley, Horace, 39
Gridley, Jeremiah, 11
Grover, Wayne C., 106, 107, 133
GSA. *See* General Services Administration
Guantanamo Bay, 217
Guggenheim, Charles, 112, 134
Gulf War, 201, 203, 217

Hackman, Larry, 110
Halbouty, Michael T., 201
Hamilton, Alexander, 19
Hamlin, Hannibal, 25, 26
Hanna, Marcus, 58, 61
Hannegan, Bob, 103

Harding, Warren G., 54, 66, 74, 80, 84, 90
Harger, Charles M., 122
Harriman, W. Averell, 110, 113
Harrison, Benjamin, *50–52*; collections and
    exhibits, 53–54; library and museum,
    52–54
Harrison, Caroline, 50, 52, 53, 54
Harrison, Mary Lord, 52, 53
Harrison, William Henry, 50, 54
Harry S. Truman Presidential Library and
    Museum, xvii, 102, 106–14, *107, 109*
Hay, Colonel John, 27
Hayes, Fanny, 46
Hayes, Lucy Webb, 44, 45, 46, 47
Hayes, Rutherford B., *44–45*; collections
    and exhibits, 46–47; and Grant, 39; home
    estate, ix; library and museum, xiii, 45–47;
    and McKinley, 57, 58
Hayes, Webb Cook, 46, 47
Heald, Edward Thornton, 62
Health, William W., 147
Hearst, William Randolph, 59
Hemingway, Ernest, 137, 138
Hemingway, Mary, 138
Hennessey, David, 52
Henry, Patrick, 13
Henry A. Wallace Visitor and Education
    Center, 98
Herbert Hoover National Historic Site, 82
Herbert Hoover Presidential Library and
    Museum, xv, xvi, 79, 81–86, *83*
Heubusch, John, 191, 194
Hinckley, John, Jr., 188, 211
Hiss, Alger, 155
Hitler, Adolf, 130, 147
Hobart, Garret A., 58, 60
Hoes, Ingrid Westesson, 15, 16
Hoes, Laurence Gouverneur, 15, 16
Hofstader, Richard, 39
Holocaust, 97, 125
Hoover, Herbert, *79–81*; collections and
    exhibits, 84–86; and Coolidge, 76; and
    FDR, 90, 95–96; Hoover Institution, xiii,
    81, 92; library and museum, xiv, xvi,
    81–86; and Truman, 107; and Wilson, 70
Hoover, Lou Henry, *79*, 80, 84, 86
Hoover Commission, 81, 85
Hoover Institution on War, Revolution, and
    Peace, xiii, 81, 92

Hoover Presidential Society, 82
Hoover Price Planetarium, 62–63
Hoover-Wilson Correspondence papers, 70
Horowitz, Daniel, 177
Horton, Willie, 199
House Un-American Activities Committee, 155
Hufbauer, Benjamin: FDR library, 93, 94; "Happy Meal"/"McPresident" library, xvii, 94, 110, 158, 190–91, 201; Johnson library, 148; Nixon library, 158; Reagan library, 190–91; Truman library, 108, 110, 112
Human Genome Project, 210
Humphrey, Hubert H., 131, 146, 147, 151, 155
Hurricane Katrina, 201, 218, 220
Hussein, Saddam, 199, 200, 203, 217, 218
Hyde, Charlie, 53

Ida Honoré Grant Correspondence, 41
Illinois State Historical Library, 27, 29
Independence and the Opening of the West (Benton mural), 107–8, *109*
Ingrid Westesson Hoes Archives, 16
Iran-Contra affair, xvii, 188–89, 190
Iraq, 199–200, 203, 217, 218
Israel, 113, 177

Jackson, Andrew, 19
Jackson, Thomas "Stonewall," 37
James Monroe Museum and Memorial Library, 13, 14–16
Jameson, J. Franklin, 68
Jay's Treaty, 2, 8
Jefferson, Thomas, 8, 9, 13, 14, 16, 82
Jimmy Carter Presidential Library and Museum, 175, 178–82, *180*, *181*
John Adams Library, 7, 9–11
John F. Kennedy Foundation, 139
John F. Kennedy Presidential Library and Museum, xvi, 129, 133–39, *135*, *137*, 148
Johnson, Alex Smith, 9
Johnson, Andrew, *32*–34; collections and exhibits, 34–35; library and museum, 34–35; and Lincoln, 26
Johnson, Claudia Alta "Lady Bird" Taylor, *144*, 145, 147, 150, 201
Johnson, Eliza, 32

Johnson, Lyndon Baines, *144*–47; collections and exhibits, 149–51; Hoover library, 82; and Kennedy, 131, 133, 139; library and museum, xiv, xv, 147–51; and Nixon, 155
Johnson, Paul, 120, 121
Johnson, Philip, 10
Jones, William, 124

Karzai, Hamid, 217
Katzenbach, Nicholas, 147
Kazin, Michael, 58, 59, 60
Keeler, Lucy Elliot, 47
Kefauver, Estes, 131
Kellogg–Briand Act, 75
Kempton, Greta, 108
Kennan, George F., 113
Kennedy, Caroline, 131, 208
Kennedy, Edward, 134, 136, 178
Kennedy, Jacqueline Bouvier, 131, 133, 134, 136, 138
Kennedy, John F., *129*–33; collections and exhibits, 136–39; death of, 133, 134, 149, 150; and Eisenhower, 122; Harrison library, 54; and Johnson, 33, 145, 148, 149, 150; library and museum, 133–39; and Nixon, 155, 161; Reagan library, 189
Kennedy, John F., Jr., 131
Kennedy, Joseph, Jr., 129, 136
Kennedy, Joseph P., 129, 136, 138
Kennedy, Robert F., 134, 136, 138, 139
Kennedy, Rose Fitzgerald, 138
Kerry, John, 208, 218
Keynes, John Maynard, 67
Khomeini, Ayatollah, 178
Khrushchev, Nikita, 122, 155
King, Martin Luther, Jr., 136, 179
King, Rufus, 14
Kinzer, Stephen, 122
Kissinger, Henry, 161, 173
Korean War, 105, 114, 120, 121, 176
Ku Klux Klan, 38–39, 75
Kurowsky, Agnes von, 138
Kuwait, 199, 200, 203

Landon, Alfred M., 91, 96
Lane, Rose Wilder, 86
Lantzer, Jason S., 110
Larson, Jess, 106
Laura Ingles Wilder Website Index, 86

League of Nations, 67, 68, 70

Lee, Robert E., 26, 38

Lenroot, Irvine, 74

Leone, Ambrogio, 11

Leuchtenburg, William E., 80, 96

Library of Congress, xiii, 4, 27, 68, 92

Lieberman, Joe, 216

Lincoln, Abraham, *24*–27; collections and exhibits, 28–29; death of, 27, 38; and Grant, 38; Harrison library, 54; Hayes Library, 46; and Johnson, 33, 34; library and museum, 27–29

Lincoln, Mary Todd, 25, 27, 28, 29

Lincoln, Robert Todd, 27

Lincoln-Douglas debates, 25

Lindbergh, Charles, 84, 110

Link, Arthur S., 69, 70

Little Rock Nine, 210

Lloyd, David D., 106, 107

Lloyd George, David, 67

Lodge, Henry Cabot, Jr., 130, 131, 145, 155

Lodge, Henry Cabot, Sr., 67

Long, Huey, 90

Lorentz, Pare, 98

Louisiana Purchase, 15

Lowe, Alan, 219

Lubell, Sam, 105

Lusitania (ship), 66

Lyndon Baines Johnson Presidential Library and Museum, 144, 147–51, *148*, *150*

MacArthur, General Douglas, 105, 114, 120

Maddox (ship), 146

Maddox, Lester, 176

Maine (ship), 59

Mandela, Nelson, 209

Manson, Charles, 168

Marist College, 94

Marshall, George, 104, 113, 120

Marshall, Thomas, 66, 68

Marshall Plan, 104

Marszalek, John F., 40

Matthews, Chris, 182

McAdoo, Eleanor Wilson, 69

McAllister, Ted, 190

McCain, John, 216, 218

McCarthy, Eugene, 147

McCarthy, Joseph, 155

McClellan, George B., 26, 33, 37

McCormick, Cyrus, 35

McCormick, Nettie, 35

McCullough, David, 4

McFarlane, Robert, 188, 189

McGovern, George, 157, 160

McKim, Charles Follen, 10

McKinley, Abner, 62

McKinley, Ida Saxton, 58, 62

McKinley, William, *57*–60; collections and exhibits, 62–63; and Harrison, 52, 54; memorial and musuem, 61–63; and Theodore Roosevelt, 225

McKinley Memorial, 61

McKinley Tariff Bill, 52

McKinstry, Arthur, 41

McNary-Haugen Farm Relief Bill, 75

Medicare, 145, 149

Meir, Golda, 160

Mellon, Andrew, 75, 93

Michiko, Empress, 212

Milliken, William G., 170

Mitchell Memorial Library, 40

Mondale, Walter F., 135, 176, 178, 189

Monroe, Elizabeth, 13, 16

Monroe, James, *13*–14; collections and exhibits, 15–16; and John Quincy Adams, 18; library and museum, 14–16

Monroe Doctrine, 14, 15, 16

Montgomery, General Bernard, 120

Moore, Charles, 68

Moore, Sara Jane, 168

Morton, Levi P., 51

Morton, Oliver P., 51

Mount Vernon Ladies' Association, 1, 3, 4

Mudd Manuscript Library, 68, 69

Mussolini, Benito, 120

Nader, Ralph, 216

Nash, George H., 81, 83

Nast, Thomas, 47, 54

National Archives Administration Act (1984), xv

National Archives and Records Administration, xiii, xiv, xvi, xvii

National Park Service Plains Project Oral Histories, 182

Neild, Edward F., 106

Nelson, Julie Bartlett, 77

Neustadt, Richard, 134

New Deal, 81, 90, 91, 94–95, 96, 145
Newton, Verne, 94
Nicaragua, 189
Nicolay, John G., 27
9/11 attacks, 217, 219, 220
Nixon, Pat (Thelma), 154, 157, 159, 160
Nixon, Richard Milhous, *154*–57; birthplace,
    159, 161; collections and exhibits, 159–62;
    and Eisenhower, 121, 122, 131; and Ford,
    168, 169, 176; and Johnson, 145, 147,
    148; and Kennedy, 131, 136; library and
    museum, xiv, 157–62; and Reagan, 187,
    188, 190
Nixon Foundation, 158
Nixon–Sampson agreement, xiv, 157
Noriega, Manuel, 199
North, Oliver, 188, 189
North Korea, 105, 114, 217
nuclear weapons, 122, 132, 137, 146, 189
Nye, Gerald, 86

Oakley, Frances, 41
Obama, Barack, 223, *224*; Civil Rights
    Summit, 148; and George W. Bush, 219;
    and Hillary Clinton, 208; Lincoln library,
    28; and McCain, 218; presidential library,
    ix, xiii, xiv, xv, 223–24
Obama, Michelle, 148, 223, *224*
Obata, Gyo, 27
Office of Presidential Libraries, xiv
Onassis, Aristotle, 133
Onassis, Jacqueline Kennedy, 131, 133, 134,
    136, 138
Operation Desert Storm, 200, 203
Operation Iraqi Freedom, 217
Operation Menu, 156
Operation Overlord, 120
Operation Torch, 120
oral histories, 126, 138–39, 150–51, 162,
    181–82, 194
O'Reilly, Henry, 14
Orlando, Vittorio Emanuele, 67
Orville Elias Babcock Diaries, 41
Oswald, Lee Harvey, 133

Pare Lorentz Center, 98
Patterson, Andrew Johnson, 34
Patterson, Roscoe C., 103
Patton, George S., 120

Pearl Harbor, 92, 96
Pei, I. M., 134
Pendergast, Tom, 103, 111
Perkins, Francis, 94, 97
Perot, H. Ross, 200, 207, 208
Pershing, John J., 120
Peters, Andrew, 74
Phillips, Andrew, 69, 70
Pietrusza, David, 104, 105
Pinckney, Charles, 8, 9
Pinkall, Bryan, 124
Plakos, Marie, 181
Polshek, James, 208
Potter, Lee Ann, xvi
Pound, Ezra, 138
Powell, Colin, 4, 201
Powers, Francis Gary, 122
President Andrew Johnson Museum and
    Library, 32, 34–35
Presidential Libraries Act, xiv, xv, 106, 123, 133
presidential libraries and museums:
    educational programs, xv, xvi; exhibits, xvi,
    xvii; future libraries, 223–26; history of,
    xiii–xvii
Presidential Recordings and Materials
    Preservation Act, xiv, 158
Presley, Elvis, 110, 162
Princip, Gavrilo, 66
Profiles in Courage (Kennedy), 131, 138
Pusey, Nathan M., 133
Putnam, Herbert, 27, 68

Quayle, Dan, 199, 200, 203
Quintero, Frederick S., 94

race relations, 75, 96, 132, 145, 210
Rayburn, Sam, 150
Reagan, Michael, 187
Reagan, Nancy, 179, 187, 189, 192, 201
Reagan, Ronald, *186*–89; assassination
    attempt, 188, 211; and Carter, 178, 179;
    and Ford, 168, 169, 170; and George H. W.
    Bush, 199, 200, 203; library and museum,
    190–94; manuscripts and audiovisuals,
    193–94; museum and exhibits, 191–93;
    Nixon library, 158; Ronald Reagan
    Foundation, 194; *39 Men* exhibition, 83
Reed, Albert, 122
Reed, Thomas, 58

Reese, Edward Herbert, xiv
Research Library at the Benjamin Harrison
    Presidential Site, 50, 52–54
Reykjavik Summit, 189
Reza Shah (Pahlavi), Mohammed, 177, 178
Richard Nixon Presidential Archive
    Foundation, 158
Richard Nixon Presidential Library and
    Museum, 154, 157–162
Richards, Ann, 216
Richardson, Elliot, 157
Richardson, Henry Hobson, 10
Rives, Tim, 124, 126
Rockefeller, Nelson A., 126, 146, 168
Rockwell, Norman, 113
Rodham, Dorothy Howell, 211
Rommel, General Erwin, 120
Ronald Reagan Foundation, 194
Ronald Reagan Presidential Library and
    Museum, xvii, 186, 190–94, *191, 192, 193*
Roosevelt, Eleanor, 89, 92, 94, 95, 96, 97, 107
Roosevelt, Franklin Delano (FDR), *89*–92;
    collections and exhibits, 95–97; and
    Coolidge, 74; death of, 103, 111; and
    Eisenhower, 120; Harrison library, 54;
    Hayes library, 46; and Hoover, 81, 85;
    and Johnson, 145; library and museum,
    xiii, 92–98, 106; presidential terms, 2; and
    Truman, 103; and Wilson, 69
Roosevelt, Sara, 89, 96
Roosevelt, Theodore, *225*; and Coolidge,
    74; and FDR, 89, 96; library foundation,
    225–26; and McKinley, 59, 60, 61; and
    Wilson, 66, 70
Rose Wilder Lane collection, 86
Ross, Edmund G., 33, 34
Rossiter, Clinton, 106
Rothstein, Edward, 95
Rothstein, Steven, 135
Rough Riders, 59
Ruby, Jack, 133
Ruckelshaus, William, 157
Rush-Bagot Treaty, 14
Rutherford B. Hayes Presidential Library and
    Museums, xiii, 44, 45–47, 53, 92

Sadat, Anwar, 160, 177
Sampson, Arthur F., xiv, 157
Saxe, William B., 157

Schlesinger, Arthur, 96
Schlesinger, Arthur M., Jr., 134
Schwartz, Thomas, 29, 83
Scott, Dred, 25
Sermon, Roger, 106
Service, Robert, 188
Seymour, Horatio, 34, 38
Shafter, William, 59
Shepard, Alan B., 136, 137
Sherman, William Tecumseh, 37, 51
Sherman Anti-Trust Act, 51–52, 225
Shipman, Fred W., 94
Shlaes, Amity, 74, 96
Simon, John Y., 40, 41
Simon, William E., 158
slavery, 1, 2, 4, 19, 25–26
Smith, Alfred E., 80
Smith, Jerrold, 182
Smith, Richard Norton, xvi, 82–83
Smoot-Hawley Tariff, 80
Sorensen, Theodore, 134
Soviet Union, 98, 104, 108, 113, 121–22, 160,
    188–89, 199
space race, 122, 136, 156
Stalin, Joseph, 92, 96, 104
Stanton, Edwin, 33, 34
Staunton Presbyterian Manse, *69*
Stein, Gertrude, 137
Stevens, Thaddeus, 33
Stevenson, Adlai E., 121, 131, 155
Stewart, David O., 33
Stone Library, 10, 18, 20–22, *21*
Strategic Defense Initiative (SDI), 188, 189
suffrage movement, 53, 66

Taft, William Howard, 66
Taylor, Zachary, 54
Teapot Dome Scandal, 74
Tet Offensive, 146
Theodore Roosevelt Center, 225
Theodore Roosevelt Presidential Library
    Foundation, ix, 225–26
39 Men exhibition, xvi, 82–83
Thomas Crane Library, 10
Thompson, Heather Ann, 181
Thurmond, Strom, 104
Tilden, Samuel J., 44, 45
Tippit, J. D., 133
Toombs, Henry J., 93

Torresola, Griselio, 105
Townsend, Dr. Francis, 91
Treaty of 1818, 14
Treaty of Ghent, 18
Treaty of Versailles, 67, 68, 70
Trefousse, Hans L., 33
Troy, Gil, 207
Trudeau, Pierre, 170
Truman, Bess, 103, 105, 111, 112
Truman, Harry S., *102*–5; collections and
    exhibits, 110–14; death of, 105, 108; and
    Eisenhower, 120; and FDR, 92, 98; and
    Hoover, 81, 82; library and museum, xiii,
    106–14; Nixon library, 161; and Reagan,
    187
Truman, Margaret, 105, 111, 112
Truman Committee, 103
Truman Library Institute, 114
Trump, Donald J., xv, 208, 223, 226
Tsongas, Paul, 204
Tusculum College, 32, 34, 35
Tyler, Letitia, 54

Ulysses S. Grant Collection, 41
Ulysses S. Grant Presidential Library, 37,
    39–41, *40*
United Nations, 97, 105
United States Food Administration, 84, 85
Updegrove, Mark K., 148

Victor Emmanuel III, King, 120
Victoria, Queen, 46
Vietnam War, 146–48, 150, 156, 158, 160–61,
    168, 177
von Seldeneck, Robin, 69
Voorhis, Horace Jeremiah "Jerry," 155

Walch, Timothy, xv, xvi, 82, 83, 85
Walesa, Lech, 199
Wallace, George, 155
Wallace, Henry A., 91, 98, 103, 104, 105
Walt Disney Archives, 193
Warren, Earl, 107, 110, 126, 133
Warren Commission, 133
Washington, George, *1*–3; American
    Revolution, 2, 4, 8; and John Adams, 22;
    library and museum, xiii, 3–4; Monroe
    Library, 16; War of 1812, 14
Washington, George Corbin, 4

Washington, Martha, 1, 3, 4
Watergate scandal, xiv, 156–57, 160, 162, 168,
    169, 176
Weatherford, Robert P., 106
Weinberger, Casper, 188
Weisberg, Jacob, 189
Weissenbach, Karl H., 124
While England Slept (Kennedy), 130
Whisky Ring, 39, 41
Whitaker, John C., 158
White, R. B., 106
White House Staff Photographers collection,
    182
Wilder, Laura Ingles, 86
Wilkie, Wendell, 91, 97
William J. Clinton Foundation, 208
William J. Clinton Presidential Library and
    Museum, 206, 208–12, *209*
William McKinley Presidential Library and
    Museum, 57, 61–63
Williams, Frank J., 40, 41
Williams, James D., 51
Williamsburg (ship), 111
Wilson, Edith, 68, 69
Wilson, Ellen, 54, 65, 66, 69
Wilson, Joseph Ruggles, 65, 70
Wilson, Woodrow, *65*–68; collections and
    exhibits, 70; and FDR, 90; library and
    museum, 68–70; and Theodore Roosevelt,
    225
Wing, Donna, 54
women's suffrage, 53, 66
Wood, Robert E., 86
Woodrow Wilson Presidential Library and
    Museum, 65, 68–70
Woodward, Bob, 156–57
Woodward, C. Vann, 45
World Trade Center, 217, 220
World War I, 66–67, 70, 80, 85, 90
World War II, 81, 91–92, 96–97, 103–4, 120,
    124, 125, 130
Wyman, Jane, 187

Young, John Russell, 39

Zamperini, Louis, 124
Zangara, Giuseppe, 96
Zhou Enlai, 160
Zorbist, Benedict, 108

About the Author

Christian A. Nappo teaches for the Lee County, Florida, School District and holds an MA in library and information science from the University of South Florida. He also holds an MS in criminal justice from the University of Alabama and an MA in history from the University of Nebraska–Kearney. His previous book, *The Librarians of Congress*, was published by Rowman and Littlefield in 2016.